Radical Spaces

Radical Spaces

Venues of popular politics in London, 1790–c. 1845

CHRISTINA PAROLIN

Published by ANU E Press
The Australian National University
Canberra ACT 0200, Australia
Email: anuepress@anu.edu.au
This title is also available online at: http://epress.anu.edu.au/radical_spaces_citation.html

National Library of Australia
Cataloguing-in-Publication entry

Author: Parolin, Christina.

Title: Radical spaces : venues of popular politics in london, 1790 -1845 / Christina Parolin.

ISBN: 9781921862007 (pbk.) 9781921862014 (eBook)

Notes: Includes bibliographical references.

Subjects: Radicalism--Great Britain--18th century.
            Great Britain--Politics and government--18th century.
            Great Britain--Social life and customs--18th century.

Dewey Number: 320.53

All rights reserved. No part of this publication may be reproduced, stored in a retrieval system or transmitted in any form or by any means, electronic, mechanical, photocopying or otherwise, without the prior permission of the publisher.

Cover design and layout by ANU E Press

Cover image: Architectural view of the Surrey Rotunda, Sir Ashton Lever's Museum in Blackfriars Road, London. Artist and date unknown.
Copyright Wellcome Library, London.

Printed by Griffin Press

This edition © 2010 ANU E Press

Contents

Acknowledgments	vii
Illustrations	ix
Abbreviations	xiii
Introduction	1
1. 'Honourable House of Blasphemers': The radical public of Newgate in the early nineteenth century	17
2. 'Bastilles of despotism': Radical resistance in the Coldbath Fields House of Correction, 1798–1830	49
3. The 'She-Champion of Impiety': Female radicalism and political crime in early nineteenth-century England	83
4. Radicalism and reform at the 'Gate of Pandemonium': The Crown and Anchor tavern in visual culture, 1790–1820	105
5. 'Fresh Crown and Anchor sentiments': Radical reform in the Strand, 1817–1847	147
6. 'Temple of Knowledge and Reason': Culture and politics at 3 Blackfriars Road, Surrey	179
7. 'Bitten with the Rotunda notions': Audience, identity and communication 1830–1832	213
8. 'Pythoness of the Temple': Eliza Sharples and the gendered public of the Rotunda	243
9. Conclusion	273
Bibliography	289
Index	329

Acknowledgments

My opening thanks must go to Iain McCalman—who first introduced me to British radicalism during my undergraduate years—for his unfailing encouragement, generosity and guidance. At a chance meeting at a Canberra restaurant some years ago, Iain encouraged me to pursue further study and welcomed me to the rich intellectual climate of the Humanities Research Centre (HRC) at The Australian National University (ANU). This book is the outcome of research undertaken at that time.

At the HRC, I found another mentor to whom I owe an immeasurable debt. The support provided by Paul Pickering—both during and since completing my PhD—has been outstanding. His intellectual generosity and insight, encouragement, advice and friendship have been appreciated more than he knows. I have simply learnt so much from him.

I was fortunate to have undertaken this research at the ANU for many other reasons besides, including the friendship and support of my fellow PhD travellers. I am immensely grateful to the College of Arts and Social Sciences at the ANU for the prize which supported the publication of this book. I am also honoured that the ANU awarded this work the J.G Crawford prize for 2009.

The assistance of staff at various London libraries and archives has been greatly appreciated, including the British Museum, the City of London Archives, the Wellcome Library, the Guildhall Library, the British Library, the Southwark Local History Library, the Bishopsgate Institute, the City of Westminster City Archives and the Hastings Museum. Considerable thanks are owed to those institutions that granted permission to publish the images contained herein for both the e-book and hardcopy version of this study. Particular mention must go to the staff of the Arundel Castle Archive who retrieved records, provided a beautiful space in which to peruse the title deeds and other records of the Crown and Anchor tavern and shared with me their tea, fruitcake and good humour. Sources from Arundel Castle Archives are reproduced by kind permission of His Grace the Duke of Norfolk.

More recently, my colleagues at the Australian Academy of the Humanities are also owed a great deal of thanks for their support, encouragement and patience as I entered the final stages of writing.

Of course, one's personal life never stops to make way for a study of this kind. I am indebted to many family members: in particular, my parents, Robyne and Bruno, for their unwavering support and love, for reading drafts and for going well above and beyond their duties as grandparents.

To Jordan, Keelan and Jenna, who endured my absences—both in spirit and in person—and lived the stresses of the book far more than they ought to have, I offer my love and my thanks for inspiring me so much.

To Wes goes my deepest gratitude for reasons beyond measure. He never once doubted that I would complete this book.

Finally, I dedicate this book to the memory of my brother Michael, who faced his own, much more profound, challenges during the writing of this volume. His courage in the face of the most heartbreaking adversity is a more enduring testimony than anything I could hope to achieve in these pages.

Illustrations

1.1   Newgate from Old Bailey Road. Thomas Malton, 1792. Copyright Trustees of the British Museum

1.2   Newgate prison, following reconstruction after the Gordon riots. Drawing by George Dance, the Younger. Copyright Trustees of the British Museum

1.3   *Preparing for an Execution*, Unknown artist, c. 1846. Copyright Trustees of the British Museum

1.4   *Soulagement en Prison, or Comfort in Prison*, Richard Newton, 1793. Courtesy of The Lewis Walpole Library, Yale University

1.5   *'A Trifling Mistake'…Corrected…*, George Cruikshank, London, 1820. Copyright Trustees of the British Museum

2.1   *An Exact Representation of the Principal Banners and Triumphal Car, which conveyed Sir Francis Burdett to the Crown and Anchor Tavern on Monday June 29th, 1807*, Artist unknown. Copyright Trustees of the British Museum

2.2   *Citizens Visiting the Bastille, vide Democratic Charities*, James Gillray, 1799. Copyright Trustees of the British Museum

2.3   Elevation and section of Coldbath Fields House of Correction. Samuel Alken, 1800. Copyright City of London, London Metropolitan Archives

2.4   Interior view of Coldbath Fields. Thomas Ranson, 1819. Copyright City of London, London Metropolitan Archives

4.1   An early street view of the Strand and St Clement Danes Church, 1753. Copyright Trustees of the British Museum

4.2   Horwood's map of the Strand showing the Crown and Anchor before the renovation, c. 1799. Copyright Guildhall Library

4.3   Horwood's map of the Strand showing the extended site of the tavern, 1807. Copyright Guildhall Library

4.4   Arundel Street entrance of the Crown and Anchor tavern. T. H. Shepherd, 1852. Copyright Trustees of the British Museum

4.5 Ground-floor plan of the Crown and Anchor tavern. From the Deed of the Arundel Buildings Estate, Middlesex, R. & H. R. Abraham Architects, 1836. Duke of Norfolk Papers, Copyright His Grace the Duke of Norfolk (per the Archivist, Arundel Castle)

4.6 *Revolution Anniversary or Patriotic Incantations*, William Dent, 1791. Copyright Trustees of the British Museum

4.7 *Alecto and her Train at the Gate of Pandemonium…or…The Recruiting Sargeant enlisting John Bull into the Revolution Service*, James Gillray, 1793. Copyright Trustees of the British Museum

4.8 *'The Hopes of the Party, prior to July 14th…"From such wicked Crown and Anchor Dreams, good Lord deliver us"'*, James Gillray, 1791. Copyright Trustees of the British Museum

4.9 *The Chancellor of the Inquisition marking the Incorrigibles*, James Gillray, 1793. Copyright Trustees of the British Museum

4.10 *Sola 'Virtus Invicta'…'Vitue* [sic] *Alone is Invincible'*, Richard Newton, 1798. Copyright Trustees of the British Museum

4.11 *The Crown and Anchor Desperdado or the Cracked Member belonging to the Bedlam Rangers*, Charles Williams, 1803. Copyright Trustees of the British Museum

4.12 *Scene in the Crown and Anchor*, J. T. Smith, 1802. Copyright Trustees of the British Museum

4.13 *The Grand Reform Dinner*, Samuel De Wilde, 1809. Copyright Trustees of the British Museum

4.14 'This is the House that Jack Built', *The Political House that Jack Built*, William Hone and George Cruikshank, London, 1819. Copyright Trustees of the British Museum

4.15 'This is the House that Jack Built', *The Real or Constitutional House that Jack Built*, London, 1819. Copyright Trustees of the British Museum

4.16 'These are the Radicals—Friends of Reform', *The Real or Constitutional House that Jack Built*, London, 1819. Copyright Trustees of the British Museum

4.17 *The Man in the Moon*, William Hone and George Cruikshank, 1820. Copyright Trustees of the British Museum

4.18 *The Loyal Man in the Moon*, Anon., 1820. Copyright Trustees of the British Museum

4.19	'Crown and Anchor', *The Loyal Man in the Moon*, Anon., 1820. Copyright Trustees of the British Museum
5.1	*To Be…or…Not to Be the Clare MP: O'Connell and the Minister at the Bar of the (Crown) and (Anchor)*, Charles Williams, 1828. Copyright Trustees of the British Museum
5.2	Great Room, Crown and Anchor Tavern, Whittington Club Soiree, *Illustrated London News*, 1848.
6.1	Map of Blackfriars Road, Parish of Christchurch, Surrey, c. 1820. Copyright Southwark Local History Library
6.2	Front Facade of the Leverian Museum, 3 Blackfriars Road. V. Davis, 1805. Copyright Wellcome Library, London
6.3	Floorplan of the Leverian Museum, prepared by a visitor, c. 1807. Possibly drawn by Richard Cuming. From the Cuming Collection. Copyright Southwark Local History Library
6.4	Rotunda, Leverian Museum, drawn by Sarah Stone, from *A Companion to the Museum Late Sir Ashton's*, 1790. Copyright City of London, London Metropolitan Archives
6.5	'Surrey Institution', Thomas Rowlandson, from Rudolph Ackermann, *The Microcosm of London*, 1809. Copyright Wellcome Library, London
7.1	Architectural view of the Surrey Rotunda, Sir Ashton Lever's Museum in Blackfriars Road, London. Copyright Wellcome Library, London
8.1	Eliza Sharples with a copy of *Isis*, c. 1832, from Theophila Carlile Campbell, *The Battle for the Freedom of the Press*, London, 1899. Courtesy of the Barr Smith Library, Adelaide
8.2	Eliza Macauley, 1819. Copyright Wellcome Library, London
8.3	South London Rational School meeting in the Large Theatre of the Rotunda. Copyright Wellcome Library, London
9.1	Fire at the Crown and Anchor, *Illustrated London News*, 9 December 1854.
9.2	Front right corner of the Temple Club, following rebuilding on the same plan as the Crown and Anchor, c. 1880, Strand Estate Collection. Copyright His Grace the Duke of Norfolk (per the Archivist, Arundel Castle)
9.3	Demolition of the Rotunda site in January 1958. Copyright Southwark Local History Library

Abbreviations

Add. MS	Additional manuscript
BDBA	*Biographical Dictionary of British Architects*
BDMBR	*Biographical Dictionary of Modern British Radicals*
HO	Home Office Papers
LCS	London Corresponding Society
NPU	National Political Union
NUWC	National Union of the Working Classes
ODNB	*Oxford Dictionary of National Biography*
SDUK	Society for the Diffusion of Useful Knowledge

Introduction

On 4 March 1838, the life of veteran English radical John Gale Jones came to an end at his home at 32 Middlesex Street, Somers Town, London. He was aged sixty-eight.[1] In many ways, his was an archetypal radical life, lived during the efflorescence of radical culture in the age of reform of the late eighteenth and early nineteenth centuries. A surgeon and apothecary by training, his enthusiasm for the principles of the French Revolution soon saw him abandon his profession to become a prominent member of the London Corresponding Society (LCS).[2] Jones entered the political fray during tumultuous times in Britain and in 1795 he undertook a famous tour of the country with fellow LCS member John Binns. Together they advised provincial reform societies how to evade new anti-radical legislation, the *Treasonable Practices and Seditious Meetings Acts*, introduced that same year.[3] With his 'great powers of declamation', he became a leading orator in London radicalism, particularly in the borough of Westminster. Jones was a prominent figure at the traditional liberal-Whig Westminster political headquarters in the Crown and Anchor tavern in the Strand, where he accompanied the legendary Charles James Fox as he entered the Great Room of the tavern for Fox's 1798 birthday celebrations attended by 2000 guests.[4] The

---

1   There is no full biography of Jones, despite him being a prominent participant in London radical politics over so many years. Fragments of his story, however, can be found in almost every text of British radicalism focusing on the 1790s through to the time of his death. See, for example, W. D. Jones, 'Jones, John Gale', in Joseph Baylen and Norbert Gossman (eds), *Biographical Dictionary of Modern British Radicals* [hereafter *BDMBR*], vol. 1 (Sussex: Harvester Press, 1979), pp. 269–73; E. P. Thompson, *The Making of the English Working Class* (London: Penguin, 1968), chs 5, 15 and 16, passim; J. Ann Hone, *For the Cause of Truth: Radicalism in London 1796–1821* (Oxford: Clarendon Press, 1982); Iain McCalman, *Radical Underworld: Prophets, revolutionaries and pornographers in London, 1795–1840* (Cambridge: Cambridge University Press, 1988), pp. 45, 89–90, 114; Iowerth Prothero, *Artisans and Politics in Early Nineteenth Century London, John Gast and his Times* (Folkestone: Dawson, 1979), passim. For obituaries for Gale Jones, see *Gentleman's Magazine*, August 1838, p. 218; *Manchester Times and Gazette*, 10 March 1838; *Examiner*, 11 March 1838; *Newcastle Courant*, 16 March 1838.
2   On the London Corresponding Society, see John Barrell, 'London and the London Corresponding Society', in James Chandler and Kevin Gilmartin (eds), *Romantic Metropolis: The urban scene of British culture, 1780–1840* (Cambridge: Cambridge University Press, 2005), pp. 85–112; Michael T. Davis (ed.), *London Corresponding Society, 1792–1799*, 6 vols (London: Pickering & Chatto, 2002); Benjamin Weinstein, 'Popular Constitutionalism and the London Corresponding Society', *Albion*, vol. 34, no. 1 (2002), pp. 37–57; Mary Thale, 'London Debating Societies in the 1790s', *Historical Journal*, vol. 32, no. 1 (1989), pp. 57–86; John Barrell, *Imagining the King's Death: Figurative treason, fantasies of regicide, 1793–1796* (Oxford: Oxford University Press, 2000).
3   As a result of the tour, Binns and Gale Jones were indicted for 'seditious practices' at a meeting they assembled in Birmingham. See *Evening Mail*, 25 July 1796; *Whitehall Evening Post*, 26 July 1796. For accounts of their trial in Warwick, see *London Chronicle*, 1 April 1797; *The Times*, 8 May 1797. They were eventually confined in Birmingham Prison. For a discussion of the *Treasonable Practices Act*, see Barrell, *Imagining the King's Death*, pp. 551–603.
4   *Morning Post*, 12 January 1798.

same tavern hosted many of the deliberations of the British Forum, a debating club Jones helped establish after the eventual demise of the LCS at the turn of the century.[5]

In 1810, Jones was imprisoned in the detested and feared Newgate prison after posting a placard condemning a Member of Parliament, Charles Yorke, for seeking to exclude visitors to the Strangers Gallery in the House of Commons during a debate.[6] Yorke had Jones charged with a breach of privilege and confined indefinitely in Newgate. Despite the support of many other MPs—notably the independent Whig Sir Francis Burdett (who in turn was committed to Newgate for his support of Jones)—Jones was not released from prison until four months later.[7] Newgate evidently proved little deterrent for Jones's radical proclivities; later the same year he was committed to a new prison on the London penal landscape: the Coldbath Fields House of Correction. Here Jones was confined for 12 months for a libel on Lord Castlereagh, a man loathed by the radical community for his role in the harsh suppression of the Irish Uprising in 1798, as well as for his vehement stance against political reform.[8] By 1810, Coldbath Fields had become notorious for its harsh administration of justice, and the conditions experienced by its radical prisoners, including Jones, gained wide publicity.

By 1819, Jones can be found among the 3000 other shocked and distressed Londoners who thronged to the Crown and Anchor tavern upon hearing the news of the Peterloo massacre—the now infamous episode in British history in which the Manchester magistrates authorised the local yeomanry to disperse a peaceful mass protest for political reform in St Peter's Fields.[9] On 16 August, the yeomanry drew their sabres as their horses pushed through the crowds, killing more than a dozen people and injuring hundreds of others. Jones later wrote:

---

5   For a discussion of the British Forum, which generally operated out of Lunt's Coffeehouse, Clerkenwell Green, see J. W. Hudson, *A History of Adult Education* (1851; reprinted, New York: A. M. Kelley, 1969), p. 49; Iain McCalman, 'Ultra-Radicalism and Convivial Debating Clubs in London 1795–1838', *English Historical Review*, vol. 102, no. 403 (1987), pp. 329–30; *Black Dwarf*, 18 June 1823. On debating societies more generally, see Donna T. Andrew (ed.), *London Debating Societies, 1776–9* (London: London Record Society, 1994).
6   W. D. Jones, 'Jones, John Gale', pp. 270–1; Hone, *For the Cause of Truth*, p. 197.
7   On Jones's confinement in Newgate, see *Morning Chronicle*, 17 April 1810; *Leeds Mercury*, 21 April 1810. For Burdett's speech to the House of Commons calling for Jones's release, see *Morning Chronicle*, 13 March 1810. Following the printing of the speech in *Cobbett's Weekly Political Register*, Burdett was accused of a breach of privilege. See *Cobbett's Weekly Political Register*, 24 March 1810. On Sir Francis Burdett, see J. R. Dinwiddy, 'Sir Francis Burdett and Burdettite Radicalism', *History*, vol. 65 (1980), pp.17–31; Hone, *For the Cause of Truth*, pp. 117–219. For more on Burdett, see Chapters 2 and 5 of this study.
8   *Jackson's Oxford Journal*, 1 December 1810.
9   For a contemporary account of events in Manchester in 1819, see Samuel Bamford, *Passages in the Life of a Radical* (Oxford: Oxford University Press, 1984), pp. 134–59. See also Joyce Marlow, *The Peterloo Massacre* (London: Rapp & Whiting, 1969); M. L. Bush, *The Casualties of Peterloo* (Lancaster: Carnegie, 2005); Robert Poole, 'The March to Peterloo: Politics and festivity in late Georgian England', *Past & Present*, no. 192 (2006), pp. 109–53. On women's involvement in Peterloo, see Anna Clark, *Struggle for the Breeches: Gender and the*

> From that fatal day when the sword was drawn and war declared against the people of England, by the bloody and unavenged massacre of the defenceless men, women and children of Manchester, I was one of those, who made up their mind that all further praying and petitioning ought to be at an end, that the *time for Reform was past and the hour of revolution had come*.[10]

Peterloo was a galvanising moment for new and old radical followers alike, and it consolidated the rapidly emerging leadership provided by aspiring Member of Parliament and Peterloo's key platform orator, Henry Hunt.[11] Jones shifted his own political support from Burdett to the immensely popular Hunt, whose enduring support of universal male suffrage mirrored Jones's own political raison d'être.

Jones was again at the Crown and Anchor later that year to deliver a British Forum oration protesting against the imprisonment of leading radical publisher and champion of the freedom of the press, Richard Carlile.[12] Jones developed a close friendship with Carlile over the next decade, supporting the controversial advocate of Thomas Paine's works during his recurrent terms of imprisonment. Jones's commitment to republican principles was also cemented by this time: 'What then was mere youthful predilection, is now deliberate conviction, and will, I doubt not, continue so till the end of my days.'[13]

The friendship between the radical stalwarts saw Jones again rise to prominence as a key player in Carlile's post-prison venture at the Blackfriars Road Rotunda in South London. Now a veteran of the radical movement, Jones continued to delight Rotunda audiences with his political oratory during 1830 and 1831. With the closure of the venue in 1832, however, he appears to have retired from public life. Like most of the prominent male radicals of this period, little is known of Jones's family, though we know he was married. Mrs Jones is briefly visible in the public record during John's time in Coldbath Fields prison, but it is unclear whether she survived him when he died in 1838. The end of his life was also typical of many radicals of the period: he died without seeing his political convictions realised and his final years were 'embittered by poverty'.[14]

---

making of the British working class (Berkeley: University of California Press, 1995), pp. 161–73; M. L. Bush, 'The Women at Peterloo: The impact of female reform on the Manchester meeting of 16 August 1819', *History*, vol. 89, no. 2 (2004), pp. 209–32.
10 *Republican*, 28 June 1822.
11 On Henry Hunt, see John Belchem, *'Orator' Hunt: Henry Hunt and English working-class radicalism* (Oxford: Clarendon Press, 1985); Henry Hunt, *Memoirs of Henry Hunt, Esq., Written by himself in his majesty's jail at Ilchester*, 3 vols (London, 1820–22).
12 *The Speech of John Gale Jones, Delivered at the British Forum, held at the Crown and Anchor in the Strand* (London, 1819). For more on Carlile, see Chapters 1, 3 and 6–8 of this study.
13 *Republican*, 6 June 1822.
14 *Manchester Times and Gazette*, 10 March 1838.

This biographical snapshot of John Gale Jones reveals a life that traversed radical London, both literally and metaphorically. There were many common elements to his experience, but one feature that has received only limited attention in the scholarship of early nineteenth-century radicalism is the venues in which it occurred: from the ostensible restrictions of incarceration and the conditional space of the public house—occupied under the capricious eye of the authorities and at the whim of the licensee—to the tenuous liberty of a venue owned and operated by radicals themselves. Thus, it is not Jones's radical life, per se, that is of primary interest to this study, but how his story illuminates some key sites of radical activity in the period of his radical career.

As the drive for political reform gathered pace in the late eighteenth and early nineteenth centuries, alongside London's increasing urban sprawl and emerging public sphere, the geography of the capital became patterned with political spaces. This book examines the relationship between radical activity and the spaces in which it operated from the 1790s through to the beginnings of Chartism in the early 1840s. It is guided by two overarching questions. Were sites of radical assembly more than simply physical structures within which to assemble or did the space itself affect the activity taking place therein? And what does this reveal about radical culture of the early nineteenth century and its place within the wider public sphere?

The issue of space is a particularly salient one for early nineteenth-century radical culture. Jones himself faced difficulties securing premises for his Westminster Forum—the earlier incarnation of the British Forum.[15] The view of one of Jones's close Rotunda associates, the Reverend Robert Taylor, encapsulates the importance of such sites to the radical community itself. In 1829, before the opening of Carlile's Blackfriars Road premises, Taylor had identified the importance of establishing a dedicated space from which to operate. What radicalism needed, he felt, was 'to see and feel a tangibility of our great cause about us, a substance and a nucleus; around which support may wreath itself; a place, a house…I cannot dream of an Infidel College, but some place'.[16]

Taylor's yearning for this 'tangibility' highlights the importance of access to spaces in which to assemble and communicate, to organise, gain inspiration and to embrace followers. It also speaks of a significance much deeper than merely a physical structure under which to gather.

The authorities recognised the importance of radical spaces too. Taylor's plea for a 'substance and nucleus' for the radical community spoke to the immense challenge of finding sites for political assembly during this period. When the government witnessed overt popular discontent on an unprecedented scale, its

---

15 McCalman, 'Ultra-Radicalism and Convivial Debating Clubs', pp. 311–12.
16 *Lion*, 23 January 1829.

attempts to cripple the burgeoning radical movement had a key spatial element. The two incarnations of the *Seditious Meetings Act*, passed in 1795 and in 1819, placed severe restrictions on the numbers allowed at political meetings to only 50. The acts were introduced alongside a raft of other legislation, including the *Treasonable Practices Act* (1795), the suspension of habeas corpus (1794 and 1817), the *Newspaper Stamp Duties Act* (1819) and the *Blasphemous and Seditious Libels Act* (1819), which together formed Britain's domestic security architecture—supported further by a growing network of spies and informers to monitor and survey the key radical players at their sites of assembly.[17] Despite recent scholarly debate over the reach and effectiveness of the legislation,[18] when the approach of the authorities is considered as a whole, it is evident that a key aim was to restrict outlets for expression, including access to spaces in which to assemble, in order to curtail the expansion of the political nation beyond the narrow confines of the aristocratic elite.

Moreover, it must be remembered that the period encapsulated by this study was one in which property equalled not only wealth and prestige, but also political power. Inclusion in the political nation was predicated precisely on the ownership of property, entitling a minority of men access to official spaces of political power. For those excluded from the formal arenas of the political nation, then, the association of space with power—and deliberate attempts of the authorities to restrict access to spaces for political purposes—helps account for Taylor's impassioned appeal for a 'substance and nucleus' for the radical movement. For women, the issue of access to space in this period takes on an added layer of complexity, for, as many scholars argue, women became increasingly marginalised both in radical culture and in the wider public sphere.

The issue of space and its social dimension has captured the scholarly imagination for the past several decades. Scholars from a range of disciplines, including political theory, architecture, philosophy, human geography, sociology, anthropology and history, have all turned their attention to the interplay between spaces, social organisation and social movements.[19] Library shelves

---

17 For a discussion of the 1790s legislation including the suspension of habeas corpus, the *Treasonable Practices Act* and the seditious libel laws, see Barrell, *Imagining the Kings Death*, passim. See also Clive Emsley, 'An Aspect of Pitt's Terror: Prosecutions for sedition during the 1790s', *Social History*, vol. 6 (1981), pp. 155–84; idem, 'Repression, "Terror" and the Rule of Law in England During the Decade of the French Revolution', *The English Historical Review*, vol. 100, no. 397 (1985), pp. 801–25; Philip Harling, 'The Law of Libel and the Limits of Repression, 1790–1832', *The Historical Journal*, vol. 44, no. 1 (2001), pp. 107–34; Michael Lobban, 'From Seditious Libel to Unlawful Assembly: Peterloo and the changing face of political crime, c.1770–1820', *Oxford Journal of Legal Studies*, vol. 10, no. 3 (1990), pp. 307–52.
18 See Emsley, 'An Aspect of Pitt's Terror', pp. 155–84; idem, 'Repression, "Terror" and the Rule of Law', pp. 801–25; Harling, 'The Law of Libel and the Limits of Repression', pp. 107–34.
19 Although the literature in the field is too vast to undertake a thorough survey, take, for example: Henri Lefebvre, *The Production of Space*, trans. D. Nicholson-Smith (1974; reprinted, Oxford: Blackwell, 1996); Michel de Certeau, *The Practice of Everyday Life* (Berkeley: University of California Press, 1984); Derek Gregory and John Urry (eds), *Social Relations and Spatial Structure* (Bassingstoke: Macmillan, 1985); Charles

now groan under the weight of a plethora of works that interrogate the notion of space, its definitions and varieties, and its importance to human activity and communities.[20] The concept of 'space' has been cast widely, from virtual landscapes to abstract and disembodied arenas in which discourse occurs, from human occupation of natural locales to tangible spaces of the built environment.

Analysis of the built environment, which most directly concerns this study, has traditionally fallen within the purview of the architectural scholar. The earliest sense that architecture was something more than the unison of 'form and function' saw the rise of the notion of *architecture parlante*—that architecture speaks, that it is expressive.[21] Concomitantly, the expressive nature of the built environment enabled architecture to be 'read', as one might read a painting or other form of art. Within the field of architectural studies, such readings of the built environment focus largely on the fabric and aesthetics of the site, and the role of the architect in a particular historical or spatial context, rather than the interactions and interplays between the space and its inhabitants. As Jonathon Hill argues, architects and architectural historians often view the occupants of a space as the 'intruder'—manifested, he contends, most evidently by the practice of the architectural photograph, in which the 'most obvious and important action is…to empty architecture of its inhabitants'.[22]

Many scholars in the humanities and social sciences now consider that a 'reading' of architecture and other spaces—to appreciate the way they are used,

---

Tilly, 'Spaces of Contention', *Mobilization: An International Quarterly*, vol. 5, no. 2 (2000), pp. 135–59; P. Howell, 'Public Space and the Public Sphere: Political theory and the historical geography of modernity', *Society and Space*, vol. 11 (1993), pp. 303–22; Richard Sennet, *The Fall of Public Man: On the social psychology of capitalism* (Cambridge: Cambridge University Press, 1978); Edward W. Soja, 'The Spatiality of Social Life: Towards a transformative retheorisation', in Gregory and Urry, *Social Relations and Spatial Structure*; Peter Stallybrass and Allon White, *The Politics and Poetics of Transgression* (Ithaca, NY: Cornell University Press, 1986); Allan Pred, *Making Histories and Constructing Human Geographies* (Colorado: Westview Press, 1990); Doreen Massey, *For Space* (London: Sage, 2005); Jane Rendell, Barbara Penner and Iain Borden, *Gender Space Architecture: An interdisciplinary introduction* (London: Routledge, 2000).

20 Another such work, coincidentally, shares the name of this study. The political theorist Margaret Kohn's *Radical Space: Building the house of the people* was published after I began the study for my PhD thesis on which this book is based. It also uses space as the guiding paradigm for a study of the democratic movement in pre-Fascist Italy. Her study undertakes a more overtly theoretical approach to spatial analysis and provides a very useful overview of the development of spatial theory and politics. Margaret Kohn, *Radical Space: Building the house of the people* (Ithaca, NY: Cornell University Press, 2003).

21 For a discussion of the change within French architectural theory that saw architecture become seen in terms of an expressive language—'something more than a mixed art uniting beauty and utility'—see Remy G. Saisselin, 'Architecture and Language: The sensationalism of Le Camus De Mezeieres', *British Journal of Aesthetics*, vol. 15, no. 3 (1975), pp. 239–53. See also Richard Wittman, 'Architecture, Space, and Abstraction in the Eighteenth-Century French Public Sphere', *Representations*, vol. 102, no. 1 (2008), pp. 1–26, especially p. 16.

22 Jonathon Hill, *Occupying Architecture: Between the architect and the user* (London: Routledge, 1988), p. 139. Some architectural historians, however, consider that 'the interpretation of people's social experience of spaces and buildings' is paramount in understanding architecture's 'relationship to the rest of the world'. See the forward by Adrian Forty as well as the contributions to Iain Borden, Joe Kerr, Alicia Pivaro and Jane Rendell (eds), *Strangely Familiar: Narratives of architecture in the city* (London: Routledge, 1996).

formed and transformed by their inhabitants—is a crucial avenue of inquiry. Sites of human activity are no longer seen merely as passive contexts in which the human experience is played out, but rather, as Derek Gregory and John Urry argue, 'as a medium through which social relations are produced and reproduced'.[23] Further, recognition of the cultural conventions that determine behaviour within a particular site has also gained wide traction. Peter Stallybrass and Allon White maintain that 'each "site of assembly" constitutes a nucleus of material and cultural conditions which regulate what may and may not be said, who may speak, how people may communicate and what importance must be given to what is said'.[24] The relationship between culture and space, to borrow from Allan Pred, has the potential to lead to 'a better understanding of human and social phenomena, past and present'.[25]

Historians of the late eighteenth and early nineteenth century radical movements have long sensed, at least implicitly, that space mattered to radical culture. Among the seminal works in the genre are those involving the narrative of radical culture told through its spaces. In his chronicle of the formation of a class-consciousness among the English working class, E. P. Thompson documented the sites in which radical life unfolded. He recognised that the working-class 'public market' consisted of two important elements: not only the market of the printed word expressed through the burgeoning radical press, but also the 'market for spoken debate'.[26] Iain McCalman's rich and detailed portrayal of the radical underground illuminated the less prominent and less respectable side of radical culture, including its taverns, coffee houses, bookshops and other meeting places.[27] For all that works such as those by Thompson, McCalman and others have provided a window onto radical culture, subsequent work by Dorothy Thompson, Barbara Taylor, Catherine Hall and Anna Clark (among others) has become their essential scholarly companion by bringing to the fore the issue of the gendered nature of radicalism in the age of reform. Their work has identified the spaces in which women either experienced or were denied

---

23 Gregory and Urry, *Social Relations and Spatial Structure*, p. 3.
24 Stallybrass and White, *The Politics and Poetics of Transgression*, quoted in James Epstein, *In Practice: Studies in the language and culture of popular politics in modern Britain* (Stanford: Stanford University Press, 2003), p. 113.
25 Pred, *Making Histories and Constructing Human Geographies*, p. 1.
26 Thompson, *The Making of the English Working Class*, p. 843.
27 McCalman, *Radical Underworld*. Other historians have, of course, noted the importance of such spaces to extra-parliamentary agitation. Take, for example, James Walvin's work on the anti-slavery campaigns and his argument that Exeter Hall 'came to symbolise anti-slavery'. James Walvin, 'The Propaganda of Anti-Slavery', in James Walvin (ed.), *Slavery and British Society 1776–1846* (London: Macmillan, 1982), p. 53. See also Gillian Russell's contention that the Beaufort Buildings in London represented a 'potent political space'. Gillian Russell, 'Spouters or Washerwomen: The sociability of Romantic lecturing', in Gillian Russell and Clara Tuite (eds), *Romantic Sociability: Social networks and literary culture in Britain, 1770–1840* (Cambridge: Cambridge University Press, 2002), pp. 126–9; and Paul A. Pickering and Alex Tyrrell's recognition of the importance of the Manchester Free Trade Hall in the Anti-Corn Law campaign. Paul A. Pickering and Alex Tyrrell, *The People's Bread: A history of the Anti-Corn Law League* (London: Leicester University Press, 2000), pp. 41, 44, 88.

access to the venues of political culture.[28] Although these studies, and the many more that followed, returned the sites of radical activity to the historical map, the spaces themselves were implicit to the narrative, rather than its driving force.

James Epstein was among the first to explicitly invoke the paradigm of spatial analysis in his studies on British radicalism. Strongly informed by work in other disciplinary fields, Epstein's work has focused on the 'logic of spatial practices' in the production of cultural and political meanings. Epstein chides historians for their tendency to give 'short shrift' to space as a 'dimension of historical agency' when 'human action takes place within time and space'.[29] He presents a series of vignettes of the coffee house and the courtroom to illustrate the connections between radical activity and space, anticipating the possibilities of 'writing histories of the economics of social and discursive space, not as a supplement—as background and context—to meaning, but as part of a complex, active process bound to the production of meaning'.[30]

This study seeks such ground. It is concerned principally with enriching our understanding of radicalism by narrowing the lens on specific sites of radical assembly to provide both a deep and a broad reading of the venues in order to explore how these spaces shaped, or were shaped by, radical culture. The following pages populate the spaces of the public sphere with their historical actors through the use of public records—both textual and visual—of the period, as well as private correspondence and secret service reports to the Home Office. In so doing, it perhaps could be categorised as a study invoking the so-called 'spatial turn', however, it does not aim to do so at the expense of other key categories of analysis, such as class and gender, but rather to complement and inform these other explorations of the complex relations between politics, culture and plebeian agency.[31]

The English tavern and coffee house have gained much celebrity as transformative political spaces with the seminal theory of the public sphere penned by Jürgen

---

28 Dorothy Thompson, 'Women and Nineteenth-Century Radical Politics', in Juliet Mitchell and Ann Oakley (eds), *The Rights and Wrongs of Women* (London: Penguin Books, 1976); Anna Clark, *Struggle for the Breeches*; Barbara Taylor, *Eve and the New Jerusalem: Socialism and feminism in the nineteenth century* (London: Virago, 1983); Catherine Hall, *White, Male and Middle-Class: Explorations in feminism and history* (Oxford: Polity Press, 1992).
29 Epstein, *In Practice*, p. 107.
30 Ibid. Other scholars have followed Epstein's lead. Take, for example, James Vernon, *Politics and the People: A study in English political culture, c. 1815–1867* (Cambridge: Cambridge University Press, 1993), especially chs 2 and 6. References to other works appear throughout this study.
31 For a good overview of the often rigorous debates among historians about class and gender in the pre-Chartist and mid-Victorian period, see the introduction in Neville Kirk, *Change, Continuity and Class: Labour in British society, 1850–1920* (Manchester: Manchester University Press, 1998), pp. 1–20. For another take on the debate, see also the introduction to Vernon, *Politics and the People*, pp. 1–14.

Habermas.³² Habermas envisaged these urban institutions of the eighteenth and nineteenth centuries as part of the fabric that enabled the formulation of a public sphere, distinct both from the authority of the state and the court on the one hand and from the private world of the family on the other. The public sphere, Habermas wrote, was the arena that 'mediates between society and state, in which the public organizes itself as the bearer of public opinion'.³³ In Habermas's conception of the public sphere, rational-critical discourse and debate among the emergent bourgeois about the common good helped formulate public opinion, shifted power from the state and the court and in so doing provided the genesis of democratic decision making. Though Habermas considers that the public sphere was born in the 'world of letters' as an 'apolitical form', he points to such public spaces as the tavern and coffee house as critical sites that enabled the transformation to a 'public sphere in the political realm'.³⁴

The English edition of Habermas's *The Structural Transformation of the Public Sphere* (published 17 years after the German-language original) soon captured the attention of scholars of Britain, both because of the prominence of the British Isles in Habermas's account of the historical conditions that enabled the public sphere to emerge and for what were perceived as its crucial historical omissions—based in large part on who Habermas considered as participants in the public sphere. For Habermas, the public sphere emerged with the rational discourse and exchange of the bourgeoisie, and he therefore dismissed the plebeian public sphere as a 'variant' that was 'suppressed in the historical process', which failed to ever 'attain dominance' and instead 'oriented itself to the intentions of the bourgeois public sphere'.³⁵ Students of British history, such as Craig Calhoun, Geoff Eley, Jon Klancher, Kevin Gilmartin and Terry Eagleton, swiftly took exception to Habermas's dismissal of the plebeian public sphere in the British context.³⁶ As Eley suggests, 'private people putting reason to use' could be found

---

32 Jürgen Habermas, *The Structural Transformation of the Public Sphere: An inquiry into a category of bourgeois society*, trans. Thomas Burger (Cambridge, Mass.: MIT Press, 1989). Richard Sennet also considered the coffee house as a transformative social space due to its egalitarian ideals and forum for free speech. Sennet, *The Fall of Public Man*, pp. 80–4. There are many scholarly works that focus on Habermas and the British coffee house. See, for example, the recent paper by Brian Cowan, 'Publicity and Privacy in the History of the British Coffeehouse', *History Compass*, vol. 5, no. 4 (2007), pp. 1180–213. For further discussion of the coffee house and the tavern as spaces of the public sphere, see also Chapter 5 of this study.
33 Jürgen Habermas, 'The Public Sphere: An encyclopedia article', in Stephen Eric Bronner and Douglas Kellner (eds), *Critical Theory and Society* (New York: Routledge, 1989), p. 137.
34 Habermas, *The Structural Transformation of the Public Sphere*, pp. 33–6, 51–9.
35 Ibid., p. xviii.
36 See Craig Calhoun's introduction in Craig Calhoun (ed.), *Habermas and the Public Sphere* (Cambridge, Mass.: MIT Press, 1992); and the contribution in that volume by Geoff Eley, 'Nations, Publics, and Political Cultures: Placing Habermas in the nineteenth century', pp. 289–339; Terry Eagleton, *The Function of Criticism, From the Spectator to Post-Structuralism* (London: Verso, 1984); Jon Klancher, *The Making of English Reading Audiences, 1790–1832* (Madison: University of Wisconsin Press, 1987). For an overview of the scholarship that has sought to restore the place of the plebeian public sphere, see Kevin Gilmartin, 'Popular Radicalism and the Public Sphere', *Studies in Romanticism*, vol. 33, no. 4 (1994), pp. 549–57; idem, *Print Politics: The press and radical opposition in early nineteenth-century England* (Cambridge: Cambridge University Press, 1996), pp. 1–10.

beyond the confines of the bourgeoisie, and the public sphere quickly acquired 'broader democratic resonance' than Habermas's bourgeois construct allowed.[37] And, as Calhoun adds, the discourse of 'artisans, workers and others' cannot be understood as simply 'derivative of the bourgeois public sphere'.[38] Moreover, he continues, 'the absence of social movements from Habermas's account thus also reflects an inattention to agency, to the struggles by which both the public sphere and its participants are actively made and remade' or, further, the ability to 'permeat[e] it with demands from below'.[39]

The revisionist case to re-situate plebeian players in the public sphere has fostered further scholarly debate about the nature of their participation. Did the plebeian public arena constitute a counter-public sphere, or spheres, which either operated beyond, or overlapped with, the mainstream?[40] Or does Habermas's classical public sphere require reframing to take account of a wider breadth of participants? Terry Eagleton, for instance, considers that 'the whole epoch of the intensive class struggle' presented by E. P. Thompson constituted 'nothing less than a "counter-public sphere"'.[41] James Epstein also contends that 'radical dining during the early nineteenth century can be viewed as an aspect of the attempt to fashion an autonomous and distinctly working-class or plebeian "public sphere"', which operated in parallel with the bourgeois public sphere.[42] Kevin Gilmartin, for one, considers this position is overstating the independence of the radical sphere and is concerned that the tendency of revisionist theorists to '"pluralize" and "multiply" as well as spectralize the concept of the public sphere' is at odds with the radicals' own desire for 'unity in opposition and for a limit to counter-publicity', and their own testing of the boundaries of the public sphere, which closer resembles Habermas's 'relatively monolithic theory of the classical public sphere'.[43]

This study heeds Gilmartin's warning to 'remain sensitive to historical variations' in its consideration of the counter-sphere argument as it populates these radical spaces. It also remains mindful of Eley's proposition that the 'public sphere makes more sense as the structured setting where cultural and ideological contest or negotiation among a variety of publics takes place'.[44] This analysis of radical spaces traces the expanding political nation and in so doing interrogates

---

37   Eley, 'Nations, Publics, and Political Cultures', p. 304.
38   Calhoun, 'Introduction', in his *Habermas and the Public Sphere*, p. 38.
39   Ibid., p. 39.
40   For an overview of the debate, see Gilmartin, 'Popular Radicalism and the Public Sphere', pp. 547–9; Orrin N. C. Wang, 'Romancing the Counter-Public Sphere: A response to Romanticism and its publics', *Studies in Romanticism*, vol. 33, no. 4 (1994), pp. 579–88.
41   Eagleton, *The Function of Criticism*, p. 36.
42   James Epstein, *Radical Expression: Political language, ritual and symbol in England, 1790–1850* (Oxford: Oxford University Press, 1994), p. 150.
43   Gilmartin, 'Popular Radicalism and the Public Sphere', p. 556.
44   Eley, 'Nations, Publics and Political Culture', p. 306.

both Habermas's contention that the plebeian public sphere was merely an imitation of the bourgeois sphere and the dichotomy inherent in the analysis of Epstein (and others) between the bourgeois and plebeian spheres. As we can see in the opening biographical snapshot of John Gale Jones, he moved within and between many institutions of the public sphere, and the chapters that follow also make the case for a more integrated and symbiotic relationship than perhaps the bourgeois–plebeian or the counter-mainstream dichotomies allow.

By populating the spaces of the public sphere, this study also aims to address a second major criticism of the Habermas vision: his neglect of the issue of gender in the construction of the public sphere. The English translation of *Structural Transformation* in 1989 drew sustained criticism from feminist scholars, such as Joan Landes, who argued that the gendered exclusion was not merely incidental to the formation of the public sphere, but rather that its masculine construction was crucial to its very formation.[45] Many scholars also took Habermas to task for the relegation of women to the private sphere of the family as a new 'source of subjectivity'.[46] There is now a growing body of knowledge that situates women within the public sphere and views the boundaries between the private sphere of the family and the public sphere as more fluid than Habermas originally envisaged. As Brian Cowan notes, 'the public sphere was (and is) imagined in a manner quite different from the ways in which [it] was enacted in daily life'.[47] In the pages that follow, we will find women where none were thought to gather.

Habermas's neglect of both the issue of gender and plebeian participation can be partly attributed, as Calhoun notes, to his 'general lack of attention to the nineteenth-century public sphere' as well as 'thinness of attention to matters of culture and the construction of identity'.[48] This relationship between identity and radical culture and the public sphere is another central tenet of this book. The radical movement was a loose collective at this time, fractured by ideological affiliation, allegiances to prominent leaders, tensions over religious dissent and the means by which to effect change. This study explores how various venues across London allowed both leaders and followers a collective identity in the years before the disparate working-class movements were encompassed under the umbrella of Chartism or trade unionism.

Despite the paucity of attention to the plebeian public sphere, its gendered nature or its construction of identity, Habermas's work has opened a rich and

---

45   Joan Landes, *Women and the Public Sphere: In the age of the French Revolution* (Ithaca, NY: Cornell University Press, 1988); idem, *Women and the Public Sphere in the Age of Enlightenment* (Ithaca, NY: Cornell University Press, 1994).
46   For a thorough overview of the debates around gender, Habermas and the public sphere, see Jane Rendall, 'Women and the Public Sphere', *Gender & History*, vol. 11, no. 3 (1999), pp. 475–88.
47   Brian Cowan, 'What was Masculine about the Public Sphere? Gender and the coffeehouse milieu in post-Restoration England', *History Workshop Journal*, vol. 51 (2001), p. 133.
48   Calhoun, 'Introduction', p. 34.

wide vein of inquiry and debate.[49] Although historians such as Cowan lament the overuse of the concept of the public sphere as an impetus to inquiry—'every era has had its own public sphere', making the term 'so fluid that with a little imagination it can be applied to almost any time and any place'[50]—and others such as Ruth Bloch anticipate that the concept has come 'perilously close to dissolving into mush',[51] or David Waldstreicher, who considers the theory 'half swallowed and half dead'[52], I argue that the use of the concept of the public sphere still has much to offer scholars of early nineteenth-century radical culture and of wider society.

A thorough survey of all of London's radical sites—or indeed the thousands beyond the metropolis—lies beyond the scope of this book. There clearly exist a multitude of such spaces, some of which have been highlighted in other scholarship—from courtrooms, taverns, coffee houses and radical bookshops to the open spaces of streets, fields and parks, or the world of the radical family home where ideologies were debated and discussed in private.[53] Instead, this study offers a sample of key radical spaces from London's political landscape of the early nineteenth century, indicated by the calculated selections from the life of John Gale Jones surveyed earlier. These were important sites in and of themselves, but here they also serve another purpose: they provide an index of the types of space in which radical politics happened.

The book is divided into three sections. Section one is concerned with a pre-eminent radical space of the late eighteenth/early nineteenth century, though not one of any radical's choosing: the prison cell. Although the punitive and

---

49 The legion of studies focusing on the public sphere and the nature of its formation is too great to list here. Aside from the works already noted, Harold Mah's overview of the reception and use of the public sphere theory in Britain and beyond provides a very useful survey of the field. Harold Mah, 'Phantasties of the Public Sphere: Rethinking the Habermas of historians', *The Journal of Modern History*, vol. 72, no. 1 (2000), pp. 153–82.
50 Cowan, 'What was Masculine about the Public Sphere?', p. 128.
51 Ruth H. Bloch, 'Inside and Outside the Public Sphere', *The William and Mary Quarterly*, vol. 62, no. 1 (2005), pp. 99–106.
52 David Waldstreicher, 'Two Cheers for the "Public Sphere"…and one for historians' skepticism', *The William and Mary Quarterly*, vol. 62, no. 1 (2005), pp. 107–12.
53 See, for example: on outdoor spaces and radical culture, John Michael Roberts, 'Spatial Governance and Working Class Public Spheres: The case of a Chartist demonstration at Hyde Park', *Journal of Historical Sociology*, vol. 14, no. 3 (2001), pp. 305–35; Vernon, *Politics and the People*, pp. 208–14. For the later Victorian period, see Antony Taylor, '"Commons-Stealers", "Land-Grabbers" and "Jerry-Builders": Space, popular radicalism and the politics of public access in London, 1848–1880', *International Review of Social History*, vol. 40, no. 3 (1995), pp. 383–407. On the coffee house as a venue for political discourse, see John Barrell, 'Coffee-House Politicians', *Journal of British Studies*, vol. 43 (2004), pp. 206–32. On the courtroom as a radical forum, see Uwe Böker, 'Institutionalised Rules of Discourse and the Courtroom as a Site of the Public Sphere', in Uwe Böker and Julie A. Hibbard (eds), *Sites of Discourse—Public and private spheres—legal culture* (Amsterdam, NY: Rodopi, 2002), pp. 35–66; Epstein, *In Practice*, pp. 59–82; Kevin Gilmartin, *Print Politics: The press and radical opposition in early nineteenth-century England* (New York: Cambridge University Press, 1996), pp. 115–57. On radical culture and taverns in the second half of the nineteenth century, see Antony Taylor, '"A Melancholy Odyssey Among London Public Houses": Radical club life and the unrespectable in mid-nineteenth century London', *Historical Research*, vol. 78, no. 199 (2005), pp. 74–95.

isolated space of the prison might at first appear incongruent with a study of rational exchange of the public sphere, the plethora of convictions for political crime in the period and the number of radical voices that can be heard in the historical record from within the prison warrant an investigation of the prison as a radical space. Chapter 1 utilises Iain McCalman's study of the intellectual culture of the 1790s Newgate radicals as a springboard to explore and compare the experience of a later generation of radical prisoners within the ancient penal site. It focuses on the 1820s, when Newgate not only housed radical prisoners of a more plebeian rank than their 1790s counterparts, but at a time when Newgate's long-established subculture and unique prison economy, based largely on the ability to pay to secure comforts, was rattled by the tenets of the prison reform movement. How did Newgate fare within this new penal regime and what effect did it have on its radical prisoners? Were they able to effect a radical counterculture within the prison walls as their 1790s predecessors had or did the new prison environment impede their participation in the discourse and exchange of the wider public sphere?

These questions are revisited in Chapter 2 within the context of a new prison on the penal landscape: Coldbath Fields House of Correction. This was one of the earliest prisons built to implement the prison reform ideals of separate and solitary confinement, and the chapter explores the architectural changes engendered by the prison reform movement and their impact on the radicals' relationship to the prison space. It considers the theory of Michel Foucault and the work of British penal historian Michael Ignatieff, who contend that the impetus of prison reform had more to do with social control than it did with humanitarianism. However, the radical experience of the reformed prison space remains the central concern; how the changes in architectural configuration affected the ability to forge a radical identity and resist that ascribed by the prison space, and further, whether the new spatial configuration of the prison proved an impediment to the participation of its radical prisoners in the public sphere beyond its walls.

The issues of gender and political crime provide the focus of Chapter 3, which offers a case study of a female radical prisoner, Susannah Wright, imprisoned in both the 'unreformed' Newgate and the 'reformed' Coldbath Fields prisons during the 1820s. It considers how her experience of these prison spaces compared with her male colleagues, particularly in a period when female criminality was associated with liminality and prostitution—the very antithesis of the feminine ideal. Wright's story also highlights the connections between different types of radical spaces that were scattered across London at this time and provides a lens through which to view how women negotiated these spaces.

Section two of the book focuses on a more likely institution in the public sphere: the Crown and Anchor tavern—one of the great cultural and political centres of the metropolis. From the 1790s through the first half of the nineteenth century, the Crown and Anchor was a vibrant, visible and tangible embodiment of the public sphere. As an established space on London's cultural landscape, the tavern was appropriated by successive generations of radicals throughout the period of this study. Chapter 4 traces the representation of the Crown and Anchor in visual culture—specifically in caricature, or graphic satire—through the late eighteenth century to the period of Peterloo. Through an analysis of these visual records of the past, it charts how the tavern came to be understood in the public sphere as a radical space, but also as a site of legitimate political opposition. It examines how, over time, the tavern generated its own language, protocols and practices. The venue's nomenclature, like its symbolic counterpart, the tavern emblem, became a form of political shorthand.

The story of the Crown and Anchor in the first half of the nineteenth century is taken up in Chapter 5. In this period, the tavern's clientele shifted considerably from its association with elite politics of liberal Whiggish and parliamentary radicals to a space embraced by London's expanding political nation. By examining the tavern's radical clientele, the chapter explores who was participating in public discourse at the venue and how the radical relationship with the tavern was affected following the 1832 *Reform Act*.

The third section of this study focuses on Richard Carlile's Blackfriars Road Rotunda as both a unique radical space and a venue of the public sphere. The Rotunda was one of the first spaces controlled and operated by the radical movement itself and it drew on both new and traditional forms of radical communication and urban sociability. Chapter 6 documents the site's prehistory, as first the Leverian Museum and later the Surrey Institution, before it became a haven for working-class radical culture under Carlile's tutelage between 1830 and 1832. In Chapter 7, we meet the multivalent identities associated with the Rotunda, enabled by Carlile's success, albeit briefly, to combine all the elements of plebeian radicalism under the one roof. It also explores the tensions inherent in London radicalism at this period and how these impacted on the space of the Rotunda and wider radical culture.

The final chapter in this study again brings the gendered nature of such sites of assembly to the fore and explores the participation of women at the Rotunda, both as platform orators and as audience members, in a venue whose dominant public identity was essentially masculine. At a time when the feminine ideal was increasingly celebrated as apolitical, and in a period when scholars consider women were increasingly marginalised from the public sphere, the Rotunda's emphasis on gender inclusion and its repercussions for radical culture warrant investigation.

The book argues the case that space offers a useful unit of analysis, providing a highly focused index of radical culture and experience over time. It takes a narrative approach, utilising the concepts of space, identity and the public sphere as guiding paradigms for the study of radical spaces. Intermittently, it engages in a conversation with relevant theoretical concepts, rather than offering a sustained analysis of any one theory itself. The radical spaces themselves are of uppermost concern and drive the analysis, along with the historical actors who populated them—both the few who are identified and the many more who remain anonymous. These radical spaces provided a generation of men and women excluded from the formal machinery of politics with a voice in the public sphere. We only need now to open the doors and enter.

1. 'Honourable House of Blasphemers': the radical public of Newgate in the early nineteenth century

In 1799, former Newgate state prisoner Thomas Lloyd reflected on his '1187 days' of imprisonment in London's most notorious and loathed gaol as a '[c]ourse of life [that] has tended to bring into view almost all the great political questions which have agitated the two hemispheres for five and twenty years past'.[1] A debtor in the Fleet prison in 1792, Lloyd had received a further three-year sentence to Newgate for producing and displaying a truculent political poster in the Fleet.[2] For Lloyd, incarceration in Newgate gaol allowed a period of intense intellectual development, fostered by a vibrant and eclectic radical milieu that thrived in the prison during the 1790s.[3]

Lloyd's 'political enlightenment', however, was not his only focus during his imprisonment. Apart from several works written about his experiences in the American colonies during the 1780s, he also penned a damning indictment on the management and operation of Newgate itself. Overwhelmed by what confronted him on the felons' side of Newgate, Lloyd documented the squalor and destitution of the prisoners and the venality of the Keeper in his prison tract, *Impositions and Abuses in the Management of the Jail of Newgate*.[4] The publication chronicled a litany of abuses: those with the means to pay could purchase superior accommodation, no matter what their crime; prisoners were shackled with fetters and irons until they paid to be released; the windows of

---

1   Quoted in Michael Davis, Iain McCalman and Christina Parolin (eds), *Newgate in Revolution: An anthology of radical prison literature in the age of revolution* (London: Continuum, 2005), p. 81.
2   For a brief biographical account of Lloyd, see ibid., pp. 67–8, 81. For an account of prisoners' experiences in eighteenth-century debtors' prisons, see Joanna Innes, 'The King's Bench Prison in the Later Eighteenth Century: Law, authority and order in a London debtors' prison', in John Brewer and John Styles (eds), *An Ungovernable People: The English and their law in the seventeenth and eighteenth centuries* (London: Hutchinson, 1980), pp. 251–387; Margot Finn, *The Character of Credit: Personal debt in English culture, 1740–1914* (Cambridge: Cambridge University Press, 2003), pp. 109–51. While Finn and Innes offer a view of debtors' prisons as sites of prisoner agency, Philip Woodfine offers a 'darker' vision of these prisons in his paper 'Debtors, Prisons, and Petitions in Eighteenth Century England', *Eighteenth-Century Life*, vol. 30, no. 2 (2006), pp. 1–31.
3   See Davis et al., *Newgate in Revolution*, pp. ix–xxv; Iain McCalman, 'Newgate in Revolution: Radical enthusiasm and Romantic counterculture', *Eighteenth Century Life*, vol. 22 (1998), pp. 95–110; Ralph A. Manogue, 'The Plight of James Ridgway, London Bookseller and Publisher, and the Newgate Radicals 1792–1797', *Wordsworth Circle*, vol. 27 (1996), pp. 158–66; Uwe Böker, 'Institutionalised Rules of Discourse and the Courtroom as a Site of the Public Sphere', in Uwe Böker and Julie A. Hibbard (eds), *Sites of Discourse—Public and private spheres—legal culture* (Amsterdam, NY: Rodopi, 2002), pp. 211–47; John Bugg, 'Close Confinement: John Thelwall and the Romantic prison', *European Romantic Review*, vol. 20, no. 1 (2009), pp. 37–56.
4   Thomas Lloyd, 'Impositions and Abuses in the Management of the Jail of Newgate' (London, 1794), reprinted in Davis et al., *Newgate in Revolution*, pp. 69–79.

the felons' side were unglazed so that the 'poor naked wretches [were] constantly exposed to all the rigour of this severe weather'; for several days at a time the 'cisterns and pipes of the water closets see not a drop of water, to wash off the excrement and filth'; and tubs of urine were kept standing in the yards for days at a time.[5] He despaired:

> Here, in the midst of hunger, of disease, and of nakedness, rapine finds the means of gorging its voracious maw!! Such few of the miserable tenants, as have any plunder left, which their deprecations procured, are obliged to surrender it, to the myrmidons of the place.[6]

Despite regulation, and the prison's design itself, which provided for separation of different categories of prisoners, Lloyd found that money remained '*passé-partout*, the master key' to location; he was 'forced over' to the felons' side after refusing to pay the 'extortionate demands' of the Keeper for more agreeable lodgings on the state side of the prison.[7]

Lloyd's exposé indicates the vast difference between prisons operating in the late eighteenth century and the modern penitentiaries that arose in the first decades of the following century. During Lloyd's time, Newgate operated as a private concern, essentially unregulated and unchecked by government authorities.[8] Fees were extracted from prisoners for food, bedding, favours and, remarkably, for a prisoner's release once their sentence expired. Such expenses provided the main source of income for Keepers who kept their staff to a minimum in an effort to make a profit. Almost everything was available for a price within the gaol, and from the architectural plans of the prison, it is evident that even a tap room and wine room were accessible to those with the financial means to anaesthetise their sentence. A ruthless Newgate economy centred on cheap and unrestricted alcohol and a bartering system for the most basic necessities of food and clothing.

Almost two decades before Lloyd penned his Newgate treatise, the misery, overcrowding and deep corruption inherent in Britain's prisons provided the impetus for the publication of John Howard's celebrated prison reform tract, *The State of the Prisons in England and Wales*, published in 1777.[9] Howard's

---

5   Ibid., p. 72.
6   Ibid.
7   Ibid., p. 73.
8   On the history and operation of Newgate prison, see Charles Gordon, *The Old Bailey and Newgate* (London, 1902); Hepworth Dixon, *The London Prisons: With an account of the more distinguished persons who have been confined in them* (1850; reprinted, New York: Garland Publishing, 1995); Arthur Griffiths, *The Chronicles of Newgate* (London: Chapman and Hall, 1884); Anthony Babington, *The English Bastille: A history of Newgate Gaol and prison conditions in Britain 1188–1902* (London: Macdonald & Co., 1971); Richard Byrne, *Prisons and Punishments in London* (London: Grafton, 1992), pp. 25–39.
9   John Howard, *The State of the Prisons in England and Wales, With preliminary observations, and an account of some foreign prisons* (Warrington, 1777).

groundbreaking publication was the culmination of an exhaustive research tour of hundreds of gaols by Britain's pioneer prison reformer. He chronicled the idleness, profligacy, debauchery and immorality that resulted from the cheap and easy supply of alcohol, the prevalence of gaming and the freedom of sexual exchange allowed by unrestrained movement of male and female criminals throughout the prisons.[10] Howard's *State of the Prisons* provided the catalyst for a committed and exerted campaign for changes to both criminal law and punishment in Britain. The fundamental principles for penal reform—many of which relied on a complete overhaul of prison architecture—would ultimately lead to the birth of the modern penitentiary in the nineteenth century.[11]

The images of Newgate prison presented by both Howard and Lloyd are in stark contrast with the portrait of radical civility and conviviality in the prison captured in 1793 by young radical engraver Richard Newton.[12] The centrepiece of Newton's print *Soulagement en Prison, or Comfort in Prison* is Lord George Gordon's dining table in his apartment on the state side of the prison, around which a myriad radical (and other wealthy) Newgate inmates and visitors gathered to smoke pipes, drink wine and engage in conversation. Inspired, as Iain McCalman writes, by 'radical-romantic enthusiasm' and developments in revolutionary France, Gordon and men such as James Ridgway, Henry Symonds, William Holland and Charles Piggot were confined in Newgate for publishing an array of cheap subversive writings against church and state. According to McCalman, the prison became a site of 'British Jacobin civility', a 'salon of radical philosophes'.[13]

The suppression of intellectual dissent in the 1790s proved to be the first instalment in a succession of interventions to curb political and religious heterodoxy, which continued into the early decades of the 1800s. The surge in prosecutions against radicals in the early decades of the nineteenth century has been the subject of much scholarly attention, yet the connection between the prison space and radical activity remains inconspicuous in the historiography. This chapter builds on McCalman's study of 1790s Newgate to survey these other two phases of radical imprisonment in Newgate in the early decades of the nineteenth century—a crucial period in British penal history as the prison reform ideals that emanated from the work of Howard and other prison reformers increasingly impacted on the operations and management of Britain's

---

10 For an account of this Newgate culture of the eighteenth century, see W. J. Sheehan, 'Finding Solace in Eighteenth-Century Newgate', in J. S. Cockburn (ed.), *Crime in England 1550–1800* (London: Metheun, 1977), pp. 239–45.
11 For an excellent overview of the prison reform agenda, see Randall McGowen, 'The Well-Ordered Prison: England, 1780–1865', in Norval Morris and David J. Rothman (eds), *The Oxford History of the Prison: The practice of punishment in Western society* (Oxford: Oxford University Press, 1995), pp. 79–110. For more on prison reform, see Chapter 2 of this study.
12 McCalman, 'Newgate in Revolution', pp. 95–9.
13 Ibid.

oldest prison and, necessarily, on those confined there. Although Newgate prison entered the nineteenth century without the benefit of the architectural innovations prescribed in the new vision for prison reform, it is clear that by the 1820s, prison life was being transformed by the encroaching reform ideals. Although the radical prisoners themselves were of a markedly different ilk to their earlier counterparts, particularly in terms of social rank, they too found ways to perpetuate the rigorous and effective counter-culture of the 1790s. The achievements of this later cohort of radicals within the prison warrant attention because in many ways, they relied on a measure of their tenacity rather than the depth of their pockets.

* * *

Great Old Bailey Road was part of the burgeoning metropolitan landscape in 1820s London (Figure 1.1). An entirely built environment, muted shades of sandstone and various intonations of grey coloured the three-storey buildings that dominated one of London's oldest streets.[14] Tavern signs hooked the eye with splashes of colour, with the whole landscape lifted in texture and spirit by the dome of St Paul's in the distance and various church spires spiking the horizon. One of the four ancient gates to the city, *New gate* once crowned the street but by the eighteenth century had long since been claimed by fire and urban regeneration. Residential dwellings, shops and taverns with solid and indistinguishable facades now screened one side of the street, seemingly pinned to an axis at one end by the spire of St Sepulchre's church and repelled at the other by its formidable neighbour opposite: Newgate gaol.

With no framing outer prison wall, Newgate's carceral function was not immediately betrayed by its imposing facade (Figure 1.2). Stretching 300 feet (90 m) along the street and three storeys high, Newgate had a monotonous texture and colour and an imposing magnitude that struck the eye of contemporary observers.[15] In the centre of the facade was the Keeper's residence. While hardly elaborate or elegant, the central section was the most embellished, reflecting, to some extent, the aesthetic aspirations of grand architecture and its celebrated City of London architect, George Dance, the Younger.[16] Each floor of the Keeper's

---

14 The description of the environs of Newgate that follows is drawn from the visual representations of the area such as that at Figure 1.1.
15 Dixon, *The London Prisons*, pp. 191–223. See also W. H. Leeds, *Illustrations of the Public Buildings of London: With historical and descriptive accounts of each edifice*, vol. 2, second edn (London: John Weale, Architectural Library, 1838), pp. 100–13.
16 On George Dance, the Younger (1741–1825), see H. M. Colvin, *A Biographical Dictionary of British Architects*, fourth edn (New Haven, Conn.: Yale University Press, 2008), pp. 295–8; Roger Bowdler, 'Dance, George, the Younger (1741–1825)', in *Oxford Dictionary of National Biography*, <http://www.oxforddnb.com.virtual.anu.edu.au/view/article/7096> (hereafter *ODNB*). For an extensive account of the development of Dance's design of Newgate, see Harold D. Kalman, 'Newgate Prison', *Architectural History*, vol. 12 (1969), pp. 50–61, 108–12.

section was stamped with neat rows of five arched windows. To the left and right of centre, two identical gatehouse features provided entry points—one for debtors and one for felons—to an otherwise impenetrable fortress. Half the height of the building, they were incorporated into the granite facade and stood as bookends supporting the centre. Abutting these, the outermost wings of the building abandoned any aesthetic considerations. Large granite slabs melded together to create dense walls, subdued only by arched brick recesses taunting observers with the illusion of windows. In place of casements, statues representing the figures of Justice, Fortitude and Prudence guarded the recesses.

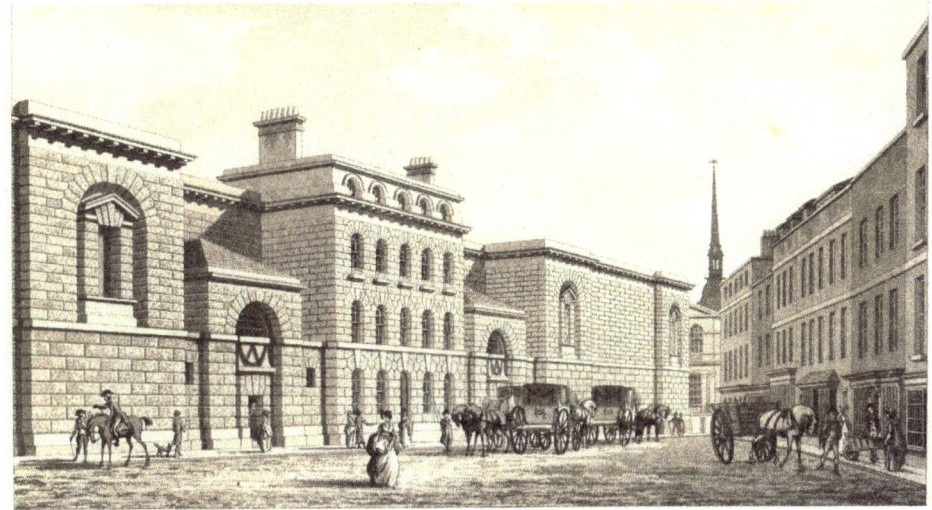

Figure 1.1 Newgate from Old Bailey Road with St Sepulchre's spire in the background.

Thomas Malton, 1792. Copyright Trustees of the British Museum.

Newgate had occupied an imposing and malevolent presence on the London townscape for centuries. The building was a phoenix, rising again on the same site on three occasions: following its destruction by London's great fire in 1666; after it was demolished to accommodate increased traffic flows in the burgeoning metropolis in 1770; and after it was razed during the Gordon riots, which enveloped the prison in 1780.[17] The fervour with which the rioting crowd ransacked and torched the prison (along with several other London gaols) reveals the extent of the revulsion for the prison in the psyche of the London populace,

---

17 For a discussion of the Gordon riots, see John Nicholson, *The Great Liberty Riot of 1780* (London: Panther Press, 1995); Iain McCalman, 'Controlling the Riots: *Barnaby Rudge* and Romantic revolution', in Michael T. Davis (ed.), *Radicalism and Revolution in Britain, 1775–1848* (London: Macmillan Press, 2000), pp. 207–28; Nicholas Rogers, *Crowds, Culture and Politics in Georgian Britain* (Oxford: Clarendon, 1998), pp. 152–75; George Rudé, 'The Gordon Riots: A study of the rioters and their victims', *Paris and London in the Eighteenth Century* (New York: Viking Press, 1971), pp. 268–92. On the rebuilding of the prison after the riot, see Babington, *The English Bastille*, pp. 39–58; Kalman, 'Newgate Prison', pp. 108–12.

particularly the London poor. The storming of the Bastille by the Parisian revolutionaries, which became the hallmark of the 1789 revolution, helped to further cement the image of Newgate—London's oldest prison—as a comparable symbol of government repression and neglect.[18] Yet as contemporary observer James Grant noted, Newgate had an appearance of 'indefinite durability' about it, to the extent that 'one would suppose that even Time himself, whom Lord Bacon personifies as the great innovator, could hardly make an impression on Newgate'.[19]

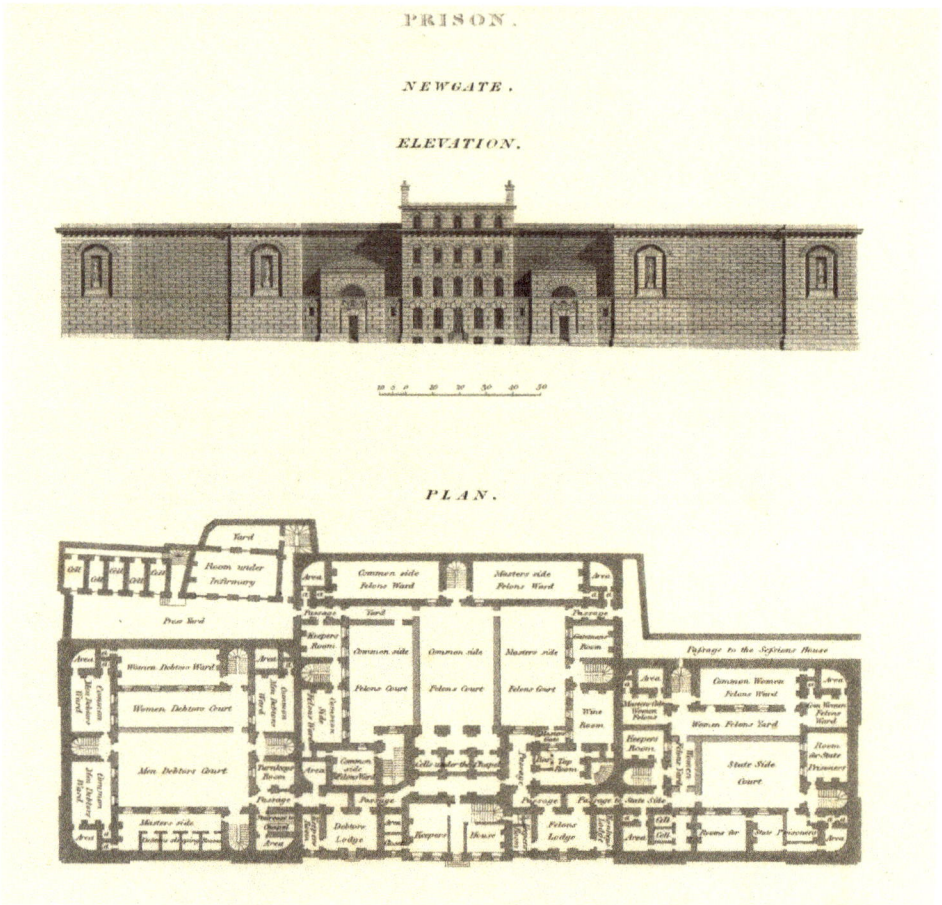

Figure 1.2 Newgate prison, following reconstruction after the Gordon riots. Ground-floor plan of Newgate showing the state side accommodation and the wine and tap rooms.

George Dance, the Younger, architect. Copyright Trustees of the British Museum.

---

18 Margaret DeLacy, 'Grinding Men Good? Lancashire's prisons at mid-century', in Victor Bailey (ed.), *Policing and Punishment in Nineteenth Century Britain* (London: Croom Helm, 1981), p. 182. For a discussion of British perceptions of the Bastille, see Norbert Schürer, 'The Storming of the Bastille in English Newspapers', *Eighteenth-Century Life*, vol. 29, no. 1 (2005), pp. 50–81.
19 James Grant, *The Great Metropolis* (London, 1837), vol. 2, p. 217.

Newgate's reputation for vitriolic punishment, despair, destitution and disease was seared on the collective memory of Londoners long after the Bastille had been demolished. As Hepworth Dixon asked rhetorically in 1850: 'Of all that busy, whirling, thoughtful throng of passengers, which daily roll beneath its massive battlements, is their one who heedlessly goes by, without bestowing on it a glance of curiosity, a shudder, or a sigh?'[20]

Figure 1.3 *Preparing for an Execution.*

Artist unknown, c. 1846. Copyright Trustees of the British Museum.

Answering his own question, Dixon observed that 'some of this interest is very probably owing to the fearful memories which float about the spot'; those traversing Newgate Street and Great Old Bailey milled on the same roadway where hundreds of lives had terminated at the end of a gallows rope. In 1783, with Britain's Bloody Code of capital punishments still in full swing, Newgate had replaced Tyburn as the site of public executions in the capital. The move had the unintended consequence of providing a new, albeit grim, source of popular metropolitan entertainment.[21] As depicted in Thomas Rowlandson's print *An Execution outside Newgate Prison* news of an impending execution brought thousands of Londoners into the street outside the prison to witness the

---

20 Dixon, *The London Prisons*, p. 191.
21 On the place of executions within both British criminal history and wider culture, see V. A. C. Gatrell, *The Hanging Tree: Execution and the English people 1770–1868* (Oxford: Oxford University Press, 1994).

macabre drama and spectacle that surrounded the public hangings.[22] The print *Preparing for An Execution* reveals that the gruesome appeal of an execution would last well into the nineteenth century (Figure 1.3).

The Rowlandson print is but one example of the prominent place of Newgate in the print culture of the period.[23] Such prints were forms of public commentary accessible to the literate and illiterate alike. The fascination with Newgate, and the mystique surrounding the prison, is also evident in written forms of print culture, including the metropolitan newspapers, which increasingly reported events concerning the prisons, and in the immense popularity of the *Newgate Calendar*.[24] Editions of the *Newgate Calendar*, originally a monthly bulletin of executions published by the Keeper of Newgate, were produced in 1774, 1824 and 1826 and chronicled, in often macabre detail, the crimes of those brought to trial, imprisoned in the gaol or sentenced to be executed.

Newgate also held a central place in prison narratives of the eighteenth century, most prominently in Daniel Defoe's famous novels *Robinson Crusoe*, *Moll Flanders* and *John Sheppard*.[25] Moll Flanders' traumatic response to Newgate, following her committal for stealing two pieces of silk, speaks of the dread of the space:

> 'Tis impossible to describe the terror of my mind, when I was first brought in, and when I look'd round upon all the horrors of that dismal Place: I look'd on myself as lost, and that I had nothing to think of, but of going out in the world, and that with the utmost Infamy; the hellish Noise, the Roaring, Swearing, and Clamour, the Stench and the Nastiness, and all the dreadful croud of Afflicting things that I saw there; joyn'd together to make the Place seem an Emblem of Hell itself, and a kind of Entrance into it.[26]

John Bender writes that for Moll Flanders, Newgate 'signifies liminality at its most concentrated'.[27] The novel encapsulated the fear, loathing and terror

---

22 For a fascinating firsthand account of the spectacle surrounding an execution, see Dixon, *The London Prisons*, pp. 193–7.
23 For an overview of the place of Newgate, and prison in general, in the print culture and popular imagination, see John Bender, *Imagining the Penitentiary: Fiction and the architecture of mind in eighteenth-century England* (Chicago: University of Chicago Press, 1987); Uwe Böker, 'The Prison and the Penitentiary as Sites of Public Counter-Discourse', in Böker and Hibbard, *Sites of Discourse*, pp. 211–47.
24 See Simon Deveraux, 'From Sessions to Newspaper? Criminal trial reporting, the nature of crime, and the London press, 1770–1800', *London Journal*, vol. 32, no. 1 (2007), pp. 1–27.
25 Bender, *Imagining the Penitentiary*, p. 44. See also Sean Grass, *The Self in the Cell: Narrating the Victorian prisoner* (London: Routledge, 2003), pp. 22, 46–50. Newgate continued to be of great interest to novelists of the nineteenth century, including Charles Dickens. See 'A Visit to Newgate', in *Sketches by Boz* (London: Chapman & Hall, 1877), pp. 114–22. For an overview of the literature, see Keith Hollingsworth, *The Newgate Novel 1830–47: Bulwer, Ainsworth, Dickens, & Thackeray* (Detroit: Wayne State University Press, 1963).
26 Quoted in Bender, *Imagining the Penitentiary*, p. 45.
27 Ibid.

generally associated with the prison in the print culture of the period. The image of Moll's Newgate was also enduring, reinforcing the horror and awe of the prison for generations of readers.

Given Moll Flanders' experience of the prison, she might well have agreed with the suggestion of architectural historian Harold Kalman that Newgate achieved 'sublimity as much as may be expected in solid stone'.[28] Kalman argues that Dance's design for Newgate was influenced by Edmund Burke's aesthetic of the sublime, outlined in his 1757 publication, *Philosophical Enquiry into the Origin of our Ideas of the Sublime and Beautiful*. Burke proposed that sublimity was derived from the emotions of pain and terror: 'Terror is in all cases whatsoever', wrote Burke, 'the ruling principle of the sublime'.[29] Dance admired Burke's treatise as 'a very excellent work' and the 'dark and gloomy' presence of Newgate, its 'greatness of dimension' and the 'succession and unity of parts', all correspond with Burke's definition of the sublime in built form. Further, Kalman maintains that Burke's description of one of the emotional characteristics of the sublime, as the 'idea of bodily pain, in all the modes and degrees of labour, pain, anguish, [and] torment', can also be used to 'read' Newgate as a site embodying the principles of the sublime.[30] In this sense, Dance, as architect, played a key role in building not only the physical attributes of the space, but the awe and mystique associated with London's most notorious prison.

Though the facade of the building was calculated to hold terrors for passers-by, as Moll Flanders discovered, the real horrors awaited those immured within. The dominance of such emotional responses to the prison experience by inmates and visitors alike has tended to replace purely descriptive accounts of the interior so that it is harder to gain a sense of the internal material structure of the prison. The architectural plans for the prison, however, provide some insight into the internal arrangements of the prison in this period (see Figure 1.2). The northern side of the prison was allocated to male and female debtors and consisted of two small courtyards surrounded by three storeys of wards, which housed the prisoners.[31] The state side was located on the southern end of the prison, along with the felons' quadrangle and the women's ward. According to contemporary observers, the large open wards for accommodating prisoners were of similar

---

28 Kalman, 'Newgate Prison', p. 55.
29 Edmund Burke, *Philosophical Enquiry into the Origin of our Ideas of the Sublime and Beautiful* (1756; reprinted, J. T. Bolton [ed.], London: Routledge and Kegan Paul, 1958), p. 59.
30 The ability of the prison space to elicit such emotions in the populace, according to both Kalman and Bender, also meant that Newgate conformed to the premise of *architecture parlante*, described as 'narrative architecture', which 'stressed the capacity…to foster emotion in its spectators as much as narrative paintings did'. Dance's use of real chains and shackles above the prison's two entry doorways provides further evidence of the building conforming to the mode of *architecture parlante*. See Bender, *Imagining the Penitentiary*, p. 241.
31 A good overview of the layout of Newgate is provided in James Neild, *State of the Prisons in England, Scotland and Wales…Together with some useful documents, observations, and remarks, adapted to explain the conditions of prisoners in general* (London, 1812), pp. 412–29. See also Griffiths, *The Chronicles of Newgate*, vol. 1, pp. 70–101; George Wilkinson, *The Newgate Calendar* (Leeds: Panther, 1965), vol. 3, pp. 9–11.

proportions on both the debtors' side and the state side of the prison.[32] Stone walls divided a central court into three sections: 'yards for the male felons who could afford a bed, for poorer ones who could not, and for women; and the south quadrangle received a separate enclosed area for state prisoners.'[33] According to Dance's intentions, then, the spatial hierarchy of the prison was determined both by the capacity to pay and according to the nature of the offence.

The configuration of Newgate lent itself to the development of the well-known radical culture of the 1790s, many of whose members were independently wealthy gentlemen.[34] Newgate keepers had a long tradition of renting out the rooms available on the state side of the prison where most radicals were housed for the majority of their sentence. The prison economy also allowed radical prisoners to enjoy alcohol and to purchase coal, furniture and food. Lord George Gordon had a seemingly limitless capacity to pay for his own apartment, to be attended by two personal maids and, as Newton's *Soulagement* print depicts, to entertain and dine with guests (Figure 1.4).[35] The spatial hierarchy of the prison reflected that of the outside world: money allowed wealthy prisoners to buffer their prison experience and to be separated from their poorer prison counterparts—the criminal underworld—depicted so menacingly in the literature of the period.[36]

As McCalman argues, the ability of the 1790s radicals to forge a distinct presence in the prison facilitated the sense of collectivity and resistance as prisoners had to fortify, entertain, advise and rely on each other.[37] They were united by their convictions under William Pitt's 'reign of terror' for publishing a barrage of subversive writings including Paine's most prosecuted political works, numerous records of the French National Assembly, pro-Gallic addresses and petitions from all major metropolitan radical clubs and several scathing attacks on Edmund Burke's *Reflections on the Revolution in France*.[38] In Newgate, they

---

32 Wilkinson, *The Newgate Calendar*, pp. 9-11.
33 Neild, *State of the Prisons in England, Scotland and Wales*, p. 412.
34 See McCalman, 'Newgate in Revolution'. The dissenting minister Reverend William Winterbotham was confined to Newgate for four years for seditious preaching. He complained that everything bar liberty was available in Newgate for a fee. See Manogue, 'The Plight of James Ridgway', p. 162. There were claims of neglect by some radical prisoners such as William Hodgson and Joseph Gerrald, but these appear not to have been the norm in this period.
35 For a discussion of Gordon's term in prison, see William Hazlitt (ed.), *Memoirs of the Late Thomas Holcroft* (London, 1816), vol. 1, p. 78; Babington, *The English Bastille*, p. 139.
36 For an interesting discussion of the concept of the 'deviant underworld' and attitudes towards crime and criminals, see Victor Bailey, 'The Fabrication of Deviance: "Dangerous classes" and "criminal classes" in Victorian England', in John Rule and Robert Malcolmson (eds), *Protest and Survival: The historical experience: essays for E. P. Thompson* (London: Merlin Press, 1993), pp. 221–56.
37 McCalman, 'Newgate in Revolution'.
38 See Clive Emsley, 'An Aspect of Pitt's Terror: Prosecutions for sedition during the 1790s', *Social History*, vol. 6 (1981), pp. 154–84; T. A. Jackson, *Trials of British Freedom* (London, 1940), p. 35; Jon Mee, '"Examples of Safe Printing": Censorship and popular radical literature in the 1790s', *Essays and Studies*, vol. 46 (1993), pp. 81–95; Ian Haywood, *The Revolution in Popular Literature: Print, politics and the people, 1790–1860* (Cambridge: Cambridge University Press, 2004), pp. 81–111.

formed a prison publishing collective that generated such iconic enlightenment texts as Paine's *Age of Reason*, Helvetius's *Catechism of Man*, Rousseau's *Social Contract* and Volney's *Ruins of Nature*.[39] Aimed especially at disseminating each other's work, the 1790s makeshift publishing house of Newgate produced dozens of polemical, satirical and philosophical publications from prisoners and their friends and fostered long associations between writers and publishers. Radical publishers James Ridgway and Henry Symonds formed a partnership to produce Newgate radical publications that lasted four years and, despite their own incarceration for publishing, Ridgway and Symonds remain amongst the most prolific publishers of radical writings in this period.[40] By transforming a prison into a site of significant literary production, the 1790s milieu produced what McCalman describes as an 'enthusiastic cultural revolution'.[41]

Figure 1.4 *Soulagement en Prison, or Comfort in Prison.*

Richard Newton, 1793. Courtesy of The Lewis Walpole Library, Yale University.

Because visitors to Newgate moved freely in and out of the prison in this period, the 1790s radical milieu also extended well beyond the prison walls. Historians have documented the extensive network of radical intelligentsia who regularly visited the state-side apartments, such as the doctor and radical James Parkinson and 'prison breakfaster' William Godwin, whose diaries record some

---

39 Manogue, 'The Plight of James Ridgway'. For a sample of the publications produced by radicals such as Charles Piggot and William Hodgson within Newgate, see the anthology of prison writings edited by Davis et al., *Newgate in Revolution*.
40 Manogue, 'The Plight of James Ridgway'.
41 McCalman, 'Newgate in Revolution', p. 107.

of the 'intricate webs of radical and literary sociability associated with Newgate culture'.[42] In his study, McCalman has identified women such as Maria Reveley and Amelia Alderson among those 'taking the lead in Newgate sociability'.[43] The free movement of visitors within the prison allowed the prison publication enterprises to flourish and generally ensured that prisoners were well maintained and sustained by friends and family.[44] The sociability within the prison also meant that radicals could re-create familiar spaces from the world of the radical intelligentsia outside prison such as the tavern and the coffee house.

By depicting Newgate as a site of radical conviviality and sociability, there is a risk of trivialising the suffering that undoubtedly accompanied imprisonment. To borrow from McCalman, the 'unfreedom of Newgate' as well as the ever-present threat of the lethal gaol fever cannot be lightly dismissed. Yet despite the physical and psychological hardships endured by the 1790s Newgate radicals, many clearly had the financial means, or at least the backing of wealthier patrons such as Whig leader Charles James Fox, to cushion the effects of the harsher aspects of prison life.[45] As a consequence, it is helpful to think of at least two 'Newgates' in operation at this time: that of relative comfort for those with the means to pay, and that faced by the majority of the Newgate population, who lived a harsh and crippling existence in the 'mansion of misery'.[46]

The horrors of Newgate for most of the prison population had not gone unnoticed during the eighteenth century. Although the subject of prison reform is addressed in greater detail in Chapter 2, a survey of the basic premises of the reform is crucial if we are to appreciate the changes that impacted on the subsequent waves of radical prisoners in Newgate. Though Howard's *State of the Prisons* initiated the call for wide-reaching changes to penal practice in Britain, other vocal British agitators soon joined the fray, including James Neild, Sir Samuel Romilly, Sir George Onesiphorus Paul and Jeremy Bentham. The British reform movement was also heavily influenced by Italian philosopher Cesare Beccaria, who campaigned against the death penalty and penned the famous treatise *An Essay on Crimes and Punishment*, published in 1764. Other influences included the work of French philosopher Baron de Montesquieu on crime, punishment and the law.[47]

---

42 Ibid., p. 98. On Godwin's involvement in the Newgate circle, see also Mark Philp, *Godwin's Political Justice* (Ithaca, NY: Cornell University Press, 1986), chs 4–5. On Parkinson, see A. D. Morris, *James Parkinson: His life and times* (Boston: Birkhauser, 1989); Roy Porter, *Doctor of Society: Thomas Beddoes and the sick trade in late Enlightenment England* (London: Routledge, 1992), pp. 157–66.
43 McCalman, 'Newgate in Revolution', p. 102.
44 See Davis et al., *Newgate in Revolution*, p. xiii.
45 Manogue, 'The Plight of James Ridgway', pp. 159, 165.
46 The phrase belongs to Thomas Lloyd. See Lloyd, 'Impositions and Abuses in the Management of the Jail of Newgate', p. 72.
47 For an overview of the philosophies of Montesquieu and Beccaria, see Frank McLynn, *Crime and Punishment in Eighteenth-Century England* (London: Routledge, 1989), pp. 42–4, 252–9.

British reformers were generally united in visualising a new approach to criminals, which held out the possibility of reform and redemption of even the most immoral, deviant and wayward. Custodial sentences were advocated in place of the death penalty for many serious offences. A new and rigid disciplinary system centred on mandatory religious instruction, often pernicious hygiene measures and forced labour as the means by which even the most hardened criminal could be delivered back to society a redeemed and reformed citizen.[48]

The physical space of prison came under close scrutiny in the effort to envisage a new era in the approach to crime and punishment. The issue of prisoner accommodation was a crucial aspect of reform, and also the most contentious. Bentham and Paul were particularly focused on the need to reform prison architecture as a means to realise the changes advocated by Howard. Although reformers agreed on the separation of men and women within the prison, the extent to which a prisoner should be consigned to solitary cells was more controversial. Howard considered that each prisoner should have a small room in which to sleep alone at night but should spend the day in a common ward in the company of other prisoners. Bentham's model for the panopticon—Greek for 'all seeing'—proposed confinement based on extreme solitude and continuous surveillance.[49] The design—a circular structure with a central tower at its axis—meant the prison staff could observe each of the single-occupant cells that formed the building's circumference. Although the panopticon was never built, its influence can be seen in the many nineteenth-century prisons that continue to hold a presence on the British urban landscape.

The configuration of older prisons such as Newgate, with large wards rather than single cells, made it easier to resist prison reform. Dance's original design for the 1770 rebuild of the prison, and the laying of the foundations for it, predated Howard's landmark exposé in 1777. When Newgate was rebuilt following the Gordon riot fires in 1780, however, Dance made only minor modifications to his original plan. Howard despaired at the time that no design could have been worse for 'unless room be given for the separation of prisoners', he predicted, 'an audacious spirit of profaneness and wickedness will continue to prevail'.[50] The immediate changes demanded by reformers to the operation and culture of

---

48 For an overview of the chronology and ideology of prison reform, see Clive Emsley, *Crime and Society in England 1750–1900* (London: Longman, 1996), pp. 248–92; J. E. Thomas, *House of Care: Prisons and prisoners in England 1500–1800* (Nottingham: University of Nottingham, 1988), pp. 147–81; Babington, *The English Bastille*; Michael Ignatieff, *A Just Measure of Pain: The penitentiary in the Industrial Revolution, 1750–1850* (New York: Columbia University Press, 1980), pp. 44–79. On the relationship between prison reform and radical culture, see J. Ann Hone, *For the Cause of Truth: Radicalism in London 1796–1821* (Oxford: Clarendon Press, 1982), pp. 249–50.
49 For more on Bentham and prison reform, see Chapter 2 of this study.
50 Howard is quoted in H. G. Bennet, *A Letter to the Common Council and Livery of the City of London, on the Abuses Existing in Newgate*, second edn (London, 1818), p. 3. See also Dixon, *The London Prisons*, p. 209.

Newgate stood little chance in a space that simply could not accommodate the necessary separation or solitary confinement of prisoners, and in an institution that had functioned largely unchecked for hundreds of years.[51]

* * *

William Pitt's 'reign of terror' against the radicals of the 1790s did little to dissuade radical followers. As political dissidence continued to gain momentum in Britain after the turn of the century, Newgate hosted another wave of radical prisoners. William Cobbett's experience of the prison in 1810 suggests little had changed since Lord George Gordon's time. Cobbett, a radical writer, publisher and farmer, was prosecuted for publicly criticising the flogging of five militiamen who had been involved in a mutiny at Ely. Cobbett was tried and convicted for seditious libel in June 1810 and sentenced to Newgate for two years.[52] Immediately after arriving at the prison, Cobbett agreed to pay five shillings a week to the turnkey for a single apartment in the state side of the prison. The intervention of Matthew Wood, Sheriff of London and Middlesex and radical sympathiser, however, was a boon for Cobbett.[53] For 12 guineas a week in rent and another eight guineas in fees, he was moved to an even more comfortable abode on the top floor of the Governor's residence.

Separated from other prisoners, he was allowed to entertain as many visitors as he chose each day between midday and 10 o'clock in the evening. Friends dined with him, or took refreshments, and his family was permitted to stay with him in his room. In the tradition of the 1790s radicals, he continued his writing and publishing endeavours, editing and managing *Cobbett's Weekly Register* from the prison. 'In fact', G. D. H. Cole noted in his biography of Cobbett, 'there was no restriction on his freedom save that he could not move beyond the prison walls'.[54] In his autobiography, Cobbett recalled that a hamper which travelled between his farm in Botley and the prison provided for his every need: carrying letters of support, providing 'fruit and all sorts of country fare', the necessary materials to keep a journal, plants, bulbs and the most 'beautiful flowers…

---

51 Unlike that for many eighteenth-century prisons, Dance's design had allowed for separate quarters for men and women, but the separation was rarely enforced during the late eighteenth century until the intervention of prison reformer Elizabeth Fry (see Chapter 3).
52 Cobbett also faced an extraordinary £3000 in fines and two sureties of £1000 each for good behaviour for seven years to be paid on his release. For an account of his trial, see *Morning Chronicle*, 16 June 1810. On William Cobbett, see George Spater, *William Cobbett: The poor man's friend*, 2 vols (Cambridge: Cambridge University Press, 1982); William Cobbett, *The Autobiography of William Cobbett: The progress of a plough-boy to a seat in Parliament*, William Reitzel (ed.) (London: Faber, 1967); G. D. H. Cole, *The Life of William Cobbett* (London: Collins, 1924).
53 Spater, *William Cobbett*, p. 246. On Matthew Wood, see Anita McConnell, 'Wood, Sir Matthew, First Baronet (1768–1843)', in *ODNB*, <http://www.oxforddnb.com/view/article/29889>. On Wood's involvement in London radical culture, see Hone, *For the Cause of Truth*, pp. 8–9, 186–9, 347–9.
54 Cole, *The Life of William Cobbett*, p. 161.

everything that they thought calculated to delight me'.[55] Cobbett's detention, to borrow Cole's words, was 'irksome enough', but it was the 'mildest that well can be imagined'.[56] Nevertheless, it would be a mistake to make light of such a period of 'unfreedom'. As Philip Harling notes, Cobbett suffered financially from his period of imprisonment, which could account for his decision to flee to America following the *Habeas Corpus Suspension Act* in 1817 to avoid any repeat prison term.[57]

The imprisonment of another prominent radical of the period closely coincided with Cobbett's release in 1812. Daniel Isaac Eaton, the veteran radical publisher who was part of the early 1790s Newgate milieu as a regular visitor, had managed to avoid a prison term during the 'reign of terror' despite successive prosecutions.[58] His publication of the third part of Paine's *Age of Reason* in 1812 finally gave the authorities the verdict they had long sought. Eaton's imprisonment was clearly less agreeable than Cobbett's. In 1813, he published a damning account of the gaol, *Extortions and Abuses of Newgate*, which, like Lloyd's exposé, documented a corrupt prison economy in which prisoners continued to remain vulnerable to the profit making of keepers and turnkeys.[59]

One of Lloyd's key complaints was that men judged guilty of felonies but 'possessed of financial means' could pay their way into the superior rooms of the state side.[60] Similarly, Eaton raged that despite laws that then provided for the separation of prisoners into classifications of debtors, felons and misdemeanours (with state prisoners in the last), 'in rapacity of fees, Felons of all descriptions are admitted into [the state side], and the accommodation [is] distributed to them in a partial, unjust, and oppressive way'.[61] It remains unclear why Eaton was not afforded the luxury of the Keeper's residence as Cobbett had been. Eaton's growing impoverishment could have meant he simply did not have the financial means to warrant special privileges. His fractious relationship with the

---

55   Cobbett, *The Autobiography of William Cobbett*, p. 124.
56   Cole, *The Life of William Cobbett*, p. 161.
57   Philip Harling, 'The Law of Libel and the Limits of Repression, 1790–1832', *The Historical Journal*, vol. 44, no. 1 (2001), pp. 118–19.
58   On Daniel Isaac Eaton, radical publisher, see Michael T. Davis, '"Good for the Public Example": Daniel Issac Eaton, prosecution, punishment and recognition, 1793–1812', in Davis, *Radicalism and Revolution in Britain*, pp. 110–32; Michael T. Davis, '"I Can Bear Punishment": Daniel Issac Eaton, radical culture and the rule of law, 1792–1812', *Criminal Justice History*, vol. 18 (2003), pp. 89–106; D. McCue, 'The Pamphleteer Pitt's Government Couldn't Silence', *Eighteenth-Century Life*, vol. 5 (1978–79), pp. 38–49.
59   Daniel Isaac Eaton, *Extortions and Abuses of Newgate* (London, 1813), reprinted in Davis et al., *Newgate in Revolution*, pp. 145–66. This is supported by Henry Mayhew, who later reported that from 1788 to 1810, 'Newgate continued in a wretched, misguided condition'. Henry Mayhew and John Binny, *The Criminal Prisons of London and Scenes of Prison Life* (London: Griffin, 1862), p. 591.
60   Lloyd, *Impositions and Abuses in the Management of the Jail of Newgate*, p. 73.
61   Eaton, *Extortions and Abuses of Newgate*, p. 152.

Radical Spaces

Keeper could also account for his treatment, for, as we will see in Chapter 2, this relationship was a crucial factor in determining the prisoner's experience of the prison space.

In many ways, Eaton was the exception that proved the rule. In the first two decades of the nineteenth century, the resistance of the informal prison economy to the reform process generally continued to benefit those incarcerated for political offences. Five years after Cobbett vacated the Governor's rooms, John Cam Hobhouse, radical Westminster MP, took up residence. In 1819, Hobhouse was imprisoned in Newgate after suggesting that if soldiers did not protect the Parliament, 'members of that House [of Commons] would be pulled out by their ears'.[62] At a time of pressing social discontent, and in the highly charged atmosphere that followed Peterloo, his comments were deemed to be inciting unrest. As it had been for Cobbett, Newgate was to be a site of confined comfort for Hobhouse. It was reported that he 'lived in the governor's rooms, and in splendid style' (Figure 1.5).[63]

Figure 1.5 *'A Trifling Mistake'…Corrected…*, a satirical depiction of John Cam Hobhouse's accommodation in Newgate.

George Cruikshank, London, 1820. Copyright Trustees of the British Museum.

---

62   On John Cam Hobhouse, see Robert E. Zegger, *John Cam Hobhouse: A political life, 1819–1852* (Columbia: University of Missouri Press, 1973).
63   Dixon, *The London Prisons*, p. 210.

1. 'Honourable House of Blasphemers'

Most startling was Hobhouse's ability to continue his political affairs from the prison in full public view. In an advertisement placed in *The Times* in early January 1820, a 'Metropolitan and Central Committee' announced a meeting to decide on the dispersal of funds collected for Peterloo victims. 'The place of the meeting', the advertisement announced, 'will be Mr Hobhouse's apartments on the State side of Newgate, the time for the meeting 12 for 1 o'clock on Monday 10th January 1820'.[64] As it had been for the 1790s radicals, the prison space proved no impediment to either Cobbett's or Hobhouse's participation in the political life of the nation. Moreover, the fact that the propriety of conducting a public meeting in a prison was not questioned suggests a tacit recognition that prison should not impede participation in the mainstream public sphere, at least for elite radical politicians such as Hobhouse.

Hobhouse's ability to conduct his political activity from Newgate, almost two decades after that of the 1790s radical prisoners, provides a useful index of the slow pace of change within the old prisons. According to Henry Grey Bennet MP, this is also true of the conditions facing the general prison population. Bennet conducted his own inquiry into Newgate in 1818, and published his findings the same year.[65] He reported that corruption remained rampant in the prison, despite the payment of an annual salary to the Keeper. He noted that the sale of alcohol continued and that gaming and 'freedom of exchange and movement' within the prison were prevalent; 'drunkenness prevailed to such an extent, and was so common, that unaccompanied with riot, it attracted no notice'.[66] He also noted that despite male and female prisoners being housed in separate parts of the prison, local prostitutes and other women were still permitted to stay during the night. This was easily accomplished, Bennet maintained, by claiming to be the wife of a prisoner and slipping a shilling to the turnkeys.[67]

Given that Newgate generally appeared impervious to prison reform for the gentlemen radicals such as Cobbett and Hobhouse, and in turn for the wider prison population, what of the conditions that faced the next cohort of radical prisoners in the 1820s? This decade was marked by the renewed suppression of political and religious dissidence, with the London radical bookshop of Jane and Richard Carlile a key target. Their Fleet Street bookshop and publishing enterprise played a crucial role in circulating a range of radical texts, not only in the metropolis, but throughout Britain via an extensive regional network of print sellers.[68] The bookshop became a marked site; Richard and Jane were both

---

64 *The Times*, 8 January 1820. For further accounts of Hobhouse in Newgate, see *Morning Chronicle*, 2 February 1820, 7 February 1820; *Examiner*, 6 February 1820.
65 Bennet, *A Letter to the Common Council and Livery of the City of London*.
66 Ibid., p. 6.
67 Ibid., p. 8.
68 For further discussion of Jane and Richard Carlile's contribution to London radical culture, see Iain McCalman, Popular Radicalism and Freethought in Early Nineteenth Century England, Unpublished MA thesis (Canberra: The Australian National University, 1975); Joel Wiener, *Radicalism and Freethought*

imprisoned in the early 1820s, and the shopmen and women who answered the call to keep the bookshop open did so at great peril. The provisions of the Six Acts combined with the suspension of habeas corpus in 1817 saw almost 150 workers, distributors and volunteers associated with the Carliles' bookshop imprisoned throughout the country during the 1820s—the sum of their sentences totalling a staggering 200 years.[69]

The years between 1820 and 1824 saw the most intensive suppression of the Carliles' bookshop. Volunteers Susannah Wright (to whom I will return in Chapter 3), Humphrey Boyle, Joseph Rhodes, William Holmes, William Tunbridge, William Haley, Thomas Jeffries, Thomas Ryley Perry, Richard Hassell, John Clarke, William Campion, William Cochrane and John Christopher all spent time in Newgate, either for the entirety of their sentence or for a holding period before they were moved to another prison.[70] Bennet B. Jones, a London radical and key supporter of radical prisoners in the period, later recalled that 'no sooner did a person stand behind the counter in the shop, than he was taken to Newgate. We had one week seven taken, and lodged [there].'[71]

One consequence of the dichotomy between the earlier radical experience of Newgate and that of the general prison population was that those radicals who followed Hobhouse into prison were primed to expect more amicable conditions by virtue of their status as state prisoners. This could account for the boldness exhibited by one of the Carliles' shop workers, William Haley. He defiantly advised the judge that

> we have every reasonable prospect of being consigned to the company of the Newgate beetles, for some five or six and thirty moons: yet no title in the gift of the proud sovereign of these realms is more eagerly sought, than a situation of so honourable a nature.[72]

---

in *Nineteenth-Century Britain: The life of Richard Carlile* (Westport, Conn.: Greenwood Press, 1983); Guy Aldred, *Richard Carlile, Agitator: His life and times* (London: Pioneer Press, 1923); James Epstein, *Radical Expression: Political language, ritual and symbol in England, 1790–1850* (Oxford: Oxford University Press, 1994), pp. 100–46; Angela Keane, 'Richard Carlile's Working Women: Selling books, politics, sex and *The Republican*', *Literature & History*, vol. 15, no. 2 (2006), pp. 20–34; Iain McCalman, *Radical Underworld: Prophets, revolutionaries and pornographers in London, 1795–1840* (Cambridge: Cambridge University Press, 1988), pp. 156–60, 181–217; E. P. Thompson, *The Making of the English Working Class* (London: Penguin, 1968), pp. 791–846. See also Chapters 6–8 of this study.

69 Thompson, *The Making of the English Working Class*, p. 757.

70 William Campion (Lancaster shoemaker), John Clarke (an ex-Methodist preacher), Thomas Ryley Perry (an actor-comedian) and William Haley (shoemaker) all received the harshest sentences of 36 months. For reports on the trials of William Haley, see *Leeds Mercury*, 19 June 1824; on William Holmes, see *Morning Chronicle*, 20 February 1824; on the trials of the seven other men, see *Morning Chronicle*, 8 June 1824, 10 June 1824; also the *Examiner*, 13 June 1824. See also McCalman, *Popular Radicalism and Freethought in Early Nineteenth Century England*, pp. 76–7; Wiener, *Radicalism and Freethought in Nineteenth-Century Britain*, pp. 89–95.

71 B. B. Jones, 'The Peoples' First Struggle for Free Speech and Writing', *The Reasoner*, 5 June 1859, pp. 178–9.

72 Quoted in Wiener, *Radicalism and Freethought in Nineteenth-Century Britain*, p. 89.

It appears Haley, as a prison martyr, had discovered his raison d'être.

If Haley and the other shop workers expected the comforts enjoyed by earlier radicals, their hopes were soon quashed. The reality of life in Newgate reported by the Carliles' shop workers during this third wave of radical imprisonments suggests a discernable shift in approach towards those imprisoned for political and religious offences. In 1822, Humphrey Boyle, a shoemaker from Leeds, reported that he had been held in conditions similar to those facing the general prison population.[73] After five months, he claimed, he was still sleeping on a hempen mat on the floor of the apartment, with 'only three rugs for covering'—the standard issue for prisoners in Newgate. Furthermore, he was forced to share his ward with up to 10 other prisoners, including felons.

The shopmen convicted of blasphemous libel in 1824 related similar conditions. Richard Carlile printed an 'exact account' of the men's treatment, expressing his outrage at the conditions that faced his men on their arrival in Newgate. Confined with 10 men in a room measuring 22 ft x 16 ft (7 m x 5 m), they were given three 'door mats' to lie on, the rugs constituting the 'whole of bed and bedding'.[74] For sustenance, they received only the new prison food allocation, described as the 'the most wretched stuff': 'one pound of bread and one pint of gruel each day' with six ounces of beef each alternate day. This, they claimed, was no better than 'dog's meat'.[75] Carlile reported that his men were denied 'all means of procuring proper food' from friends and relatives, as 'undressed food' was not allowed in the prison, leaving that which had been 'mangled...by some filthy men and women employed for that purpose'—the only option to avoid starvation.[76]

In one of the most notable departures from earlier practice towards state prisoners, radicals in this period reported that they were no longer permitted to receive visitors in their wards. Relatives were forced to 'converse between bars', with friends excluded altogether without *'lying like a Christian*, by saying they are relatives'.[77] Carlile further claimed that men's visitors were insulted and were often refused entry to the prison altogether. Most galling, however, was that even the 'most respectable' female visitors 'must submit to be stripped, by two of the most disrespectable' turnkeys and then were permitted only 'to talk through a double row of iron gratings four feet apart!'.[78]

These conditions are in stark contrast with the scenes of conviviality and sociability in the 1790s and the comforts enjoyed by Cobbett and Hobhouse.

---

73   *Republican*, 7 June 1822.
74   Reports on the men's treatment also appeared in the *Morning Chronicle*, 30 June 1824 and 9 July 1824.
75   *Republican*, 25 June 1824.
76   *Republican*, 6 August 1824.
77   *Republican*, 25 June 1824, 6 August 1824; *Newgate Monthly Magazine*, 1 November 1824.
78   *Republican*, 6 August 1824, 3 June 1825.

What, then, accounts for the shift in the treatment of radical prisoners after 1820? Part of the answer lies in the headway finally being made by British prison reformers. Although reforms were designed to improve the conditions of the most disadvantaged of the prison population, they appear to have had an inverse effect on the treatment of state prisoners. At the heart of reform was an egalitarian approach, which, theoretically, treated all inmates without favour. Tighter controls on prison management now existed, with visiting prison committees and visiting magistrates overseeing the work of the Governor and attempting to stamp out the old prison economies and profit making from prisoners. While the system of classifying prisoners according to the nature of their crime still meant prisoners who were convicted of sedition, blasphemy or libel could be housed in the state side, separation from other classifications of prisoners within the state side was never assured as Newgate became at times breathlessly overcrowded.[79] Furthermore, visiting rights were now regulated and restricted as reformers considered that personal reform and redemption could not be achieved if the prisoner continued to be surrounded by their unsavoury milieu.[80]

That the prison was finally succumbing to the reform endeavour, however, is not the complete picture. The generous concessions paid to Hobhouse only a year or so earlier suggest that other factors could account for the conditions faced by the 1820s radical milieu. At the same time that prison reform was finally making progress, the face of radicalism was also undergoing dramatic change. Many of the 1790s radicals, and those imprisoned before the 1820s, had the capacity to purchase superior accommodation and other comforts because of their social rank: either they were independently wealthy or they had the financial backing of a wealthy supporter. By the 1820s, the rapid dissemination of radical principles among the people resulted in the first wave of popular, as opposed to parliamentary, radicalism. Spurred on by the events at Peterloo and the Queen Caroline affair,[81] the shopmen and women who rallied to the Carliles' cause represented a 'microcosm of the thousands of artisans and mechanics', who, Joel Wiener notes, were drawn to the popular radical movement in this period.[82] Significant numbers of the volunteers were shoemakers or in the print

---

79 Several contemporary reports observed the overcrowding in the prison. See, for example, Neild, *State of the Prisons in England, Scotland and Wales*, pp. 412–14.
80 Ignatieff, *A Just Measure of Pain*, p. 102.
81 The Queen Caroline Affair, which engrossed the country during 1820, involved the attempt by newly anointed King George IV to deprive Caroline, his estranged wife, of the title of queen. Her cause attracted overwhelming popular support, and many in the radical community also took up her cause. See Anna Clark, 'The Queen Caroline Affair and the Sexual Politics of Popular Culture in London, 1820', *Representations*, vol. 31 (1990), pp. 47–68; John Stevenson, 'The Queen Caroline Affair', in John Stevenson (ed.), *London in the Age of Reform* (Oxford: Blackwell, 1977), pp. 117–48.
82 Wiener, *Radicalism and Freethought in Nineteenth-Century Britain*, pp. 87–8. See also Thompson, *TheMaking of the English Working Class*, passim.

trade, with half from London and the newly industrialised centres of Leeds and Manchester, and the remainder from smaller towns and villages across England.[83]

It is not my intention here to reduce either the complexities of radical imprisonment or the intentions of reformers to a cursory class analysis. The shift in social status of prisoners, however, clearly had implications given the intricate dynamics of social ranks within British society, the threat posed by the rapid spread of radicalism among the 'masses' and the central role that both money and status played in securing the comforts of earlier cohorts of radical prisoners. The impact on the relationships with the staff, and the magistrates, who oversaw the management of the prison, is but one example. Where earlier radical prisoners were of an eminently higher social standing than those who staffed the prisons,[84] the plebeian radicals of the 1820s encountered markedly different power relations within the prison space. Though beyond the scope of this study, a survey of political convictions across the broader nineteenth century would help illuminate the extent to which social status impacted on the radical experience of the prison space.[85]

Irrespective of the reasons behind the harsher treatment faced by radicals in the 1820s, a clear consequence of the shift in approach to their imprisonment was a rigorous effort to construct a distinctive radical collective within the prison. This was designed to directly counter that of the criminal identity, which was being increasingly prescribed by both the authorities and the prison space itself. One of the key radical strategies in this regard was to agitate for sole access to the state-side accommodation. Of all the complaints reported by radicals between 1790 and 1830, their confinement with felons was the most galling. The presence of 'real criminals' in the state side of the prison first prompted the exposé by Eaton, who maintained that his Keeper had disregarded and departed from the 'immemorial usage' that saw felons excluded from the state side of the prison.[86]

Despite the system of classifying prisoners, which legislated for their separation within new and old prisons, H. G. Bennet noted in 1818 that little attempt had been made to implement the regulations so that the 'political libeller was confined with the perjured, fraudulent and persons convicted for attempts to commit abominable crimes'.[87] For Humphrey Boyle, despite having slept on the

---

83 Wiener, *Radicalism and Freethought in Nineteenth-Century Britain*, pp. 87–8.
84 For an account of the changing nature of prison staff from 'keepers' to 'gentlemen governors' in this period, see Shane Bryans, *Prison Governors: Managing prisons in a time of change* (Cullompton: Willan Publishing, 2007), pp. 14–19.
85 To date, there is no comprehensive study of British political prisoners across either the eighteenth or the nineteenth centuries.
86 Eaton, *Extortions and Abuses of Newgate*, p. 158.
87 Bennet, *A Letter to the Common Council and Livery of the City of London*, p. 6. See also *Morning Chronicle*, 13 November 1818.

floor for much of his sentence, the issue of separate accommodation remained paramount during his imprisonment in Newgate in 1822. Admitting that 'good beds were much to be desired', he reported that what he and fellow radical prisoners Joseph Rhodes and William Holmes hoped for most was a room of their own.[88] Though their demands were never met in Newgate, they were later moved to another prison, the Giltspur Street Compter, where they gladly reported that they secured a 'good room' for themselves.[89]

It is unclear what prompted the three men's move to the Compter, although reports from within Newgate suggest that the issue of accommodation could have forced the authorities' hand. Following the initial complaints of the 1824 cohort, the men soon reported that they had won some concessions regarding their accommodation. By July 1824, the *Morning Chronicle* reported that the shopmen's complaints prompted an investigation by the magistrates and officials who formed the City Gaol Committee.[90] Despite finding that the men's allocated room was 'not crowded to inconvenience', the committee determined that the group of radical prisoners 'should be allowed the use of another room'. The committee also addressed the men's complaints regarding their lack of proper bedding, acknowledging that 'horse bedsteads should be allowed to the complainants' despite the committee's concern that such a concession 'might be regarded as a violation of the discipline'.[91]

The victory in securing separate accommodation was a major coup for the radicals. Not only did it distance the men physically from the remaining prison population, it assisted with creating a moral divide from the criminals, whom radicals generally appear to have regarded with disdain. Richard Hassell, for instance, remarked dispassionately in 1826 that he had 'never felt the least interest in the fate of any one who was executed' in Newgate.[92] Prompted by their own contempt for the criminal other, particularly felons, radicals in Newgate appear to have avoided any extensive contact or communication

---

88   *Republican*, 7 June 1822.
89   Ibid.
90   *Morning Chronicle*, 9 July 1824.
91   Ibid.
92   *Newgate Monthly Magazine*, 1 March 1826. Hassell, a farm labourer from Dorset, was entirely self-taught and continued his education in prison, where he excelled in mathematics and French. His work on political economy while in Newgate had a marked impact on Carlile's thinking, and Patricia Hollis contends it was the first time the 'interweaving of economic and political power' was presented in the popular press. See Patricia Hollis, *The Pauper Press: A study in working-class radicalism of the 1830s* (Oxford: Oxford University Press, 1970), p. 210. See also Aldred, *Richard Carlile, Agitator*, pp. 130, 183; Joel Wiener, 'Hassell, Richard', in Joseph Baylen and Norbert Gossman (eds), *Biographical Dictionary of Modern British Radicals* [hereafter BDMBR] (Sussex: Harvester Press, 1979), vol. 1, pp. 213–15; McCalman, *Popular Radicalism and Freethought in Early Nineteenth Century England*, p. 158. Tragically, Hassell was to die within months of his release, aged twenty-five. Carlile was devastated. He genuinely anticipated that Hassell would become a future leader with the potential to unite the generally fractured radical movement. See Wiener, *Radicalism and Freethought in Nineteenth-Century Britain*, p. 136.

with the remaining prison population.[93] It was not, however, simply their own exertions that led to the separation from other prisoners. The surge in popular radicalism in the intervening decades since the 1790s gave the 1820s radicals a key advantage: the authorities were now even more concerned by the dangers of exposing the criminal classes to the apostasy of radical views and publications.[94]

Contagion was an ever-present danger in the unreformed prison, but here was the threat of contamination of a different sort. Paradoxically, it was the risk of contagion *from* the state prisoners to the wider prison population that in many cases secured these radicals the separate accommodation they demanded. The concern of the authorities was not without basis. When Gilbert Wakefield was imprisoned in Dorchester during the late 1790s for a 'seditious utterance' (suggesting that the English people were in such a state of misery they had little to lose from a French invasion), he assisted felons with writing petitions, paid some fines and debts of prisoners and debtors and sometimes purchased food for those without.[95] Convicted Peterloo orator Henry Hunt used his imprisonment in Ilchester during 1820–21 to publicly advocate for an improvement in the situation of debtors and also assisted with petition writing.

Nevertheless, many radicals scoffed at the fears of the prison authorities, believing that other prisoners were incapable of understanding even the most basic tenets of radicalism. In 1826, the radicals' brief contact with a fellow prisoner, Edward Cockerill, however, both challenged the general disdain of radicals for their prison counterparts and affirmed the authorities' fears of the potential for contagion from state prisoners to the wider prison community. Cockerill had been awaiting execution in Newgate for his crime of forgery, when, following the release of Thomas Jeffries, and for the six weeks before his execution, he shared the state-side accommodation with Campion, Clarke and Hassell. They reported that Cockerill 'had the free use of our library, and the benefit of some philosophical and blasphemous conversations' and, despite being a 'stranger' to infidelism, Cockerill read with 'avidity'. By the time of his execution, the radicals reported that he had 'imbibed our principles'.[96]

To the disgust and despair of the prison chaplain, Cockerill refused religious consolation and shunned God during the entire proceedings at the gallows.

---

93   Michael Ignatieff notes the same of the radicals imprisoned in Gloucester during the late 1790s. See Ignatieff, *A Just Measure of Pain*, p. 125.
94   Ibid., p. 123.
95   See ibid., p. 126. See also the campaign by Henry Hunt to improve the situation of debtors while he was imprisoned in Ilchester during 1820–21, in John Belchem, *'Orator' Hunt: Henry Hunt and English working-class radicalism* (Oxford: Clarendon Press, 1985), pp. 8–9, 134–43; Margot C. Finn, 'Henry Hunt's "Peep into a Prison": The radical discontinuities of imprisonment for debt', in Glenn Burgess and Matthew Festenstein (eds), *English Radicalism 1550–1850* (Cambridge: Cambridge University Press, 2007), pp. 191–216. As Finn notes, imprisoned debtors, because of their status as civil prisoners rather than criminals, had been seen as 'fitting objects of radical solicitude since the seventeenth century'.
96   *Newgate Monthly Magazine*, 1 March 1826.

His radical roommates instead had prepared him with the 'consolation of philosophy' to see his fate as the 'inevitable result of life', as 'merely the termination of sensation, a perfection of that state of unconsciousness which he nightly experiences in an inferior degree'.[97] The incident made news across Britain with the mainstream press reporting Cockerill's long and painful death on the gallows as a consequence of his impiety, juxtaposing it with the instant death of a fellow condemned prisoner who had allowed the presence of God during his final days.[98] Perhaps unsurprisingly, the radicals instead related a different version of events, in which the two men suffered equally at the gallows.

Such a public conversion to the infidel cause was abhorrent to orthodox early nineteenth-century society on several levels. First, it occurred at a moment so sacred in the Christian faith—that of preparing to face God upon death. It was also a direct affront to the central tenets of prison reform, which claimed that even the most wanton and fallen criminal could be redeemed through religious instruction. The separate and solitary system advocated by prison reformers could well have prevented the contagion of Edward Cockerill. The space of the old prison was once again the radicals' ally.

The incident, Campion reported, 'occasioned the consultation of a coterie of Alderman'.[99] This committee determined that 'no more prisoners were to be mixed with us, and that all communication between us and any other prisoners should, as far as possible, be prevented'.[100] The risk posed by the seepage of such heretical views through the wider prison population created a spatial conundrum for the prison authorities. The four rooms that housed the remaining three radical prisoners in Newgate in 1826 would have otherwise accommodated between 40 and 50 prisoners in other parts of the prison. As Campion quipped, the prison authorities had only three choices: send in more prisoners to share the space and risk their 'souls be[ing] lost to Jehovah—or keep the yard solely for us—or send us to another prison'.[101] Despite being an 'orderly set of fellows', wrote Campion, 'we have been more trouble to our Keepers than all the other prisoners who have been in the place since our arrival', claiming the Keeper had 'wanted to get them out' as soon as they arrived at the prison.[102] His observations suggest that state prisoners had become a troublesome anomaly in the old prisons, which, despite reform ideals, generally housed many more inmates than room allowed.

---

97   Ibid.
98   The *Ipswich Journal*, 25 February 1826, claimed the hangman was forced to pull on Cockerill's legs until he died. For a similar account, see *The Times*, 22 February 1826; *Aberdeen Journal*, 1 March 1826.
99   *Newgate Monthly Magazine*, 1 July 1826.
100 Ibid.
101 Ibid.
102 Ibid.

If Cockerill's conversion to atheism was trumpeted as a triumph in the 'Honourable House of Blasphemers', their bluster was to be short-lived. As Cockerill was being enlightened 'on the real value of religion', one of their own was rescinding his radical principles in favour of Christianity. William Haley, the defiant shopman who scoffed at the prospect of his confinement with the 'Newgate beetles', received one of the longest sentences in the 1824 prosecutions, and had become one of the most vocal complainants from within the prison. The reality of life in London's 'mansion of misery', however, eventually tested both Haley's bravado and his commitment to the radical cause. The authorities shortened his sentence by 15 months after he renounced the infidel views that led to his prosecution.[103] When Hassell discovered the petition Haley had penned to Home Secretary, Robert Peel, advising of his conversion to Christianity, he quickly relayed his find to Richard Carlile.

The betrayal drew an acerbic response from the radical leader. Characteristically, Carlile went on the attack, not only labelling Haley a 'bad principled fellow', a 'thief' and a 'traitor', but also claiming to have countered Haley's move by forwarding his own doubts of the shopman's recant directly on to Peel. Carlile crowed publicly that his efforts had 'kept Haley a prisoner through the last winter'.[104] On Haley's eventual release from Newgate, Carlile reported that

> I heartily rejoice at his release from prison, that we may say that we are fairly rid of him, well assured, that his habits and character, notwithstanding his ability with the pen, will lead him to his former rags and wretchedness.[105]

Although Carlile's spiteful treatment of Haley raised the ire of the wider radical community, we cannot underestimate the depth of feeling Haley's defection engendered in the small Newgate community; it dealt a heavy blow to the collective political identity that the men had forged despite the ordeal of imprisonment. Solidarity was crucial to their resistance. Haley's recantation also drew the radicals back into the criminal ether of the prison; his conversion suggesting that radicals, like other prisoners, could be reformed and find redemption under the right prison conditions.

Haley's actions were also the very antithesis of what Carlile expected from his shopmen and women. Carlile's own experience of prison was as an unparalleled opportunity for self-improvement and knowledge, which deepened his commitment to the radical cause.[106] He expected his fellow radicals to make similar use of the opportunity. Richard Hassell's liberation three months after

---

103 Reports of the events appeared in the *Republican*, 31 March 1826.
104 Ibid.
105 Ibid.
106 McCalman, *Radical Underworld*, p. 187.

the Haley affair gave Carlile the opportunity to praise him as the model radical prisoner, celebrating his dedication to self-improvement and instruction during his incarceration.[107] Prison reformers believed that mandatory religious instruction would result in reform and redemption, but Hassell's educative achievements were of an entirely different order. Just as the 1790s radicals utilised Newgate as a 'virtual college', Hassell found the prison gave him an opportunity for political enlightenment, and Carlile reported Hassell had 'diligently spent his time in various modes of self-improvement' developing his 'literary, mathematical, linguistical, and philosophical talents'.[108] Carlile could boast that Hassell left prison 'well prepared to take a lead in assisting to reform those who sent him there'.[109]

Education led to greater political awareness, which was another means of resistance within the prison space. Hassell's prison education was not an isolated occurrence for the 1820s radicals. Carlile's correspondence with other imprisoned radicals also urged them to use the opportunity presented by their prison sentences to further their education. Carlile wrote to Boyle in 1823, expressing his earnest wish that he would use the remainder of his imprisonment to 'conquer [his] antipathy towards to the complete study of Grammar', hoping that following Boyle's release he could be employed 'in the superintendence' of Carlile's publishing business.[110] The study of grammar, however, was not to Boyle's taste; his preference instead was 'amusing [himself] in arithmetic'.[111] The promise of self-improvement was also a way for radicals to come to terms with the 'unfreedom' of prison. Boyle considered that his '18 months imprisonment shall not be 18 months of my life lost; I think in 18 months I can gain some little knowledge of geometry'.[112] Carlile taunted the authorities for facilitating the education of his shopmen; had more prosecutions been effected, he claimed, 'we should have had more Philosophers in our Gaols than debtors, smugglers or poachers'.[113] As George J. Holyoake would later recall, Carlile 'suspected the qualifications of every man who had not taken out a diploma from the Attorney General'.[114]

The educative possibilities presented by imprisonment also endowed radicals in the 1820s with the skills and confidence to embark on their own publishing enterprise. In one of the most striking and overt forms of resistance and

---

107 *Republican*, 2 June 1826.
108 Ibid. See also E. P. Thompson, who noted that debtors' prisons also functioned as 'finishing schools for Radicals'. Thompson, *The Making of the English Working Class*, p. 692.
109 *Republican*, 2 June 1826.
110 Richard Carlile to Humphrey Boyle, 18 January 1823, Humphrey Boyle Papers, WYL623/5, West Yorkshire Archive Service, Leeds.
111 *Republican*, 7 June 1822.
112 Ibid.
113 *Republican*, 20 January 1826.
114 George J. Holyoake, *The Life and Character of Richard Carlile* (London, 1849), p. 39.

renegotiation of the Newgate prison space, the men produced their own prison publication, the *Newgate Monthly Magazine*, from within their ward. Modelled on Carlile's *Republican* (and produced with Carlile's assistance), the first edition was issued shortly after their initial incarceration in 1824. In addition to providing a public vehicle in which to air their grievances about their conditions and expose 'life in Newgate', the publication was used to defy their containment in the prison space by continuing to disseminate their trenchant views on social, theological and political issues. Despite the altered conditions for political prisoners, the existence of the *Newgate Monthly Magazine* highlights the continuities with older radical prison traditions.

As Kevin Gilmartin has observed, the 'ability to work through repression, and especially imprisonment, became a litmus test for the viability of radical protest in print'.[115] It was, but prison publications also suggest much more. The editorial collective of the magazine was drawing on a long tradition of literary pursuit and prison publications that was a manifest form of prisoner resistance and expression of political identity—a defiance of their forced removal from society. As radical poet Elijah Ridings wrote to the *Newgate Monthly Magazine* editors:

> Your thoughts are not confined either in your own cranium or within the walls of your prison, but are wandering around the Island of Albion… almost persuading me that you are at large, once in each month at least, perambulating and disputing, confabulating and philosophising.[116]

Gilmartin notes that the prison name itself 'hovered over the production and reception of the magazine, but its impact was not entirely negative, since prison called attention to injustices that demanded reform'.[117] In fact, from the radical perspective, there was little that was negative about the use of 'Newgate' in the magazine's title. It was shrewdly selected as a means of resistance, announcing clearly to the wider public that the walls of the prison would not serve to silence radical voices. The *Newgate Monthly Magazine* also serves as an important reminder to historians that public discourse and exchange occurred beyond those institutions typically described as outlets of rational communication in Habermas's original conception of the bourgeois public sphere.

The very existence of the magazine demonstrates how the prison space afforded radicals a measure of protection from prosecution throughout this period. As the ultra-conservative *New Times* newspaper protested, imprisonment did not 'in the slightest degree check the publication of fresh blasphemies on [Carlile's]

---

115   Kevin Gilmartin, *Print Politics: The press and radical opposition in early nineteenth-century England* (New York: Cambridge University Press, 1996), p. 90.
116   *Newgate Monthly Magazine*, 1 April 1826.
117   Gilmartin, *Print Politics*, p. 90.

part'.[118] Prison allowed for a freer expression than was able on the outside. The *Newgate Monthly Magazine* was heralded by supporters as a publication of 'the greatest utility' and as a 'medium for the interchange of sentiments uncorrupted by the prejudices of the times, and untainted by servility'.[119] It tapped into the groundswell of popular radicalism, and the imprisoned men believed that instruction in rational thought and reason was vital in order to effect their political and social aims. It appears particularly incongruent that the authorities should be so concerned with containing the possibility of radical contagion within the prison walls and yet approached the prison publications with such leniency. Part of the explanation lies in the rights claimed by radical prisoners, which will be explored in detail in Chapter 2. It also suggests that regardless of prison reform, the authorities considered the prison space and state prisoners themselves as legitimate elements of both the radical public sphere and the wider compass of political discourse.

Nevertheless, it is clear that the literary production of the 1820s radical prisoners never matched that of the 1790s milieu. Several factors worked against a more prolific output in the period, not the least of which involved both the education levels of the new cohort of radicals and their working-class status, which directly impacted on their financial means to fund such production. Unlike their earlier counterparts, most did not enter prison primed with the knowledge or skills to produce a prison tome. Another crucial impediment to the 1820s group was that which proved the 1790s milieu's greatest ally: the unhindered entry of visitors to the prison space. Despite securing some concessions in terms of accommodation and beds, Newgate radicals of the 1820s never succeeded in having the restrictions on the entry of visitors lifted. In 1825, Perry complained in a petition to Parliament that 'the regulations of the prison place your Petitioner under the treatment of a convicted felon; all which annoyances, and degrading regulations amount to a total exclusion of all your Petitioners friends'.[120] This provided less opportunity for the creation of a 'salon of radical philosophes' for engaged discussion and debate for developing and testing novel thoughts and ideas.

In this light, prison newspapers such as the *Newgate Monthly Magazine* and the *Republican* also played a vital role in providing physical contact with the outside world. Both the prisoners and their families depended on the subscriptions generated by and encouraged in the radical press. A particularly generous offer from one region could encourage support from another. The magazine also served as reminder to the radical community that its advocates and leaders

---

118 Reproduced in *Republican*, 14 January 1825. See also complaints printed in *The Times* of the *Courier* newspaper lamenting the 'fresh blasphemies' shortly after Carlile's imprisonment. *The Times*, 26 October 1819.
119 *Republican*, 15 April 1825.
120 *Republican*, 3 June 1825.

were paying a heavy price in pursuit of a new political and social order for the nation. As one subscriber to the *Republican* noted, the Newgate magazine had 'a double claim for patronage upon every friend of truth and reason: coming as it does from the shrine of virtue and containing the sentiments of her invincible votaries'.[121]

The restrictions on visitors entering the prison also impacted on the ability of the 1820s radicals to emulate the sociability and conviviality of the earlier radical imprisonments. During the 1790s, and during Cobbett's and Hobhouse's confinements, the entry of visitors to the state-side apartments allowed radicals to re-create the familiar radical spaces of the tavern, the coffee house or the dining room of the radical home. Despite the restrictions on visitors to the prison, the 1820s radicals made the most of their situation to ensure their continuing participation in important radical events. One episode in the prison in 1826 speaks volumes of the determination to maintain a radical collective and a connection with radical culture outside the prison.

In a scene that evokes the image of radical sociability depicted by Newton in his *Soulagement* print more than 30 years earlier, on the afternoon of 29 January 1826, the four remaining shopmen, Perry, Hassell, Clarke and Campion, all gathered in their state-side apartment to commemorate the birth of radical ideologue and icon Thomas Paine (a birth date serendipitously shared by Perry).[122] Belting out tunes with titles such as *The Bravest of the Brave* and *Lovely Woman Governs All*, the men reported that the gathering provided opportunity for much 'hilarity' and revelry. Assembling their own makeshift tavern, they sat down to an 'excellent leg of mutton' with all the 'expected trimmings', filled their tankards with wine at the end of each rendition and raised their cups in earnest to toast 'the immortal memory of Thomas Paine', 'Richard Carlile' and 'The Female Republicans'. In defiance of their incarceration, they reserved a toast for their adversaries: 'May our example teach the Government that Imprisonment for opinions is useless.' In a rare public avowal of the much maligned prison authorities, the men acknowledged that the prison Governor had been kind enough in this instance 'to allow us to remain together until eight o'clock, instead of being locked up as usual, at this season of the year, at five'.[123]

The anniversary of Paine's birth had become an auspicious day for the radical community in Britain. As the four men celebrated in Newgate, 75 'respectable, well dressed' radicals also met in honour of Paine's birth at the City of London tavern, where a 'half-a-guinea ticket' provided dinner, dessert and wine.[124] Mirroring events in Newgate prison that afternoon, the London tavern assembly

---

121 *Republican*, 15 April 1825.
122 *Newgate Monthly Magazine*, 1 March 1826.
123 Ibid.
124 *Republican*, 3 February 1826.

raised their glasses to honour the four men—'freedom of mind's undaunted champions'.[125] Clearly, the incarceration of Perry, Hassell, Clark and Campion was to prove no impediment to their own participation in this important radical community event. The men were as happy, they reported, as 'our friends could possibly be at the London Tavern, or elsewhere'.[126]

The observance of ceremonies such as the birth of Thomas Paine in 1826 fostered radical camaraderie and a sense of fraternity within the prison, and a shared collective identity both with earlier generations of radical prisoners and with the radical community beyond the prison walls. Like the early generation of radical prisoners, they defied their containment within the prison space by re-creating familiar radical spaces such as the tavern. Certainly, their festivities were more solitary affairs than previous radical gatherings in the prison; however, the ability of radicals to subvert the prison regime and routine and maintain contact across time and space with the wider radical community attests to the vitality and adaptability of the new generation of plebeian radicals.

The defiance with which radicals faced imprisonment, and the concessions they fought hard for and won, however, should not obscure the suffering that undoubtedly came with imprisonment. Separation from family inflicted deep emotional and financial hardship not only on those confined, but on families who were left without a breadwinner. Thomas Ryley Perry's petition to the House of Commons for a reprieve for his situation noted the 'state of extreme distress' his imprisonment had caused his wife and two infant children.[127] Despite the claim by the songsters of 1826 that the afternoon provided much hilarity, at times it also took on a particularly sombre tone. One tune, a parody on the poem *A Soldiers Dream*, spoke of 'thoughts from my prison-house' wandering back to the 'sweet home' where

> My little-ones kiss'd me a thousand times o'er
> And my wife sobb'd aloud in the fullness of heart.
> Stay, stay, with us Father, you must not return
> And fain was the thrice happy parent to stay,
> But sorrow came back with the coming of morn,
> When the heart-cheering vision had melted away.[128]

Doubtlessly, the martyrdom, radical credentials and educative possibilities of prison came at a high price for many radical prisoners.

---

125 *Republican*, 24 February 1826.
126 *Newgate Monthly Magazine*, 1 March 1826.
127 *Republican*, 3 June 1825. On Perry, radical and freethinker, see Joel Wiener, 'Perry, Thomas Ryley', *BDMBR*, pp. 372–3.
128 *Newgate Monthly Magazine*, 1 March 1826. The editors noted that the song was a 'parody on Campbell's "Soldiers Dream"'.

The *Newgate Monthly Magazine* was to be the last gasp of radical expression from Newgate prison. The remaining men—Clarke, Perry and Campion—were removed from Newgate on 25 July 1826 to the Compter, where they, like Boyle three years before them, reported more comfortable conditions.[129] Most importantly, friends were admitted each day between noon and 2 pm, and on Sundays could remain until four in the afternoon. In what Gilmartin refers to as an 'appropriate irony', their departure from Newgate saw the *Newgate Monthly Magazine* cease production.[130] This appears less ironic when the production of the magazine is viewed as an integral part of their prison resistance and assertion of a political identity rather than the criminal identity afforded by the prison space.

Although the men initially reassured their readers that relocation to another prison would simply mean a new title—the *Compter Magazine*—they finally conceded that to continue with a third volume 'would be inconvenient', for before 'twelve more numbers could be published we may be very widely dispersed'.[131] In the end, the demise of the magazine could also have been due to financial considerations. The men had complained that their own financial support through subscriptions had begun to dwindle and so too, perhaps, had interest in the publication. Carlile, never one to be beaten, claimed that the last edition of the magazine was necessitated by the fact the men had 'finished their education'.[132]

The radical relationship with Newgate, from the 1790s through to the 1820s, suggests that it was a symbiotic and dialectal one. Newgate both shaped and was shaped by its radical inhabitants. The ability of radicals in the 1820s to adapt to the encroaching impact of prison reform by forging a radical identity and retaining a voice in the public sphere remains an enduring link between two generations of radical prisoners. From the production of the *Newgate Monthly Magazine* to the fight to secure better conditions within the prison; from the opportunities for self-improvement to the revelries of January 1826—these all attest to the vitality and tenacity of radical culture, even faced with the hardship and liminality of the prison space.

As well as highlighting the need for change in older prisons such as Newgate, the rigorous drive for prison reform also resulted in the proliferation of new, purpose-built prisons on the English landscape. During the early nineteenth century, magistrates could take advantage of a greater selection of destinations for those convicted of political and religious offences. Radical prisoners could now be scattered around the metropolis and beyond—from Newgate

---

129 *Republican*, 26 July 1826.
130 Gilmartin, *Print Politics*, p. 90.
131 *Newgate Monthly Magazine*, 1 August 1826.
132 *Republican*, 20 January 1826.

to the Compter, from Coldbath Fields to Dorchester. The new prison spaces differed markedly to Newgate; they were designed and built specifically to accommodate the new ideals of separation and solitary confinement. The new spatial arrangements presented a fresh challenge for radical culture; how radical prisoners incarcerated in one such prison, the House of Correction at Coldbath Fields, responded to this challenge is examined in the following chapter.

2. 'Bastilles of despotism': radical resistance in the Coldbath Fields House of Correction, 1798–1830[1]

In the early morning of 13 July 1802, the road from London to the town of Brentford was already buzzing with a carnival atmosphere. Thousands had assembled on foot while others rode in hackney coaches; riders on horseback and bands of musicians formed a cavalcade that snaked along the roadways.[2] The 1802 elections for Middlesex had become a major spectacle in the metropolis during the month of July.[3] Crowds assembled each day at the Piccadilly home of Sir Francis Burdett to accompany their hero to the hustings. Burdett, the independent Whig MP for Boroughbridge and vocal opponent of William Pitt, had been enticed to London to contest the Middlesex elections by his close radical supporters.[4] The streetscape was a panorama of vivid deep blue: banners were draped across buildings, ribbons were tied and handkerchiefs waved in Burdett's electoral colour by thousands of supporters. The occasional hint of light blue or splatter of orange in the crowd meant supporters of rival contestants, such as Tory MP William Mainwaring, had unwisely spilled into the procession.[5]

Three horsemen led the massive entourage, each bearing a large blue banner, with the words 'No Bastille' illuminated in golden letters. The words inflamed the otherwise festive throng; angry chants of 'No magistrates' and 'No Bastille' reverberated among the crowd. Newgate, however, was not the object of scorn, but rather a new prison, the Coldbath Fields House of Correction, and the Middlesex magistrates responsible for its management. In mock scenes from the 'dungeons of Coldbath Fields', street performers were carried down the street, half-naked, writhing and crying in agony as they were 'whipped' by other actors. Other participants, scantily dressed as prisoners, imitated fainting

---

1 The term 'Bastiles of despotism' is taken from a letter from Joseph Harrison printed in *Black Dwarf*, 30 October 1822.
2 The account of the procession is taken from the report in *The Times*, 14 July 1802. See also reports in *Morning Chronicle*, 14 July 1802, 15 July 1802.
3 On the significance of the Middlesex elections to radical London, see J. Ann Hone, *For the Cause of Truth: Radicalism in London 1796–1821* (Oxford: Clarendon, 1982), pp. 133–46. On elections more generally, see Frank O'Gorman, 'Campaign Rituals and Ceremonies: The social meaning of elections in England, 1780–1860', *Past and Present*, vol. 135 (1992), pp. 79–115.
4 On Sir Francis Burdett, see J. R. Dinwiddy, 'Sir Francis Burdett and Burdettite Radicalism', *History*, vol. 65 (1980), pp. 17–31; Peter Spence, *The Birth of Romantic Radicalism: War, popular politics, and English radical reformism, 1800–1815* (Aldershot: Scolar, 1996), pp. 14–25; Hone, *For the Cause of Truth*, pp. 117–219.
5 William Mainwaring, Tory MP, was also Chairman of the Quarter Sessions for Middlesex. On Mainwaring, see Leon Radzinowicz, *The History of the Criminal Law and its Administration Since 1750* (London: Stevens and Sons, 1948–86), vol. 2, pp. 81, 195, vol. 3, pp. 186–7, 377–8.

from hunger. Others still feigned the agonies of death. Even though the street theatrics concluded at the end of the procession, 'No Bastille' banners continued to dress the streets throughout July.

Electoral fever culminated on 29 July when immense crowds again gathered at the hustings in anticipation of the final count. The announcement of Burdett's victory prompted one of the largest political processions ever seen in the metropolis.[6] Burdett's supporters had keenly anticipated the victory— an elaborate chair decorated with branches of laurel had been built to carry him all the way to London (Figure 2.1). As heavy rain fell, the entourage was forced to abandon the pageantry of 'chairing' in favour of a closed carriage.[7] The weather did nothing to diminish the occasion for the thousands assembled in celebration. The Strand, reported the *Morning Chronicle*, was 'illuminated in honour of Burdett'.[8] An observer from *The Times* struggled for words to adequately describe the mood of the crowd and the 'expressions of joy and congratulation manifested by the people all along the road'.[9]

Figure 2.1 *An Exact Representation of the Principal Banners and Triumphal Car, which conveyed Sir Francis Burdett to the Crown and Anchor Tavern on Monday June 29th, 1807*. It is unclear whether the same procession car was used for the 1802 election.

Unknown artist. Copyright Trustees of the British Museum.

---

6   *Morning Chronicle*, 30 July 1802.
7   On 'chairing' as election ritual and the theatrics of the electoral campaign, see O'Gorman, 'Campaign Rituals and Ceremonies'; John Brewer, 'Theatre and Counter-Theatre in Georgian Politics: The mock elections at Garrat', *History Today*, vol. 33 (1983), pp. 14–23.
8   *Morning Chronicle*, 30 July 1802.
9   *The Times*, 30 July 1802.

The Times correspondent observed that as the victory procession moved through respectable neighbourhoods, 'beautiful well-dressed women' waved blue silk handkerchiefs from their windows. As the entourage moved closer to central London, the correspondent noted that 'less polished damsels vociferated… "Burdett forever, and no Bastille"'.[10] On the street, young boys clenched carved wooden figurines dangling from poles with chains and bones—caricatures of prison torture and execution. Further depictions of prison cruelty were displayed by performers on makeshift stages atop carriages. Some held larger versions of the cruelty 'toys' of the boys on the street, and some pretended to flog figurines representing prisoners. Others donned the executioner's mask and menaced the crowd with parcels of chains wrapped around their hands. The intent with which the harrowing scenes were performed and the impassioned reception by the crowd disturbed *The Times* observer: never had he witnessed so large an assemblage or 'such a motley scene of disgusting folly'. According to the correspondent, the crowd had assumed the hallmarks of an unruly mob, though to his great relief, he reported that adequate precautions by the police had prevented what the French could not: the storming of London's own 'Bastille'.

If the fear and loathing evinced by Newgate gaol had accumulated in the public memory of Londoners over the centuries, the revulsion felt for the House of Correction at Coldbath Fields was achieved in only a few short years. Following its opening in 1794, the prison quickly earned a reputation for brutality and severity. Burdett first became embroiled in the abuses in the prison when 16 men from the London Corresponding Society (LCS), including former military officer Colonel Edward Marcus Despard, were imprisoned in Coldbath Fields on charges of treason.[11] They had been arrested (and eventually found guilty) for plotting to incite popular uprisings in Ireland and England in preparation for a French invasion. The harsh treatment meted out to the prisoners while awaiting trial attracted Burdett's notice and he demanded a House of Commons inquiry into their case.

---

10 Ibid. See also *Morning Chronicle*, 30 July 1802, which reported the involvement of ladies such as 'Mrs Read of Turnham Green', who waved Burdett's colours and were active during the election campaign. For a discussion of women's participation in elections, see Anna Clark, 'Class, Gender and British Elections, 1794–1818', in Michael T. Davis and Paul A. Pickering (eds), *Unrespectable Radicals? Popular politics in the age of reform* (Aldershot: Ashgate, 2008), pp. 107–24. On the involvement of aristocratic women in elections and politics more generally, see Judith Lewis, *Sacred to Female Patriotism: Gender, class and politics in Georgian Britain* (New York: Routledge, 2003); Elaine Chalus, '"That Epidemical Madness": Women and electoral politics in the late eighteenth century', in Hannah Barker and Elaine Chalus (eds), *Gender in Eighteenth Century England: Roles, representations and responsibilities* (London: Addison Wesley Longman, 1997), pp. 151–78.
11 For an account of the arrests and trials, see Edward Royle and James Walvin, *English Radicals and Reformers 1760–1848* (Brighton: Harvester, 1982), pp. 95–122; Hone, *For the Cause of Truth*, pp. 103–37; Michael Ignatieff, *A Just Measure of Pain: The penitentiary in the Industrial Revolution, 1750–1850* (New York: Columbia University Press, 1980), pp. 126–33; David Worrall, *Radical Culture: Discourse, resistance and surveillance 1790–1820* (New York: Harvester, 1992), pp. 53–67. On Despard's arrest under a Habeas Corpus Writ, see *Sun*, 26 June 1798; *True Briton*, 26 June 1798. On Despard more generally, see James Bannantine, *Memoirs of Edward Marcus Despard* (London, 1799); Marianne Elliot, 'The "Despard Conspiracy" Reconsidered', *Past & Present*, vol. 75 (1977), pp. 46–61; Clifford D. Connor, *Colonel Despard: The life and times of an Anglo-Irish rebel* (Conshohocken: Combined Publishing, 2000); Mike Jay, *The Unfortunate Colonel Despard* (London: Bantam Books, 2004).

Radical Spaces

Figure 2.2 *Citizens Visiting the Bastille, vide Democratic Charities.*
James Gillray, 1799. Copyright Trustees of the British Museum.

Burdett's visits to the prison became highly publicised, as evident by James Gillray's 1799 print, *Citizens Visiting the Bastille* (Figure 2.2). He uncovered a litany of abuses and brought them to public notice through a speech in the House of Commons, subsequently printed as a pamphlet titled *An Impartial Statement of the Inhuman Cruelties Discovered! in the Coldbath Fields Prison*.[12] Although the motivation for the pamphlet was the alleged ill treatment of the state prisoners, none of the cases it exposed appeared more shocking than the plight of Mary Rich, a fourteen-year-old girl held in the prison for a month after accusing a lawyer of attempted rape. A grim feature of the late eighteenth-century legal system made provision for witnesses in trials to be held in custody, while those actually being prosecuted could remain free until trial if they had sufficient wealth to provide for it. Mary's appearance in court a month after being committed to the prison caused a sensation: deathly pale and drawn, her emaciated frame appeared crippled from starvation. Despite being seated in a chair, she was 'scarcely able to hold herself upright'.[13] When questioned on her condition, she feebly advised the jury that she had been fed only bread and water for the month and had been left with only scanty bed coverings. Her sickly frame was exposed to a frigid cell without glazed windows or a fireplace. Further, the pamphlet relayed her claim in court that, despite being exceedingly ill for more than four days, she had been denied access to a doctor.

The *Impartial Statement* catalogued further abuses: prisoners being beaten by turnkeys; some prisoners being chained in irons for several months at a time without provocation; others confined to shattering spells of solitary confinement for only minor infractions; prisoners being fleeced of money for the most basic of necessities; and still others, along with Mary, starved 'to the point of death'.[14] With Burdett's intervention, the plight of Colonel Despard also gained significant public attention. Along with Burdett, Despard's West Indian-born wife, Catherine, commenced a campaign to elicit public sympathy, complaining to the Home Secretary, the Duke of Portland, that Despard had been treated 'more like a common vagabond than a gentleman or State Prisoner'.[15] One letter, read in the House of Commons and reported in the daily press, complained that he had been imprisoned 'without either fire or candle, chair, table, knife, fork, a glazed window or even a book to read'.[16] Despard was eventually moved to a

---

12   Sir Francis Burdett, *An Impartial Statement of the Inhuman Cruelties Discovered! in the Coldbath Fields Prison* (London, 1800), part 1, p. 6. For further discussion of Burdett's visit, see Hone, *For the Cause of Truth*, pp. 121–8.
13   Burdett, *An Impartial Statement of the Inhuman Cruelties Discovered*, pp. 14–15. See also Ignatieff, *A Just Measure of Pain*, p. 133.
14   Burdett, *An Impartial Statement of the Inhuman Cruelties Discovered*, pp. 10–12.
15   *Morning Post*, 24 December 1798.
16   See *Morning Post*, 24 December 1798; *Courier*, 24 December 1798; *Oracle and Daily Advertiser*, 27 December 1798.

room with a fire, though not before, Catherine claimed, 'his feet were ulcerated by frost'.[17] Burdett's report on the prison conditions was presented to the House of Commons for recommendation, but failed by an overwhelming majority.[18]

Nevertheless, Burdett's and Catherine's crusades against the prison quickly found a receptive public audience. Although the British populace had long been accustomed to allegations of abuse in old prisons such as Newgate, Coldbath Fields was one of the first prisons to arise in the outer London landscape as a testament to the aspirations of John Howard and other late eighteenth-century prison reformers.[19] Here was a prison intended to embody Howard's humanitarian convictions of protecting prisoners, not only from the squalor, disease and misery of old prisons such as Newgate, but also from the whims of governors and turnkeys and the ruthless prison economy. Instead, Burdett had exposed a site of neglect, barbarity and corruption. The abhorrent conditions of the prison were immortalised in poetic brevity by celebrated writers Samuel Taylor Coleridge and Robert Southey in their composition *The Devil's Thoughts*:

> As he went through Coldbath-fields, he saw
> A solitary cell;
> And the devil was pleased, for it gave him a hint
> For improving his prisons in hell.[20]

For Coleridge and Southey, the solitary cell—the keystone of new prison design sweeping Britain in the late eighteenth century—exemplified the cruelty and inhumanity of the new prison at Coldbath Fields.

Yet from the perspective of the early Middlesex magistrates charged with overseeing the prison, Coldbath Fields was a model of success.[21] They

---

17   *Courier*, 24 December 1798.
18   See Richard Brinsley Sheridan, *Speeches of the Late Right Honourable Richard Brinsley Sheridan* (London, 1816), pp. 93–107.
19   J. Ann Hone notes that the LCS men committed to Newgate at the same time had no cause for complaint, and that John Kirby, the Keeper, 'received only praise' over their treatment. See Hone, *For the Cause of Truth*, p. 124.
20   The original stanzas were penned by Coleridge and caused a scandal when they were printed in the *Morning Post and Gazetteer* in September 1799. There is some contention over whether the revised poem, retitled *The Devil's Walk*, was a collaboration of Coleridge and Southey or a work from Percy Bysshe Shelley. It has appeared under both titles in the works of the individual authors. For an account of the debate surrounding authorship, including the hoax that it was penned by a 'Professor Porson', see *Notes and Queries*, 10 March 1866. See also the tract published under the Porson pseudonym (said to be by Southey and Coleridge), *The Devil's Walk; by Professor Porson* (London, 1830). For an online edition of the poem, see also <http://www.rc.umd.edu/editions/shelley/devil/dev29vs35.html>, and Morton Paley, 'The Devil's Thoughts' and 'The Devil's Walk', Conference paper, 1997, University of California, <http://www.rc.umd.edu/villa/vc97/paley.html>
21   See the anonymous pamphlets, *The Secrets of the English Bastille Disclosed, To which is added a copy of the rules and orders by which the whole system is regulated, by a Middlesex magistrate* (London, 1799); *The Case of the New House of Correction in Coldbath Fields…Fairly and impartially stated…by a brother magistrate* (Brentford, 1801); *Considerations on the Late Elections for Westminster and Middlesex, Together with some facts relating to the House of Correction in Coldbath Fields* (London, 1802).

vehemently denied the accusations of cruelty and neglect, claiming (with almost desperate excess) an early victory for prison reform. They had, they reported, the satisfaction of hearing from their 'reformed delinquents'—those who had never 'had a serious thought in their lives'—that their imprisonment had been the 'happiest event that ever befell them'.[22] Clearly, they urged, the prison was 'wholly undeserving of that calamitous epithet *Bastille*' when in fact it was

> [a] House of Correction in its best and fullest signification: a house in which their stubborn tempers have been subdued—their hardened hearts have been softened—their ignorant minds have been instructed—their vicious habits have been overcome—new habits of diligence and sobriety have been established.[23]

The reform utopia of 'subdued stubborn tempers' in Coldbath Fields was shattered only, claimed the magistrates, by the intrusion of the state prisoners in 1798. One magistrate considered the committal of such prisoners a serious error of judgment on the part of the authorities, claiming it was 'an ill-fated hour' when

> [t]he doors of the prison were opened for the reception of a new description of offenders; and the cells were filled with turbulent, condemned mutineers; and not less turbulent, seditious, and traitorous state prisoners:—The prison was not built for these, nor fitly calculated to receive them; the rules and orders for the management of the prison were not drawn up with a view to such prisoners.[24]

Despite the magistrates' warning of the unsuitability of the prison for state prisoners, Coldbath Fields was to host many radicals convicted of political and religious offences in the early nineteenth century. Veteran radical orator John Gale Jones was imprisoned for a libel on Lord Castlereagh; John Hunt, editor of the *Examiner* and less celebrated brother of literary luminary Leigh Hunt, was sentenced to two years for seditious libel; and several of Richard Carlile's bookshop volunteers, including Samuel Waddington, James Watson, William Tunbridge and Susannah Wright, also served out their sentences in the new prison.[25]

---

22   *The Secrets of the English Bastille Disclosed*, p. 14.
23   Ibid.
24   *The Case of the New House of Correction in Coldbath Fields*, p. 5.
25   It was also to be one of the metropolitan destinations for many Chartist prisoners following the crackdown on sedition and blasphemy in the early 1840s. A survey of their experience is beyond the scope of this book, however, it warrants further attention in light of the experience of political prisoners throughout the nineteenth century. On the Chartist prisoners, see Christopher Godfrey, 'The Chartist Prisoners, 1839–41', *International Review of Social History*, vol. 24, no. 2 (1979), pp. 189–236. On the experience of Chartist prisoners, see also two recent publications concerning the prison experiences of individual Chartists: Paul A

Michael Ignatieff remains one of the few historians to resurrect Coldbath Fields prison to the historical record. His study of the rise of the penitentiary in Britain, *A Just Measure of Pain*, focuses on Coldbath Fields prison as a key institution in the transition to the modern penitentiary. His account is consistent with Coleridge's hellish depiction of the site; the brutality of the first Governor, Thomas Aris, was exceeded only by the neglect of Middlesex magistrates who ignored the abuses of Aris and his eldest son. The other Coldbath Fields Governor to feature in Ignatieff's account is the 'disciplinarian' George Laval Chesterton, who banned all 'speech and gesture among inmates' by introducing a silent system into the prison in 1834.[26] Ignatieff quotes from Chesterton's account that the

> [p]risoners are kept under constant and secret inspection day and night…every movement…is made so as to prevent their faces being turned to each other; they are never allowed to congregate or cluster together, they move in solitary lines in single file.[27]

Here, then, was a prison that not only intended, but had achieved the level of social control outlined by French philosopher Michel Foucault in his landmark study *Discipline and Punish*, which provided the theoretical framework for Ignatieff's study.[28] At the heart of Foucault's analysis of the birth of the modern prison is the idea that the corrective prison, which was widely embraced at the end of the eighteenth century, recalibrated the focus of crime and punishment. Under the old unreformed system, confinement, whippings, irons and hanging meant punishment was directed at the body. Prison reform saw many of these physical punishments replaced by mandatory religious instruction, prison labour and separate and solitary confinement, which shifted the emphasis from punishment directed at the body to that now directed at the soul. The new system, which separated, controlled and observed, rendered prisoners' bodies docile; and docile bodies could be controlled and manipulated at whim.[29]

The motivations of eighteenth-century prison reformers such as John Howard, Sir George Onesiphorus Paul and Jeremy Bentham have dominated recent writings on British criminal history and those investigating the source of the modern prison. Foucault and Ignatieff both rejected penal histories that

---

Pickering, *Feargus O'Connor: A political life* (London: Merlin, 2008), pp. 91–3; Stephen Roberts, *The Chartist Prisoners: The radical lives of Thomas Cooper (1805–1892) & Arthur O'Neill (1819–1896)* (Oxford: Peter Lang, 2008).
26   Ignatieff, *A Just Measure of Pain*, p. 178.
27   George Laval Chesterton quoted in ibid., p. 178.
28   Michel Foucault, *Discipline and Punish: The birth of the prison*, trans. Alan Sheridan (London: Penguin, 1991).
29   For a thorough survey of studies of prison reform that initially followed Foucault's watershed book, see Joanna Innes and John Styles, 'The Crime Wave: Recent writing on crime and criminal justice in eighteenth-century England', in A. Wilson (ed.), *Rethinking Social History: English society 1570–1920 and its interpretation* (Manchester: Manchester University Press, 1993), pp. 201–65.

celebrated the religious, philanthropic and humanitarian motivations of reformers. Ignatieff claimed his intention, and that of Foucault, was to 'pierce through the rhetoric that ceaselessly presents the further consolidation of carceral power as "reform"'.[30] They proffered more complex and sinister motives for the emergence of the modern prison, which centred on social-control theory and the need for a swiftly trained yet skilled workforce to meet the economic demands of industrialisation.[31]

Although the time frame of this chapter predates the opening of Mettray in France in 1844 and Britain's Pentonville prison in 1842—the time when Foucault and Ignatieff respectively argue for the realisation of the modern prison—Foucault's work has become the dominant theoretical model for historical investigations of the prison and cannot be overlooked even in the earlier period. Prisons such as Coldbath Fields, as suggested by its inclusion in Ignatieff's analysis, played an important role in the transition to the modern penitentiary. To borrow from J. Ann Hone, it was built in the 'vanguard of this movement'.[32] According to Foucault, the new prisons were designed to dominate not merely the body but also the mind, and this chapter examines the extent to which (at least in this period) the new prisons succeeded in crushing the mind, soul and spirit of these men and women of ideas.

As minorities in the prison system, radical prisoners have generally been overlooked in studies investigating the source of the modern prison, which tend to base their analyses on the male felon as the normative prison inmate. Similarly, the relationship between radical culture and the reformed prison system also remains under-explored in radical historiography. The perspective of another theoretician, Jürgen Habermas, also provides a useful framework with which to explore this terrain. The ability of radicals to forge a political identity within the new prison and, further, their ability to promote public discussion about the status of the political prisoner went beyond the condition or the standing of those convicted of political offences; they challenged the very basis by which Britishness was defined.

* * *

---

30 Ignatieff, *A Just Measure of Pain*, p. 220.
31 Ibid. In penning *A Just Measure of Pain*, Ignatieff considered it the role of history—and by default the historian—to 'combat carceral power and the coercive structures of thought that underpin it' (p. 220). See also Randall McGowen, 'A Powerful Sympathy: Terror, the prison and humanitarian reform in early nineteenth-century Britain', *The Journal of British Studies*, vol. 25, no. 3 (1986), pp. 312–34. For an alternative view of the argument, see George Fisher, 'The Birth of the Prison Retold', *Yale Law Journal*, vol. 104 (1995), pp. 1235–325. It must also be noted that Ignatieff later tempered some of the stronger assertions he made in *A Just Measure of Pain*. See Michael Ignatieff, 'State, Civil Society and Total Institutions: A critique of recent social histories of punishment', in Stanley Cohen and Andrew Scull (eds), *Social Control and the State* (New York: St Martin's Press, 1983), pp. 75–105.
32 Hone, *For the Cause of Truth*, p. 126.

Architectural innovation lay at the heart of late eighteenth-century prison reform and one of its master thinkers was Jeremy Bentham, arguably Britain's pre-eminent philosopher.[33] In his design for the panopticon—a prison that he believed encapsulated the essence of reform—Bentham marvelled that he could effect '[m]*orals reformed, health preserved, industry invigorated, instruction diffused, public burthens* [sic] *lightened, Economy seated, as it were upon a rock, the gordian knot of the Poor-Laws not cut but untied—all by a simple idea in architecture*'.[34] Bentham's panopticon was based on solitude and surveillance; his design enabled prison staff to maintain a constant watch over every one of the single-occupant cells from a central observation tower, which formed the axis of his circular design. Although the panopticon, as Bentham envisaged it, never came to fruition, the impact of its central principles of solitude and surveillance on future generations of prison architects should not be underestimated.[35]

Other prison architects such as William Blackburn and Jacob Leroux also responded to the design challenge presented by the twin reform ideals of punishment (rather than mere confinement) and redemption.[36] Cellular design—as opposed to the dormitory-style wards that accommodated Newgate prisoners—soon pervaded all new architectural interpretations of the prison. Prison reformers saw the general concept of housing prisoners separately in single cells as the best means to prevent criminals mixing with other prisoners and leaving the prison more 'depraved' and 'wretched' than when they first entered.[37] The solitude of single cells also allowed for inner reflection and repentance. Along with the mandatory attendance at regular chapel services and

---

33   Howard himself envisaged that the structure of the prison was key to improving the prison system: 'the first item to be taken into account is the prison itself.' John Howard, *The State of the Prisons in England and Wales, With preliminary observations, and an account of some foreign prisons* (Warrington, 1777), p. 40. For an overview of the scholarship focusing on Jeremy Bentham since John Dinwiddy's 1989 study, *Bentham*, see John Dinwiddy and William Twining (eds), *Bentham: Selected writings of John Dinwiddy* (Stanford: Stanford University Press, 2004). See also Gertrude Himmelfarb, 'The Haunted House of Jeremy Bentham', in *Victorian Minds* (London: Weidenfeld and Nicholson, 1968), pp. 32–81; Catherine Fuller (ed.), *The Old Radical: Representations of Jeremy Bentham* (London: University College London, 1998). For recent discussions of Bentham and radical culture, see Michael Turner, '"Arraying Minds Against Bodies": Benthamite radicals and revolutionary Europe during the 1820s and 1830s', *History*, vol. 90, no. 2 (2005), pp. 236–61; Philip Scholfield, 'Jeremy Bentham, the French Revolution and Political Radicalism', *History of European Ideas*, vol. 30, no. 4 (2004), pp. 433–61; F. Rosen, 'Jeremy Bentham's Radicalism', in Glenn Burgess and Matthew Festenstein (eds), *English Radicalism 1550–1850* (Cambridge: Cambridge University Press, 2007), pp. 217–40.
34   This phrase opens Jeremy Bentham's preface in his seminal treatise *Panopticon: Or, the Inspection House: containing the idea of a new principle of construction applicable to any sort of establishment, in which persons of any description are to be kept under inspection: and in particular to penitentiary houses, prisons, houses of industry...and schools* (1787; reprinted, London: T. Payne, 1791). The italics are from the original.
35   For a thorough account of the impact of Bentham's design on nineteenth-century prison architecture, see Robin Evans, *Fabrication of Virtue: English prison architecture, 1750–1840* (Cambridge: Cambridge University Press, 1982), pp. 195–229.
36   On William Blackburn, see ibid., pp. 118, 126–31; H. M. Colvin, *A Biographical Dictionary of British Architects*, fourth edn (New Haven, Conn.: Yale University Press, 2008), pp. 126–7 (hereafter *BDBA*). On Leroux, see Colvin, *BDBA*, pp. 645–6.
37   Howard did not advocate complete isolation of prisoners. He considered total solitude as severe, cruel and unnecessary to effect the reform intentions. See Fisher, 'The Birth of the Prison Retold', p. 1324n.

with the religious instruction afforded by newly appointed prison chaplains, the new structure of the prisons held the promise of redeeming the prisoner and correcting criminal behaviour. Prison labour was a key element of reform and was designed to inculcate the habits of industry on an otherwise indolent criminal community. Such thinking constituted a critical shift in the approach towards crime and criminals: mere confinement was no longer enough; it was now seen as possible to 'correct' offenders. As Howard remarked in his watershed treatise, *State of the Prisons*, in 1777, 'to reform prisoners or make them better as to their morals, should always be the *leading* view in any house of correction'.[38]

The House of Correction at Coldbath Fields had its genesis amidst the prison reform boom. It was completed in 1794 after six years of construction following the plan of architect Jacob Leroux.[39] The architectural features of Coldbath Fields instantly identified the site as a place of confinement. The 8 acre (3 ha) site on London's outskirts in Clerkenwell was encircled by an immense outer wall, giving the site, observed Hepworth Dixon, 'the idea of a strong fortress'.[40] Black letters carved in the painted stonework above the massive prison doorway announced 'The House of Correction for the County of Middlesex 1794', illuminated in the evening by gas lamps above. Two giant iron rings constituted the door handles and, if the imposing prison wall was not signal enough, enormous black fetters, 'big enough to frighten any sinful passer-by back into the paths of rectitude', hung as tassels from the top of each entrance pillar.[41] The only ornamental feature of the entrance was the County of Middlesex crest, which hung over the door; even then, three sabres hung 'threateningly over the heads of all who enter[ed]'. Dixon considered that, despite these grim accoutrements, and compared with Newgate, the site of the prison was 'certainly not an imposing edifice…It looks like a place of punishment, but not one of torture'.[42]

To better appreciate the architectural changes of the new prison and their impact on the prison population, it is worth lingering for a moment on the design and layout of the new prison (Figure 2.3). Encased within the prison wall, the original

---

38   Howard, *The State of the Prisons in England and Wales*, quoted in Fisher, 'The Birth of the Prison Retold', p. 1271.
39   There remains some dispute about the architect of the prison. Ackermann's *Microcosm of London* (London, 1809) records the architect as Sir Robert Taylor, and that, after his death, Sir William Chambers completed the plan. H. M. Colvin records a similar account, though also contends that the building was 'chiefly designed by Jacob Leroux'. See Colvin, *BDBA*, p. 645. See Colvin, *BDBA*, pp. 239–45 for Sir William Chambers. For a very detailed account of the procurement and building process of the prison, see C. W. Chalkin, 'The Reconstruction of London's Prisons, 1770–1799: An aspect of the growth of Georgian London', *London Journal*, vol. 9, no. 1 (1983), pp. 21–34.
40   Henry Mayhew and John Binny, *The Criminal Prisons of London and Scenes of Prison Life* (London: Griffin, 1862), p. 279. Robin Evans contends that the new trend of exposing the interior of the prison to the public gaze was a reaction against the enclosed courtyard style adopted by architects such as Dance, both father and son. See Evans, *Fabrication of Virtue*, p. 166.
41   Mayhew and Binny, *The Criminal Prisons of London and Scenes of Prison Life*, p. 279.
42   Hepworth Dixon, *The London Prisons: With an account of the more distinguished persons who have been confined in them* (1850; reprinted, New York: Garland Publishing, 1995), p. 237.

building was a prodigious structure based on parallel rows of cells separated by yards.[43] Mayhew observed that they were 'overloaded with ponderous iron gates, window frames and fastenings; while narrow entrances and passages were designed to render a sudden outburst of prisoners impracticable'.[44] The prison was designed to effect a key reform measure of separating male and female prisoners—the men housed on one side of the prison and the women on the other. The prisoners were kept in different divisions, with between 50 and 100 prisoners to each division depending on the numbers in the prison at any one time. Each division had a yard for prisoners to exercise and converse in, measuring between 70 and 100 ft by 50 ft (20–30 m x 15 m). The yards were paved with 'flag stones' so that they drained well and stayed relatively dry. Prisoners were accommodated during wet weather by a colonnade on one side of each yard, which provided a measure of protection from the elements.[45]

Figure 2.3 Elevation and section of Coldbath Fields House of Correction, 1800.
Samuel Alken. Copyright City of London, London Metropolitan Archives.

Most commentators, even those more hostile observers, agreed that the new prison design achieved a remarkably light, open, clean and well-aired environment—one commentator noting that 'in no part is the prison close

---

43   Ibid., p. 245.
44   Mayhew and Binny, *The Criminal Prisons of London and Scenes of Prison Life*, p. 280. Mayhew here is quoting Governor George Laval Chesterton's *Revelations of Prison Life* (1856; reprinted, New York: Garland, 1984).
45   Dixon, *The London Prisons*, p. 238; *The Abuse of Prisons, or, An Interesting and Impartial Account of the House of Correction in Cold-bath-Fields, and the treatment of Mr Gale Jones founded upon a minute inspection of the prison and a personal interview with him* (London, 1811), p. 3.

or gloomy'.[46] Crucially, prison reformers heralded the new cellular design of prisons as a key weapon in the fight against the virulent and sometimes lethal spread of infection and disease caused by overcrowding, freedom of movement between prisoners and squalid conditions of older prisons such as Newgate. As Howard noted 'many more prisoners were destroyed by [gaol fever] than were put to death by all the public executions in the kingdom'.[47] At Coldbath Fields, the regular application of whitewash on the inner walls, passages and cells provided a cyclical cleansing of the space.[48]

Opening immediately onto the yard, the cells for the prisoners were also lined with flagstones, with the centre of the floor slightly arched to promote drainage in an effort to keep the cells dry. Most cells were meagre in size—roughly 8 or 10 ft (2.4–3 m) square. In a significant advance on the older prisons where beds consisted of straw matting on the floor, the new cells were fitted with a wooden bench in the 'shape of a trough', about 2.5 ft (0.8 m) wide, and mounted off the floor along one wall. This was hailed as an adaptable feature—converting to a table or bench seat during the day—though some reports suggest that the bedding provided to prisoners remained desperately inadequate.[49] Each cell featured a window near the top of the room lined with thick iron bars. Like Newgate, here, the windows remained unglazed, but had a shutter outside that (theoretically) could be opened or closed at the prisoner's pleasure. The adequacy of the shutters in alleviating the often-frigid temperature in the cells is questionable; as visiting officials quizzically observed, in many cells, the mechanism to operate the shutters had been damaged by prisoners as an act of defiance.[50]

Although the new prison rules allowed for only one man to occupy each cell (though sometimes two women were permitted to live together), overcrowding meant that this was rarely achieved.[51] The possibility of such overcrowding could have prompted the inclusion of some larger cells, which was evident on

---

46   See *Courier* commentary on John Gale Jones in ibid. A similar reaction was recorded during William Hazlitt's visit to Coldbath Fields to see John Hunt, the imprisoned co-editor of the *Examiner*, where the 'extreme cleanliness of the narrow and interminable passages' of the prison was noted. See R. H. Stoddard, *Personal Recollections of Lamb, Hazlitt and Others* (New York: Scribner, Armstrong & Co., 1875), p. 153.
47   Howard, *The State of the Prisons*, p. 7. Even Burdett's initial exposé of the prison reported that 'every part of the gaol we had seen appeared to be very clean'. See Burdett, *An Impartial Statement of the Inhuman Cruelties Discovered*, p. 11.
48   The issue of disease has been relatively underplayed in many of the more recent accounts of eighteenth-century prison reform. Severe overcrowding, freedom of movement between prisoners and squalid conditions meant earlier prisons were ideal breeding grounds for disease. Gaol fever, later identified as typhus, had already proven its ability to hurdle the prison walls and transcend class lines—afflicting visitors, prison staff, magistrates and the wider community in eighteenth-century Newgate.
49   See Burdett, *An Impartial Statement of the Inhuman Cruelties Discovered*, p. 9. See also *Morning Chronicle*, 8 September 1818.
50   *Morning Chronicle*, 8 September 1818.
51   *House of Correction—Coldbath Fields—Additional Rules*, November 1823, MA/G/GEN/1271, London Metropolitan Archives, London (hereafter *Additional Rules—Coldbath Fields*).

the prison plan. Each division was also allocated a 'public room of association', which had a large fire—the only form of heating allowed to the general prison population. In an 1818 report from a 'Police Committee' tasked with visiting the prison and reporting on its conditions, the day rooms were considered 'insufficient for the number of persons who are confined there; so that it is impossible for them in the winter to be warmed by the fire which is kept up, or even to have access to the room itself'.[52]

Prisoners were allocated to the different divisions in the prison according to the classification of their crime. By the time Coldbath Fields opened its doors in 1794, prisoners were classified as felons, debtors or misdemeanours. Offences for seditious libel or blasphemy saw radical men and women treated in the last category.[53] In providing for distinct categories of prisoners, reformers hoped to separate different sorts of offenders, so that felons, for instance, could not corrupt the morals of those committed for lesser offences and for shorter stays. Changes to prison design made this theoretically possible in the new prisons, with separate cells, yards and public rooms for association, but overcrowding in the early nineteenth century often meant that such boundaries were impossible for governors to maintain.[54]

The payment of a salary to prison staff and an ostensibly egalitarian approach of introducing new regulations for the maintenance of prisoners were intended to replace the pre-reform practice of extracting fees from prisoners. Another key area of the old prison economy in the reformers' firing line was the trade in food and drink. New regulations provided for a prison food allowance, the provision and quality of which were to be a source of rigorous debate. Burdett's early exposé of the prison reported that the meagre food allocations were regularly of substandard quality and the bread, meat and gruel allocations almost always under the regulated weight.[55] Supporters of the prison described the 16-ounce (500 g) loaf of bread as 'excellent', which they observed was accompanied by a quart (1.2 L) of gruel for breakfast and, on alternate days, either 'six ounces of beef for dinner at two o'clock' or 'a due proportion of soup'.[56]

In one of the most significant departures from the old prison system, much tighter controls now governed the entry of visitors to the prisons. Architectural historian Robin Evans maintains that the new prisons were seen as the very antithesis of the old system in which prison was merely an extension of the outside world and where visitors moved freely in and out of the prison walls.[57]

---

52 For the report, see *Morning Chronicle*, 8 September 1818.
53 *Additional Rules—Coldbath Fields*.
54 Dixon, *The London Prisons*, p. 238.
55 Burdett, *An Impartial Statement of the Inhuman Cruelties Discovered*, p. 15.
56 *The Secrets of the English Bastille Disclosed*, p. 15.
57 See Evans, *Fabrication of Virtue*, pp. 47–93, on the transformation of the prison from the old to the new.

Though such restrictions were eventually implemented (at least in part) in Newgate by the 1820s, they were firmly in place from the opening of Coldbath Fields in 1794. The new rules of Coldbath Fields strictly regulated when and where friends and family could now visit: entry to the cells was not permitted and a designated visiting space maintained a wide separation between the imprisoned and the visitor.[58] The duration and frequency of visits were determined by the classification of the prisoner. Felons had the most restrictive visitation rights while for those in the misdemeanour category, visitors were allowed between noon and two o'clock each day, except on Sundays.

If the spiritual cleansing of the prisoners was provided for with regular chapel services, the physical cleansing of new arrivals was also mandatory under the new regulations. Rules at Coldbath Fields provided that each person be 'stripped and well washed…their clothes are baked in an oven, to extinguish disease, tied up in a bundle, and ticketed, ready to be returned on going out'.[59] The processing of the new prisoner was complete when he or she was outfitted in the 'gaol dress…instead of their own'. By 1818, despite the official rules, the 'Police Committee' that undertook an investigation of the prison noted the practice of allowing prisoners (with the exception of felons) with 'good clothing and linen' to wear their own garments.[60]

Descriptions of new prison spaces, regulations and reform intentions provide useful context for understanding the 'ideal' environment faced by prisoners and for theorising the motivations for change. They are of less value for illuminating a prisoner's actual experience within the new reformed prison space, particularly in a prison system in transition. A dearth of writings from within the prisons from 'common' criminals has led to a heavy reliance on the writings of prison reformers and official prison records, which often fail to consider the practical results of reform on the wider prison population, or indeed on the agency of prisoners themselves to effect changes to prison routines and regimes. Both Foucault's and Ignatieff's reliance on official sources, including the claims of Governor Chesterton in 1834, presuppose that the impositions from above provide the exclusive determinant of prison life and environment. Historians such as Peter Linebaugh, Margaret De Lacy and Lucia Zedner have challenged the approach of Foucault and Ignatieff, recognising the disparity between ideology and practice and viewing prison reality as 'multi-

---

58   See the rules of the prison appended to the pamphlet *The Secrets of the English Bastille Disclosed*.
59   *The Abuse of Prisons*, p. 4.
60   *The Times*, 24 August 1818.

faceted, often contradictory and always problematic'.[61] Ignatieff himself later conceded that Foucault's work did not allow for viewing the 'disciplinary world view—Foucault's savoir—as a site of contradiction, argument and conflict'.[62]

The gulf between theory and practice in the new prison system was most evident in relation to political prisoners. From the example of Colonel Despard in 1798, it seemed that the new prison, with its 'uniformity of plan', had heralded a new era in the treatment of those convicted of political and religious offences. When Burdett took up the case of Despard—one of the first political prisoners to be housed in Coldbath Fields—he found that the former military officer was confined in one of the prison's smallest cells, measuring a mere 7 ft (2 m) square, which, being set below ground level, flooded during rain.[63] The window of the cell was unglazed so that

> he was obliged, during the rigours of a hard winter, to jump from his table to his bed, and from his bed to the ground, in order to produce such an increased circulation of his blood as should diffuse warmth through his half-frozen veins.[64]

Despard's wife, Catherine, reported that despite the desperate physical drill, his legs bore ulcers from the extreme cold of his cell. Combined with his 'felon's diet' of bread and water, Coldbath Fields prison, she feared, had almost achieved prematurely what the hangman would later accomplish on the gallows.

Catherine's unyielding pursuit of the government to intervene in Despard's plight saw some eventual improvements in the conditions in which he was incarcerated. Despard's allies were to be found across the political spectrum. Though Horatio Nelson attended his trial as a character witness, it did little to change the outcome of the final verdict.[65] The intervention of John Reeves, former leader of a loyalist network centred on the Crown and Anchor tavern, and now a conservative magistrate, saw Despard's prison conditions somewhat alleviated. Following Reeves' intervention, Despard was moved to an upstairs room in the prison with a fire, was allowed books and papers, and Catherine was permitted to visit him in his cell.[66] When Burdett presented Despard's case to the

---

61 Lucia Zedner, *Women, Crime and Custody in Victorian England* (Oxford: Clarendon Press, 1991), p. 97; Margaret DeLacy, 'Grinding Men Good? Lancashire's prisons at mid-century', in Victor Bailey (ed.), *Policing and Punishment in Nineteenth Century Britain* (London: Croom Helm, 1981), pp. 182–216; idem, *Prison Reform in Lancashire, 1700–1850: A study in local administration* (Stanford: Stanford University Press, 1986); Peter Lindebaugh, *The London Hanged: Crime and civil society in the eighteenth century*, second edn (London: Verso, 2003), p. 3.
62 Ignatieff, 'State, Civil Society and Total Institutions', p. 95. In this paper, Ignatieff presents a very good overview of the scholarship, which, to that date, had criticised his approach, and that of Foucault.
63 *Morning Herald*, 24 December 1798; *Oracle and Daily Advertiser*, 27 December 1798.
64 *Oracle and Daily Advertiser*, 27 December 1798.
65 Jay, *The Unfortunate Colonel Despard*, pp. 324–32; Roger Knight, *The Pursuit of Victory: The life and achievement of Horatio Nelson* (Boulder, Colo.: Westview Press, 2007), pp. 433–4.
66 *The Times*, 22 December 1798.

House of Commons, the Attorney-General, John Scott, admitted that Despard had been moved to a better room because of his rank, along with other state prisoners from the LCS.[67] Scott regretted the indulgence after it was reported that the men had made the room into a '*Debating Society* of the worst possible species'.[68] He also maintained that Catherine was allowed to visit her husband and, with a thinly veiled threat, remarked that in 'speaking of *wives*', it was 'no small degree of indulgence that the Government had not imprisoned some of them also'.

The relocation of Despard and the other LCS men to another area of the prison takes on greater significance when considering the spatial context of Coldbath Fields. Where Newgate's architectural plans clearly allowed accommodation for state prisoners as a distinct category of prisoner, no such provision was made in the architectural design of Coldbath Fields. The absence of such specific accommodation could have prompted the Middlesex magistrates' desperate defence in 1798 that the 'prison was not fitly calculated to receive' state prisoners.[69] It is possible that in classifying state prisoners as 'misdemeanours', both the architects and the authorities no longer considered that such separate allocation of accommodation was necessary.

For radical prisoners, however, the repercussions were critical. As was the case with radical prisoners in Newgate throughout the period 1790–1820, separation from the remaining prison population was a crucial means of resisting the criminal identity inscribed by the prison space. Yet despite the omission of a dedicated 'state side' in the plans of Coldbath Fields, the historical record suggests that radical prisoners of the nineteenth century owed a great debt to the exertions of Catherine Despard; most reported being confined in larger, more comfortable cells and with access to their own yard. In 1811, the *Independent Whig* newspaper published an account of the imprisonment of prominent radical orator John Gale Jones for a libel on Lord Castlereagh. Reports that Jones had been denied access to visitors, books, pen and paper enraged the paper's editor, Henry White.[70] The rival conservative *Courier* newspaper sent its own representative to the prison to investigate. When the unnamed journalist arrived at Jones's room, he noted briefly that Jones's wife and child were with him and that Jones did not appear well. He was struck, however, with Jones's commodious and agreeable accommodation:

> [L]odged in the front of the prison, in a building, not built like the prison, but as a dwelling-house…The room is spacious, and neatly

---

67 See report from the House of Commons reprinted in the *Sun*, 27 December 1798.
68 Ibid.
69 *Considerations on the Late Elections for Westminster and Middlesex*, p. 20.
70 See the excerpts from the paper, and the counter-charges by the *Courier*, reprinted in *The Abuse of Prisons*.

fitted up with paper, a Bath stove fire-place, a bed, chairs, tables, writing table, carpet, &c. The furniture is Mr Jones's own. The room is about 16 feet by 14, and about nine feet high, remarkably warm and cheerful, it having a southern aspect, being very light, having sashed windows, and immediately overlooking the yard of the entrance where there is always some bustle going on.[71]

The *Courier* columnist reported that although some books had been denied by the magistrates, the Governor had advised him that as Mrs Jones had never had her person searched on entering or leaving the prison, Jones had ample opportunity to obtain books should he have wanted them. Confronted with a scene that totally contradicted that presented by the *Independent Whig*, the *Courier* published its own 'impartial' account of the prison in a public pamphlet, announcing in it their duty to expose the 'fraud' of claims of abuse and to restore the character of the 'long calumniated' prison.[72] Crucially, the *Courier* reporter observed that Jones had been removed from what it described as the 'state side' of the prison and housed in the 'dwelling house' at the front of the prison for allegedly supplying Burdett with details of the prison. Here again was 'evidence' of the radical as a source of infection. This time, the threat posed was not to the morals of the remaining prison population, but to the status and regard of the prison in the public eye.

When the correspondent toured the 'state side' of the prison, he found the 'state' yard slightly smaller than the others, but 'remarkably open and airy'. Here he found three men 'of better appearance than the rest, dressed in their own clothes, walking together briskly to and fro'.[73] The reporter briefly inspected the cell of an American named Colville, which he noted was considerably larger than other cells in the prison, measuring approximately 14 ft (4 m) long by 10 ft (3 m) wide, and 10 ft high, boarded and with a fireplace. It contained a table and chairs, shelves and a bed. The cell was generally locked and unlocked at the same time as the other prisoners', but Colville advised that he could mingle all day with the other prisoners on the 'state side'. Further, he had 'as many coals as he wished to burn' and, the *Courier* correspondent reported, 'light is frequently seen in his room as late as eleven o'clock'. Colville's cell, the journalist noted, was the same as the one that had housed Despard prior to his execution.

Reports of the treatment of other radical prisoners in the early decades of the nineteenth century lend weight to the *Courier*'s version of Jones's incarceration. When brothers John and Leigh Hunt were prosecuted in 1813 for libels printed in their *Examiner* newspaper, John was committed to Coldbath Fields for two

---

71 *The Abuse of Prisons*, p. 10.
72 Ibid., p. viii.
73 Ibid., p. 7.

years while Leigh was sent to Surrey Gaol. Leigh Hunt's outrageous decoration of his prison cell with elegant and elaborate furnishings and paintings has become legendary in literary and radical scholarship.[74] As John's biographer, Timothy Webb, has noted, the 'less glamorous imprisonment' of John Hunt has been 'less celebrated'.[75] Nevertheless, as private correspondence to his brother reveals, John Hunt was also afforded considerable, if less ostentatious accommodation. His room was simply furnished with chair and table, and a painting by his friend William Hazlitt hung over the fireplace.[76] He described having been granted one of the 'double' rooms (like that of Colville), which was being cleaned for him, and that Governor Adkins had also organised for another room to be whitewashed for him so that he would have access to two rooms, opposite each other. John Hunt was also informed by Adkins that once the 'bustle' of his imprisonment had subsided, he would have access to the Governor's garden to walk in.[77]

John found the prison's governing committee 'behaved with much civility' and 'granted what he asked of them in terms of family contact, books, pens, ink and paper'.[78] He advised Leigh that it would not be wise to test the magistrates' leniency by requesting the visit of friends. Anyway, he noted, Adkins had always allowed his friends to visit, providing they did so before lock-up. In a further departure from new prison regulations, when Hunt's friends visited they were not restricted to the same visiting times or space as the other prisoners. Hazlitt and P. G. Patmore reported that when they visited the prison, they found Hunt strolling in a 'dreary unkempt prison garden dotted with sickly cabbages and lettuce' before retiring to his cell for conversation and refreshments.[79]

Other radical prisoners also reported similar comforts. When Samuel Bamford, the Lancashire radical, was held in Coldbath Fields in 1817, he reported that Governor Adkins always behaved with humanity and civility.[80] Bamford, along with 28

---

74   On Leigh Hunt, poet and journalist, see Jeffrey Cox, *Poetry and Politics in the Cockney School: Shelley, Hunt, and their circle* (Cambridge: Cambridge University Press, 1998); Greg Kucich, '"The Wit in the Dungeon": Leigh Hunt and the insolent politics of Cockney coteries', *Romanticism on the Net*, vol. 14 (1999), <http://users.ox.ac.uk/~scat0385/cockneycoteries.html>; Philip Harling, 'Leigh Hunt's Examiner and the Language of Patriotism', *English Historical Review*, vol. 111 (1996), pp. 1159–81; Luther A. Brewer, *My Leigh Hunt Library* (New York: B. Franklin, 1970); Leigh Hunt, *The Correspondence of Leigh Hunt, Edited by his Eldest Son* [Thornton Leigh Hunt], 2 vols (London: Smith, Elder and Co., 1862).
75   On John Hunt, printer and publisher, see Timothy Webb, 'Hunt, John (1775–1848)', *Oxford Dictionary of National Biography*. See also Philip Harling, 'The Law of Libel and the Limits of Repression, 1790–1832', *Historical Journal*, vol. 44, no. 1 (2001), p. 124n. For a report of John Hunt's trial, see *Examiner*, 3 June 1821.
76   Stoddard, *Personal Recollections of Lamb, Hazlitt and Others*, p. 148.
77   Hunt, *The Correspondence of Leigh Hunt*, vol. 1, p. 72.
78   Brewer, *My Leigh Hunt Library*. John's earlier letter to Leigh reveals his distress on first being committed.
79   Stoddard, *Personal Recollections of Lamb, Hazlitt and Others*, p. 153. On Peter George Patmore, writer and journalist, see Hershel Moreland Sikes (ed.), *The Letters of William Hazlitt* (London: Macmillan, 1979), p. 181n.
80   Samuel Bamford, *Passages in the Life of a Radical* (1884; reprinted, Oxford: Oxford University Press, 1984), p. 114.

others, was arrested in Manchester on a charge of treason after he was suspected of involvement with the 'Blanketeers', the spinners and weavers who proposed to march from Manchester to London (encouraging others to join along the way) to protest against the severe distress felt in the north due to the ever-expanding factory system.[81] Bamford and several of those arrested were sent to London and housed in Coldbath Fields while awaiting trial. Bamford reported that, on entering the prison, the men were sent to a 'good room, or cell, about ten yards in length, and three in width'.[82] There they found three beds on each side of the room, placed 'in what might be termed wooden troughs'. A 'good fire was burning' and there was an ample supply of coal and wood to use at their pleasure. He later recalled that 'had it not been for the grating at the window above the door, and the arched roof, bound by strong bars of iron, we might have fancied ourselves to be in a comfortable barrack'.

The comfort in their surroundings also extended to their food provisions, which Bamford considered more than adequate. Breakfast consisted of a pound (450 g) of bread with butter, and tea and sugar, while lunch promised meat, potatoes and vegetables (at which time they were allowed a pot of porter, as well as pipes and tobacco) and the dinner allowance was tea and cold meat. 'As far as diet was concerned', reflected Bamford, 'we lived more like gentlemen than prisoners'.[83] This bounty of food, however, also caused some trepidation amongst the men, who feared that the Governor's generosity was 'only precursory to some terrible act of severity', signalling that they might soon face the ultimate sacrifice for their involvement with the Manchester march. This was later reinforced when the men received written religious instruction in the form of 'sermons for persons under sentence of death'.[84] Although the men's stay in Coldbath Fields was short—some were sent to other prisons and some, like Bamford, acquitted—they made the most of their incarceration by strategising and preparing for their trial and amusing themselves with 'no lack of songs, hymns, and love and family tales, with scraps of plots and insurrections, and droll blunders, which sometimes caused roars of laughter'.[85] In so doing, they developed a camaraderie forged not in the tavern or the coffee house, but in their prison cell.

Despite Despard's early experiences in the prison, the accounts of the relatively comfortable prison conditions experienced by later prisoners such as Jones, John Hunt and Bamford correspond closely with the reports of Cobbett's and Hobhouse's confinement in Newgate during the same period. Compare two contemporaneous prints: one depicting Hobhouse in Newgate (Figure 1.5), the other, a petty forger, Thomas Ranson, in Coldbath Fields (Figure 2.4). The prints present a remarkably

---

81 On the Blanketeers, see ibid., pp. 29–37; E. P. Thompson, *The Making of the English Working Class* (London: Penguin, 1968), pp. 709–12; R. J. White, *Waterloo to Peterloo* (Harmondsworth: Penguin, 1968), pp. 92–103.
82 Bamford, *Passages in the Life of a Radical*, pp. 88–9.
83 Ibid., p. 88.
84 Ibid., p. 89.
85 Ibid.

similar inventory of the contents of the respective cells: fireplace and mantelpiece, jugs and pots, table and chairs. Ranson has a visitor's chair, Hobhouse a pipe and even pictures on the walls (of the House of Commons and the prison itself). Of course, the accuracy of the prints cannot be verified and both were undoubtedly drawn with an axe to grind, but both suggest, almost incidentally, a consistent notion of what prison was like. They lend further corroboration to the disparate accounts of Hunt, Bamford and Cobbett.

Figure 2.4 A rare interior view of a prison cell in Coldbath Fields, 1819. The figure in the scene is the artist Thomas Ranson, who claimed to be unlawfully confined by the Bank of England for holding a forged one-pound note. It is likely that the more comfortable rooms mentioned by some state prisoners were similar in style to Ranson's room.

Thomas Ranson. Copyright City of London, London Metropolitan Archives.

Given the sudden shift in treatment towards the Carlile shopmen in Newgate in the 1820s, what then of those immured in Coldbath Fields in the 1820s? One of the first radical voices to emerge from Coldbath Fields during the 1820s was that of Carlile shopman William Tunbridge.[86] Initially incarcerated in Newgate, Tunbridge was subsequently transferred to Coldbath Fields in 1823. Tunbridge was enraged at his initial treatment in his new quarters, writing a series of letters of complaint to a variety of government officials, including the Attorney-General, Sir Robert Gifford, Home Secretary, Robert Peel and the Duke of Portland.[87] When his grievances remained unanswered, he went public; the letters were printed in the radical weekly the *Black Dwarf*.

Tunbridge claimed that he was being 'deprived of sustenance' by the Governor and that his visitors were restricted to only one visit a month, and then only for two hours duration, when they were forced to converse 'among convicted felons, in an open yard'.[88] This, he fumed, meant he was being treated worse than a felon or those under sentence of death in Newgate. It was a damning indictment of the new prison that its conditions could be worse than those in the 'mansion of misery'.

Despite, or perhaps because of, Tunbridge's initial complaints, he soon reported improved conditions within the prison, with an order from the magistrates that his friends were to be admitted to his cell and that he was allowed newspapers.[89] In private correspondence to Humphrey Boyle, another imprisoned shopman, Tunbridge admitted:

> I must say that with the exception of seeing my friends I am in every respect more comfortable than you as I have a good room with two large windows and no iron bars and a good view over Highgate Hampstead and Kentish Town.[90]

Aside from more comfortable conditions in the prison, Tunbridge's public campaign had also secured an additional benefit: he now reported being financially supported by subscriptions from Birmingham.[91]

---

86 For an account of Tunbridge's trial, see *The Times*, 7 February 1823. Little is known about William Tunbridge. He was involved in the Spencean milieu, though avoided prosecution with the Cato Street conspirators. He came to Carlile's attention with his strong support of the men imprisoned in Newgate in 1821 and was engaged to work as an assistant in the shop. See *Republican*, 24 December 1824.
87 See *Black Dwarf*, 26 March 1823, 30 April 1823.
88 *Black Dwarf*, 30 April 1823.
89 *Black Dwarf*, 28 May 1823.
90 Letter from William Tunbridge to Humphrey Boyle, 6 June 1823, WYL 632/4, West Yorkshire Archive Service, Leeds (hereafter *Boyle Papers*).
91 *Black Dwarf*, 28 May 1823. By 1824, however, relations with Carlile had soured. In October that year, Tunbridge had requested that the 'Deists, Atheists, and Materialists, as they style themselves, not to transmit him any further subscriptions, as from this period he declines all further connection with them'. Carlile found

A survey of prison correspondence from Carlile's other shopmen imprisoned in Coldbath Fields during the 1820s also suggests that those convicted of political and religious offences were still housed in separate accommodation described as 'state rooms'. William Clark, who was confined for four months in the prison for refusing to 'give up' the man he employed for printing his edition of *Queen Mab*, wrote from his 'comfortable apartment', which he referred to as the 'State Room, Coldbath Fields Prison' when he addressed the radical community through the *Black Dwarf*.[92] When James Watson was imprisoned for blasphemy in 1823 after selling Palmer's *Principles of Nature* from the Carlile bookshop, he shared a room with Tunbridge.[93] After Tunbridge's release, Watson reported that he and another unnamed prisoner read to each other for three or four hours after dark 'after which until bedtime we conversed or played at a game of cribbage'.[94]

In the clearest indication that radicals had been successful in forging a political identity within the new prison space, the Additional Rules set down for the prison in 1823 now officially recognised the existence of radical prisoners as a category distinct even from other 'misdemeanours', making specific reference to those in the 'State Rooms' and allowing special provisions for such prisoners.[95] The lingering reference to a 'state side' speaks volumes: the old system was being reinscribed on the slate of the new. Yet the new prison went even further in its concessions. The Additional Rules now also prescribed for the prisoners in Coldbath Fields that which Newgate's radical prisoners had so desperately fought for: the ability to entertain their visitors within their rooms.[96]

Despite securing two of their most sought after concessions—separate accommodation and the entry of visitors—radical prisoners in the new prisons continued to resist other measures adopted following the exertions of the prison reform movement. Radical resistance to their incarceration in the new prison space was most successful at the heart of the new prison ethos: redemption and reform through mandatory religious instruction. Though attendance at chapel was now mandated by an Act of Parliament, radicals at several different prisons reported being banned from the chapel services for proving fractious and

---

him 'so very irritable, and difficult to please' that he was 'soon compelled to drop all correspondence with him', although he admitted that Tunbridge 'has some good qualities, and I shall be ever ready to do him a service'. See *Republican*, 24 December 1824.
92 See letter from William Clark addressed from 'State Room, Coldbath Fields', *Black Dwarf*, 1 January 1823. This is possibly the same William Clark of the Spencean set identified by Iain McCalman, *Radical Underworld: Prophets, revolutionaries, and pornographers in London 1795–1840* (New York: Cambridge University Press, 1988), pp. 105, 107, 123–4.
93 On James Watson, radical bookseller and publisher, see William J. Linton, *James Watson: A memoir of the days of the fight for a free press in England and of the agitation for the People's Charter* (New York: A. M. Kelley, 1971).
94 Ibid., p. 20.
95 *Additional Rules—Coldbath Fields*.
96 Under special circumstances, the visitors of other misdemeanour prisoners could meet in the 'octagonal area under the chapel'. See *Additional Rules—Coldbath Fields*.

irreverent.⁹⁷ The political prisoners who were the subject of Burdett's original crusade against the prison reported in 1798 of being banned from attending religious services after a riot in the chapel, which led to a House of Commons inquiry.⁹⁸

The futility and danger of enforcing the chapel regulations on prisoners convicted of blasphemy during the 1820s were even more apparent to prison authorities. None of the radicals in this period reports attending chapel services or being forced to participate in them. Radicals reported that the greatest inconvenience the chapel services held for them was that the prison rules prohibited the entry of visitors on the Sabbath.⁹⁹ The reluctance of the authorities to enforce the otherwise mandatory religious instruction on his shopmen delighted Richard Carlile. Crowing from his Dorchester prison cell—another of the new prisons designed by William Blackburn—Carlile taunted that he had been 'abandoned' by his prison chaplain, considering that he had a 'claim' upon the prison chaplain's attention, and 'upon every effort' he could make 'to amend the condition, both of [Carlile's] body and mind'.¹⁰⁰

If Carlile's impervious and successful defiance of official attempts to 'amend the condition' of his mind challenges Foucault's theory of social control, the conduct of William Haley in 'unreformed' Newgate (outlined in Chapter 1) is evidence of the complexities and contradictions of a prison system in transition. Haley was one of the most trenchant and defiant early contributors to the *Newgate Monthly Magazine*. In one editorial, he raged against the conduct of those responsible for his imprisonment:

> These petty tyrants…have been foolishly led to believe, that by incarcerating the body in a prison, they could controul [sic] the mind… But they have been mistaken…Although his body is confined to the small range of a few rooms, his mind daily expands, daily towers higher above their reach, daily becomes more capable of acting to their annoyance, and daily learns more to despise their base motives and contemptible power.¹⁰¹

In light of the ferocity of Haley's attacks on those responsible for his incarceration, it is questionable whether his sudden conversion to Christianity that resulted in his early release can be attributed to the increasing impact of the reform endeavour on Newgate prison. It could simply have been that he could no longer endure being immured with the 'Newgate beetles'.

---

97 See, for example, *Newgate Monthly Magazine*, 1 October 1824.
98 Burdett, *An Impartial Statement of the Inhuman Cruelties Discovered*, p. 10.
99 *Newgate Monthly Magazine*, 1 November 1824.
100 *Republican*, 23 January 1824.
101 *Newgate Monthly Magazine*, 1 September 1824.

Like the case of Haley in Newgate prison, radical prisoners in Coldbath Fields did not always live up to Carlile's high expectations of his volunteers. The comical talents of the ex-shoemaker Samuel Waddington, known as 'Little Waddy' on account of his dwarfism, had once endeared him to the radical movement, but as Iain McCalman notes, by the 1820s, he had become an embarrassment to the movement during the earnest and respectable 'ultra-radical march of mind'.[102] Despite avoiding prosecutions in his earlier radical years, by 1822, Waddington was incarcerated in Coldbath Fields.[103] If his absurd antics in the courtroom during his trial in 1822 were not enough to alienate him from the earnest sensibilities of the other volunteers, the accusation of his sexual assault of an eleven-year-old girl collecting laundry from his cell in Coldbath Fields sealed his expulsion from respectable radical circles.[104] Despite being found not guilty of the charge of rape, some radicals feared that the publicity surrounding the scandal would have wider repercussions. Tunbridge, for instance, worried that Coldbath Fields radicals would be 'put under some restrictions more severe than at present in consequence of Waddington's affair'.[105]

If there were repercussions, they were short-lived, for Tunbridge's correspondence to Boyle makes no further mention of the incident or consequences for other radical prisoners. Rather, he continued to report favourable conditions in the prison, which were in stark contrast with those of the remaining prison population. According to Tunbridge, their conditions remained deplorable. 'I myself have witnessed', he claimed in a letter addressed to the Attorney-General, 'raw potatoe (sic) peelings being eagerly devoured' by starving prisoners, who if they dared to complain, were punished with a flogging 'til their flesh was lacerated'.[106] Writing to Boyle in April 1823, Tunbridge compared his observations of the inmates of Coldbath Fields with those in Newgate:

> I can assure you that those confined with you do not know what work, or confinement is for the poor wretches here goes to work at seven in the morning and kept at it til six at night and then locked in their cells without fire and where there is nothing before the iron bars to keep out the cold and not allowed anything but the gaol fare.[107]

---

102 McCalman, *Radical Underworld*, pp. 187–8.
103 Waddington opened his own radical bookshop in the Strand to sell Carlile's publications and was indicted on a charge of blasphemous libel for the sale of Palmer's *Principles of Nature*, which denounced Jesus as 'nothing more than an illegitimate Jew'. See McCalman, *Radical Underworld*, pp. 185–6. For an account of Waddington's treatment in the prison, see *Black Dwarf*, 1 January 1823.
104 McCalman, *Radical Underworld*, p. 188. McCalman notes that the reports of Home Office informer Abel Hall confirmed that following the incident, Waddington was forced to avoid his former radical associates for several years due to the 'obloquy of his crime'. For reports on the incident, see *Morning Chronicle*, 26 February 1823; *The Times*, 25 February 1823; *Examiner*, 2 March 1823.
105 William Tunbridge to Humphrey Boyle, 26 February 1822, WYL 623/4, *Boyle Papers*. Waddington was found 'not guilty' of the assault. See *Jackson's Oxford Journal*, 24 May 1823.
106 Letter reprinted in *Black Dwarf*, 30 April 1823.
107 William Tunbridge to Humphrey Boyle, 6 April 1823, WYL 623/4, *Boyle Papers*.

None of the radical prisoners in Coldbath Fields in this period reports being put to work with the mundane tasks of picking oakum or operating one of the first prison treadmills in Britain.[108] Rather, Tunbridge reported that after serving one-third of his sentence, he 'had no occasion to soil my hands, but of my own accord, having had a servant to wait on me at the expense of the County'.[109] The exemption from prison labour could now be added to the list of concessions gained by radical prisoners in addition to visitor rights, separate accommodation and exemption from religious instruction—all of which represented a glaring affront to the uniform approach of the new ideals of prison reform.

If we accept that political prisoners in Coldbath Fields generally fared better in terms of conditions and treatment than the wider prison population, what accounts for these concessions? The motivation for the allocation of separate space and provision of comforts to political prisoners in Coldbath Fields can be partially understood in the remarkable resilience of old prison cultures and economies and their ability to subvert the management of even the new British prisons. When Chesterton took over management of Coldbath Fields in 1829, he found 'a sink of abomination and pollution', describing his earlier colleagues as the 'thief-taking governors'. Aris, Adkins and Vickery, he maintained, held that their 'primary obligation consisted in feathering their own nests':[110]

> From one end of the prison to the other, there existed a vast illicit commerce at an exorbitant rate of profit. Wine, spirits, tea and coffee, tobacco and pipes...even pickles, preserves and fish sauce could be found within clandestine cavities in the walls or in the hollowed out basement of the cells.[111]

It was literally a case of old wine in new bottles. Chesterton recalled that prior to his appointment everything was available for a price, or denied to those without means—a strikingly similar environment to that of 'unreformed' prison spaces such as Newgate. As Randall McGowen contends, despite the 'large new prisons and the greater numbers incarcerated, the prison remained an institution strangely resistant to the intention of its designers'.[112]

---

108 As part of the prison reform process, some prisoners were subjected to periods of hard labour. Picking oakum involved the unravelling and cleaning of old rope with bare hands, and the treadmill was considered by many observers as a system of 'useless' labour as the treadmills generally served no production purpose, but rather were used merely as physical punishment; prisoners considered the only thing they were achieving was 'grinding the wind'. For an account of the hard-labour system in reformed prisons, see Mayhew and Binny, *The Criminal Prisons of London and Scenes of Prison Life*, pp. 299–311; Dixon, *The London Prisons*, pp. 244–6.
109 William Tunbridge to Humphrey Boyle, 5 October 1823, WYL 623/4, *Boyle Papers*.
110 Chesterton, *Revelations of Prison Life*, quoted in Mayhew and Binny, *The Criminal Prisons of London and Scenes of Prison Life*, p. 280.
111 Ibid.
112 Randall McGowen, 'The Well-Ordered Prison: England, 1780–1865', in Norval Morris and David Rothman (eds), *The Oxford History of the Prison* (Oxford: Oxford University Press, 1995), p. 80.

The correspondence of Tunbridge goes some way to supporting Chesterton's allegations. In his private correspondence to Boyle, he repeatedly assured his radical compatriot that he had sufficient cash to fund all his necessities in the prison.[113] Even the less wealthy artisan radicals of the 1820s could participate in the prison economy due to the support of family and friends and the subscriptions gleaned through prison publications such as the *Republican* and the *Newgate Monthly Magazine*. Such funds often enabled radical prisoners to subvert the power relations within the prison. One episode that illustrates this most strikingly occurred in the months before the incident involving Waddington. At this time, Governor Vickery approached Tunbridge to seek his approval to house Waddington in his cell. When Tunbridge accepted Waddington's company during the day, but objected to sharing his cell at night, the Governor explained that Waddington had consented 'to give up his room to one of the gamblers on exchange of remuneration'. After accepting 'near one pound of money', Waddington had reneged on the deal, leaving the two camps at 'open war'.[114] To furnish the prison economy, however, the Governor needed also to manage the committee of magistrates tasked with overseeing the operations of the prisoners. Tunbridge claimed that the Governor assured him he would 'use all his exertions with the Committee' to ensure that Waddington was not housed in his cell.

As this exchange between Tunbridge and Vickery suggests, another key determinant of radical treatment in the prison space lay with the prison staff. As Margaret DeLacy discovered in her study of the Lancashire prisons at mid-century, while the visiting magistrates wielded considerable power in the prisons, a sympathetic (or corrupt) governor could circumvent their rules.[115] In Coldbath Fields, John Hunt reported to his brother, Leigh, that despite Governor Adkins being 'much in awe' of the magistrates, he had still allowed considerable concessions to John before gaining their imprimatur.[116] Even though Chesterton held all the governors who preceded him in contempt, by most other accounts the governors who followed Aris—Adkins and Vickery—treated radical prisoners (at least) with humanity. According to James Watson, Vickery was more disposed to 'multiply [their] comforts than to restrict them'.[117]

Radicals had to tread carefully to protect their day-to-day relationship with prison staff at the same time as achieving their public aims. Complaints of mistreatment and hardship had become an intrinsic part of the prison discourse of radicals in their attempts to discredit their prosecutors and to gain sympathy in the wider community. But by exaggerating their injustices they risked alienating their

---

113 William Tunbridge to Humphrey Boyle, 6 July 1823, WYL 623/4, *Boyle Papers*.
114 William Tunbridge to Humphrey Boyle, 1 May 1822, WYL 623/4, *Boyle Papers*.
115 DeLacy, 'Grinding Men Good?', p. 205.
116 Brewer, *My Leigh Hunt Library*, p. 153.
117 Linton, *James Watson*, p. 19.

governors and losing the privileges their political status had secured. On the other hand, by publicly acknowledging their satisfaction with their treatment by the gaolers, they risked the intervention of the magistrates who were less likely to accommodate any special privileges. As John Hunt warned his brother, Leigh, among the magistrates 'there are all sorts of spirits'; it was only because of Adkins' relaxation of the rules that he 'was at all comfortable'.[118] He feared losing the 'many little indulgencies' granted by his governor, for if 'his friendly disposition towards me be made generally known, it might even make him enemies among these gentlemen, and not improbably lead to some restrictions'.[119] John Hunt forewarned Leigh to say little of his circumstances; a 'general remark' made in the *Examiner* concerning the politeness of the magistracy and the Governor would suffice.

The fear of political contagion in Newgate prison, discussed in the previous chapter, was also evident in the decision to separate radical prisoners from the remaining prison population in Coldbath Fields. In 1798, the Middlesex magistrates were particularly concerned with separating the 'most turbulent, refractory, and ungovernable' state prisoners from the remaining prison population.[120] These concerns go some way to explaining the separate accommodation afforded to radicals in the new prisons, but they clearly do not account for the often generous concessions afforded to political prisoners, particularly at a time when there was ostensibly a more egalitarian approach to prisoners in terms of accommodation, food allowances, prison dress and visitors.

The doyen of British law and criminology, Sir Leon Radzinowicz, maintains that the idea that political offenders were a unique group—'a *sui generis* species among the criminal doctrine'—did not begin to gain wide acceptance in Britain until the 1840s with the 'first wave' of political offenders: the Chartists.[121] Historians of the radical movement, however, have now documented several preceding 'waves' of popular political protest and imprisonment in the 1790s and, as examined here, throughout the early decades of the nineteenth century, which predated the crushing penological assault on the Chartists.[122]

The public record also suggests that the debate on the unique status of the political prisoner began earlier than Radzinowicz allows. As early as 1799, there was public concern over the prison treatment of the Despard conspirators. One

---

118 Brewer, *My Leigh Hunt Library*, p. 152.
119 Ibid.
120 *The Secrets of the English Bastille Disclosed*, pp. 18–19.
121 Sir Leon Radzinowicz and Roger Hood, 'The Status of Political Prisoner in England: The struggle for recognition', *Virginia Law Review*, vol. 65 (1979), p. 1421.
122 Patricia Hollis also documents an important wave of prosecutions against the unstamped press in the early 1830s. See Patricia Hollis, *The Pauper Press: A study in working-class radicalism of the 1830s* (Oxford: Oxford University Press, 1970), pp. 156–202.

Middlesex magistrate, noting that the treatment of state prisoners on the same basis as convicted felons seemed to be 'considered as a most unreasonable and disproportionate punishment', had 'no hesitation' in replying that

> whether the libel be directed against an individual or against a body of men; whether against the Constitution, or the persons engaged in the administration of public affairs...the observation will hold good, to the full conviction of the LIBELLER, as a far more mischievous member of society than the THIEF.[123]

Despite the firm conviction of this magistrate, the attitudes of the wider community towards political prisoners are crucial to understanding their special treatment within the new prison system. Regardless of whether the prosecution was for the 'misdemeanor' offences of sedition, blasphemy or libel, or for the more heinous crime of treason, there still existed a general uneasiness about punishing this category of criminal in the same way as other categories of prisoner. The *Courier*'s coverage of the imprisonment of John Gale Jones further highlights this unease. Despite the newspaper's reputation for conservatism, the editor maintained that if the allegations made by the *Independent Whig* were proved, the magistracy owed Jones a considerable apology: 'Such restraints and privations', they argued, should 'await only upon treason and the most atrocious crimes'.[124] The *Courier* maintained that the offence of libel was 'very different' from most other crimes:

> It may be necessary to place an incorrigible thief in solitary confinement with a view to reformation; but the libeller of a statesman, for his public conduct, can never be reduced in the eyes of mankind to the same degraded level. Such a libeller may be a more virtuous man and sincere patriot than the object libelled and most likely is impelled by a high sense of public duty, by an ardent love of his country. He may be convinced of his imprudence, but not of his guilt.[125]

Despite praising the prison as an appropriate site for the 'most depraved subjects' (and for effecting the reform of their past habits by denying them the ability to 'indulge miserable passions and mischievous propensities'), the *Courier*'s journalist continued to maintain that it was inappropriate to send there 'a man convicted of a libel', particularly as 'rules, wise and humane in relation to an ignorant, depraved felon, become unjust and cruel to a man of education, accustomed to the comforts and "endearing charities" of polished life'.[126]

---

123 *The Secrets of the English Bastille Disclosed*, p. 22.
124 *The Abuse of Prisons*, p. vi.
125 Ibid.
126 Ibid., p. 9. The issue had a lasting resonance for, in 1840, Sir Eardley-Wilmott, Member of Parliament and prominent penal reformer, made the case for special treatment for higher-rank prisoners to Lord

The argument held that if punishment was applied uniformly then the level of severity suffered differed according to the level of comfort the prisoner enjoyed before entering prison. In response to the neglect of the young Mary Rich in the late 1790s, for example, the magistrates charged with investigating her case argued that as Mary was from a poor and destitute family, she was already accustomed to the conditions she experienced in the prison. Therefore, in her case, her 'deprivations' did not constitute hardship or neglect.[127] Conversely, to the 'man of education', the deprivation of books, paper and pens actually magnified his suffering compared with the majority of the prison population, who were unaccustomed to such luxuries.[128] The notion was given official sanction in 1823 under the Additional Rules outlined for the prison that those in the state rooms who were 'accustomed to the use of wine' were permitted to consume up to one pint (500 ml) a day.[129]

At the heart of the unease over the treatment of political prisoners lay an even broader and deeper concern with how such treatment reflected on the nation's sense of itself. In his first speech from the hustings, Burdett stamped the electoral contest not merely as a skirmish between two political opponents, but as an engagement with the very basis of what it meant to be British. His platform was to expose the cruelties of the 'most horrible wickedness' that existed in the prison, which was symptomatic of the oppression and tyranny being exhibited by the British state. An impassioned Burdett claimed the issue struck at the very heart of the British character.[130]

This was a theme that would be revisited with each wave of political prosecutions throughout the early nineteenth century. The 'honour of the country', wrote the editor of the *Independent Whig* in 1811, demanded that the case of John Gale Jones be investigated. 'Surely it is time we ceased to boast of the hospitality, the humanity and the freedom of the English character', he argued:

> If discretionary imprisonment of the most arbitrary nature is not only tolerated among us, and witnessed with general apathy, but our prisons are suffered to be converted into the worst species of solitary confinement, to enclose torments without number…its miserable victims…are visited

---

Normanby, the new Home Secretary: 'to the man who has been accustomed to animal diet and other common indulgencies, one year's imprisonment is at least equal to two if not three years' imprisonment of the common run of offenders'; quoted in Radzinowicz and Hood, 'The Status of Political Prisoner in England', p. 1428.

127 Burdett, *An Impartial Statement of the Inhuman Cruelties Discovered*, p. 18. This was the view presented by William Mainwairing, Middlesex magistrate and Burdett's main electoral opponent, in the House of Commons debate over Burdett's allegations.

128 Leigh Hunt maintained that his own gaoler, Mr Ives, considered that if he treated Hunt like the other prisoners his punishment would be greater, as Hunt was unaccustomed to 'low living'. See E. Blunden (ed.), *The Autobiography of Leigh Hunt* (Oxford: Oxford University Press, 1928), p. 288.

129 *Additional Rules—Coldbath Fields*.

130 *The Abuse of Prisons*, pp. 24–5, 30–1.

with privations equally remote to the security of the prison, and the motive of the imprisonment, as really intended by the benign spirit of the British Constitution.[131]

In answer to the *Courier*'s charge that it had inflated the plight of Jones, the *Independent Whig* replied that their only motivation had been to rescue 'the national character from the stigma of cruelty and injustice'.[132] It was their 'public duty' to vindicate the 'rights of our fellow-countrymen, and [advocate] the cause of humanity and justice'.

The strategy of 'going public' was well rehearsed by the time the radicals of the 1820s were immured in Coldbath Fields. Tunbridge advised Boyle in 1822 to approach the magistrates overseeing Newgate with the names and offences of the prisoners confined in Boyle's ward in order to secure a room of his own. 'If they object', advised Tunbridge, 'tell them you will go public if they refuse you any redress'.[133] The tactic also set historical precedent for later radical imprisonments. In 1840, the *Northern Star* commenced a public campaign against the harsh treatment of leading Chartist agitator Feargus O'Connor, which eventually secured him more comfortable accommodation in York Castle prison.[134]

In the 1820s, radicals confined in the new prisons displayed as much confidence as their counterparts in the old prisons in their ability to influence public opinion. In theoretical terms, their ability to engage in rational discourse and exchange within both the radical sphere and the wider 'bourgeois' public arena is significant. In historical terms, it was simply clever politics. Those who publicly criticised the treatment of political prisoners in this period often placed emphasis on the denial of books, newspapers, pens and paper. Such 'necessities' were not merely tangible distractions from the monotony of prison life; they were also the tools that allowed for participation in the public sphere. The importance placed on such provisions by radicals and the authorities alike suggests a tacit recognition that radicals were legitimate participants in the public sphere despite their incarceration.

Further, the leniency with which the authorities approached prison publications and letter writing campaigns suggests that attempts to silence radicals in prison might have been regarded as contrary to a fundamental British right. During Susannah Wright's trial for the sale of a tract penned by Carlile from his prison cell, she maintained that it would be 'scandalous indeed to shut the mouth of a

---

131   Ibid., p. 28.
132   *Independent Whig*, 17 March 1811, reprinted in *The Abuse of Prisons*, pp. 32–6.
133   William Tunbridge to Humphrey Boyle, 26 February 1822, WYL 623/4, *Boyle Papers*.
134   *Northern Star*, 30 May 1840, 18 July 1840. On Feargus O'Connor, the Chartist leader and editor of the *Northern Star*, see Pickering, *Feargus O'Connor*; James Epstein, *The Lion of Freedom: Feargus O'Connor and the Chartist movement 1832–1842* (London: Croom Helm, 1982).

man in prison'.[135] Crucially, not only were radicals being deprived their liberty, they claimed, but also their natural rights of humanity, of inquiry, of reason and of truth. Through the prison discourse of radicals, the traditional rights claimed as freeborn Englishmen became fused with the natural and universal rights of radicalism. As E. P. Thompson argued in his seminal *The Making of the English Working Class*, it was the radical movement in this period that made the notion of British rights their own.[136]

In this way, radicals could question which side of the political divide had the 'truer', more authentic vision for Britain. The imprisonment of radicals and the public sympathy it elicited allowed them to promote the fact that theirs was a purer patriotism, a more legitimate claim to 'Britishness' based both on historical and rational rights.[137] The government's actions left the radicals in possession of the language of the Constitution. As the editor of the *Black Dwarf* lamented:

> No man has any right to ask of another to conform to opinions which he does not entertain, nor to suppress those which he does. To do this is to establish the basis on which all bastilles, and all inquisitions have been erected.[138]

Here was a British government operating more like the oppressive regimes on the Continent and in 'un-British' ways. As Linda Colley contends, Britishness was defined in one sense against the example of the 'repressive' regimes on the Continent.[139] As the spectacle of the 1802 electoral campaign for Middlesex reveals, employing the term 'Bastille' invoked powerful imagery and could generate equally powerful reaction. It was a 'particularly effective taunt', Ignatieff notes, to accuse a British government of behaving like French authority.[140] Following the French Revolution, the Bastille had come to symbolise state tyranny, severity and repression. It was a word, the *Courier*'s editor noted, which included 'everything cruel and horrible of a place of confinement'.[141] As early as 1794, MPs Charles James Fox and Richard Brinsley Sheridan likened Pitt's power to imprison political dissidents during the 'reign of terror' to the tyranny of Louis XVI and his use of the Bastille to crush opposition.[142] The most potent development in Burdett's contest for the 1802 Middlesex elections was

---

135 *Report of the Trial of Mrs Susannah Wright* (London, 1822), p. 13.
136 Thompson, *The Making of the English Working Class*, p. 805.
137 For a further discussion of radical prisoners and claims to both natural and historical rights, see my article, Christina Parolin, '"Let Us Have Truth and Liberty": Contesting Britishness and otherness from the prison cell', *Humanities Research*, vol. xiii, no. 1 (2006), pp. 71–83.
138 *Black Dwarf*, 20 November 1822.
139 Linda Colley, *Britons Forging the Nation 1707–1837* (New Haven, Conn.: Yale University Press, 1992).
140 Ignatieff, *A Just Measure of Pain*, p. 130.
141 *The Abuse of Prisons*, p. 24.
142 Ignatieff, *A Just Measure of Pain*, p. 130.

when he fixed upon the local working-class slang for the prison: 'the Stile'.[143] Commentators recognised how politically charged the epithet was in a climate of social unrest:

> [T]he discipline, as it is called, of the gaol, is new to this country, a free country; and calculated to excite a degree of horror among the lower orders, against the state, which, in a moment of public calamity, might dispose them to lend themselves to the most desperate men and the most atrocious purposes.[144]

It may appear ironic that the Bastille became synonymous with the new prison rather than its most evident British counterpart, Newgate. Clearly, London's oldest prison was a site loathed and feared by the London populace; to borrow words from DeLacy, Newgate and the Bastille stood as the 'two great "gothic" monuments to royal arbitrariness and official neglect'.[145] Though some radical prisoners considered Newgate as their Bastille, the new prisons were the ones linked so closely in the public psyche with state-endorsed cruelty.[146] The increasingly central role of the government in the regulation and operation of the reformed prison implied government responsibility and sanction.[147] The 'Bastille' became 'Bastilles' as other government institutions such as the workhouses also earned the bitter epithet.[148] The charge had a lasting appeal; 30 years on from the 1802 elections, radicals were referring to their places of confinement as 'Bastilles'.[149]

**

The story of radical activity in new prisons such as Coldbath Fields enhances our understanding of the way in which political prisoners and the radical community contested the authority, purpose, legitimacy and identity ascribed

---

143 Ibid., p. 141. Mayhew and Binny note that Governor Chesterton complained that the term was still in use by locals in the 1830s. See Mayhew and Binny, *The Criminal Prisons of London and Scenes of Prison Life*, p. 286.
144 *The Abuse of Prisons*, p. vii.
145 DeLacy, 'Grinding Men Good?', p. 182.
146 See, for example, John Thelwall, who wrote of Newgate and being a 'Patriot, immured in the walls of a bastille', quoted in Uwe Böker, 'The Prison and the Penitentiary as Sites of Public Counter-Discourse', in Uwe Böker and Julie A. Hibbard (eds), *Sites of Discourse—Public and private spheres—legal culture* (Amsterdam, NY: Rodopi, 2002), p. 228. The editors of the *Northern Star* soon described the new model prison at Pentonville as the 'Whig Bastille'. See *Northern Star*, 30 October 1841, 5 November 1842.
147 For example, Margot Finn maintains that the pressman Thomas Wooler 'invoked the memory of Stuart absolutism in endorsing Hunt's cause, warning readers' conditions at Ilchester meant Court of the King's Bench resembled a "Star Chamber tribunal"'. Margot C. Finn, 'Henry Hunt's "Peep into a Prison": The radical discontinuities of imprisonment for debt', in Glenn Burgess and Matthew Festenstein (eds), *English Radicalism 1550–1850* (Cambridge: Cambridge University Press, 2007), pp. 191–216.
148 See, for example, the pamphlet by Peter Simple, *The Horrible Cruelty of the New Poor Law; A scene in the Bath Union Bastile*, n.d. See also Simon Fowler, 'Pauper Bastille or Pauper Palace? Assessing the success of workhouses', *Modern History Review*, vol. 11, no. 3 (2000), pp. 10–13.
149 *Poor Man's Guardian*, 17 May 1834.

by the reformed prison space. The seemingly isolated, 'docile' and subjugated space of the reformed prison provided little impediment to radical participation in the public sphere and Habermas's model remains a useful theoretical platform on which to understand the experience of radical prisoners in both the new and the old prisons of the early nineteenth century. Radical participation in the public sphere in this period persisted despite the architectural changes and philosophical ideas designed to remove prisoners further from the public eye.

Many contemporary observers recognised the fundamental incongruity of seeking to punish a political offender. It could not be justified in principle or practice. As the *Courier* columnist investigating the case of John Gale Jones observed, such treatment did 'not amend the man or loyalize the subject, when carried to such vigorous extremes...More ill blood is created than repressed by the example'.[150] In many cases, the prison experience of radicals in this period appears to have cemented their dedication to the cause, and many returned to the movement prepared to risk repeat prison terms. The incarceration of radicals in the new prisons served to highlight the vitality, tenacity and persistence of radical culture in the early nineteenth century. This alone posed a challenge to the aim of the new prisons for reform and redemption.

The following chapter presents a case study of one such radical whose political dissidence was fortified by her experience of both Newgate and Coldbath Fields prisons. Susannah Wright, one of the few radical women incarcerated for political and religious offences in the early nineteenth century, has thus far been relegated to the periphery of radical historiography. With prison reform impacting differently on the incarceration of women, and with few historical precedents of radical female imprisonment from which to draw, Wright's experience cannot simply be read as ancillary to that of the male radical prisoner. Examining Wright's experience underscores the continuities between 'old' and 'new' prisons in this period, allows an insight into the gendered nature of public political participation and enhances our understanding of how prisons (and courts) were active sites of radical political activity.

---

150 *The Abuse of Prisons*, p. vi.

3. The 'She-Champion of Impiety': female radicalism and political crime in early nineteenth-century England[1]

In December 1822, another of Richard Carlile's imprisoned shop workers, Susannah Wright, penned a letter from her Newgate prison quarters to Carlile's wife, Jane, who was herself immured in the Carlile family cell in Dorchester prison. Susannah recounted her experience of arriving in the much maligned and feared prison, recalling that she and her seven-month-old baby were initially placed in a 'small and disgustingly filthy' ward in the section of the prison that housed the female felons.[2] Upon her arrival, Wright found the ward already occupied by five felons of 'the most wretched stamp', two of whom were facing execution for their crimes. An exchange between Wright and a turnkey provides a rare insight into the conditions in the female section of the prison.[3] Wright was infuriated by the advice of the turnkey that she and the baby were to sleep on the floor with an 'old blanket and rug…as filthy as the streets and full of holes'. She scoffed at his suggestion that there was nothing he could do to improve her situation; it was custom, he claimed, that even 'well-off' women were forced to sleep on the floor in Newgate. Wright retorted that had she been one of them 'I would have excited a rebellion against you'. Given the choice of her original cell, or another down the corridor housing two women as 'filthy with snuff as I never before saw', she reluctantly made her own way back to her first cell and spent a freezing night with her baby on the damp stone floor.

It is of little surprise that Wright was plunged into 'an atmosphere of the most offensive nature'. Although a century had passed since Daniel Defoe immured the fictional character Moll Flanders in Newgate, neither the redesign and rebuilding of the prison nor the intervention of celebrated prison reformer Elizabeth Fry altered the fact that Newgate remained oppressively overcrowded and impoverished with inadequate ventilation and fetid surroundings.

---

1 A revised version of this chapter formed the basis of my contribution to a festschrift for Iain McCalman published in 2008. See an article by the same title in Michael T. Davis and Paul A. Pickering (eds), *Unrespectable Radicals? Popular politics in the age of reform* (Hants: Ashgate, 2008), pp. 185–200. My sincere thanks to Ashgate for the permission to reproduce this version of that chapter here.
2 Letter to Jane Carlile reproduced in the *Republican*, 13 December 1822. The quotations that follow are from this letter.
3 For another account of perspectives of the female felons in Newgate, see the fascinating article by Deidre Palk, '"Fit Objects for Mercy": Gender, the Bank of England and currency criminals, 1804–1833', *Women's Writing*, vol. 11, no. 2 (2004), pp. 237–58. Her paper is based on letters from female felons convicted of forgery who requested and received regular pecuniary assistance from their prosecutors, the Bank of England.

Wright's two years as a state prisoner, served in both Newgate and Coldbath Fields prisons, afforded her some celebrity as a popular radical heroine. Her profile, however, also came with much public deprecation as the 'She-Champion of Impiety'. The imprisonment of Susannah Wright as part of the spate of radical prosecutions in the early 1820s has been noted in many studies of British radicalism, including E. P. Thompson's celebrated text, *The Making of the English Working Class*.[4] Previous scholars, however, have afforded Wright little attention, depicting her as an accessory of, and incidental to, the story of prominent radical Richard Carlile. Her story has been relegated to little more than a footnote in radical history and her experience both as a radical prisoner and of the wider radical culture remains untold. Edward Royle's approach to Wright's story in his document collection, *Radical Politics 1790–1900*, is a case in point. Royle includes an article written by B. B. Jones from the *Reasoner* of 1859, originally penned by Jones 'because no one has given any account' of the individuals who 'assisted Mr Carlile in his arduous task against despotism'.[5] Although it contained one of the most detailed accounts of Wright's experience in the radical movement, Royle reproduced it more than a century later as a record of Richard Carlile's experience; Wright's name was included but the remainder of the detail of her experience was edited out.[6]

Subsequent scholarship from Iain McCalman on radical women has gone some way to redressing this neglect.[7] McCalman argued that the women in Carlile's circle had been either neglected or misunderstood by historians, even those who were beginning to uncover the women 'hidden from history'. Opposed to the 'supplementary' role ascribed to radical women, he pointed to a radical movement 'in which women played a genuinely critical part' and where the movement enjoyed the exceptional dedication of women such as Susannah Wright.[8]

---

4   E. P. Thompson, *The Making of the English Working Class* (London: Penguin, 1968), pp. 802–3.
5   B. B. Jones, 'The Peoples' First Struggle for Free Speech and Writing', *The Reasoner*, 5 June 1859, pp. 178–9.
6   Edward Royle, *Radical Politics 1790–1900—Religion and unbelief* (London: Longman, 1971), pp. 104–5. Apart from Thompson and Royle, historians including James Epstein and Joel Wiener also mention Wright in the story of Richard Carlile but overlook her independent contribution to the radical movement. See James Epstein, *Radical Expression: Political language, ritual and symbol in England, 1790–1850* (Oxford: Oxford University Press, 1994), pp. 109, 132–3; Joel Wiener, *Radicalism and Freethought in Nineteenth-Century Britain: The life of Richard Carlile* (Westport, Conn.: Greenwood Press, 1983), pp. 89–90, 95.
7   Iain McCalman, 'Females, Feminism and Free Love in an Early Nineteenth Century Radical Movement', *Labour History*, no. 38 (1980), pp. 1–25.
8   Ibid., pp. 6–13. Historians who have followed McCalman's lead in documenting radical women have neglected to fully explore Wright's contribution to early nineteenth-century radicalism. See, for example, the brief mention of Wright in the most thorough account of women in the radical movement, Anna Clark, *Struggle for the Breeches: Gender and the making of the British working class* (Berkeley: University of California Press, 1995), p. 186. See also Ruth Frow and Edmund Frow, *Political Women, 1800–1850* (London: Pluto Press, 1989), pp. 35, 41, 48–149. A recent paper on the women in the Carlile circle again offers only a short mention

This chapter aims to give full justice to the story of Susannah Wright, to not only extricate her from Richard Carlile's shadow, but to restore her to her rightful place in the historical record. Her experience shows how a woman negotiated various spaces of political activity and forged a radical identity, and how her involvement provided a platform for other women to express their radicalism. Her experience cannot simply be read as a subsidiary to that of the radical male narrative; a woman prepared to forsake her young family for repeated prison terms for the radical cause deserves recognition as a viable political actor in her own right. Her prison experience allows us to examine the extent to which gender impacted on the radical relationship with both the 'unreformed' and the 'reformed' prison space. Moreover, her story places radical women in the evolving scholarship of the alternative or radical public sphere; Wright's experience broadens our understanding of how courts, bookshops and prisons were active sites of radical political activity. Finally, Susannah Wright's story highlights the complex and often contradictory nature of contemporary attitudes to gender. As a freethinker and a woman, how did her experience fit with newly emerging notions of femininity, which were often imbued with deeply religious undertones?

* * *

A native of Nottingham, and a lace worker, Susannah Wright was an active participant in radical politics well before she was first arrested for blasphemy in 1821. She attributed the formation of her political principles to the 'distinguished spirit' of local reformers in Nottingham and, in the years before her arrest, she, and her husband, William Wright, published many politically charged caricatures (in his name).[9] Wright's early participation in radicalism occurred in a key, though less visible, radical space: the private world of the radical family.[10] The account from B. B. Jones in the *Reasoner* details the participation of the Wrights in the regular Sunday gatherings of radicals at the home of Jones and his wife. These evenings, Jones recalled, were spent feasting on the latest in radical and heterodox literature with their 'Atheistical friends'—an ideological challenge to Christianity on its most sacred of days.[11]

---

of Wright, although it provides a valuable account of Jane Carlile's story. See Angela Keane, 'Richard Carlile's Working Women: Selling books, politics, sex and *The Republican*', *Literature & History*, vol. 15, no. 2 (2006), pp. 20–34.

9 *Republican*, 23 August 1822. There was a strong tradition of political organisation among women in Nottingham. As Nicholas Rogers notes, in 1811, women employed in Nottingham's lace trade organised themselves into a combination to raise wages. See Nicholas Rogers, *Crowds, Culture, and Politics in Georgian Britain* (Oxford: Clarendon Press, 1998), p. 234.

10 On the concept of the radical family, see Dorothy Thompson, 'Women and Nineteenth Century Radical Politics: A lost dimension', in Juliet Mitchell and Ann Oakley (eds), *The Rights and Wrongs of Women* (Harmondsworth: Penguin, 1976), pp. 118–20. See also Brian Harrison, 'A Genealogy of Reform in Modern Britain', in Christine Bolt and Seymour Drescher (eds), *Anti-Slavery, Religion and Reform: Essays in memory of Roger Anstey* (Folkestone: Dawson, 1980), pp. 119–48.

11 *The Reasoner*, 5 June 1859.

Such gatherings were reminiscent of the dinner parties held by the 'radical intelligentsia' of the late eighteenth century, which provided a safer forum for expressing one's heterodoxy during repressive years.[12] As we will see in coming chapters, when many of the public outlets for radical assembly acted to preclude women's involvement—the clandestine or masculine milieu of the tavern and the coffee house, for example—and when exposing one's political views to the public gaze could be perilous, the private space of the family home provided a safe arena in which women could express their radicalism.

It was one such gathering that led to Susannah becoming one of Carlile's key recruits in the radical cause. As members of the London radical community, both Jones and Wright were well acquainted with the radical bookshop of Jane and Richard Carlile.[13] Following the arrest and imprisonment of the Carliles, management of the shop passed to Richard's sister, Mary-Ann, though she too was soon arrested for her work in the shop. The 'not guilty' verdict from her first trial provided an immense boost for a besieged radical movement, although the triumph, and her freedom, was short-lived.[14] After being successfully prosecuted for a second time, she joined the Carlile family cell in Dorchester gaol, which already housed Richard, his heavily pregnant wife, Jane, and the couple's young son.

Despite the obvious perils, Susannah was among the first to answer Carlile's call for volunteers to keep the shop open. She vowed to 'attend to the business at all risk'.[15] The Society for the Suppression of Vice, a group established in 1802 to counter all manner of 'vice' in the metropolis and the leading instigators of prosecutions against the Carlile set, moved swiftly to ensure Wright gained little traction in her new role.[16] An agent for the Vice Society gained much needed evidence when he purchased from Wright a tract penned by Richard Carlile from his prison cell. She was soon charged with blasphemy and in December 1821 faced court for the first of three appearances. Released on bail after her first hearing, her trial was delayed until July 1822 by which time she had given birth to another child. These months provided a vital period of preparation, for, as Carlile noted in the *Republican*, Wright was 'determined to defend herself, and read her own defence, and will not allow [Judge] Best to silence her'.[17]

---

12   For an account of such dinner parties, see James Epstein, *In Practice: Studies in the language and culture of popular politics in modern Britain* (Stanford: Stanford University Press, 2003), p. 91.
13   In 1822, Carlile observed that Wright was one of the few volunteer shop workers who was known personally to him prior to his imprisonment. See *Republican*, 5 April 1822.
14   Wiener, *Radicalism and Freethought in Nineteenth-Century Britain*, pp. 84–90.
15   *The Reasoner*, 5 June 1859.
16   For an account of the early activities of the Vice Society, see Michael Roberts, 'The Society for the Suppression of Vice and its Early Critics, 1802–1812', *The Historical Journal*, vol. 26, issue 1 (1983), pp. 159–76.
17   *Republican*, 15 March 1822.

On 8 July, Susannah was escorted to the court of the King's Bench by her children, B. B. Jones and his wife and a tight-knit band of unnamed female radical supporters. Jones recalled that Wright defended herself against the charge of bringing the 'Christian religion into disbelief and contempt among the people' with 'an ease peculiar to herself'. He assisted her in the dock, keeping her place in her notes when she was frequently interrupted by the judge disapproving of her line of defence or during the commotion in the public galleries caused by heckling from several youths.[18] Jones recalled that the plan from the outset was to get as much of the defence read as possible, which entailed reading the offending tracts so as to 'prove' their innocence.[19] This was a pattern by now familiar at political trials, where the accused radicals utilised the courtroom as a radical space through which to convey their message to a wider public audience.[20]

Wright was so absorbed in the trial that Jones had to remind her to request a break to attend to her baby. She emerged from the court to the cheers of the crowd who had gathered outside and retired for refreshments to nearby Castle Coffee House accompanied by a group of 20 close supporters. Returning to the court, Wright concluded almost four hours of defence by advising the jury to 'be firm and do your duty', concluding that she both 'scorn[ed] mercy and demand[ed] justice'.[21] Despite such bravado, her supporters were determined to avoid her being taken into custody pending sentencing and ushered her swiftly out of the court before the guilty verdict was announced minutes later.

Four months later, Wright returned to court for sentencing. On this occasion, the notoriety of a woman arrested for blasphemy and the defiance she exhibited at her first trial attracted more of the public gaze in both crowd numbers and interest from the press. Wright continued to challenge the validity of her guilty verdict and, under the pretext of addressing the court in 'plea of mitigation of punishment', she instead argued that her conviction was invalid, as Christianity had no place in the law. Clearly agitated by the content of her statement, the

---

18 Criminal trials attracted audiences from all walks of life and spectators could prove difficult for magistrates to control. For an account of the courtroom crowds, see Peter King, *Crime, Justice, and Discretion in England 1740–1820* (Oxford: Oxford University Press, 2000), pp. 253–7.
19 *The Reasoner*, 5 June 1859.
20 For other accounts of radicals using trials and courtrooms as extensions of the public sphere, see James Epstein, '"Our Real Constitution": Trial defence and radical memory in the age of revolution', in James Vernon (ed.), *Re-Reading the Constitution: New narratives in the political history of England's long nineteenth century* (Cambridge: Cambridge University Press, 1996), pp. 22–51; Kevin Gilmartin, *Print Politics: The press and radical opposition in early nineteenth-century England* (New York: Cambridge University Press, 1996), pp. 115–57; Uwe Böker, 'Institutionalised Rules of Discourse and the Courtroom as a Site of the Public Sphere', in Uwe Böker and Julie A. Hibbard (eds), *Sites of Discourse—Public and private spheres—legal culture* (Amsterdam, NY: Rodopi, 2002), pp. 35–66; Olivia Smith, *The Politics of Language, 1791–1819* (Oxford: Clarendon, 1984), pp. 176–201.
21 See *The Times*, 9 July 1822; *John Bull*, 15 July 1822. A report that the 'avenues of the Court of the King's Bench were much crowded' on account of Susannah's trial appeared in *Bell's Life in London*, 14 July 1822.

Chief Justice issued repeated warnings that he would not suffer such profanity against the law or the church in his court. This only spurred Susannah to greater defiance, retorting: 'You, Sir, are paid to hear me.'[22] To the great amusement of the crowded courtroom, she continued to ignore his interruptions. Exasperated by her recalcitrance, the judge sentenced Wright (and by default her infant) to be confined for 10 weeks in the loathed Newgate prison to deliberate on her plea.

Early nineteenth-century courtrooms were undoubtedly gendered spaces; only the public galleries were open to women and the business of the court was performed and controlled by men.[23] It was therefore no accident that it was Jones who assisted Wright with her notes, rather than one of her numerous female attendants. James Epstein has argued, in relation to the courtrooms of the 1790s, 'all those who spoke were men'.[24] Wright's experience suggests that by the early 1820s this was no longer the case. Her trial reveals ways that women could circumvent and contest the unequal power relations implicit in the early nineteenth-century legal process.[25]

Although women were undoubtedly absent as officers of the courts, they were not absent from the courtroom. During political trials, courtrooms provided a legitimate public arena for women to participate in radical culture. By all accounts, Wright was surrounded by women in her trials—from her close circle of female friends to the unknown supporters in the public galleries, some of whom travelled long distances to attend the trial. This support was also not unique to Wright's trial; she reported herself attending Jane Carlile's trial every day for a week to 'watch the conduct of her inhumane Judges'.[26] Most importantly, she was not silent—nor did she allow herself to be silenced. Her defence in the July trial lasted almost four hours and in her November trial she countered the judge's interruptions by claiming that 'nothing but absolute force shall prevent me reading'.[27]

---

22 *The Times*, 22 November 1822.
23 Epstein, *In Practice*, p. 111.
24 Ibid.
25 There are other examples where women defended themselves in the courts in this period. See the case of Mary Ann Tocker, who successfully defended herself in a libel case by invoking constitutionalist language and the principles of English liberty. On Tocker, see Frow and Frow, *Political Women*, pp. 2–14; Jonathon Fulcher, 'Gender, Politics and Class in the Early Nineteenth-Century English Reform Movement', *Historical Research*, vol. LXVII (1994), pp. 57–74; Malcolm Thomis and Jennifer Grimmett, *Women in Protest 1800–1850* (London: Croom Helm, 1982), p. 90. On women's participation in the courtroom, see also Margaret Anne Doody, 'Voices of Record: Women as witnesses and defendants in the Old Bailey Sessions Papers', in Susan S. Heinzelman and Zipporah B. Wiseman (eds), *Representing Women: Law, literature, and feminism* (Durham, NC: Duke University Press, 1994), pp. 287–308.
26 *Republican*, 23 August 1822.
27 *The Times*, 15 November 1822.

Wright's preparation for her own trial was doubtless assisted by her experience of the machinations of the courtroom prior to her own trial. Aside from her attendance at Jane Carlile's trial, it is clear from the historical record that she attended at least one other trial of an indicted shopman. In February 1822, she was called as a witness in the trial of William Holmes.[28] Explaining that she was the 'housekeeper at Mr Carlile's' the night Holmes was arrested, she characteristically proved a difficult witness. When questioned whether she herself had the 'misfortune to be indicted' for selling pamphlets from the bookshop, she replied 'if you call it misfortune, Sir, I have', adding that she would 'rather enjoy my own opinion, of course, and be indicted for it'.[29] She infuriated the legal counsel by refusing to give Holmes's name, referring to him only as the 'man unknown', and frustrated the counsel by refusing to be drawn into details about the evening when Holmes was arrested. In a further act of defiance—and evidence of her aptitude for the combat of the courtroom—she refused to be drawn on the question of her belief in the holy 'Scriptures'. 'I shall not answer that', she tersely replied, 'When I am brought to trial, perhaps I may give my opinion'. Such prior experience in the courtroom goes some way to explaining why most accounts speak of the ease and comfort with which she negotiated the courtroom during her own trial and her confidence in defending herself from the outset.

The court appearances of Carlile's imprisoned shopmen and women have tended to be downplayed in radical historiography with the suggestion that Richard was responsible for writing their defences. Carlile did mention working on Susannah's defence in private correspondence with another imprisoned shopman, yet much of it accords with the style and language of her correspondence to the *Republican*. The prison correspondence that flowed freely within the network of imprisoned bookshop volunteers reveals that radical defences at this time were a collective effort—learning from and building on each subsequent iteration, honing ways to circumvent the legal arguments against them and to utilise the arena to publicise the radical agenda.[30]

The question of authorship is further redundant when Wright's performance of the defence is taken into account. One female supporter who travelled from Manchester for the trial recorded her awe at Wright's performance: 'never will the impression be effaced from my memory; the firmness she evinced and her resolution not to be silenced.'[31] This was not the case of an uneducated or docile

---

28   *Old Bailey Proceedings*Online, <www.oldbailey.org>, February 1822, trial of William Holmes (t18220220-204), hereafter cited as *OBP*. See also *Examiner*, 10 March 1822.
29   *OBP*, February 1822, William Holmes (t18220220-204).
30   See, for example, the correspondence between Humphrey Boyle and Richard Carlile and the development of Boyle's defence. Richard Carlile to Humphrey Boyle, 27 May 1822, WYL623/5, West Yorkshire Archive Service, Leeds.
31   *Republican*, 20 September 1822.

woman regurgitating the words of an astute leader; she performed her defence in an exemplary manner—unsettling the prosecution with her legal tactic and understanding, challenging the jury on their own understanding of the Christian faith and frustrating the judges with the force and persistence of her defence and her refusal to yield. Surprisingly, not even the most conservative of newspapers took the opportunity to question the right or the propriety of a woman to conduct her own defence.[32] Given her notoriety, the absence of any criticism suggests that it is time to look again at the British courtroom not only as a platform for political radicalism but also as a contested site of power and gender relations.

Wright's performance on the courtroom stage, as well as the harshness of her treatment, helped establish her identity as a popular radical heroine. Details of her trials circulated around the country through newspaper reports.[33] Veteran ultra-radical and poet Allen Davenport was clearly enamoured with her efforts in the poem he dedicated to her, *The Captive*:[34]

> Ah! Great was my surprise rely on't,
> When I beheld thy slender form;
> 'Is this,' me thought, 'the mighty giant,
> That battl'd in the *legal* storm!
> And was it she that brav'd the fury,
> Of the ruthless bench and bar,
> And scorn'd the verdict of a jury,
> *Empanell'd* for religious war!'[35]

Despite Wright's popular radical appeal, the nature of her crime and its moral implications polarised press opinion in the metropolis. Both the *Morning Chronicle* and *The Times* remarked that she and her attendants were 'very respectably dressed'.[36] In the courtroom, Wright described herself as a respectable woman in the 'genteel' occupation of lace worker—a stinging taunt to the aristocracy who were mocked by radicals as the 'useless' classes. Describing a working woman charged with blasphemy as 'respectable' infuriated the conservative *New Times*, which countered with a savage invective against Susannah Wright,

---

32 During Jane Carlile's trial, one provincial newspaper accused her of taking her 'child in arms' to court 'to excite, we presume, the tender sympathies of the jury'. *Trewman's Exeter Flying Post or Plymouth and Cornish Advertiser*, 25 January 1821.
33 See, for example, *Trewman's Exeter Flying Post or Plymouth and Cornish Advertiser*, 21 November 1822; and for her later trial, *Jackson's Oxford Journal*, 8 February 1823; *Hampshire Telegraph and Sussex Chronicle*, 10 February 1823; *Plymouth and Cornish Advertiser*, 13 February 1823.
34 On Allen Davenport, see Allen Davenport, *The Life and Literary Pursuits of Allen Davenport...Written by himself*, Malcolm Chase (ed.) (Hants, UK: Scolar Press, 1994); Iowerth Prothero, 'Davenport, Allen', in Joseph Baylen and Norbert Gossman (eds), *Biographical Dictionary of Modern British Radicals* [hereafter BDMBR] (Sussex: Harvester Press, 1979), vol. 1, pp. 111–13.
35 Printed in *Republican*, 9 January 1824.
36 *The Times*, 15 November 1822; see also *Morning Chronicle*, 15 November 1822.

aligning her with the most maligned and liminal of the female population: the prostitute. Wright, the columnist sneered, was a 'wretched and shameless woman', an 'abandoned creature' who had 'shunned all the distinctive shame and fear and decency of her sex'.[37] John Stoddart's *New Times* saw itself as the voice of a deeply religious conservatism in which blasphemy was akin to prostitution in terms of the moral outrage and danger it posed, particularly from the mouth of a woman: 'Blasphemy from any lips is shocking, but from those of a female it is beyond expression horrible.' Stoddart was not alone in his views; in the House of Commons, William Wilberforce castigated Mary-Ann Carlile as 'fallen and wretched…without one ray of hope to cheer amidst the dark and desolate prospect of eternity'.[38]

Although the courtroom provided women with a legitimate public arena in which to participate as audience members, the trial of Susannah Wright demonstrated that such attendance could also prove perilous. Not satisfied with castigating Wright, Stoddart (or 'Dr Slop' as radicals had dubbed him) broadened his attack to include her female supporters.[39] Women choosing openly to support Wright were left in no doubt that they would be tarnished as the lowest form of 'public woman'.[40] Noting the 'several females' in attendance with Wright at her trial, the *New Times* editor ranted:

> [T]his is the first time…that a *body of women* has defied all shame, and trampled upon all decency, in so profligate and daring a manner—in a manner at which the lowest prostitutes would shudder…It is manifest that these female brutes came prepared, not only to applaud what the She-Champion of Impiety had already done; but to hear her load with fresh insults the law of her country and the law of her GOD.[41]

Stoddart had prior form with such voracious attacks against female reformers. When the Blackburn Female Reform Society gained national prominence in 1819 with their involvement at one of the great reform meetings in Blackburn, the *New Times* compared the women with the murderous 'Poissardes of Paris, those furies in the shape of women' and likened Mrs Alice Kitchen, who addressed

---

37 *New Times*, 16 November 1822. The quotes that follow originate from the same edition. See also Thompson, *The Making of the English Working Class*, p. 803.
38 Wilberforce here is commenting on a petition from Mary-Ann Carlile appealing for her release and presented to the House of Commons by Joseph Hume. See reports in *New Times*, 27 March 1823.
39 Such scathing attacks on female reformers helped fuel the loathing of radical publisher and satirist William Hone towards Stoddart. Hone, in collaboration with George Cruikshank, dedicated his immensely successful satire, *The Political House that Jack Built*, to Stoddart. Hone dubbed him 'Dr Slop' and the *New Times* the 'Slop Pail'. In 1820, the pair produced another satire, *A Slap at Slop*, which ran to four editions. See Edgell Rickword, *Radical Squibs and Loyal Ripostes: Satirical pamphlets of the Regency period, 1819–1821* (Bath: Adams and Dart, 1971), pp. 9–10, 37. For more on Hone, see Chapter 4 of this study.
40 Clark, *Struggle for the Breeches*, pp. 140–57. Clark argues that where 'public man' represented a notion of citizenship and civility, 'public women' was a term employed to describe prostitutes, p. 51.
41 *New Times*, 16 November 1822.

the meeting, to a 'hardened and shameless Prostitute'.⁴² The vehemence of the *New Times* attack was a stark warning for women who were beginning to find a place in public politics: participation put reputation and moral standing at grave risk.⁴³ Significantly, Wright's supporters—inside and outside the court—included many men, but they received no mention in the *New Times* report. The commentary conflated the moral heresy of radicalism firmly with its women.

Just as the conservative press linked Wright firmly with the maligned figure of the prostitute, so too did the authorities when they criminalised her heterodoxy and confined her and her baby to Newgate prison with the most marginal of the prison population: the female felons.⁴⁴ Wright embarked on her prison term at a time when Newgate women had been thrust into the public eye by the highly celebrated work of Quaker prison reformer Elizabeth Fry.⁴⁵ Appalled by her first visit to Newgate in 1813, Fry commenced a sustained public campaign to reform prison conditions for women—a program that had the dual purpose of improving the living conditions within the prison and effecting the reformation of those previously deemed beyond redemption, the women prisoners themselves.

The work of the Quaker Ladies focused public attention on the female prison population, who had been demonised as the most wretched and unruly of the entire prison population. In 1812, James Neild's visit to the prison uncovered the desperate overcrowding of the female wards. The eight wards of the female section contained 90 prisoners, allowing 'a space of 20 inches for each', where they slept on bare floorboards without 'any bedding whatsoever'.⁴⁶ While the perceived deviance, depravity and danger led criminals to be classified as non-subjects, forfeiting their rights and privileges, female criminality contained an

---

42   See Epstein, *Radical Expression*, pp. 88–9. Even more mainstream newspapers, such as *The Times*, considered women who participated in the society as 'of the most abandoned of their sex'. See *The Times*, 13 July 1819.
43   Eileen Yeo documents the 'dangerous territory' that faced women entering the political public sphere in the nineteenth century. See her introduction in Eileen Yeo (ed.), *Radical Femininity: Women's self-representation in the public sphere* (Manchester: Manchester University Press, 1998), pp. 1–24. See also Clark, *Struggle for the Breeches*, pp. 35–7, 51–3.
44   In the debates of the Seditious Meetings Bill 1819, Lord Castlereagh considered the involvement of women in political protest as the antithesis of femininity, pointing to the involvement of French prostitutes in the 'bloody orgies' of the Revolution, and appealing to his countrywomen to retain their 'innate sense of modesty' and refrain from political activism. *Parliamentary Debates*, vol. 41 (23 November 1819 – 28 February 1820), p. 391, quoted in Rogers, *Crowds, Culture and Politics in Georgian Britain*, p. 238n.
45   Most contemporary and historical accounts of Newgate prison recall the work of Elizabeth Fry and the Quaker Ladies. See, for example, Arthur Griffiths, *The Chronicles of Newgate* (London: Chapman and Hall, 1884), vol. 1, pp. 143–211; Hepworth Dixon, *The London Prisons: With an account of the more distinguished persons who have been confined in them* (1850; reprinted, New York: Garland Publishing, 1995), p. 222. For the most detailed secondary accounts, see June Rose, *Elizabeth Fry, A Biography* (Philadelphia: Quaker Books, 1994); Anthony Babington, *The English Bastille: A history of Newgate gaol and prison conditions in Britain 1188–1902* (London: Macdonald, 1971), pp. 148–60; Lucia Zedner, *Women, Crime and Custody in Victorian England* (Oxford: Clarendon Press, 1991), pp. 116–22.
46   James Neild, *State of the Prisons in England, Scotland and Wales…Together with some useful documents, observations, and remarks, adapted to explain the conditions of prisoners in general* (London, 1812), p. 416.

extra layer of 'otherness'. Lucia Zedner, who has to date produced the most comprehensive survey of women and crime in Victorian England, suggests that since women were generally considered more pure and moral by nature than men, the women who fell from this elevated pedestal through criminality were considered the very 'negation of femininity', and, as such, could be dehumanised and demonised as 'monsters'.[47]

Further, Zedner argues that because of the inherently unfeminine nature of crime, there was a reluctance to accept that women were capable of its barbarities.[48] Some evidence of this attitude can be seen in the case of Susannah Wright and Jane Carlile. Much was made of Wright's countenance because it seemed so incongruous that a woman with respectable appearance, even from a humble occupation, was capable of crime, particularly one as abhorrent as blasphemy. In both women's cases, the judges voiced their reluctance to have to pass sentence on the defendants and were 'most anxious' to hear any mitigating circumstances that could alleviate harsh sentences. It was reported that, before passing sentence on Jane Carlile,

> His lordship admitted the painful nature of the duty which was cast upon the Court and upon the jury...he could not but be astonished at seeing a woman stand forward as the opponent of that system from which everything valuable to woman was derived.[49]

The magistrates were unprepared for the fierce resolve of these radical women who would 'submit with pleasure and with joy to any pains and penalties' in defending their principles.[50]

In Wright's case, the judge provided her time to reflect on her plea with 10 weeks in the 'mansion of misery', Newgate gaol. If Susannah's judge felt any angst at sentencing her to the most feared and detested of London's prisons as punishment, it was apparently short-lived. Her treatment as a felon upon arrival in Newgate, claimed the prison's Governor, accorded with the wishes of the judges. Once again, however, Wright refused to be silenced. She demanded

---

47   Zedner, *Women, Crime and Custody in Victorian England*, pp. 11–12. On female criminality, see also Lucia Zedner, 'Wayward Sisters: The prison for women', in Norval Morris and David J. Rothman (eds), *The Oxford History of the Prison: The practice of punishment in Western society* (New York: Oxford University Press, 1995), pp. 295–324; Deidre Palk, *Gender, Crime, and Judicial Discretion, 1780–1830* (Woodbridge: Boydell Press, 2006); King, *Crime Justice and Discretion in England 1740–1820*, pp. 196–207. For accounts of similar attitudes towards female criminality beyond Britain, see L. Mara Dodge, '"One Female Prisoner is of More Trouble than Twenty Males": Women convicts in Illinois prisons, 1835–1896', *Journal of Social History*, vol. 32, no. 4 (1999), pp. 907–30; Ann-Louise Shapiro, *Breaking the Codes: Female criminality in fin-de-siecle Paris* (Stanford: Stanford University Press, 1996).
48   As Garthine Walker has shown, this attitude was evident in the early modern period in England, when women were often treated more leniently than men. See Garthine Walker, *Crime, Gender and Social Order in Early Modern England* (Cambridge: Cambridge University Press, 2003).
49   *The Times*, 24 October 1821.
50   *Report of the Trial of Mrs Susannah Wright* (London, 1822), p. 10.

that she be moved to the prison infirmary where she was aware that 'good beds' existed. Despite advising a bed was 'against the rules', the Governor did defer to the visiting Sheriff with whom Wright successfully negotiated an upgrade to more agreeable lodgings.

The concession of more comfortable accommodation was predicated, once again, upon a fear of contagion within the prison. When Wright vowed to the Sheriff that she would desist from 'unfold[ing] the object of religion to the prisoners', she gained a sense of her bargaining power within this otherwise powerless space: 'I cannot describe the difference this expression made on their countenances', she wrote.[51] Prison officials long feared the spread of radical views of political prisoners within prisons, and as we saw in earlier chapters, radical men were generally housed separately from other prisoners to ensure that their views were contained within their prison cells. Even though prison authorities considered female criminals already morally destitute, the strength of Wright's character perhaps convinced them that even such wayward women were in need of protection from the 'She-Champion of Impiety'.

That Wright succeeded in securing this concession is particularly significant given that the structure of Newgate itself worked against her. As we have seen, the prison's floorplan allowed for some male prisoners, with the necessary financial means, to be housed in the less crowded 'Masters Side', which had rooms specifically designated for state prisoners. There were no such rooms allocated in the recently segregated female section of the prison.[52] In the case of Jane and Mary-Ann Carlile, the problem had been resolved by housing them in Richard's apartment, but Susannah Wright was on her own in her battle to be afforded a different status to that of the female felons.[53] Wright's negotiation of her accommodation in Newgate forced a change to the rules to place her on a similar footing to her radical male counterparts. We should not underestimate the significance of a working-class woman's struggle to circumvent the rules normally applied even to wealthier women, to defy the stigma of the female criminal and to forge a radical identity. Wright's challenge to both the spatial and the regulatory boundaries of the prison saw her achieve recognition within the prison that often eluded other radical women; prison officials saw Wright first and foremost as a radical; her gender became of secondary significance.

It is difficult to gauge whether the turnkey's suggestion on that occasion—that 'well-off' women were forced to sleep on the floor—was the result of a

---

51 Susannah Wright to Jane Carlile, reproduced in *Republican*, 13 December 1822.
52 Until the work of prison reformers such as John Howard and Elizabeth Fry, male and female felons mixed freely in Newgate although their sleeping quarters were designated separately on Newgate's architectural plans.
53 According to Richard Carlile, Jane had a 'long fight' with the Dorchester prison authorities to secure these accommodation arrangements for herself and her fifteen-month-old child. See *Republican*, 10 October 1823.

misogynistic approach to female criminals or whether the sustained work of prison reformers to realise an egalitarian approach to all prisoners could have filtered down even to unreformed Newgate. Then again, it might simply have been a result of severe overcrowding, for pecuniary enticements still operated in the prison, despite the efforts of prison reformers who agitated against the practice of prison staff extracting fees from prisoners. Indeed, for Wright and the baby, the ability to pay for food and other privileges was not only a means to separate herself from the common criminals, but it also meant the difference between surviving and perishing in the fetid environment. B. B. Jones recalled in 1859 that he developed a way of ensuring that Susannah received a hot meal each week. Officially, only cooked food was allowed into the prison, but by searing the outside of a joint of meat, Wright could 'cut the outside off and [have] it roasted over again', which he noted 'a shilling or two would always accomplish'.[54]

Wright issued further challenges to the prison regime and to her status as a female felon by insisting on special visiting rights rather than those more restrictive rules enforced with the female felons. She also vehemently refused the religious instruction and redemption efforts of the Quaker Ladies. These she dismissed as mere entertainment: 'I know you would help me to laugh at them if you were here', she wrote to Jane Carlile.[55] It is not surprising that she reported the Ladies were 'afraid to have anything to say' to her; Wright's most biting insult was to label an opponent 'Christian'.

* * *

Despite the concession granted to Susannah with her accommodation, it is clear that the mire of Newgate and the daily ritual of standing in an open-air yard 'with snow burying her shoes and icy water running into the clogs' left her health severely compromised.[56] She was too ill on the date originally scheduled for her return to court to reappear in front of her judge.[57] When she appeared a week later on 6 February 1823, the *Morning Chronicle* reported that she was 'genteelly dressed' but exhibited 'infirm health'.[58] Wright nevertheless showed remarkable resolve, for she was determined to 'see the old women of the bench go into hysterics' by continuing to challenge the very basis of Christianity and its place in the law. She took her battle directly to them, sending copies of her statement to their private residences. The appearance was a short one;

---

54 *The Reasoner*, 5 June 1859.
55 *Republican*, 13 December 1822.
56 *Republican*, 7 February 1823, 16 July 1824.
57 *Morning Chronicle*, 1 February 1823. This was confirmed in private correspondence of the Carlile shopmen. See William Tunbridge to Humphrey Boyle, February 1823, WYL623/4, West Yorkshire Archive Service, Leeds, in which Tunbridge reports that Susannah was too ill to attend court.
58 *Morning Chronicle*, 7 February 1823; *Examiner*, 9 February 1832.

once it was clear to the judges that she would not yield by pleading mitigating circumstances, they immediately pronounced sentence. She was ordered to be held in Coldbath Fields prison for a further 18 months with heavy penalties: a fine of £100 and £200 in sureties for good behaviour—an impossible sum for Susannah and William. Despite her ill health, she retorted: 'then your Lordship must have the kindness to give me a cheque for the £100, and provide me with provisions during my imprisonment.'[59] She then managed to leave the court with a 'laugh of triumph' and a 'contemptuous smile on her countenance'.[60] Perhaps there was some small measure of satisfaction that, once again, her gender failed to come into play; her sentence rivalled that of the harshest afforded to male radicals in the period.

Wright's committal to Coldbath Fields presented a new challenge to resist the identity of the female felon. Unlike Newgate's ancient presence in the landscape of inner London, Coldbath Fields was sited further away from the centre of London in nearby Clerkenwell. Distance meant supporters such as the Joneses, who had previously visited three or four times a week, now could visit only on the weekend. From her letters published in the *Republican*, it is clear that Wright regarded the relative geographic isolation from family and friends as a small price to pay; in Coldbath Fields she was quickly afforded higher standing than the female felons. Just as other male radical prisoners reported, and in contrast with other prisoners, she was permitted to receive her female friends within her ward in a 'manner quite satisfactory'. She reported that she was housed in 'the best part' of the prison. Even so, this caused problems when she had to share her ward with those committed for short periods; the 'vagrants and other disorderly persons…unhappy beings, wretchedly filthy and diseased…disease which is attendant upon a want of cleanliness and bad living, or a connection with persons in that state'. Despite all her care, she despaired that she could not keep herself and her infant free from 'that disease'.[61] Carlile reported in the *Republican* that compared with her experience in Newgate, here Wright was 'treated with kindness approaching to paternal attention' by the magistrates and by Mr Vickery, the Keeper, his family and the newly appointed matron, Mrs Adkins.[62] Other than the issues of hygiene and space, and the continuing health problems from her stay in Newgate, Wright could defiantly claim from Coldbath Fields that 'prison has no terrors for me'.[63]

Her ability to cross the gender-divided walls of the prison to meet with male radicals imprisoned in Coldbath Fields also attests to her success in forging a

---

59   *Plymouth and Cornish Advertiser*, 13 February 1823.
60   *The Times*, 7 February 1823; *Morning Chronicle*, 7 February 1823.
61   *Republican*, 11 April 1823.
62   *Republican*, 16 July 1823.
63   *Republican*, 11 April 1823.

radical identity.⁶⁴ Despairing that 'prejudice and ignorance were so fast rooted in the minds of the people', she was reassured by a fellow radical prisoner, James Watson, that *'perseverance on our part will work wonders'*.⁶⁵ Her contact with Watson was reminiscent of the radical collectives forged decades earlier in both Newgate and Coldbath Fields, where, as we have seen, many radical men had continued their publishing endeavours and transformed their prisons into virtual colleges that offered unprecedented opportunities for self-improvement.⁶⁶

Though there is no record of Wright utilising the educative possibilities of prison, the improved conditions at Coldbath Fields did not mean she acquiesced quietly in her confinement. She continued to rage against the conduct of the magistrates, 'mostly religious men', whose 'order is the law, until another comes and contradicts it by some new whim'.⁶⁷ Like her radical male counterparts, Wright defied her containment in the private prison space by maintaining a presence in the public eye through letters to radical journals. She also continued trenchant public assaults against those responsible for her incarceration. In a caustic public letter to Judge Bayley, published in the *Republican*, Wright cursed the 'Christian' judge and threatened that when justice presided in the country he would 'be a criminal at her bar', if he failed to first follow the suicide of his 'late patron *Castlereagh* and inflict justice on [himself] prematurely'.⁶⁸ After almost six months in prison, her defiance continued unabated and she concluded her letter: 'Conscious in my opinion that I am right: cheerful in my dungeon's solitude; happy even in my widowhood; proud in being the Christian's victim: smiling on each pang as you inflict them, I remain, Yours, &c. Susanna [sic] Wright.'⁶⁹

Wright might have made the best of her incarceration—politically and personally—but women were particularly vulnerable to the moral scarring of prison at a time when an emerging middling class increasingly equated feminine ideals with passivity, gentleness and childrearing. Jane Carlile remained defiant when she wrote that 'neither me nor my children will ever have occasion to blush as the cause of my incarceration'.⁷⁰ Similarly, Susannah Wright gave no

---

64 Separation of male and female prisoners appears to be one of the few reform measures that was successfully introduced from the beginning in Coldbath Fields.
65 *Republican*, 18 September 1826.
66 See Iain McCalman, 'Newgate in Revolution: Radical enthusiasm and romantic counterculture', *Eighteenth Century Life*, vol. 22 (February 1998); Michael Davis, Iain McCalman and Christina Parolin (eds), *Newgate in Revolution: An anthology of radical prison literature in the age of revolution* (London: Continuum, 2005).
67 *Republican*, 11 April 1823.
68 Radicals detested Lord Castlereagh for his quashing of the Irish Uprising (1798) and his keen support of Home Secretary, Lord Sidmouth's, suspension of habeas corpus (1817) and the Six Acts (1819). The Cato Street conspirators planned to march the streets with the pair's heads on pikes. The radical community viewed his suicide in 1822 as a cause for celebration. See, for example, the letter to the *Republican*, 18 April 1823, by a 'poor surgeon' congratulating Castlereagh for knowing 'where the carotid artery lay'.
69 *Republican*, 13 June 1823.
70 *Republican*, 10 May 1822.

hint of concern as to her reputation. Interestingly, none of the accounts of Susannah accuses her of abandoning or disgracing her family, or of failing to fulfil the duties of wife and mother. Even the ultra-conservative *New Times*, so afraid of her monstrous influences on a generation of unsuspecting and unthinking mothers and their infants, passed no judgment on Wright's own role in this sense.

Nonetheless, the attempts to question the morality of Susannah, Jane and Mary-Ann through both their imprisonment and the public press attacks provoked a counter-assault from radical supporters. The pages of radical journals such as the *Republican* and *Black Dwarf* assured the women that their actions were seen as both praiseworthy and virtuous. Many men and women showed their support with financial subscriptions, addressing their offerings to 'Susannah the Chaste' or to 'the heroine in the cause of Free Discussion', with some offering 'a small token of my admiration of your virtuous conduct'.[71] Relief funds were organised all over the country and subscriptions were often accompanied by letters from group leaders such as Alfred Cox of Nottingham, who wrote to Susannah Wright: 'you may assure yourself of the sympathy of every virtuous character as well as the approving testimony of a good conscience, of which no earthly power can deprive you.'[72] Allen Davenport celebrated her moral inspiration in his poem *The Captive*:

> Hail child of truth! Hail glorious woman!
> Whom tyranny could not subdue;
> Since all the pow'rs that she could summon,
> Were baffled, and defied by you.
> What tho' the Christian bigots blame thee,
> What tho' they frown upon thee still;
> While truth is thine they cannot shame thee,
> Rail and bluster how they will.[73]

The financial contributions and letters of support confirmed the contribution of these women as equals of men. The radical martyr was becoming a familiar trope in radical literature; correspondence about Susannah, Jane and Mary-Ann showed that women could be radical martyrs as well and that their contribution to the cause was no less valued because of their gender. Susannah, Jane and Mary-Ann were toasted at radical meetings throughout Britain along with male heroes such as Thomas Paine. Similarly, when Adam Renwick, a Sheffield silversmith, sent a gift to Richard Carlile in the form of an elegantly fashioned 16-blade penknife, he allocated a blade each to Susannah, Jane and Mary-Ann Carlile, forging them into the radical movement as equals alongside the names

---

71   *Republican*, 20 December 1822, 6 February 1824.
72   *Republican*, 23 August 1822.
73   *Republican*, 9 January 1824.

of radical icons such as Mirabaud, Paine, Volney and Richard Carlile.[74] 'More than our thanks are due', he wrote, 'to your wife, sister, brave shopmen, and that heroine Mrs Wright'.[75]

Importantly, many women independently offered their support through financial subscriptions, gifts and letters of support. The prosecution and martyrdom of radical women provided an opportunity for a wider circle of women to participate through that hitherto essentially masculine medium of the printed word. While the public exposure of their support at a trial risked the moral outrage of the *New Times*, women found a more generous atmosphere in Carlile's *Republican*. The harsh treatment of these women—Susannah Wright having been wrenched from the love of her family, and Jane Carlile enduring both pregnancy and childbirth in prison—enticed female radicals out of the private world of the family and provided the platform on which women could join the radical public sphere. Letters of support came in from around the country and were reproduced in the *Republican* (along with their replies).[76] Subscription lists were printed weekly and featured women's names more prominently than at any other time during the 1820s (and dropped off noticeably after their release).[77] While some subscribers preferred to remain anonymous—'a female republican'—others listed specific donations against their own name, and that of their daughters, alongside their husband and sons. For Richard Carlile, it was glaringly obvious that Susannah, Jane and Mary-Ann had given a 'kind of zest' to the struggle for free expression. Carlile clearly saw Wright and the female support she engendered as a means to mobilise women more widely to join the cause. The transcript of her defence was dedicated to the 'Women of the Island of Great Britain' for 'their example, consideration [and] approbation'.[78]

In early July 1824, Susannah received the news she was no longer a prisoner; she was released one month early from her 18-month sentence and with her fine waived. Despite flaunting her apparent comfort with prison life, Wright left prison in a 'dreadful state with the loss of sight in one eye' and a spate of 'nervous disorders'.[79] After visiting her radical colleagues in Newgate in October 1824, she disappeared from the radical scene during the winter of 1824–25, and Carlile feared that she had succumbed to the raft of 'disorders' with which she left prison.[80] By the end of 1825, however, Wright had sufficiently recovered in strength to battle with yet another prison keeper when she was refused entry to

---

74   *Republican*, 23 October 1823.
75   *Republican*, 23 August 1822.
76   See, for example, the letter to Jane Carlile from the 'female republicans of Manchester' (who also noted their support for 'our brave Mrs Wright'), *Republican*, 14 March 1823.
77   McCalman, 'Females, Feminism and Free Love in an Early Nineteenth Century Radical Movement', pp. 7–8n.
78   *Report of the Trial of Mrs Susannah Wright*.
79   *Republican*, 24 September 1825.
80   Ibid.

Dorchester gaol to visit Richard Carlile. Admonished for arriving at the prison without a letter requesting a visit, she was then denied the use of pen and paper to comply with the Keeper's edict. Like so many before, he underestimated her indomitable spirit. Wright made the arduous trip back to the village to compose the letter and eventually gained entry to see Carlile. At that time, he enthused, she 'so delighted me with the detail of the particulars of her share of the campaign since 1821' that for 10 days the radical luminary 'neglected everything to listen to her'.[81]

Ironically, William Wright must continue to be accorded the fate in the historical record that normally falls to the female spouse in a radical family.[82] William and the children were ignored in the public accounts and in private correspondence as much as many radical wives and children were. We know little of his involvement in the radical movement, or of his relationship with Susannah. The fact that she was married was even ignored by all the press accounts. We do know that he had a short stint as a radical bookseller in Fleet Street, although his name disappears in publishing circles after 1821. From the accounts of both the newspapers and reflections of Susannah's closest friends, William was absent from all the court proceedings. We know the Wrights had more than the one child who endured Susannah's prison experience with her; perhaps it was William who attended to the day-to-day task of child care. And we know of William's death, 18 months after Susannah was finally released from prison. The intimate details of their relationship are lost, yet there is a sense that William supported Susannah's radical role, and that the radical community supported him, both by providing him with a home (with the Joneses) during her imprisonment and financially. The Wrights are a reminder that the concept of a radical couple is a hazardous one if it is used to imply a hierarchy of dedication or service.

***

Susannah Wright's prison experience evinced neither reform nor redemption. After William's death, she returned with her children to Nottingham to live with her mother. By August 1826, Wright caused an uproar when she established her own radical space in Nottingham by opening a bookshop trading in politically extreme and heretical publications.[83] She reported to Carlile that 'large crowds of Christians' assembled in protest each night outside the shop. Wright wrote

---

81 *Republican*, 18 November 1825.
82 For an insightful article that recovers the experience of the female spouse of a radical couple, see Eileen Janes Yeo, 'Will the Real Mary Lovett Please Stand Up?: Chartism, gender and autobiography', in Malcolm Chase and Ian Dyck (eds), *Living and Learning, Essays in Honour of J. F. C. Harrison* (Brookfield, Vt: Scolar Press, 1996), pp. 163–81. See also Catherine Hall, *White, Male and Middle Class: Explorations in feminism and history* (Cambridge: Polity Press, 1992), pp. 124–50, who explores the different experiences of working-class culture of Samuel and Jemima Bamford.
83 *Republican*, 29 August 1826.

that she found herself in the 'midst of a Christian storm' when angry crowds, affronted by the caricatures of God and the King adorning the front window, made repeated attempts to break into the bookshop and to drag her out into the street. Correspondents to the *Republican* reported that Wright was subjected to 'profane curses' and 'horrid imprecations', and Wright herself reported receiving several death threats. While evening produced the largest wrathful gatherings, her radical friends were able to rally around the shop in support. During the day, however, she was forced to take all means to defend herself. Faced with two youths who used the 'most dreadful language' against her, she reached for the pistol that she kept on the front counter and advised that she would most certainly fire it if they did not leave. They hurriedly 'scampered off'. The trouble came to a head by the end of the month when 'furious' crowds attempted to break into the shop five or six times in one evening and by nine o'clock her friends sent for the police. The irony must have struck many. Initially an inadequate force was sent and reinforcements were needed to quell the riot outside the shop. After several arrests, the police succeeded in clearing the streets by 11 o'clock.[84]

By mid-September, however, she reported to the readers of the *Republican* that she had witnessed a remarkable turnaround in her situation. The riots, death threats and curses had ceased and even some of her most vehement opponents, she claimed, were now inquiring for her publications. In what seems to be her last entry in the public record, Wright jubilantly announced that 'the Victory is ours' for she had succeeded in establishing free discussion in Nottingham—a triumph indeed for the 'She-Champion of Impiety'.

In 1899, Richard Carlile's daughter wrote a biography of her father in which she listed the most important people who aided her father in the battle for reform.[85] Susannah Wright earned a place alongside radical stalwarts such as Francis Place, Julian Hibbert and George Holyoake.[86] Carlile himself had publicly praised Wright for her 'enthusiasm, her perseverance, her undauntedness, her coolness' during the 'hottest part' of the radical struggle. Following Wright's liberation from prison, Carlile earnestly hoped that she would recover her

---

84 Ibid.
85 Theophila Carlile Campbell, *The Battle for the Freedom of the Press as Told in the Story of the Life of Richard Carlile* (London: 1899), pp. 254–6.
86 On Francis Place, radical and master tailor, see the introduction by Mary Thale in Francis Place, *The Autobiography of Francis Place, 1771–1854*, Mary Thale (ed.) (Cambridge: Cambridge University Press, 1972); Dudley Miles, *Francis Place, 1771–1854: The life of a remarkable radical* (Brighton: Harvester, 1988). On George Holyoake, freethinker and journalist, see George J. Holyoake, *Life of Holyoake: Sixty years of an agitator's life* (London: T. Fisher Unwin, 1906); Lee E. Grugel, *George Jacob Holyoake: A study in the evolution of a Victorian radical* (Philadelphia: Porcupine Press, 1976); Edward Royle, *Victorian Infidels: The origins of the British secularist movement 1791–1866* (Manchester: Manchester University Press, 1974), passim. Far less is known of Julian Hibbert, though he was a crucial radical organiser and financial supporter of Carlile throughout his radical life. He was also involved in the formation of the National Union of the Working Class. See Campbell, *The Battle for the Freedom of the Press*, pp. 245–50; Joel Wiener, 'Hibbert, Julian', *BDMBR*, pp. 221–2.

health and 'some day receive that great reward from the public, to which she is eminently entitled'.[87] He was not alone in the esteem he held for Wright as the woman who had done 'more public good than any other one'. Allen Davenport clearly thought her efforts worthy of a place in history:

> 'That captive,' said the friendly spirit,
> 'With pallid cheeks, and tender frame,
> Has won the laurel wreath of merit,
> And purchased everlasting fame.
> 'For not a name in his'try's pages,
> Shall be found more fair and bright,
> Which may descend to future ages,
> Than the name of—Susan Wright.'[88]

Despite the prominent role Wright played in the radical movement of the 1820s, and the wish of some leading radicals that she be afforded an eminent place in the history of the movement, she remains a relatively obscure figure in both the broader radical literature of the period and the subsequent historiography. Wright's close association with Richard Carlile goes some way to explaining the dereliction by her contemporaries, as the case of Eliza Sharples, examined in a later chapter, also attests. Even among those who admired Carlile's struggle for a free press were many who were disgusted by his anti-religious zeal and by the most marginal of his advocacies: birth control.[89] A woman imprisoned for blasphemy, who continued her trenchant attacks upon Christianity and supported Carlile's most extreme tenets, was a direct affront to a newly evolving moral code, from which a radical movement struggling for a place in the hegemonic order was not immune.[90] Despite Carlile's 'most anxious wish' to impress on his female readers that 'religion has nothing to do with morality',[91] Wright's early public announcement that she wished her rejection of Christianity to be 'as notorious' as that of Carlile undoubtedly curbed her influence among mainstream radicals, both male and female. While she engendered popular support during her imprisonment, her defenders still lamented: 'Alas! How few of her countrywomen have attained to such an honour, and how very few there are of her own sex, who have even thought her worthy of notice.'[92]

---

87 *Republican*, 16 July 1824.
88 *Republican*, 9 January 1824.
89 For a discussion of Carlile's philosophies regarding sex and birth control, see M. L. Bush, *What is Love? Richard Carlile's philosophy of sex* (London: Verso, 1998); Iain McCalman, Popular Radicalism and Freethought in Early Nineteenth Century England, Unpublished MA thesis (Canberra: The Australian National University, 1975), pp. 163–71. For the reception of Carlile's ideas on birth control, see Clark, *Struggle for the Breeches*, pp. 181–5; Hera Cook, *The Long Sexual Revolution: English women, sex and contraception 1800–1975* (Oxford: Oxford University Press, 2005), pp. 70–6.
90 Yeo, *Radical Femininity*, p. 3. As Yeo notes, the rising middling classes made religious family life a key factor in their claim to moral superiority.
91 *Republican*, 29 November 1822.
92 *Republican*, 30 July 1824.

Wright's independent contribution to extreme postwar radicalism has also been largely overlooked in radical historiography. Susannah Wright's story helps advance our understanding of the radical relationship with the prison space. In many ways, her experience of the prison space shaped her experience of radical culture. It expedited and cemented her identity as a radical, above and beyond her gender—a status that often eluded women in the radical movement. Wright's story also highlights the experience of women within the radical spaces associated with the prison—that of the courtroom and the radical bookshop—and adds to our growing understanding of women's involvement in the radical public sphere; how they negotiated and operated within the radical movement not only as radical wives and daughters but as women with independent agency. Further, her experience of both Newgate and Coldbath Fields prisons highlights the continuities between the old system and the new in this transitional period of prison reform as well as the resilience and vitality of radical culture in this period. The often fierce encounters between the London press such as the *Courier*, *The Times*, the *New Times* and the *Morning Chronicle* over the rights and treatment of prisoners such as Wright, and the debates within the very centre of political power in the House of Commons, suggest that the radicals were not simply speaking to one another from their prison cells, but were capable of intersecting and interacting with the discourse of the mainstream public sphere.

The radical relationship with the prison space highlighted the adaptability, vitality and tenacity of radical culture, but, of course, it was never a site of choice. The next chapters in this study take a spatial leap beyond the prison walls to examine the interplay between radical culture and other spaces *chosen* by radicals as sites of assembly in the early nineteenth century. Where the issue of prison reform played a central role in the penal experience of radicals, it was to be another reform agenda that would pervade all manner of discourse of, and provide key motivation for, radicals meeting in the London venues featured hereon. The demand for sweeping political reform of Britain's exclusive parliamentary system in this period dominated the social and political aspirations of a generation of radical men and women. The extent to which these other types of radical spaces constituted an alternative public sphere, or enabled radical participation in the mainstream public sphere, is also further explored.

4. Radicalism and reform at the 'Gate of Pandemonium': the Crown and Anchor tavern in visual culture, 1790–1820

On the morning of 28 February 1820, John Cam Hobhouse sat down to write what he hoped would be his last diary entry from his Newgate prison quarters. Rumour had it, he noted, that his 'den' would be 'adjourned this day'.[1] Later in the afternoon, as Hobhouse enjoyed a stroll on the top of the gaol, he received news from the Governor of his release. Paying the watchman a pound, he descended to his apartments,

> sent [his] boy for a horse…put on breeches and boots…packed up letters &c…and at half-past five p.m., after shaking hands with Mr Brown [the Governor] I *repassed the door of Newgate*, got on my horse and trotted away.

Hobhouse, who had been confined in Newgate for his inflammatory comments following Peterloo, immediately retired to the family estate at Whitton, where his attention was devoted to 'thinking what I should say at the dinner to be given to me tomorrow at the Crown and Anchor on my liberation'.[2]

After only a day's respite from London, Hobhouse rode back to the metropolis to rendezvous with Sir Francis Burdett, the veteran radical ally, who accompanied his new charge to the Crown and Anchor tavern. After the disappointment of having 'a dozen or so gentlemen' reject his request for them to act as stewards for the dinner, Hobhouse was delighted to find many others unconcerned at the prospect of associating with the newly released prisoner. When he arrived at five o'clock on the afternoon of 2 March 1820, about 450 guests had gathered in the tavern for dinner and Hobhouse recorded that he was 'received in a most affectionate manner'.[3] An observer from *The Times* reported the 'immense cheering' on the entry of the reform duo to the Large Dining Room of the tavern. The diners, the correspondent noted acerbically, were 'superior to those who usually attend dinners of this description'.[4] Following the meal, the formalities began. The first toast of the evening, usually reserved for the health of the sovereign, was defiantly given to '[t]he people; the only free source of

---

1 For a digitalised version of the Hobhouse diaries, see <http://www.hobby-o.com/newgate.php> For a discussion of John Cam Hobhouse, see Robert E. Zegger, *John Cam Hobhouse: A political life, 1819–1852* (Columbia: University of Missouri Press, 1973).
2 *The Times*, 3 March 1820.
3 <http://www.hobby-o.com/newgate.php>
4 *The Times*, 3 March 1820. The description of the events that follows is sourced from this report.

legitimate power' and was met with loud and sustained applause, and 'three times three'. Defying the suspension of habeas corpus and the climate in which careless words could lead to immediate imprisonment, subsequent toasts served to remind the King of his duty to the people of England, while others advocated the 'thorough reform of parliament'. Each toast was followed with a bellowing 'three times three' and was interspersed with songs such as *Rule Britannia* and *Kick the Rogues Out*.

With the revelry of the toasts dispensed with, Hobhouse rose to address the crowd amid 'waving handkerchiefs and the loudest cheers'. In a lengthy and defiant address, he admonished those in the government responsible for his imprisonment as 'eavesdroppers, spies, men without character, men who could only command respect by means of corruption'. He invoked the tropes of nationalism and constitutionalism, reminding the assembly that despite conquering the land, not the Romans, the Danes or the Normans could destroy the 'free institutions and the free laws' that belonged to England.[5] Englishmen, he proudly noted, were not destined to 'fall by such hands'—then or now—'for even an assembly, met as they were at present, to protest against the acts of tyranny which had been committed, was sufficient to show that the people of England were not thus to be subdued'.

The gendered nature of these public celebrations is apparent when we consider the release of Susannah Wright; when she left prison, she did so quietly and with little ceremony.[6] Suffering from ill health, she later reaffirmed her dedication to the radical cause by supporting those still in prison and by disseminating the radical message through her Nottingham bookshop. Hobhouse, however, was following in the footsteps of other male radical 'martyrs' when his release from imprisonment was celebrated at the venue. Along with Hobhouse (and Burdett himself), many other imprisoned male radicals, including William Cobbett, William Holmes and John Ward, found a different expression of defiance when they testified to their continued commitment in the public arena of the Crown and Anchor tavern.

For Hobhouse, the tavern provided a fitting venue to reaffirm his radical political opinions. What better way to close a period of 'unfreedom' than with a public

---

5   The tropes of nationalism and constitutionalism remained contested territory throughout the early nineteenth century. For a discussion of radicals invoking the discourse of natural and historical rights, see the various contributors to James Vernon (ed.), *Re-Reading the Constitution: New narratives in the political history of England's long nineteenth century* (Cambridge: Cambridge University Press, 1996); E. P. Thompson, *The Making of the English Working Class* (London: Penguin, 1968), pp. 84–110; James Epstein, *Radical Expression: Political language, ritual and symbol in England, 1790–1850* (Oxford: Oxford University Press, 1994), pp. 3–28; Iain McCalman, 'Popular Constitutionalism and Revolution in England and Ireland', in Isser Woloch (ed.), *Revolution and the Meanings of Freedom in the Nineteenth Century* (Stanford: Stanford University Press, 1996), pp. 138–72.
6   My research failed to uncover an instance where an imprisoned female radical enjoyed similar public recognition upon her release.

rebirth at the venue he once described as a 'Temple of Liberty'—a space that Hobhouse believed embodied the very freedoms denied (theoretically at least) by the prison space.[7] In the same year, *The Times* newspaper saw a natural synergy between the prison space and the Crown and Anchor—albeit in less celebrated terms. In 1817, the paper caustically reported on a speech delivered in the tavern by veteran radical Major Cartwright advocating a political reform agenda:

> How soothing a doctrine for the many who are now 'fast bound in misery and iron', in those receptacles of guilt, Newgate and Coldbath Fields, and all the other prisons of the kingdom; the tenants of which, if they should come out tomorrow, would, like those gentlemen who met at the Crown and Anchor, be much more inclined to reform the State than to amend their own lives.[8]

The Crown and Anchor had joined Newgate and Coldbath Fields in a triumvirate of radical spaces now clearly mapped on the early nineteenth-century public sphere.

In the long period of popular discontent that stretched from the 1790s through to the mid-nineteenth century, the Crown and Anchor tavern was a seminal site in the campaign for political reform. The historical record is rich in episodes of popular radical involvement with the tavern and countless scholarly works documenting the climate of political discontent of the period feature meetings held in the venue.[9] Yet these works invariably set the Crown and Anchor as merely a backdrop (if they mention it by name at all) to the meetings of the day, rarely exploring the significance of the site and its intimate connections with popular radical culture in these years.

The following two chapters explore the Crown and Anchor tavern itself as a central site of London radicalism, charting how it became a central institution in the public sphere, so ubiquitous that its name became a form of shorthand in the language of politics. Although there are ample text-based references to the Crown and Anchor, this chapter will first focus on the representation of the tavern in the popular political prints of the period, when the Crown and Anchor became part of the caricaturists' palette of symbols with which to communicate,

---

7   *The Times*, 10 February 1819.
8   *The Times*, 24 January 1817.
9   Some studies of British radicalism mention the venue explicitly, such as J. Ann Hone, *For the Cause of Truth: Radicalism in London 1796–1821* (Oxford: Clarendon, 1982), passim; and Epstein, *Radical Expression*, pp. 107, 219; David Worrall, *Radical Culture: Discourse, resistance and surveillance, 1790–1820* (New York: Harvester, 1992), pp. 25, 144, 161; Iain McCalman, *Radical Underworld: Prophets, revolutionaries and pornographers in London, 1795–1840* (Cambridge: Cambridge University Press, 1988), p. 29. In other studies, the name of the venue is often overlooked in the narrative. Take, for example, John Belchem, *'Orator' Hunt: Henry Hunt and English working-class radicalism* (Oxford: Clarendon Press, 1985).

Radical Spaces

and in so doing embedded the tavern on London's political landscape. The prints also record the changing nature of the tavern's clientele over time and as such provide an important commentary on the development of radicalism.

* * *

The Crown and Anchor tavern was located in London's bustling central business area of the Strand—opposite Christopher Wren's seventeenth-century church of St Clement Danes and only a short distance from London's locus of power in Westminster. The tavern was situated on the Strand estate of the Dukes of Norfolk—the prominent English Catholic dynasty of the Howard family. Title deeds survive for the tavern as far back as 1731 when it existed in a modest form (Figures 4.1 and 4.2).[10] In 1787, then incumbent to the title of the Duke of Norfolk, Charles Howard, extensively renovated the site, rebuilding the venue to formidable proportions. By 1790, the tavern stretched the entire block from Arundel Street to Milford Lane—running parallel with the Strand—though set back behind the houses and shopfronts of the southern side of the bustling London artery (Figure 4.3).

Figure 4.1 An early street view of the Strand and St Clement Danes Church, 1753. On the right is the original entrance to the building with the Crown and Anchor tavern sign visible.

Copyright Trustees of the British Museum.

---

10   See the title deed, dated 25 March 1731, in the collection of documents concerning the tavern in the estate of the Duke of Norfolk, D7415, Arundel Castle Archives, Arundel. There are earlier reports of an auction in the 'Great Room' at the Crown and Anchor 'near St Clements Dane' in the *Daily Journal*, 6 November 1723.

4. Radicalism and reform at the 'Gate of Pandemonium'

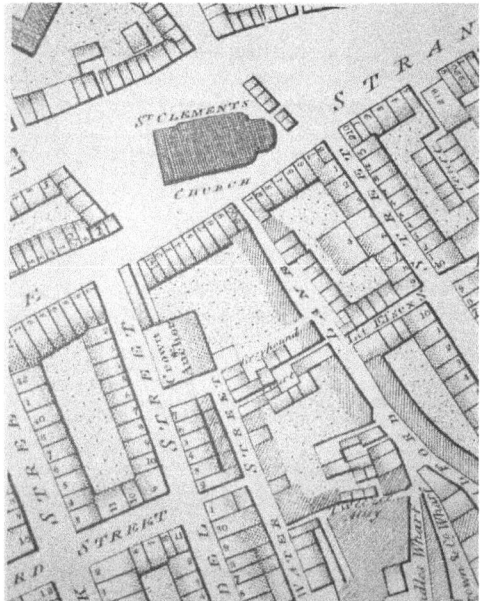

Figure 4.2 Horwood's map of the Strand showing the Crown and Anchor before the renovation, c. 1799.

Copyright Guildhall Library.

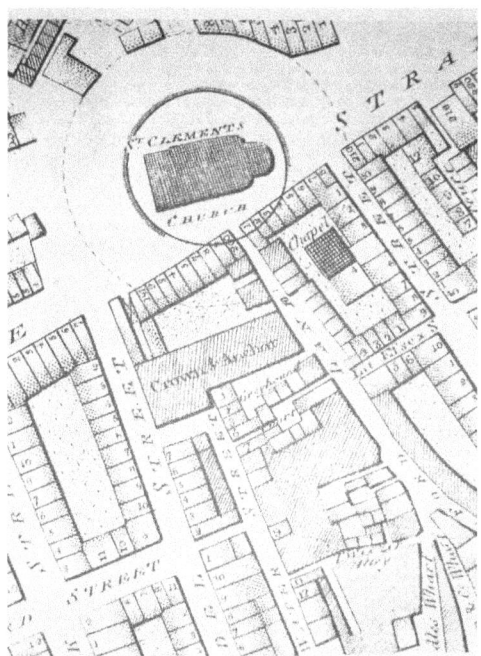

Figure 4.3 Horwood's map of the Strand showing the extended site of the tavern, 1807.

Copyright Guildhall Library.

Radical Spaces

Despite the immense size of the tavern, the front facade, which faced Arundel Street, was modest in appearance with the proportion and balance typified by Georgian architecture (Figure 4.4). Seven windows on each floor of the four-storey building were symmetrically aligned—the ground floor distinguished from the upper floors by arched windows and rusticated stonework. Iron balconies, each with their own iron lamps, dressed the windows of the first floor. Pilasters intersected each of the windows and stretched the height of the building. The whole effect provided an understated face to the streetscape. The tavern's principle entrance faced Arundel Street, and the subtle restraint evident in the facade was reflected by the narrow passageway that dissected two Strand shopfronts, allowing ingress from the major London thoroughfare (Figure 4.5).

Figure 4.4 Arundel Street entrance of the Crown and Anchor tavern.

Thomas H. Shepherd, 1852. Copyright Trustees of the British Museum.

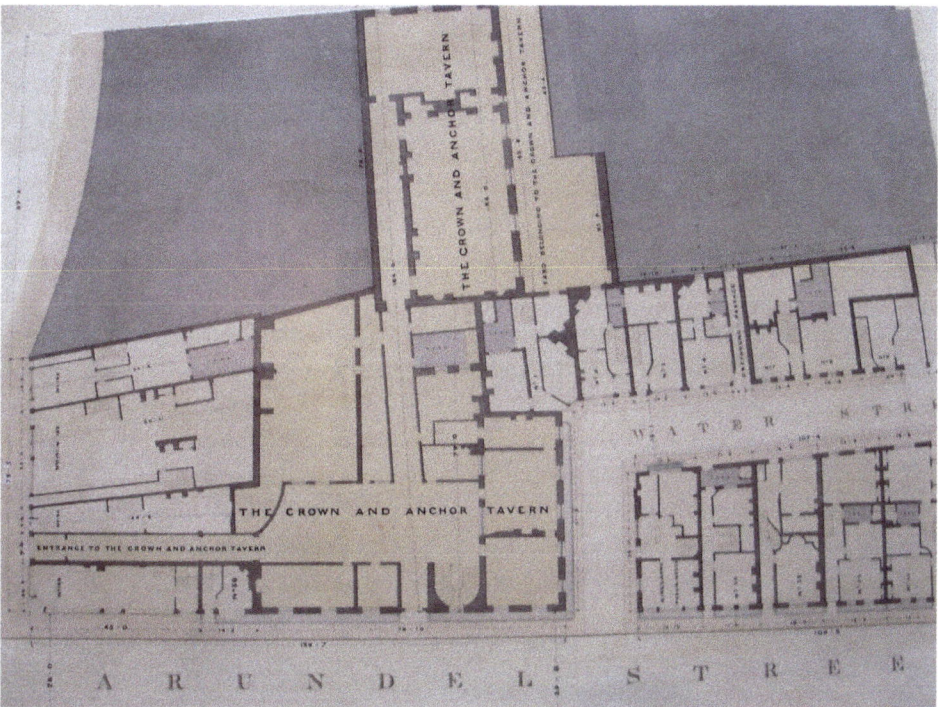

Figure 4.5 Ground-floor plan of the Crown and Anchor tavern, 1836.

From the Deed of the Arundel Buildings Estate, Middlesex, R. and H. R. Abraham Architects. Copyright His Grace the Duke of Norfolk (per the Archivist, Arundel Castle).

Entering the building from Arundel Street, visitors were greeted by an elegant foyer, paved with stone and dominated by four large Doric columns, which supported a gallery above. The entry was light and spacious, effected by a large lantern that hung overhead.[11] The tavern's considerable kitchen facilities were located on the ground floor, providing convenient access to the aptly named Large Dining Room, which, as evidenced by the Hobhouse liberation dinner, could seat upwards of 500 guests. The room was simply but elegantly appointed. Enriched carved cornices circled the ceiling, which featured two large moulded centrepieces of carved flowers supporting the room's chandeliers. Two substantial fireplaces framed with marble and wood dressings provided winter warmth. Festoons (carved chains of flowers, leaves or ribbons hung in curves) cascaded from the walls of an arched recess at the western end of the room, with the walls adorned with a frieze of eight panels.

---

11 This description of the interior of the Crown and Anchor has been taken from the title deeds to the tavern held at the Arundel Castle Archives. I owe a great debt to the staff of the Arundel Castle Archive who retrieved these records, some of which were uncatalogued at the time of my visit. Since that time, an illustrated catalogue of the collection has become available. See Heather Warne (ed.), *The Duke of Norfolk's Deeds Vol II—Properties in London and Middlesex* (London: Phillimore, 2010). Sources from Arundel Castle Archives are reproduced by kind permission of His Grace the Duke of Norfolk.

A prodigious staircase constructed of stone, framed by continuous ornamental iron rails and topped with mahogany handrails, led to the upper floors. Ascending the staircase to the second floor, visitors to the tavern could momentarily catch their breath in the small second-floor lobby—described as a 'large well hole', lit both by natural light drawn into the space by two conical skylights and, in the evenings, by a huge lantern raised six feet, six inches (1.98 m) high. The lobby provided an area for guests to assemble before making their entrance into the Crown and Anchor's premium asset: the 'Great Assembly Room'. The room was one of the largest available in the metropolis, measuring an immense 2969 sq ft (276 sq m) and was reportedly capable of hosting concerts, balls and banquets for at least 2000 people.[12] The room was elegantly appointed with chandeliers, marble fireplaces and intricately carved architraves and cornices, and the centre of the immense ceiling was garnished with an ornate domical centrepiece of formidable proportions from which grasped an enormous chandelier. Like the Large Dining Room, here an enriched moulded frieze and cornice encircled the entire room with 'ornamental panels, medallions and festoons' featured on four walls. These were further detailed with Doric pilasters mirroring the facade of the building. A raised music gallery for orchestras was situated at the western end of the room, surrounded by iron railings and supported by three fluted Doric columns. Three substantial arched windows at the eastern end of the room allowed for illumination by daylight.

In its extended configuration, the venue provided an immediate outlet for the flourishing social and cultural energies of the city.[13] The building was both expansive and immensely versatile as its many meeting rooms were capable of accommodating diverse gatherings of varying sizes at the one time. Apart from rooms for staff and for the major dining operations of the tavern, the architectural plans and title deeds for the tavern detail a large drawing room, a smoking room, a news room, a library, a reading room, several 'class' rooms and a ladies room. The building had developed strong cultural associations during its long eighteenth-century history and, by the turn of the century, it had emerged as one of the cultural icons of the city. It was the eighteenth-century birthplace of the Academy of Ancient Music and the Academy of Musicians, of

---

12 *Epicure's Almanack* (London, 1815), p. 115. This source also records that two other rooms in the tavern measure 1200 sq ft (111 sq m) and 1500 sq ft (139 sq m), along with 'numerous elegant rooms'. See also E. B. Chancellor, *The Annals of the Strand: Topographical and historical* (London: Chapman & Hall, 1912), pp. 333–6.
13 There are many works that discuss the nature of urban sociability in this period. See, for example, Gillian Russell and Clara Tuite, 'Introducing Romantic Sociability', in Gillian Russell and Clara Tuite (eds), *Romantic Sociability: Social networks and literary culture in Britain, 1770–1840* (Cambridge: Cambridge University Press, 2002), pp. 1–24; Peter Clark, *British Clubs and Associations 1580–1800: The origins of an associational world* (Oxford: Oxford University Press, 2000); John Brewer, *The Pleasures of the Imagination: English culture in the eighteenth century* (London: Harper Collins, 1997); Raymond Williams, *Culture and Society 1780–1950* (1953; reprinted, New York: Columbia University Press, 1983); Iain McCalman (ed.), *An Oxford Companion to the Romantic Age: British culture 1776–1832* (Oxford: Oxford University Press, 1999).

which Handel was a founding member, as well as the Society of Musicians.[14] The Great Assembly Room's orchestra gallery continued to accommodate promenade concerts by the Philharmonic Orchestra and other musical groups throughout the first half of the nineteenth century.[15]

The tavern also had strong affiliations with London's medical and scientific establishments throughout the decades that straddled the turn of the eighteenth century.[16] It was the customary dining venue for fellows of the Royal Society, who would retire to the tavern's dining room following their meetings.[17] It was the birthplace of the Pharmaceutical Society of Great Britain, and meetings of the foundation organisations, which would later combine as the British Medical Association, were also held in its rooms. The tavern also developed an association with the diffusion of knowledge, hosting both scientific and literary lectures throughout the late eighteenth century and into the nineteenth century. It was a key metropolitan establishment for London's literary elite as a venue for sociability and conviviality, and for the lectures by such literary greats as Samuel Taylor Coleridge and William Hazlitt.[18]

Observers of London later in the nineteenth century remembered the tavern as 'one of the most famous houses in London' during the earlier part of the century, and much of this reputation was owed to the venue's political affiliations.[19] Its status as a cultural centre was surpassed only by its renown as a thriving venue for political debate, discussion and dissent. As both J. Ann Hone's study of London

---

14   Peter Clark notes that the academy attracted '[l]ords, gentry, clergy and artists like William Hogarth'. Clark, *British Clubs and Associations 1580–1800*, p. 79. For an overview of the musical associations of the Crown and Anchor, see Robert Elkin, *The Old Concert Rooms of London* (London: Arnold, 1955), pp. 50–7. For an account of the formation of the Society of Musicians, see also Pippa Drummond, 'The Royal Society of Musicians in the Eighteenth Century', *Music & Letters*, vol. 59, no. 3 (1978), pp. 268–89.
15   Elkin, *The Old Concert Rooms of London*, p. 56.
16   For a discussion of these connections, see T. D. Whittet, 'The Crown and Anchor and the Arts and Sciences, Part 1', *Pharmaceutical Historian*, vol. 13, no. 3 (1983), pp. 2–6, and 'Part 2', *Pharmaceutical Historian*, vol. 13, no. 4 (1983), pp. 5–8; Alec Lawrence Macfie, *The Crown and Anchor Tavern: The birthplace of Birkbeck College* (London: Birkbeck College, 1973). See also the many histories of the area that detail the early use of the tavern. For example, Walter Thornbury, 'The Strand (Southern Tributaries)', *Old and New London*, vol. 3 (1878), pp. 63–84; Peter Cunningham, *Hand-Book of London* (London, 1850), p. 480; Henry C. Shelley, *Inns and Taverns of Old London* (Boston, 1909), ch. 4.
17   See *London Chronicle*, 28 November 1789. The Royal Society continued to hold their dinners at the tavern until 1848. See, for example, *The Times*, 1 December 1831; *Morning Chronicle*, 10 December 1832. For a discussion of the dinners of the Royal Society, see H. G. Lyons, 'The Anniversary Dinner', *Notes and Records of the Royal Society of London*, vol. 1, no. 2 (1938), pp. 96–103.
18   On Coleridge's Crown and Anchor lectures, see Kathleen H. Coburn, 'S. T. Coleridge's Philosophical Lectures of 1818–19', *The Review of English Studies*, vol. 10, no. 40 (1934), pp. 428–37. See also Peter J. Manning, 'Manufacturing the Romantic Image: Hazlitt and Coleridge lecturing', in James Chandler and Kevin Gilmartin (eds), *Romantic Metropolis: The urban scene of British culture, 1780–1840* (Cambridge: Cambridge University Press, 2005), pp. 227–45.
19   See, for example, the clipping headed 'Some Account of the Parish of St Clement Danes' (n.d.) and other early references to the tavern compiled by D. Foster in the 82-volume 'scrapbook': D. Foster, *Inns, Tavern, Alehouses, Coffee Houses etc, In and Around London*, vol. 20, c. 1900, City of Westminster Archives, pp. 230–301. The compilation is a remarkable resource for the history of London meeting places.

radicalism and Marc Baer's more recent study of Westminster political dinners reveal, the Crown and Anchor had a long association as the headquarters and the favoured dining establishment of the reform-minded or radical Westminster politicians and electors.[20] During the 1790s, the figure of Charles James Fox was synonymous with Crown and Anchor politics.[21] Apart from countless meetings and appearances at the tavern, supporters of the indomitable Whig grandee gathered on 10 October each year to celebrate his 1780 election victory, and on 13 January for festivities to mark his birthday. Such high-profile events helped propel both the tavern and its clientele into the broader public sphere. By the turn of the century, Fox's failing health saw him retreat from public life and the Crown and Anchor baton passed to Sir Francis Burdett. As we saw in an earlier chapter, the tavern became the headquarters for Burdett and his supporters, and celebrations of his electoral victories occurred annually in May throughout the early decades of the nineteenth century.

Though newspapers in this period are strewn with accounts of political meetings and events at the Crown and Anchor (as we shall see in the next chapter), visual culture also has much to offer as evidence of the venue's importance on the political landscape. Vic Gatrell maintains that 'just as a cluster of texts is read', so too prints, whose themes tend to 'cluster chronologically', can provide a 'clue to the preoccupations of a moment'.[22] Prints of this period offer particularly rich rewards for those investigating cultural communication through visual form, as artists brought their satirical skills to an increasingly politically aware public, providing sharp political commentary in amusing and often ribald fashion.[23] H. T. Dickinson observes that in the late eighteenth century, printmaking became professionalised, with artists who 'read newspapers and periodicals, listened to parliamentary debates and sought out political gossip in order to find topics

---

20   The Whig Club met at the tavern as early as 1786. See *Morning Herald*, 6 February 1786; *General Evening Post*, 30 March 1790; *Morning Chronicle*, 11 January 1790, 8 December 1790. A meeting in November 1795 was reported as one of the largest assemblies ever held, with more than 50 lords and members of the House of Commons in attendance. See E. W. Brayley, *Beauties of England and Wales, London and Middlesex* (London, 1810), vol. 1, p. 567.
21   On Charles James Fox, see Leslie G. Mitchell, *Charles James Fox* (Oxford: Oxford University Press, 1992); John Dinwiddy, *Radicalism and Reform in Britain 1780–1850* (London: Hambleton Press, 1992), pp. 1–18.
22   V. A. C. Gatrell, *City of Laughter: Sex and satire in eighteenth-century London* (New York: Walker & Co., 2007), p. 14.
23   There are now many scholarly works that have utilised this rich resource to illuminate aspects of British culture throughout the seventeenth, eighteenth and nineteenth centuries. See, for example, Gatrell, *City of Laughter*; Tamara Hunt, *Defining John Bull: Caricature, politics and national identity in late Georgian England* (Aldershot: Ashgate, 2003); Diana Donald, *The Age of Caricature: Satirical prints in the reign of George III* (New Haven, Conn.: Yale University Press, 1996); Marcus Wood, *Radical Satire and Print Culture, 1790–1822* (Oxford: Clarendon, 1994). See also the seven-volume Chadwyck-Healy series, *The English Satirical Print 1600–1832* (Cambridge: Chadwyck Healy, 1986), including contributions by John Brewer, *The Common People and Politics, 1750–1790s*; H. T. Dickinson, *Caricatures and the Constitution 1760–1832*; Michael Duffy, *The Englishman and the Foreigner*; John Miller, *Religion in the Popular Prints, 1600–1832*; J. A. Sharpe, *Crime and the Law in English Satirical Prints*.

which they could make relevant and interesting to a large body of opinion'.²⁴ Caricatures, or graphic satires, provide an insight into the social and political climate of the period. Moreover, they remind us that the language of the public sphere also involved visual forms.²⁵

The use of caricature to investigate the political temper of the day, however, is not without peril. As John Brewer notes, 'the assumption that political prints provide an unrefracted image of political life produces its own distortions'.²⁶ To approach visual culture as 'visual realism' is, for Brewer, an ahistorical assumption; we cannot grasp the meaning and significance of visual culture for a historical audience, he contends, without understanding the 'visual and perceptual conventions' employed by artists and graphic satirists of the day.²⁷ Similarly, both Roy Porter and Vic Gatrell remind us that visual culture is no 'less value laden than verbal' material.²⁸ The caution with which the modern scholar approaches visual records owes much to the humanist training to tread carefully with every source—image, text or oral—and recognise each as a social construct. It also owes much to the field of semiotics, which, at its crudest definition, involves the study of 'signs'.

The Swiss linguist Ferdinand de Saussure first posited the idea of studying the role of signs as part of social life—not only the visual, but also words, sounds and even body language.²⁹ Saussure's thesis sparked myriad responses from philosophers and theoreticians, most notably Charles Peirce and Roland Barthes, and semiotics has become a dense and rigorously debated area of study.³⁰ Though the scope of this chapter precludes chronicling the points and counterpoints of this increasingly vast field, semiotics' most basic premises remain fruitful

---

24 Dickinson, *Caricatures and the Constitution 1760–1832*, p. 19.
25 An immeasurable debt is owed to the seminal work of F. G. Stephens and M. D. George in describing, documenting and cataloguing the immense holdings of popular prints (more than 17 000) in the British Museum. Their groundbreaking work has allowed subsequent scholars much scope in utilising this once-neglected print medium. My own debt to their detailed cataloguing and description of prints associated with the Crown and Anchor tavern is apparent in this chapter. The prints identified here by the prefix 'BM' refer to the entries in their catalogue. See F. G. Stephens, *Catalogue of Prints and Drawings in the British Museum. Division 1: Political and personal satires*, 4 vols (1870–83); M. D. George, *Catalogue of Political and Personal Satires Preserved in the Department of Prints and Drawings in the British Museum* (1935–54): all 11 vols reprinted (London: The Trustees of the British Museum, 1978).
26 Brewer, *The Common People and Politics*, p. 16.
27 Ibid.
28 Roy Porter, 'Seeing the Past', Review article, *Past and Present*, vol. 118, no. 1 (1988), p. 200; see also Gatrell, *City of Laughter*, p. 14, who maintains that the reading of such prints depends on the 'historian's insight and intuition, and will never be comprehensive'.
29 On Saussure, see Roy Harris, *Saussure and His Interpreters* (New York: New York University Press, 2001). On semiotics and the arts, see Jessica Evans and Stuart Hall (eds), *Visual Culture: The reader* (London: Sage Publications, 1999).
30 On Peirce, see James Hoopes (ed.), *Peirce on Signs: Writings on semiotics* (Chapel Hill: University of North Carolina Press, 1991). See also the many debates regarding Peirce in the journal dedicated to his work, *Transactions of the Charles S. Peirce Society*. On Roland Barthes, see Annette Lavers, *Roland Barthes, Structuralism and After* (Cambridge, Mass.: Harvard University Press, 1982). For an overview of the debates, see Harris, *Saussure and His Interpreters*.

for the analysis of the visual; it alerts us to the constructed meanings inherent in visual imagery, to the ability of different signs within an image to interact and produce layers of meaning, and to the polysemic nature of many prints—their ability to embody multiple meanings.[31] This is particularly relevant to the diverse range of images, symbolism and meaning embodied in caricatures of the late eighteenth and early nineteenth centuries.[32]

Three of the earliest prints to feature the Crown and Anchor evolved out of one seminal event held at the tavern in 1791: a celebration to mark the anniversary of the storming of the Bastille.[33] British reformers initially welcomed the Revolution with much enthusiasm and news that they were publicly celebrating the tumultuous events across the Channel caused a shudder amongst conservative London and prompted a flurry of public commentary, including contributions from graphic satirists.[34] The publicity surrounding the impending event was sufficient to induce William Dent's graphic response, *Revolution Anniversary or Patriotic Incantations* (Figure 4.6).[35] The print is set inside an amorphous space, though it is given a spatial grounding by the addition of an invitation titled 'Crown and Anchor', which sits curled at the bottom left corner of the print. The walls are dominated by four posters that link the organisers of the 1791 meeting with historic English rebels: 'WAT TYLER' depicts the famous English leader of the Peasants' Revolt in 1381 and 'JACK CADE', the leader of the Kentish rebellion against Henry VI in 1450, appears alongside present-day reformer and Dissenting minister Dr Joseph Towers, shown attacking the crown and the sceptre with an axe in the poster titled 'REPUBLICISM'. The historical allusion is unambiguous: the caricaturist saw Tyler, Cade and Towers as part of an unbroken tradition of rebellion in the British past.

The fourth wall poster, titled 'FANATICISM', depicts a winged and cloven-footed devil setting fire to a church, while in the foreground prominent Whig

---

31 For a discussion of the 'indeterminate meanings associated with signs' in respect to radical politics, and specifically the cap of liberty, see Epstein, *Radical Expression*, pp. 70–99.
32 As Epstein argues, 'Struggles to enforce or destabilise such meanings often define the contested terrain of politics.' Epstein, *Radical Expression*, p. 71.
33 For reports of the meeting, see *Evening Mail*, 1 July 1791, 12 July 1791; *London Chronicle*, 12 July 1791.
34 For a discussion of British responses to the French Revolution in print culture, see David Bindman, *The Shadow of the Guillotine: Britain and the French Revolution* (London: British Museum Publications, 1989); Hunt, *Defining John Bull*, pp. 87–90, 97–110. For responses more generally, see the entries in Mark Philp (ed.), *The French Revolution and British Popular Politics* (Cambridge: Cambridge University Press, 1991); H. T. Dickinson (ed.), *Britain and the French Revolution 1789–1815* (Basingstoke: Macmillan, 1989); Clive Emsley, 'The Impact of the French Revolution on British Politics and Society', in Ceri Crossley and Ian Small (eds), *The French Revolution and British Culture* (Oxford: Oxford University Press, 1989), pp. 31–62; Michael T. Davis, 'Le radicalisme Anglaise et la Revolution Française', *Annals Historiques de la Revolution Française*, vol. 342 (2005), pp. 73–99.
35 BM 7890. For M. D. George's description of the print, see George, *Catalogue of Political and Personal Satires*, 1791, vol. 6, pp. 808–9. William Dent, a self-taught artist, produced hundreds of political caricatures in the period. See David Bindman, 'Prints', in Iain McCalman (ed.), *An Oxford Companion to the Romantic Age* (Oxford: Oxford University Press, 2001), p. 210.

reformers Joseph Priestley, Charles James Fox and Richard Brinsley Sheridan join Towers in a pagan-like dance around a cauldron as they summon both 'French Spirits' and that of radical ideologue Thomas Paine: 'Oh! choice Spirit of dauntless Paine/Make, make our Cauldron blaze again.' Imps play music around the base of the steaming boiler and in the top left a demon sets fire to a church as it treads upon a bishop's mitre. The conflation of radicalism with devilry makes Dent's print one of the early examples of the satirical convention identified by Brewer—the 'satanic radical'[36]—in which caricaturists attempted to demonise and blacken the individuals espousing reform. The print offers a visual instance of what Norbert Elias so eloquently refers to as the 'threshold of repugnance' by which radicals were measured.[37]

Figure 4.6 *Revolution Anniversary or Patriotic Incantations.*

William Dent, 1791. Copyright Trustees of the British Museum.

The satanic connotations of the Crown and Anchor milieu are evident again in James Gillray's mordant response to news of the July celebrations.[38] Arguably the leading caricaturist of the period, Gillray's *Alecto and her train, at the*

---

36 Brewer, *The Common People and Politics*, pp. 39–40.
37 Nobert Elias, *The Civilizing Process: Sociogentic and psychogenetic investigations* (1965; revised edn, Oxford: Blackwell, 2000), quoted in Michael T. Davis, 'The Mob Club? The London Corresponding Society and the politics of civility in the 1790s', in Michael T. Davis and Paul A. Pickering (eds), *Unrespectable Radicals? Popular politics in the age of reform* (Aldershot: Ashgate, 2008), pp. 21–40.
38 On James Gillray, see Draper Hill, *Mr Gillray, The Caricaturist: A biography* (London: Phaidon Press, 1965); George, *Catalogue of Political and Personal Satires*, vols 5–8; Christiane Banerji and Diana Donald, *Gillray Observed: The earliest account of his caricatures in 'London und paris'* (Cambridge: Cambridge University Press, 1999).

Gate of Pandemonium…or…The Recruiting Sargeant enlisting John Bull into the Revolution Service was published on 9 July 1791, immediately prior to the meeting at the tavern (Figure 4.7).[39] The central figure in the scene is Alecto, one of the three grotesque goddesses (or Furies) of vengeance in Greek mythology, known for inflicting famines and pestilences. As generally represented in mythology, she has been draped with snakes by Gillray, although the serpents suckling at her haggard breasts were surely an indication of his desire to shock. The scene is set outside the Crown and Anchor—designated in the print as the 'Gate of Pandemonium', referring to the capital of hell depicted in John Milton's *Paradise Lost*. Smoke and flames bellow ominously from the doors of the tavern while demons circle within. Here the space of the tavern is imbued with satanic connotations rather than the reformers themselves. Gillray stamps the Crown and Anchor as an iniquitous space; one can hardly imagine a more brutal appellation than the capital of hell.

Figure 4.7 *Alecto and her Train at the Gate of Pandemonium…or…The Recruiting Sargeant enlisting John Bull into the Revolution Service.*

James Gillray, 1793. Copyright Trustees of the British Museum.

---

39 BM 7889. For M. D. George's description of the print, see George, *Catalogue of Political and Personal Satires*, vol. 6, pp. 807–8.

The symbolism employed by caricaturists, observes Paul Pickering, was an effective 'form of social or cultural shorthand: a public mode of communication'.[40] Symbols were an essential tool of the graphic satirist for communicating a message in a succinct and immediate fashion. They also allowed the caricaturist to play with meaning in their prints and, by combining different symbolic elements, the artist could also alter meanings. For instance, seminal events across the Channel were connected with those occurring at the Crown and Anchor by visually endowing the tavern clientele with the key symbols of the Revolution—primarily the 'bonnet rouge' (or red cap of liberty) and the tricolour cockade. A combination of the symbols of the French Revolution and the convention of the satanic radical saw the Crown and Anchor portrayed as a venue seething with danger and revolutionary possibility.

This is particularly evident in the Crown and Anchor prints with inclusion of symbols firmly associated with the French Revolution. Though Dent's print makes fleeting reference to the threat of revolution by depicting the reformers wearing the French Grenadiers' cap and summoning 'French spirits' from the cauldron, Gillray endows Alecto as the embodiment of revolutionary France. Wearing a French cocked hat with a tricolour cockade, she holds a long pike topped with a bonnet rouge. British caricaturists seized on the symbols of the French Revolution to indict the activities of local reformers, many of whom (as the July 1791 meeting itself suggests) were fervent supporters of the Revolution and were easily targeted as revolutionaries-in-waiting. The hapless Whigs were conflated with bloodthirsty French Republicans with a few careful strokes of Gillray's pen.

Despite these connotations, neither print deterred the organisers or supporters from proceeding with the celebrations. More than 1500 'gentlemen' are said to have gathered to dine on such typical Crown and Anchor fare as stewed pigeons, roasted beef and venison and gooseberry tart.[41] As generous quantities of wine were imbibed, their reforming spirits were stirred as the provocative ode celebrating the fall of the Bastille by eminent Della Cruscan poet Robert

---

40 Paul A. Pickering, 'Class Without Words: Symbolic communication in the Chartist movement', *Past & Present*, no. 112 (1986), p. 155. On symbolic practices as an integral part of political language, see also Lynn Hunt, *Politics, Culture, and Class in the French Revolution* (Berkeley: University of California Press, 1984), chs 1–3; Epstein, *Radical Expression*, pp. 70–99; John Brewer, *Party Ideology and Popular Politics at the Accession of George III* (Cambridge: Cambridge University Press, 1976), pp. 163–201; idem, 'Theatre and Counter-Theatre in Georgian Politics: The mock elections at Garrat', *Radical History Review*, no. 22 (1979–80), pp. 7–40.
41 The description is taken from the sample menu for July from the tavern published in a commercial cookbook prepared by the 'Principal Cooks at the Crown and Anchor'. Francis Collingwood and John Woollams, *Universal Cook, and City and Country Housekeeper* (London, 1792). It is unclear whether the 'Bill of fare for July' was from 1791 or 1792. For a report of the meeting, see *Morning Herald*, 15 July 1791; *Morning Post and Daily Advertiser*, 15 July 1791; *Star*, 15 July 1791.

Merry was read to the assembly.⁴² The meeting itself presented Gillray with an opportunity too good to ignore, and in the days following he sketched a second print, *The Hopes of the Party* (Figure 4.8).⁴³

Figure 4.8 'The Hopes of the Party, prior to July 14th… "From such wicked Crown and Anchor Dreams, good Lord deliver us."'

James Gillray, 1791. Copyright Trustees of the British Museum.

Although the print depicts less satanic associations, it firmly conflates the Crown and Anchor with treachery and revolution, and seals the notion of the tavern as the headquarters for a British rebellion. In a setting reminiscent of the execution prints outside Newgate prison, Gillray sets the scene around a platform erected outside the tavern's Strand entrance, with a mob cheering and waving their hats in anticipation of the beheading of King George III by Charles James Fox. Radical veteran John Horne Tooke⁴⁴—in a pose suggestive of sodomy—grasps

---

42 The reading of the poem became part of the publicity for the event. See *Whitehall Evening Post*, 12 July 1791. On Robert Merry and Della Cruscan poets, see Jon Mee, '"Reciprocal Expressions of Kindness": Robert Merry, Della Cruscanism and the limits of sociability', in Russell and Tuite, *Romantic Sociability*, pp. 104–22; William Hargreaves-Mawdsley, *The English Della Cruscans and Their Time, 1783–1828* (The Hague: M. Nijhoff, 1967); John Strachan, 'Gifford and The Della Cruscans', in John Strachan (ed.), *British Satire 1785–1840* (London: Pickering and Chatto, 2003), vol. 4, p. 384.
43 BM 7892. For M. D. George's description of the print, see George, *Catalogue of Political and Personal Satires*, vol. 6, pp. 810–11.
44 On Tooke, a veteran of the radical movement of the late eighteenth century, see Christina Bewley and David Bewley, *Gentleman Radical: A life of John Horne Tooke, 1763–1812* (London: Tauris Academic Studies, 1998); John Barrell, *Imagining the King's Death: Figurative treason, fantasies of regicide, 1793–1796* (Oxford: Oxford University Press, 2000), pp. 285–7, 366–98, 403–5.

by the legs King George, whose head rests on a block. Sheridan grips the King's ears in preparation for Fox to take an axe to the Monarch's head. Queen Charlotte and the Prime Minister, Pitt, have been summarily dispensed with as they hang limply from the Crown and Anchor's lampposts. In the background, heads appear on spikes atop a burning Temple Bar as the winged figure of Liberty watches from above. Gillray's caustic commentary on the revolutionary intent of the reforming Whigs also mocks the King, who appears confused by the whole situation: 'What! What! What!—what's the matter now.'[45] Despite the undoubtedly scandalous suggestion of beheading the King, the print might have had less ominous undertones for eighteenth-century audiences. They were to wait another two years before the guillotining of Louis XVI—arguably the most famous beheading of the period. The conflation of the Crown and Anchor with both devilry and revolutionary possibility gave credence to the prospect of a British rebellion; a home-grown revolution had been given a spatial context.

Though the three 1791 prints associated the Crown and Anchor with a threat to the political order, the meaning of the Crown and Anchor as a symbol in popular prints was not fixed throughout the decade. This was largely a result of a loyalist campaign to appropriate the tavern in the early 1790s in response to the threat of London's flourishing radical groups and associations who increasingly found a home at the venue. Only five years before his intervention in Colonel Despard's plight in Coldbath Fields prison, then London barrister John Reeves took a decidedly unfavourable view of the tavern's growing radical association when he formed his own loyalist counter-society.[46] In a masterly coup, he appropriated not only the Crown and Anchor site for his meetings but also its name for his association. Originating under the cumbersome title the 'Association for Preserving Liberty and Property against Republicans and Levellers', it soon became known in the public sphere as the 'Crown and Anchor Society'.[47] Reeves' usurpation of the Crown and Anchor site and nomenclature can be seen as an attempt to sanitise the space that had bred the 'nefarious designs…[of] the wicked and senseless Reformers of the present time'.[48] Its mandate to 'discourage and suppress Seditious Publications' predated that of the Vice Society, which, as we saw in an earlier chapter, was to lead the prosecutions

---

45 George, *Catalogue of Political and Personal Satires*, vol. 6, pp. 810–11.
46 On Reeves and the Crown and Anchor Association, see Kevin Gilmartin, 'In the Theater of Counterrevolution: Loyalist association and conservative opinion in the 1790s', *Journal of British Studies*, vol. 41 (2002), pp. 291–328; Michael Duffy, 'William Pitt and the Origins of the Loyalist Association Movement of 1792', *Historical Journal*, vol. 39, no. 4 (1996), pp. 943–62; Mark Philp, 'Vulgar Conservatism, 1792–3', *English Historical Review*, vol. 110, no. 435 (1995), pp. 42–69; Worrall, *Radical Culture*, pp. 9–17.
47 *Association for Preserving Liberty and Property Against Republicans and Levellers: Association papers* (London, 1793), part 1. Almost 30 years later, Sir Francis Burdett alluded to Reeves' society in one of his anniversary of election dinners at the tavern: 'it was…strange to see how times had altered. If there should now be a Crown and Anchor Association, it would be not to put down the liberty of the press, but to support that, and to preserve whatever of public liberty still remained to the people.' *The Times*, 24 May 1821.
48 *Association for Preserving Liberty and Property Against Republicans and Levellers*.

of radicals in the early decades of the nineteenth century. The Society spawned several allied provincial societies and generated a mass of correspondence to its headquarters at the Crown and Anchor.[49]

Reeves' relationship with the Crown and Anchor itself, however, was short-lived; the tavern's radical brethren did not acquiesce so easily.[50] In May 1792, leading reform activist John Horne Tooke revived Major Cartwright's 'Society for Constitutional Information' to agitate for parliamentary reform and they actively promoted and published cheap editions of Thomas Paine's *Rights of Man* from their headquarters at the Crown and Anchor.[51] Another radical counter-society was launched at the tavern in the month following Reeves' first meeting. The 'Friends to the Liberty of the Press', led by prominent barrister Thomas Erskine, also established the venue as their base.[52] At times, the rival groups even met on the same day, though on different floors of the tavern.[53] Although Reeves' society considered they had successfully prevented England from being engulfed by revolution as early as 1793, the 'perverted and evil men' that the Crown and Anchor Society were formed to resist successfully reappropriated the tavern as a site to further their reform agenda. Reeves' failure to expunge the tavern's radical affiliations was to lead to an enduring legacy of radical and political reform at the venue.

Despite the brevity of Reeves' intervention at the Crown and Anchor, the loyalist champion was also captured in the print culture of the period—due largely to a close, though often fractious, relationship between Reeves and Gillray.[54] Reeves commissioned the master caricaturist to produce several anti-radical prints early in the decade, such as *The Blessings of Peace, The Curses of War* (1795). Only two years earlier, Gillray had been more contemptuous of the association, producing in 1793 the uncommissioned print *The Chancellor of the Inquisition*

---

49   Philp, 'Vulgar Conservatism', p. 58.
50   The formation and conduct of the association prompted several hostile text-based responses from the radical community. See, for example, the anonymously printed pamphlet *Truth and Reason Against Place and Pension; Being a candid examination of the pretensions and assertions of the society held at the Crown and Anchor, and of similar associations in various parts of the metropolis. Addressed to John Reeves, Esq, and his Associates* (London, 1793); Joseph Towers, *Remarks on the Conduct, Principles, and Publications, of the Association at the Crown and Anchor, in the Strand, for preserving liberty and property against republicans and levellers* (London, 1793).
51   For more on Major Cartwright, see Chapter 5 of this study.
52   Thomas Erskine, *Declaration of the Friends of the Liberty of the Press; Assembled at the Crown and Anchor tavern* (London, 1793). Erskine became one of the key figures in radical culture of the 1790s for his prominent, and often highly successful, defence of radicals prosecuted in this period, including Lord George Gordon in 1780 and Thomas Paine (*in absentia*) in 1792, as well as his remarkable defence of radicals during the treason trials of 1794, where he secured 'not guilty' verdicts for all those he represented. See Gillian Russell, 'The Theatre of Crim. Con.: Thomas Erskine, adultery and radical politics in the 1790s', in Davis and Pickering, *Unrespectable Radicals*, pp. 57–70; David Lemmings, *Professors of the Law: Barristers and English legal culture in the eighteenth century* (Oxford: Oxford University Press, 2000).
53   See *True Briton*, 28 July 1794.
54   Donald, *The Age of Caricature*, p. 147; Hill, *Mr Gillray*, p. 54.

Marking the Incorrigibles (Figure 4.9).[55] The print depicts Edmund Burke (the fierce opponent of the French Revolution responsible for the 'swinish multitude' epithet) walking in legal robes to the door of the Crown and Anchor, over which a sign reads 'British Inquisition' in reference to the activities of Reeves' society.[56] According to Dorothy George, the bag hanging from Burke's waist resembles the chief seal of the Crown, used to show the Monarch's approval of important state documents, and is employed by Gillray to indicate that the work of the Society came with the government's imprimatur.[57] Gillray replaces the royal arms of the Great Seal with a crown and an anchor, and features a skull at each corner. The 'anonymous letter box' at the door of the tavern refers to the correspondence the Society attracted, and also its call for information about the activities of reformers from spies and informers. In a brilliant sleight of hand to indicate the change in ideological complexion of the venue, Gillray has placed royal crowns on top of its lamps.[58]

Just as the change in occupation of the venue could be signified by the use of the crown in this way, the tavern emblem itself could also be manipulated by caricaturists to communicate meaning. The binary of the Crown and Anchor, in both nomenclature and emblem, was a coup for caricaturists. In Dent's *Revolution Anniversary*, the anchor from the tavern's emblem is magnified and assumes centre stage. Long regarded as the symbol for 'hope', the anchor assumed an altogether different meaning when placed in the context of the tavern and amongst the tangible weapons of rebellion—the cannons, swords, axes and the flag of liberty. The symbol of the anchor was now imbued with threat and danger.

The tavern's radical clientele also embraced the possibilities presented by the binary symbols of crown and anchor in the venue's emblem. The reported plan by organisers of the 1791 anniversary celebrations to ceremoniously remove the crown from the emblem (thereby disassociating any connection with monarchical rule), allowing only the anchor to remain, attracted much public attention.[59] In Dent's print, amid the steam rising from the cauldron, he depicts a crown being propelled from the cauldron—a clever visual metaphor for the intentions of the evening, and for radical plans for society at large.

---

55 BM 8316. For George's description of the print, see George, *Catalogue of Political and Personal Satires*, vol. 7, pp. 20–1.
56 Ibid. See also Nicholas Robinson, *Edmund Burke: A life in caricature* (New Haven, Conn.: Yale University Press, 1996), pp. 167–9. Robinson notes that Burke's association with the Crown and Anchor is also evident in another print by William Dent, *An Alarming Anniversary!!!*. Burke is depicted as Don Quixote (and Pitt as Sancho) 'mounting a dead-of-night reconnaissance' of the tavern (p. 169).
57 George, *Catalogue of Political and Personal Satires*, vol. 7, pp. 20–1.
58 Gillray employs the device again in his 1795 print, *Crown and Anchor Libel, Burnt by the Public Hangman* (BM 8699). Gillray produced the print after a dispute with Reeves involving payment for an earlier commissioned print. See George, *Catalogue of Political and Personal Satires*, vol. 7, p. 207.
59 See the reports of the events in *Evening Mail*, 11 July 1791.

Figure 4.9 *The Chancellor of the Inquisition marking the Incorrigibles.*
James Gillray, 1793. Copyright Trustees of the British Museum.

4. Radicalism and reform at the 'Gate of Pandemonium'

The binary elements of the tavern emblem also allowed caricaturists more sympathetic to the radical cause to manipulate meaning in their images with the simple stroke of a pen. Richard Newton's 1798 satirical print *Sola 'Virtus Invicta'* (the motto of the Duke of Norfolk) was a response to the highly publicised 1798 birthday celebrations for Charles James Fox, and the prominent, and soon infamous, role of the Duke of Norfolk in the events.[60] The festivities were an annual event, and 1798 saw one of the largest assemblies ever held at the tavern. The Duke's penchant for drinking and revelry was renowned in London society, as were his liberal political views, despite his close friendship with the Prince Regent.[61] At the request of the chair of the occasion, the Duke of Bedford, the Duke of Norfolk proposed a string of toasts to the 2000-strong audience.[62] Though convention stipulated the first toast at such a public occasion be offered as a salutation to the Monarch, the Duke raised his glass and gave instead to 'the rights of the people'.[63] The flagrant disregard of custom and etiquette met a mix of cheers and murmured disgruntlement. When the room quieted, the Duke continued with an altogether scandalous line-up of toasts bordering on the treasonous: 'to constitutional redress for the wrongs of the people'; to 'a speedy and effectual reform in the representation of the people in parliament'; to 'the genuine principles of the British Constitution'; and to 'the people of Ireland—may they be speedily restored to blessings of law and liberty'. When he finally offered a toast to the King, it contained a thinly disguised rebuke reminding the Monarch of his duty—to 'Our Sovereign's health—the majesty of the people'.

In his print *Sola 'Virtus Invicta'*, Newton shows a tumultuous scene outside the Crown and Anchor with the foreground dominated by the image of the Duke of Norfolk arriving in spectacular and triumphant fashion driving a horse chariot, crowned with the cap of liberty (Figure 4.10).[64] The front wheel of the chariot crushes the neck of Prime Minister Pitt and the King, whose bald head (lower left) has been de-crowned, as the bishops and clergy wait with fearful anticipation of a similar fate. The tavern emblem can be seen in the upper left, though Newton has inverted its symbolic elements; the crown is turned on its head while the anchor stands erect. It is unclear whether Newton's use of phallic

---

60 Richard Newton's artistic talents were evident from an early age when at fourteen he was employed by radical print publisher William Holland. It was during Holland's imprisonment in Newgate that Newton sketched the *Soulagement* print noted in Chapter 1. For a discussion of Newton's works, see David Alexander, *Richard Newton and English Caricature in the 1790s* (Manchester: Manchester University Press, 1998).
61 The architectural enhancements of the Arundel estate during the eleventh Duke's tenure illustrate the connection between liberal politics and entertainment for the nobleman. He oversaw the construction of an elegant dining room at the Howard family castle in Arundel, which he named the 'Barons Hall'—in honour of the Barons of Runnymead—a contentious title during such anxious times for Britain's monarchy. See John Martin Robinson, *The Dukes of Norfolk*, revised edn (Chichester: Phillimore & Co, 1995), pp. 174–5.
62 John Russell, Sixth Duke of Bedford. For an account of the meeting, see Thomas Wright, *Caricature History of the Georges* (London: John Camden Hotten, 1868), pp. 514–15.
63 Ibid., p. 514.
64 BM 9177. For George's description of the print, see George, *Catalogue of Political and Personal Satires*, vol. 7, pp. 424–5.

symbolism was a purely satirical tool or indicative of some deeper commentary on the vitality and fertility of radicalism and reform at the Crown and Anchor. Either way, it serves as an apt visual metaphor for the starkly gendered nature of Crown and Anchor politics, which will be discussed further in the following chapter.

Figure 4.10 *Sola 'Virtus Invicta'... 'Vitue* [sic] *Alone is Invincible.'*

Richard Newton, 1798. Copyright Trustees of the British Museum.

Neither the government nor George III could allow Norfolk's public display of disloyalty and perfidy to go unnoticed. The Duke was dismissed from all his official positions, including his position on the Privy Council and the Lord Lieutenancy of the West Riding.[65] Signalling that the Duke's powerful friendships would not protect him, the notification of dismissal was sent during a dinner with the Prince Regent. Despite eventually satisfying the King with proclamations of loyalty, he was not reinstated to his official post until 1807.[66] The publicity aroused by the meeting helped cement the image of the Crown and Anchor as an oppositional political space; and despite the penalties imposed on the Duke, it set a precedent for the toasting conventions of the venue, as evidenced by Hobhouse's own toasts following his prison release more than 20 years later.

---

65 See *Whitehall Evening Post*, 1 February 1798; *The Times*, 2 February 1798.
66 Robinson, *The Dukes of Norfolk*, p. 176. Details of the dismissal are held in the Arundel Castle manuscripts, AC MSS, Howard Letters and Papers, 1636–1822, II.

Although historian Lawrence H. Streicher considers that caricature 'presupposes the existence of relatively fixed iconographic types in art',[67] Newton's graphic interpretation of the events serves again to remind us that the meaning of the symbols employed by the caricaturist were not fixed during this period. For example, as James Epstein suggests, the cap of liberty did not always signal revolutionary intent; indeed, in the century before the French Revolution there was 'no iconographic incompatibility between the cap of liberty and patriotic sentiment'.[68] Following 1792, however, when Louis XVI was 'symbolically decrowned and forced to don the emblem of the revolution' the meaning of the cap altered dramatically. For loyalists and conservatives in Britain, the cap of liberty, particularly when coloured red, soon came to represent the 'antithesis of British constitutional "liberty" and patriotism'.[69] Just as the claims to liberty, to the Constitution and to Britishness were contested, so too were their symbolic representation.[70] Newton's radical sympathies are evident in *Sola 'Virtus Invicta'* by the positive use of the symbols traditionally employed against radicals, with Liberty (in angelic female form) floating above the Duke, preparing to crown him with a wreath of laurel.[71] Her staff bears an illuminated cap of liberty and reveals a tricolour cockade. Fox and the Duke of Bedford stand at the door of the tavern cheering on the Duke of Norfolk, and behind them the tavern crowd wildly wave their hats.

Newton's resolution to recast the meaning of symbols such as the cap of liberty in a positive light coincided with a discernable move in conservative caricature away from the 'satanic radical' conventions and the symbolism invoking revolutionary France. Though the familiar tropes of Jacobin treachery and the symbols of the French Revolution continued to play a part in some prints—as Charles William's 1803 print, *The Crown and Anchor Desperdado or the Cracked member Belonging to the Bedlam Rangers* (Figure 4.11)—reveals, the threat of radicalism is now firmly directed at the individual reformers themselves, indicting their 'levelling' intentions and defiance of the social order.[72] In the print, Burdett leans from a ground-floor window of the tavern, addressing a crowd of soldiers and onlookers. He calls to them:

---

67 Lawrence H. Streicher, 'On a Theory of Political Caricature', *Comparative Studies in Society and History*, vol. 9, no. 4 (1967), p. 437.
68 Epstein, *Radical Expression*, p. 78. See also James Vernon, *Politics and the People; A study in English political culture c.1815–1867* (Cambridge: Cambridge University Press, 1993), pp. 113–16. For a discussion of the liberty cap pre-nineteenth century, see J. David Harden, 'Liberty Caps and Liberty Trees', *Past & Present*, no. 146 (1995), pp. 66–102.
69 Epstein, *Radical Expression*, p. 72.
70 For an excellent account of the contested nature of claims to the Constitution in this period, see Barrell, *Imagining the King's Death*.
71 Similarly, the notions of 'Justice' and 'Britannia' are also gendered, the former given female form carrying her sword and scales while the latter proudly bares a shield and spear. Dickinson, *Caricatures and the Constitution 1760–1832*, pp. 20–1.
72 BM 10054. For George's description of the print, see George, *Catalogue of Political and Personal Satires*, vol. 8, pp. 173–4.

Radical Spaces

I say don't Arm—don't enter into the Volunteer Corps, don't support the Minister, don't oppose the French—but you sailors all demand to be Captains, You soldiers to be Colonels, you people to be Baronets in short now is your time to insist upon everything your hearts can wish, and then—.

The crowd, however, is contemptuous: 'why then the Rascally French will be here, and we shall have nothing left to ask for.' The print is a satire on Burdett's speech at his election celebrations at the tavern on his return for Middlesex, during which he suggested that the government ministers did not warrant 'an honest man to come forward in their defence, or to be justified in lending an assisting arm in defence of their country'.[73] The title of the print—a play on Burdett's support of Colonel Despard—and the image itself reveal that the new generation of reformers who emerged in the early decades of the nineteenth century meant a new cast of characters for satirists and caricaturists. With Fox's death in 1806, and his retirement from public life in the years preceding it, the name of Sir Francis Burdett came to be synonymous with Crown and Anchor radicalism—an association that was duly reflected in the print culture of the period.

Figure 4.11 *The Crown and Anchor Desperdado or The Cracked Member belonging to the Bedlam Rangers.*

Charles Williams, 1803. Copyright Trustees of the British Museum.

---

73 M. W. Patterson, *Sir Francis Burdett and His Times* (London, 1931), quoted in George, *Catalogue of Political and Personal Satires*, vol. 8, pp. 173–4.

A key feature of the prints examined thus far is the prominence of the elite gentlemen radicals such as Fox and Burdett who occupied leading roles in events held in the tavern. Any plebeian figures featured in the prints assemble outside the venue's walls. The Crown and Anchor, at least in the caricatures, is a venue of the bourgeois public sphere, populated—as Habermas would suggest—by the British bourgeoisie. In Gillray's 1791 *Alecto* print, the character of John Bull—the archetypal or representative figure of the English common man—is first introduced to the milieu of the tavern, although he is placed at a distance from its front door.[74] Alecto attempts to entice him with a pile of Assignats, the paper currency of the revolutionary government, placing John Bull in a quandary: 'and yet I is half in love with the sound of your drum; & wishes to leave off Ploughing & dunging, & wear one of your vine cockades, & be a French Gentlemen.' Alecto reassures him:

> [N]ay, man, never talk about your old Master the Farmer, I'll find you Hundreds of Masters as good as he; Zounds I'll make you one of the Masters of England yourself…the glorious 14th of July is approaching, when Monarchs are to be crush'd like maggots, & brave men like yourself are to be put in their places.

Alecto and her British political allies are connected spatially with the tavern by locating them directly outside the venue; John Bull is recruited as a passer-by, rather than a participant in the Crown and Anchor affairs.

The character of John Bull was another satirical convention employed by caricaturists in the period, though during the 1790s he was increasingly represented as contemptible and ludicrous by artists such as Gillray. As Brewer notes, prior to this, the image of the 'patriotic pleb' involved a far more 'indomitable and stout-hearted Briton'.[75] By the 1790s, John Bull came to be represented as a 'broad grimacing baboon, a dim witted, grossly overweight glutton, or the child-like simpleton—a gross caricature of the rustic fool' and became a stock character in British print for many years to come.[76] As Tamara Hunt argues, the use of the image of John Bull changed again over time, whereby the figure increasingly replaced the image of Britannia as the national symbol.[77]

By examining the Crown and Anchor prints over time, it is possible not only to survey the changing representation of characters of different social rank, but to trace discernible changes in their spatial placement within the prints.

---

74 On the character of John Bull, see Brewer, *The Common People and Politics*, pp. 40–3; Miles Taylor, 'John Bull and Iconography of Public Opinion in England c.1712–1929', *Past & Present*, no. 134 (1992), pp. 93–128; Hunt, *Defining John Bull*, passim; Donald, *The Age of Caricature*, ch. 5.
75 Brewer, *The Common People and Politics*, p. 40.
76 Ibid., p. 43.
77 Hunt, *Defining John Bull*, pp. 121–69. Hunt argues that the figure of Britannia lost public favour due to the close association forged by the Foxites between the Duchess of Devonshire and the Britannia icon.

Radical Spaces

Figure 4.12 *Scene in the Crown and Anchor.*

J. T. Smith, 1802. Copyright Trustees of the British Museum.

Newton's 1798 print is one of the first to depict a broader, albeit faceless, crowd assembled at the Crown and Anchor. Similarly, J. T. Smith's *Scene in the Crown and Anchor Tavern* (Figure 4.12), produced as an engraving to accompany verses by satirical poet George Huddesford, *Scum Uppermost*, in 1802, is among the first to venture inside the tavern.[78] The print provides one of the few graphic images of the interior of the venue in the public record in this early period. Although we must be wary of interpreting the print as a realistic depiction of the actual venue, some of the features accord with those described in other public records—namely, the large arched window at the end of the room and the sense of the venue's capacity for assembling large crowds in the 'Great Assembly Room'. The four busts that adorn the walls—reform icons Mirabeau, Talleyrand, Bonaparte and O'Connor—are fictitious additions to the interior; they nevertheless provide an immediate key to the ideological mood of the venue.[79] Fox holds centre place, standing on an oversized chair in the centre of the immense table, while Burdett is depicted as a small figure standing by the left-hand corner of the table. Fox holds aloft a flaming globe, the sign of a 'World's End' tavern. Apart from the title of the print, there are no identifying symbols or signs to mark the space. Yet the size of the assembly, the prominence

---

78   BM 9885. For George's description of the print, see George, *Catalogue of Political and Personal Satires*, 1791, vol. 8, pp. 91–2.
79   Ibid.

of the key characters and the fictitious busts combine to identify the venue, suggesting a more intimate knowledge of its space in the wider public sphere. It also provides a sense of wider participation at the venue, beyond the key gentlemen figures of Fox, Burdett and the Duke of Norfolk.

It is not until Samuel de Wilde's satire of the 1809 Grand Reform Dinner, however, that we begin to see the Crown and Anchor brethren diversify in terms of social standing (Figure 4.13). De Wilde seized on the reports of debauchery and drunkenness at the dinner. Speakers were reportedly howled down by intoxicated members of the audience and the meeting is said to have illustrated the growing gulf between the Burdett reformers and the Whigs.[80] The meeting was reportedly attended by men of 'some consideration', including Matthew Wood, who was made one of the two Sheriffs of London and Middlesex in 1809, Robert Waithman, political reformer and later Lord Mayor of London, and members of the parliamentary reformers' movement including Lord Cochrane, George Byng and William Smith, Member for Norwich, alongside 1200 other 'friends of liberty'.[81] Significantly, among the gallery is Francis Place, a ubiquitous figure in the machinery of radical London.[82] What makes Place stand apart among this crowd is the fact that he was an artisan—a tailor—of humble birth; he was born in a debtors' prison.

Where once John Bull stood bemused and detached from the space of the tavern, in De Wilde's print, a butcher joins in the revelries with the aristocratic reformers. The figure of the butcher, Brewer notes, was a familiar one in the caricature of the eighteenth century, and stood alongside that of the sailor as the archetypal figure of the 'liberty-loving Englishman' before the adoption of the character of John Bull.[83] In the print, not only is the butcher placed amongst the reformers, De Wilde also gives him a voice. He is depicted making a speech and holding a pamphlet, 'The Wae Ow too Rifform the Parl[iament]', while a grinning chimney sweep 'decked out in the cocked hat and gold paper epaulets of May-day' points to Gwyllym Lloyd Wardle's *Plan for a New Government*.[84]

---

80 Not all newspapers reported the meeting in this way. *Jackson's Oxford Journal*, 6 May 1809, provided a detailed report of the meeting, which excluded any mention of reports of drunkenness or riotous behaviour.
81 Michael Roberts, *The Whig Party* (London: Macmillan, 1939), pp. 246–7.
82 On Francis Place, see Dudley Miles, *Francis Place 1771–1854: The life of a remarkable radical* (Brighton: Harvester, 1988). For more on Place, see Chapter 5 of this study.
83 Brewer, *The Common People and Politics*, pp. 41–2. The butcher—seemingly an incongruous choice as the representative figure of the English common man—Brewer reminds us, linked 'national identity to culinary and dietary habits', for the butcher 'presided over the preparation and sale of that most distinctive of English dishes, the roast beef of England'.
84 Wardle, a parliamentary backbencher, caused a public scandal when he exposed corruption involving the Duke of York in the awarding of army contracts. His further exposé of the Duke's mistress, Mary Anne Clarke, eventually led to the resignation of the Duke as commander-in-chief. See Philip Harling, 'The Duke of York Affair (1809) and the Complexities of War-Time Patriotism', *Historical Journal*, vol. 39, no. 4 (1996), pp. 963–84; Peter Spence, *The Birth of Romantic Radicalism: War, popular politics and English radical reformism, 1800–1815* (Aldershot: Scolar Press, 1996), ch. 6.

De Wilde's print demonstrates that some of the familiar symbols of the previous century remained embedded in popular political prints of the early decades of the nineteenth century, as he depicts Burdett raising a glass in one hand and a bonnet rouge with tricolour cockade in the other. The binary of the tavern's emblem is again put to good use: Lord Cochrane is the figure mounting the oversized tavern emblem to slash at the crown with his sabre.[85]

Figure 4.13 *The Grand Reform Dinner*.

Samuel De Wilde, 1809. Copyright Trustees of the British Museum.

I am mindful again here of Brewer's warning about 'visual realism'. As he notes, during the 1790s, there was a tendency to remove plebeians from scenes where we should 'expect their presence' so that many of the crowds depicted in early political cartoons consist 'almost entirely of gentlemen'.[86] It is possible that De Wilde's use of the butcher and chimney sweep is the inverse of this phenomenon, and is merely intended as a metaphor for the levelling dangers inherent in the intentions of the Crown and Anchor reformers, rather than actual evidence of working-class participation in its events. Place's presence, however, suggests otherwise. He provides context for the generic figures, which suggests that the shift of placement of plebeian figures from outside to inside was recognition by the caricaturists of the day that the tavern's more plebeian identities were legitimate participants in the public sphere. Although the aristocratic reformers so intimately connected with the tavern still dominate the prints after the turn of the century there is an increasing association of the Crown and Anchor as the headquarters of a burgeoning, newly politicised and unruly rabble. With both De Wilde's and Smith's prints among the first to depict the interior of

---

85 George, *Catalogue of Political and Personal Satires*, 1791, vol. 8, pp. 91–2.
86 Brewer, *The Common People and Politics*, p. 18.

the building, it appears that by the early nineteenth century, the doors of the tavern, if only metaphorically, have opened to accommodate the expanding political nation.

* * *

The use of print culture to explore the cultural understanding of the Crown and Anchor tavern inevitably raises a question about the consumption of such prints and the extent to which they were circulated in London at the turn of the nineteenth century. Produced as works of art, they were intended for commercial gain and for sale to private buyers. Did this then mean they were accessible only to a political elite who could afford to purchase the prints, or did the caricaturists' sphere of influence extend beyond a bourgeois public? What role did the phenomena of the caricature shop—such as that of Mrs Humphrey's, which displayed and sold Gillray's works—play in extending the reach of the caricaturist beyond a paying clientele?

The question of the circulation of the prints is a vexed issue among scholars of print culture in this period.[87] H. T. Dickinson questions the veracity of claims of mass audiences, arguing that it is 'impossible' to be certain of the press runs of any of the prints.[88] Though he allows that some prints were displayed in publishers' shop windows, Dickinson argues that only about 10 such shops existed, and they were limited to metropolitan viewers so that most political prints found an audience in the politically aware inhabitants of London and Westminster.[89] He concedes that there are examples where prints gained wider circulation than that suggested purely by print run alone. When the middle classes feared revolution, for example, Dickinson maintains, they 'pasted political prints on the walls of taverns, shops, and workshops in an effort to influence the lower orders'.[90] Roy Porter and Diana Donald are less cautious in their assessments; Donald considers that the dissemination of caricatures was far wider, socially and geographically, than previous scholars (such as Dickinson) 'have thought likely'.[91]

---

87 Many scholars have written about the market for and the consumption of political prints. In addition to those already noted, see Vincent Caretta, *The Snarling Muse: Verbal and visual satire from Pope to Churchill* (Philadelphia, 1983), pp. 243, 255. For an overview of the debate, see Eirwen E. C. Nicholson, 'Consumers and Spectators: The public of the political print in eighteenth-century England', *History*, vol. 81, no. 261 (1996), pp. 5–21; and Porter, 'Seeing the Past'.
88 Dickinson, *Caricatures and the Constitution 1760–1832*, p. 17. Nicholson also remains sceptical of the reach of the caricaturist, arguing that 'the evidence presently available' does not support the status it has been accorded by historians—'that of a "mass" and potentially demotic medium'. Nicholson, 'Consumers and Spectators', p. 21.
89 Dickinson, *Caricatures and the Constitution 1760–1832*, p. 15.
90 Ibid.
91 Donald, *The Age of Caricature*, p. 184. Porter, 'Seeing the Past', p. 200. Tamara Hunt also argues against Dickinson's position. See Hunt, *Defining John Bull*, pp. 7–10.

Clearly, however, conjecture over circulation should not preclude the importance of the prints for illuminating the past. Crucially, as Vic Gatrell reminds us, 'textual evidence presents the same difficulties'.[92] 'In any case', he continues, 'the historian of mentalities is concerned with what was thinkable and doable in the past, regardless of the assumed numbers of people involved, or its assumed normative standing'. Given the uncertainty over circulation numbers, it is perhaps more prudent to focus on the availability of the prints in the public arena. The display of the prints in the caricature shops such as that operated by Hannah Humphrey meant that many prints were exposed to the public gaze.[93] Visitors to London, such as Johann Christian Hüttner, noted the extreme popularity of the 'caricature shops'.[94] He observed they were 'always besieged by the public' with the exception of 'Mrs Humphrey's shop, where Gillray's works are sold'. Here he found the audience were people of 'high rank, good taste and intelligence'.[95] In 1791, *The Times* lamented the public display of the prints as a public menace:

> [T]he scandalous caricatures in many of the print shops of this metropolis, hung out to debauch the minds of an unwary youth, and libel the most exalted characters. They attract so many passengers that it is difficult to pass the streets without being obliged to go on the carriageway to avoid pickpockets, who generally plant themselves in the way to practice their callings.[96]

Reeves' loyalist members of the short-lived Crown and Anchor Society certainly recognised the power of prints to rouse popular discontent. One correspondent to the Society considered that '[s]uch prints make stronger Impressions in the minds of Comon [sic] people than many times reading accounts of the subject'.[97] The appeal of the popular print to the illiterate public accounts for much of the moral panic over their content. Although political discontent framed as published text proliferated in this period in the form of books, pamphlets and newspapers, there was a certain safety in that these forms of cultural communication presupposed a literate (and largely bourgeois) audience.[98] Their perceived ability to influence the unpredictable, unstable and poorly educated

---

92 Gatrell, *City of Laughter*, p. 14.
93 Cindy McCreery, 'Satiric Images of Fox, Pitt and George III: The East India Bill crisis of 1783–84', *Word and Image* (1993), p. 164.
94 Johann Christian Hüttner, *London und Paris*, 1798, quoted at <http://www.npg.org.uk/live/arccari5.asp>
95 Ibid.
96 *The Times*, 22 December 1791.
97 Quoted in Donald, *The Age of Caricature*, p. 142.
98 As Ian Haywood notes, the attitude also prevailed amongst gentleman radicals such as William Godwin. See Ian Haywood, *The Revolution in Popular Literature: Print, politics and the people, 1790–1860* (Cambridge: Cambridge University Press, 2004), pp. 41–2. See also Brewer, *Party Ideology and Popular Politics at the Accession of George III*, pp. 140–2; Donald, *The Age of Caricature*, pp. 142–6.

'mob' was seen as more limited than publicly displayed graphic satire.[99] Even where the prints of the 1790s involved text as complex verses or explanatory notes, the symbolism and imagery utilised in popular prints meant members of the illiterate, or less politically aware, public could still appreciate their message.[100] Regardless of the impasse about the consumption of prints, as a cultural communicator, the caricaturist clearly did not rely solely on the skills of a literate audience.

Moreover, when the Crown and Anchor prints are viewed over time, the sharp reduction in the use of text over a relatively short time frame is evident. This appears paradoxical, for it occurs precisely at the time when literacy levels are on the rise.[101] There is little doubt that over time the caricaturist honed his skills to communicate more effectively and succinctly in purely visual form and therefore relied less heavily on the use of text. The reduction in the use of text also suggests that the collective understanding of the identities, images and symbolism featured in the prints was maturing. The caricaturist relied on an audience who instantly recognised and understood the meaning attached to the multitude of symbols that was so vital a part of the caricaturist's work. The reduction in the use of text, paradoxically perhaps, was reflective of the political sophistication of the audience—a populace well versed in the political iconography of the day.

Perhaps the clearest evidence of the broadening reach of the caricaturist lies in the increasing appropriation of the medium by radicals themselves. Prior to the 1790s, most caricatures and graphic satires were critical of government personalities and political events. The French Revolution, however, turned the caricaturists' lenses firmly on those who sought to change the British political and social system. Although Newton's *Sola 'Virtus Invicta'* is one of the few prints exhibiting any radical sympathies referred to in this chapter, there were many other prints in the period that were scathing in their criticism of those in power.[102] The iconic print by George Cruikshank of the shackled and impoverished 'Freeborn Englishman', gagged with a padlock through his lips, was inspired by a 1795 print, *A Lock'd Jaw for John Bull*, which shows Pitt padlocking John Bull's lips with the reassurance that he would soon become

---

99   Donald, *The Age of Caricature*, p. 147; Dickinson, *Caricatures and the Constitution 1760–1832*, p. 11.
100 Dickinson, *Caricatures and the Constitution 1760–1832*, p. 20.
101 See Haywood, *The Revolution in Popular Literature*, chs 1 and 2; Richard Altick, *The English Common Reader: A social history of the mass reading public 1800–1900* (Chicago: University of Chicago Press, 1957), ch. 2; David Vincent, *Literacy and Popular Culture: England 1750–1914* (Cambridge: Cambridge University Press, 1989).
102 For a discussion of the use of caricature and visual culture by the radicals in this period, see Wood, *Radical Satire and Print Culture*, ch. 2; Gatrell, *City of Laughter*, ch. 16; Alexander, *Richard Newton and English Caricature in the 1790s*.

'used to it'.¹⁰³ Nevertheless, it was the anti-radical prints from artists such as Gillray that arguably dominated the satirical world of the late eighteenth century.¹⁰⁴

That domination, however, was shattered with the entry of radical publisher William Hone onto the satirical landscape in the second decade of the nineteenth century.¹⁰⁵ Hone's work saw a resurgence of radical print propaganda and led to a pamphlet war with loyalist commentators. Amidst the stoush, we again find the Crown and Anchor has a central place in visual representations of the political landscape. Hone's brilliant political satire had a hiatus of almost two years following his three (unsuccessful) prosecutions under the suspension of habeas corpus in 1817 for earlier publishing work.¹⁰⁶ If Hone was buoyed by his defeat of the authorities, the Peterloo massacre would cement his dedication to the radical cause and reinvigorate his satirical juices. The events of 1819 inspired a remarkable period of satire as Hone produced a series of political parodies he devised while reading nursery rhymes to his children.

Engaging the sharp talents of a new caricaturist, George Cruikshank, to illustrate the pamphlet, the *Political House that Jack Built* saw an evolution of the medium of satire by combining simple rhythmic verse with accompanying images.¹⁰⁷ The collaboration produced one of the most successful satirical works seen in England—from either side of the political divide. It was first published in December 1819 and, by March the following year, it was in its fifty-second edition, with a deluxe colour edition also on sale. The shilling pamphlet tapped into a popular market and is reported to have sold 100 000 copies.¹⁰⁸

Although Hone's pamphlet itself does not feature the Crown and Anchor, a brief outline of the *Political House* parody is necessary if we are to appreciate the context of the prints in which the tavern featured in this period. The introductory image of the *Political House* represents the Constitution—or the 'House' of the parable's title (Figure 4.14). Cruikshank utilises the traditional graphic representation of the Constitution as a temple supported by three

---

103   See Gatrell, *City of Laughter*, pp. 489–90; Hunt, *Defining John Bull*, p. 224.
104   Brewer rightly notes that the 'genteel' provenance of the print collection of the British Museum might not present the 'complete picture of radical engraving'. Brewer, *The Common People and Politics*, p. 45.
105   On William Hone, see Kyle Grimes, 'Spreading the Radical Word: The circulation of William Hone's 1817 liturgical parodies', in Michael T. Davis (ed.), *Radicalism and Revolution in Britain, 1775–1848* (London: Macmillan Press, 2000), pp. 143–56; Wood, *Radical Satire and Print Culture*, pp. 96–154; Edgell Rickword, *Radical Squibs and Loyal Ripostes: Satirical pamphlets of the Regency period, 1819–1821* (London: Redwood Press, 1971), pp. 1–23.
106   See Philip Harling, 'The Law of Libel and the Limits of Repression, 1790–1832', *Historical Journal*, vol. 44, no. 1 (2001), p. 128n.
107   George Cruikshank was the son of prominent eighteenth-century caricaturist Isaac Cruikshank. For a discussion of George Cruikshank, see Robert L. Patten, *George Cruikshank's Life, Times and Art*, 2 vols (New Brunswick, NJ: Rutgers University Press, 1992); John Buchanan-Brown, *The Book Illustrations of George Cruikshank* (Newton Abbot: David & Charles, 1980).
108   Rickword, *Radical Squibs and Loyal Ripostes*, pp. 23–4.

columns, titled Commons, King and Lords. Liberty (again, in Romanesque female form) crowns the temple. The 'Wealth' of the nation is symbolised by a treasure chest, which holds scrolls symbolising 'Habeas Corpus', 'Bill of Rights' and 'Magna Carta'—a holy trinity of radical claims to Britishness.[109] Both verse and text censure the British elite, or the 'Vermin' who 'Plundered the Wealth/That lay in the House/That Jack built'. The 'People', all 'tatter'd and torn', are represented as ragged and starving as they are slaughtered by the yeomanry at Peterloo. Just as the radicals who questioned which political side had the truer vision for Britain from their prison cells, Hone's pamphlet called for the restitution of the ancient rights of the freeborn Britain, which had been 'plundered' by the 'vermin' in political power. *The Political House that Jack Built* provided the most powerful answer to the fear-driven, 'Jacobin treachery' message of the conservative prints in circulation in the previous decades by inverting the threat to the British nation. The danger lay not with the reformers and radicals who assembled at the Crown and Anchor, but with the British government itself.

The immense success of Hone's *Political House* parody pamphlet enraged conservative Britain and provoked a volley of loyalist ripostes. These works generally imitated both the style and the imagery of Hone's original; in *The Real or Constitutional House that Jack Built*, the Constitution is again represented as a temple, with three pillars of Monarch, Lords and Commons, although in this print the figure of 'Liberty' is replaced by 'Justice', also in female form, carrying in one hand the scales of justice and in the other a book symbolising 'LAW' (Figure 4.15).[110] The riposte focuses on William Pitt as the leader—or 'the PILOT'—who has prevented the 'plundering' of the treasures of the 'HOUSE that Jack Built'. Lords Wellington, Nelson, Burke and Castlereagh are denoted as the 'PATRIOTS', and their portraits hang on an English oak surrounded by laurel leaves—again indicating the contested nature of political iconography in the period.[111] The absence of the figure of Liberty in the riposte, however, suggests that by 1819 radicals had successfully appropriated that icon as their own.

---

109   See Thompson, *The Making of the English Working Class*, p. 805. As I argued in Chapter 2 of this study, although Linda Colley's account of the forging of a British identity argues that Britishness was an expression of difference from an alien 'other'—from France, from Catholicism and later from races encountered in the Empire—she does concede that internal schisms had a role to play in the formation of a national identity. See Linda Colley, *Britons Forging the Nation 1701–1837* (New Haven, Conn.: Yale University Press, 1992), p. 342.
110   *The Real or Constitutional House that Jack Built*(London, 1819), reproduced in Rickword, *Radical Squibs and Loyal Ripostes*, pp. 59–82.
111   As Marcus Wood notes, loyalist publishers who imitated Hone's style had the difficult task of presenting the Regent and the cabinet as 'astute and benevolent leaders'. Wood, *Radical Satire and Print Culture*, p. 259.

Radical Spaces

Figure 4.14 'This is the House that Jack Built', *The Political House that Jack Built.*

William Hone and George Cruikshank, London, 1819. Copyright Trustees of the British Museum.

Figure 4.15 'This is the House that Jack Built', *The Real or Constitutional House that Jack Built.*

London, 1819. Copyright Trustees of the British Museum.

Radical Spaces

Though the Whigs are mentioned in the riposte, they are dismissed as 'HYPOCRITES', and the 'RADICALS' are the focus of censure and scorn. The detail of the illustrated 'radical' scene and accompanying verse is worth pausing over (Figure 4.16). The page depicts a scene of eight men meeting in a small room. Gathered around a table, on which is placed a large sheet titled 'Petition of the Unrepresented', are all the leading radicals of the period. Veteran radical leader Major Cartwright signs his name to the petition while Richard Carlile, his hair drawn cleverly into devilish horns, looks over his shoulder. T. J. Wooler is represented symbolically by the title of his journal the *Black Dwarf* and sits on the lap of Sir Francis Burdett, represented in his electoral sash but who appears to be bearing the new radical symbol of the early nineteenth-century radicalism: Henry Hunt's white hat.[112]

Figure 4.16 'These are the Radicals—Friends of Reform', *The Real or Constitutional House that Jack Built.*

London, 1819. Copyright Trustees of the British Museum.

---

112   On the adoption of Hunt's white hat as a plebeian radical symbol, see Epstein, *Radical Expression*, pp. 94–5, 115, 199n.

Further symbols are scattered throughout the scene. On the wall behind the assembly hangs a picture of an axe being held to the base of an English oak.[113] A procession banner, 'Liberty or Death' (an image that emerged following its prominence at Peterloo), lies slumped against the wall. Joining the symbolic incarnations of radicalism (from the conservative perspective) is the crude, yet immediately identifiable, tavern sign of the Crown and Anchor placed above the doorway. Where once artists used text and graphics to locate their tavern scene, now the tavern emblem alone suffices. That a new generation of graphic satirists could represent the Crown and Anchor in symbolic form alone speaks volumes of the cultural understanding of the venue on the political landscape, and the enduring associations of the tavern and radical politics first formulated a generation earlier. Like the bonnet rouge and tricolour cockade, the tavern had assumed its own political identity; it had become a symbol in its own right.

The Crown and Anchor featured again in the loyalist responses to Hone's sequel to the *Political House* pamphlet, *The Man in the Moon*.[114] Prompted by both the inflammatory speech of the Regent at the opening of Parliament in November 1819 and the new legislative powers of the Six Acts, Hone and Cruikshank's second collaboration was published in January 1820. By March, the parody—which took the form of a dream narrative—was in its twenty-sixth edition. The poem is set in a parallel society on the Moon, 'Lunataria', and is a parody of the Regent's speech. Hone indicts the existing political and social system, the increases in taxation of the poor and the alliance between the military, the church, Parliament and the monarchy. It is interspersed with Cruikshank's illustrations, all pointedly irreverent, such as the opening image depicting the Regent facing a lunar parliament (Figure 4.17). The members are faceless and, with the royal star replacing both their heads and genitalia, they are depicted as pawns of the monarchy. In imagery consistent with the radical representations of the yeomanry at Peterloo, the Regent is charged with complicity as he triumphantly holds a sabre aloft. Outside parliament, however, a storm is brewing. The printing press shines from the sun above and the cap of liberty with a comet tail of 'reform' is about to descend on the Regent's head.

Loyalist ripostes soon followed Hone's publication, and the Crown and Anchor again featured in their counter to Hone's shrewd and pointed censure of the political system. Although the format of the *The Loyal Man in the Moon* again imitated Hone's original, the content, notes Edgell Rickword, was focused more closely on the upcoming Westminster election.[115] There is a clear return to the familiar tropes of the 1790s in *The Loyal Man in the Moon*, as the figure of the

---

113   On the oak as a symbol of liberty, see Harden, 'Liberty Caps and Liberty Trees', pp. 66–102.
114   *The Man in the Moon* (London, 1820), reproduced in Rickword, *Radical Squibs and Loyal Ripostes*, pp. 83–106.
115   Rickword, *Radical Squibs and Loyal Ripostes*, p. 314.

Radical Spaces

Regent is replaced with that of Burdett, wearing a cap of liberty with a tricolour cockade and bearing another symbol of the French Revolution—a dagger—in one hand and a 'Liberty or Death' banner in the other (Figure 4.18). In the loyalist incarnation, a radical parliament is pictured as faceless and is symbolised by daggers and bonnet rouge. A dove, stabbed by a dagger, descends with a trailing comet tail of 'Peace'. The devil, who sits atop the printing press, evokes the tropes of the 'satanic radical' from the 1790s, though it could also be an allusion to the freethinking tenets of prolific radical publisher Richard Carlile.[116]

Figure 4.17 *The Man in the Moon.*

William Hone and George Cruikshank, 1820. Copyright Trustees of the British Museum.

---

116 The date of the print coincided with Carlile's high-profile trial and imprisonment.

Figure 4.18 *The Loyal Man in the Moon.*

Anonymous, 1820. Copyright Trustees of the British Museum.

The loyalist dreamer narrating the riposte fondly reminisces about 'Moonarian Law' of which 'true Lunarians had no cause to grieve/The want of good and wholesome regulations/Such as are found in all enlightened nations'. The dreamer's contentment is shattered, however, when he finds 'the great extent of vice!'—that 'Radicals were in the moon'.

> For very shortly after my arrival,
> There happen'd in the Moon a great revival
> Of what they call the spirit of reform;
> In other words, a signal for a storm...

The dreamer quickly discovers that 'exploits of this community' have a spatial element:

> Accordingly, these Moonites, full of rancour,
> Met in a house, just like the
> CROWN AND ANCHOR;

The page is illustrated with the scene of a small tavern room (Figure 4.19). Burdett is atop the table addressing a motley bunch of reformers with tankards in hand. The imagery is reminiscent of the prints that first featured the expanding political nation with the unruly rabble of men endowed with ape-like or grotesque features—a familiar trope of artists of the 1790s who employed the technique of distorting or exaggerating the character and appearance of public figures for further satirical edge.[117]

Despite the reactionary intent of such ripostes, Donald is perhaps too quick to dismiss them as 'feeble'.[118] While they do appear to be 'lacking in penetrative power', as Rickword suggests of *The Loyal Man in the Moon*,[119] their value to the social historian lies in the sense of the political climate they also provide and of the multiple voices that could be heard in the public sphere. Juxtaposed against the originality and sophistication exemplified by Hone's work, they undoubtedly appear 'feeble' to the modern eye. They also, however, hold valuable insights into how imagery can be manipulated to produce meaning and alter identity. Take as an example the different representations of the space of the Crown and Anchor over time. Both loyalist responses depict the tavern meetings as the shadowy and intimate underground reminiscent of De Wilde's 1809 print, rather than the commanding tavern space that housed Fox in J. T. Smith's *Scene in the Crown and Anchor Tavern*. In the latter print, despite the association with political opposition, the space commands a sense of legitimacy. In the loyalist

---

117 Dickinson, *Caricatures and the Constitution 1760–1832*, p. 20.
118 Donald, *The Age of Caricature*, p. 198.
119 Rickword, *Radical Squibs and Loyal Ripostes*, p. 312.

4. Radicalism and reform at the 'Gate of Pandemonium'

ripostes, however, the depiction of a small and seedy space implies secrecy and sedition, and reinforces an image of radicalism operating on the margins of the public sphere.

Figure 4.19 'Crown and Anchor', *The Loyal Man in the Moon.*
Anon., 1820. Copyright Trustees of the British Museum

Hone's works produced such viperous responses from loyalists because of the danger inherent in their political sophistication. As Donald notes, while Hone and Cruikshank drew on the work of eighteenth-century caricaturists, Hone 'had a new and dangerous objective of indicting a political system, not simply its office holders'.[120] Hone's pamphlet changed the way satire worked. Cruikshank's illustrations were no longer the comical features of the 1790s Gillray mould.

---

120 Donald, *The Age of Caricature*, p. 198.

The ironic and often ambiguous form of the eighteenth-century print with its 'polysemic imagery', as Donald argues, 'could not serve the purposes of those bent on the conversion of public opinion to the cause of political and social reform'.[121] Radicals not only appropriated the form, they refashioned it for their own purposes, leaving the conservative responses seemingly locked in the past by revisiting the old tropes first formulated by their eighteenth-century forebears. The success of Hone's work also spoke to the growing politicisation of the plebeian classes; William M. Thackeray later recalled the 'grinning mechanics' who gathered at Hone's own shop window and who read the satires to the assembled crowd.[122] Samuel Bamford also recollected the delight with which a group of soldiers read Hone's work: 'they burst into fits of laughter.'[123]

Both Thackeray's and Bamford's observations confirm that the work of the graphic satirist was often consumed collectively. We cannot imagine that the throngs who assembled outside the shop windows in the 1790s did so in reverential or reflective silence. That people from all ranks related to and enjoyed the caricaturists' work suggests a broad cultural understanding of the symbols and imagery at the heart of graphic satire. It is clear from this survey of prints that over time, the Crown and Anchor became part of the caricaturists' palette of symbolic and political shorthand devices, which artists drew upon for the communication of their ideas. Set amongst the other (often also contested) symbols of Britishness and those of the French Revolution, the venue came to be associated with devilry, subterfuge and sedition. Beyond this, in print, it performed a function analogous to the building itself: it provided a framework, a location, a venue. The action took place at the Crown and Anchor, whether in flesh and blood, bricks and mortar or pen and ink.

Despite attempts to marginalise its radical inhabitants, the recurrence of the venue in prints of the period, as well as its early liberal Whig traditions, allowed it a prominent and legitimate place on the national political landscape. By tracing the representation of the tavern in visual culture throughout this period, it is evident that the venue was not simply an innocuous landscape backdrop to create a spatial context for prints. The venue transcended its function as a tavern; it assumed a political identity in its own right.

---

121   Ibid., p. 185.
122   William M. Thackeray, 'An Essay on the Genius of George Cruikshank', *Westminster Review*, vol. 34 (1840), pp. 6–7, quoted in Donald, *The Age of Caricature*, p. 198.
123   Samuel Bamford, *Passages in the Life of a Radical* (Oxford: Oxford University Press, 1984), p. 24.

5. 'Fresh Crown and Anchor sentiments': radical reform in the Strand, 1817–1847

Despite some caricaturists' attempts to associate the Crown and Anchor with devilry, subterfuge and sedition, the prominence of the tavern in the visual culture of the period helped ascribe it a legitimate, if not always celebrated, place on the political landscape. This is also evident in the representation of the tavern in the text-based print mediums of the early nineteenth century. If we return momentarily to Sir Francis Burdett's first victory in the Middlesex elections in 1802, when the deep-blue cavalcade brandishing 'No Bastille' banners crawled its way from Brentford to London, *The Times* report of events illuminates far more than simply the logistics of the proceedings. '*Suffice it to observe*', they wrote, 'that the motley cavalcade passed along the Strand to the Crown and Anchor Tavern where Sir Francis was met by his Committee'.[1] If the tavern had taken on its own symbolic meaning in the visual culture of the late eighteenth and early nineteenth centuries, its nomenclature also provided political commentators in the mainstream press a form of political shorthand. That Britain's leading newspaper should use the tavern as a metonymy speaks volumes both of its salience on the London political landscape and of the cultural understanding of the venue at the turn of the century.

Not only did the print culture of the period (both visual and text) help embed the cultural understanding, legitimacy and identity of the venue as a site of political opposition, it also informed the cultural and social conventions by which the space operated, or could at least be expected to operate. Peter Stallybrass and Allon White refer to the 'cultural conditions' of a space determining 'what may and may not be said, who may speak, how people may communicate and what importance must be given to what is said'.[2] By the early nineteenth century, the Crown and Anchor had been accruing such conventions for at least half a century.

How these conventions affected the radical relationship with the space in the years leading up to the 1832 *Reform Act*, and in the years immediately following, forms the overarching focus of this chapter. It examines how, by conforming to the established conventions of the Crown and Anchor, a new generation of radicals gained vital access to a venue during a period when few public spaces were available to them. In the early nineteenth century, the increasingly

---

1 *The Times*, 30 July 1802. The italics are mine.
2 Peter Stallybrass and Allon White, *The Politics and Poetics of Transgression*, quoted in James Epstein, *In Practice: Studies in the language and culture of popular politics in modern Britain* (Stanford: Stanford University Press, 2003), p. 113.

politicised (though disenfranchised) middling and plebeian classes sought a voice in the political public sphere, and this chapter explores how the Crown and Anchor—seemingly an archetypal venue of Habermas's bourgeois public sphere—accommodated the ranks of its increasingly plebeian radical tenants. Nor were the new inhabitants passive users of the space; plebeian radicals often contested and refashioned many of the conventions for their own gain. The status of the venue provided radicals an avenue through which to challenge the formal machinery of government and allowed them to fashion a collective political identity. Crucially, those excluded from formal political power found in the tavern their own locus of power—an alternative parliamentary space. By populating the venue and examining its use over time by a variety of groups, including the interactions between them, it is evident that the habitation of the public sphere was more complex than a bourgeois–plebeian binary allows.

***

Taverns such as the Crown and Anchor had existed as radical sites of public discourse, conviviality and political exchange in Britain well before the early nineteenth century. As Peter Clark reminds us, they can be traced back at least as far as the twelfth century, to be joined in the seventeenth century by the new social urban phenomenon of the coffee house; together they drew urban sociability into the public arena as never before.[3] As wine and coffee were imbibed, business was transacted, gossip exchanged and newspapers perused. The coffee house and the tavern, observes John Brewer, were involved in

> all the processes by which culture were shaped: the creation of works of art and the imagination, their communication, reception and consumption. Groups of writers, artists and performers debated their ideas and projects, criticized their friends and rivals, and penned their polemics in coffee-house booths.[4]

By drawing together the networks of the reading public, the tavern and the coffee house developed a reputation for encouraging a 'polyphony of public conversations which challenged the voice of the crown'.[5] The right to this

---

[3] Peter Clark, *The English Alehouse: A social history 1200–1830* (London: Longman, 1983). See also Brian Cowan, *The Social Life of Coffee: The emergence of the British coffeehouse* (New Haven, Conn.: Yale University Press, 2005); John Barrell, 'Coffee-house Politicians', *Journal of British Studies*, vol. 43 (2004), pp. 206–32; John Brewer, *The Pleasures of the Imagination: English culture in the eighteenth century* (London: HarperCollins, 1997), p. 34; Epstein, *In Practice*, pp. 90–105; Steve Pincus, '"Coffee Politicians Does Create": Coffeehouses and Restoration political culture', *Journal of Modern History*, vol. 67, no. 4 (1995), pp. 807–34.

[4] Brewer, *The Pleasures of the Imagination*, p. 50. John Barrell, however, warns against idealising the coffee house as an egalitarian institution, as Habermas implies, and questions 'how far distinctions of rank could possibly have been suspended in public coffee rooms'. Barrell, 'Coffee-House Politicians', p. 212.

[5] Brewer, *The Pleasures of the Imagination*, p. 37. See also E. P. Thompson, *The Making of the English Working Class* (Harmondsworth: Penguin, 1968), p. 675, who argues that 'the informal club and the tavern meeting was one part of the democratic process which had survived the repression of 1796–1806'.

exchange and dissent was also fiercely protected. In 1675, Charles II attempted to close all coffee houses, but, following a public outcry, he was forced to rescind his order and allow the venues to reopen.

The size and location of the Crown and Anchor tavern, coupled with its patronage by liberal-minded aristocratic reformers, made it a natural venue for the Whig and radical political dinners that became a key feature of tavern operations from the late eighteenth century. The phenomenon of the political dinner has received much attention from historians, including J. Ann Hone's in-depth study of London radicalism and Marc Baer's recent, more localised study of Westminster dinners, as well as broader studies focusing also on the regional incarnations of such events by Frank O'Gorman, James Epstein and Peter Brett.[6] These studies emphasise the procedures and protocols of the meetings, and how, as Brett notes, such dinners were used as a platform for Members of Parliament, providing a 'half-way house' between Westminster and broader public opinion.[7]

Baer finds continuities between the 'five quintessential types' of dinners from parties across the political spectrum. The first three typologies relate to various stages of the electoral process—where dinners were held for returning or new candidates prior to elections, during the campaign itself to rouse support and publicity, and post-electoral victory dinners. The anniversary dinner and gatherings unrelated to an election but of a political nature (such as the prison release celebrations) make up the quintuplet.[8] Despite their logistical differences, such dinners were highly ritualised affairs, and many conventions established at such events during the eighteenth century continued through the first half of the nineteenth. Hobhouse's toast to 'the People' at his liberation dinner was starkly reminiscent of those scandalous offerings for which the Duke of Norfolk was heavily censured by his King in 1798. As Epstein found with a radical dinner in Ashton in Lancashire in 1822, the Duke's toasts also had an enduring influence well beyond the walls of the Crown and Anchor and the bounds of the metropolis.[9]

Given the locale of his analysis, Baer's study reinforces the unequivocal relationship between the Crown and Anchor and key radical Whig

---

6 J. Ann Hone, *For the Cause of Truth: Radicalism in London 1796–1821* (Oxford: Clarendon, 1982); Marc Baer, 'Political Dinners in Whig, Radical and Tory Westminster, 1780–1880', *Parliamentary History*, vol. 24, no. 1 (2005), pp. 183–206; Peter Brett, 'Political Dinners in Early Nineteenth-Century Britain: Platform, meeting place and battleground', *History*, vol. 81, no. 264 (1996), pp. 527–52; James Epstein, *Radical Expression: Political language, ritual, and symbol in England, 1790–1850* (Oxford: Oxford University Press, 1994), pp. 147–65; Frank O'Gorman, 'Campaign Rituals and Ceremonies: The social meaning of elections in England, 1780–1860', *Past and Present*, vol. 135 (1992), pp. 79–115.
7 Brett, 'Political Dinners in Early Nineteenth-Century Britain', p. 547.
8 Baer, 'Political Dinners in Whig, Radical and Tory Westminster', p. 186.
9 Epstein, *Radical Expression*, pp. 154–8. As Baer also observes, the recurrence of the toast suggests that 'the nexus between patrician and plebeian politicians has been underestimated'. Baer, 'Political Dinners in Whig, Radical and Tory Westminster', p. 192.

parliamentarians involved with the Westminster constituency such as Charles James Fox and, later, Sir Francis Burdett. After Burdett switched to the seat of Westminster, the tavern was the pre-eminent venue for meetings of electors in the lead-up to election campaigns, and for subsequent electoral victory processions during his long parliamentary career. By 1820, Burdett was still being 'chaired' through the streets of London—not to Parliament, but to the Crown and Anchor.[10]

The prints examined in the previous chapter suggest that in the minds of some commentators at least, an increasingly plebeian, strident and 'disloyal' radical clientele had begun to occupy the building, but Baer's reading of the political dinners suggests the opposite; he points to a shift in the political milieu and contends that by the 1820s 'this contentious political machine in the most significant political centre in the nation was at its heart less radical than moderate, whiggish or loyal'.[11] Yet as Baer notes, the political dinner required the purchase of a ticket, and as such excluded many plebeian radicals. Although 'Whiggish' and 'moderate' elements undoubtedly continued at the tavern throughout the early nineteenth century, a broader sweep of political gatherings reveals that activity at the Crown and Anchor extended well beyond the extra-parliamentary affairs of those already embraced by formal political power and supports the case for viewing the venue as an integral part of radical culture for more than half a century.

The sense of a widening political nation at the Crown and Anchor was reflected, as we have seen, in visual culture at the turn of the nineteenth century. If we return briefly to the loyalist ripostes spawned by William Hone's brilliant political satire, we find that the shift in purpose and milieu at the venue was clearly apparent by 1820. In *The Loyal Man in the Moon*, the narrator of the parody discovers to his horror that a venue 'just like the Crown and Anchor' was operating on Lunaria. The function of the venue was clear to the narrator, for here, in this parallel Lunar tavern,

> it was resolv'd, by this committee
> To hold a meeting, somewhere in the city,
> To which all sorts of folks should be invited,
> To see, as they declar'd, 'the people righted;'[12]

---

10   See, for example, *The Times*, 14 July 1818.
11   Baer, 'Political Dinners in Whig, Radical and Tory Westminster', p. 196.
12   *The Loyal Man in the Moon* (London, 1820), reproduced in Edgell Rickword, *Radical Squibs and Loyal Ripostes: Satirical pamphlets of the Regency period, 1819–1821* (London: Redwood Press, 1971), pp. 107–34.

With the ascension of the dazzling orator Henry Hunt on the radical London scene, the issue of universal male suffrage to see 'the people righted' entered Crown and Anchor dialogue.[13]

Moreover, under Hunt's tutelage, those excluded from the formal machinery of government found in the venue their own locus of power. The tavern's long-established political and parliamentary-like culture provided the ceremony, formality and legitimacy reminiscent of the parliamentary space. At meetings, a chair was invariably appointed, resolutions were debated and speakers took turns to address the audience, who, in turn, verbalised their approval ('hear hear') or disapproval. According to Hunt, however, there was a crucial difference between the operations of the official centre of political power and those of the Crown and Anchor. When he addressed his supporters in the tavern in 1819, Hunt spoke directly to a constituency excluded from formal political power and he sought to unsettle the convention that saw the parliamentary elite take centre stage on the Crown and Anchor platform. Though entry to the meetings sometimes involved the purchase of a ticket (in order to pay for the hire of the room), Hunt assured 'every man that had paid for his ticket' that they were 'as much entitled to address them as he or any other friend of universal suffrage who at that moment happened to be in the room'.[14] If the voice of the people was excluded from Whitehall, radicals could argue that it could be heard resonating through the walls and corridors of the Crown and Anchor.

The status of the tavern as an analogue to Parliament is particularly evident in the choice of the Crown and Anchor for meetings of national assemblies of plebeian reformers. In January 1817, several newspapers reported on a meeting of '[d]elegates from various Petitioning Bodies in Great Britain, for Reform in Parliament', which met at the Crown and Anchor.[15] Delegates travelled from small and large towns across England, including Bristol, Norwich, Middleton, Lynn, Manchester, Lancashire and Liverpool. Radical luminary Major Cartwright stood in as the delegate for Glasgow, Scotland's radical stronghold.[16] Before starting the meeting, the delegates from Westminster—Hunt, William Cobbett and Mr Brooks[17]—ceremoniously received 'vouchers' from each of

---

13 See *The Triumphal Entry of Henry Hunt Esq. into London on Monday September 13, 1819…A full report of the speeches at the Crown and Anchor* (London, 1819). On Henry Hunt, see John Belchem, *'Orator' Hunt: Henry Hunt and English working-class radicalism* (Oxford: Clarendon Press, 1985).
14 *The Times*, 14 September 1819.
15 *Morning Chronicle*, 24 January 1817; *The Times*, 24 January 1817; *Leeds Mercury*, 25 January 1817.
16 On Major John Cartwright, see F. D. Cartwright (ed.), *The Life and Correspondence of Major Cartwright* (1826; reprinted, New York: A. M. Kelley, 1969) 2 vols; Rachel Eckersley, 'Of Radical Design: John Cartwright and the redesign of the reform campaign, c.1800–1811', *History*, vol. 89, no. 296 (2004), pp. 560–80; John Osborne, *John Cartwright* (Cambridge: Cambridge University Press, 1972).
17 This is likely to have been Samuel Brooks, the veteran Westminster reformer. See Alice Prochaska, 'Brooks, Samuel', in Joseph Baylen and Norbert Gossman (eds), *Biographical Dictionary of Modern British Radicals* [hereafter *BDMBR*] (Sussex: Harvester Press, 1979), vol. 1, pp. 65–6; Iowerth Prothero, *Artisans and Politics in Early Nineteenth-Century London, John Gast and his Times* (Kent: Dawson, 1979), pp. 74, 108–9.

the country delegates entitling them to represent the reformers of their towns. The representatives of the regional areas had assembled at the request of Major Cartwright and Jones Burdett (brother of Sir Francis) as representatives of the Hampden Club, a network of reform groups initiated by Cartwright to advance the cause of parliamentary reform.[18] Cartwright and Jones Burdett had been deputed by the Hampden Club to

> lay before the assembled delegates of the petitioning bodies of the country in favour of reform, the heads of a bill for that measure, which it was intended in March next to lay before the whole body of that society, previous to its being submitted to Parliament.[19]

The Hampden Club members were generally regarded as moderate middle-class reformers and the bill reflected their temperate approach to parliamentary reform. The bill declared that members of the House of Commons should be elected by householders; that the counties and cities be divided into electoral districts, with each district returning one member; and that elections should be conducted annually.

The Crown and Anchor meeting debated and discussed the three tenets of the resolution for hours. Finally, they rejected the notion of limiting suffrage to householders (owners of property), voting by a majority to instead support Hunt's resolution for universal male suffrage. Buoyed by his success, Hunt pressed further. Despite vocal opposition from Cobbett, he convinced the meeting to support vote by ballot, which was also carried. With two blows against moderate reform measures, the more radical members of the meeting pushed on. The delegate from Manchester, Mr Mitchell, launched the third strike when his proposal that 'property ought form no part of a Member of Parliament's qualifications' as 'virtue and talents were sufficient' was carried by a 'considerable majority'. The democratic processes in the Crown and Anchor altered the original proposal to such a degree that the meeting agreed to omit any reference whatsoever to the Hampden Club in the bill.

Whether Cartwright or Jones Burdett anticipated the strength of the venue's radical temper is unclear, as is their reaction to the viperous attack on the club launched by Cobbett. Though he held the individual members of the club such as Cartwright and the Burdetts in the 'highest regard', Cobbett nevertheless

---

18 For a discussion of the Hampden Club, and this meeting in particular, see Samuel Bamford, *Passages in the Life of a Radical* (1884; reprinted, Oxford: Oxford University Press, 1984), chs 1 and 3; Thompson, *The Making of the English Working Class*, pp. 691–710; Naomi C. Miller, 'Major John Cartwright and the Forming of the Hampden Club', *Historical Journal*, vol. 17, no. 3 (1974), pp. 615–19. In this, her second paper on Cartwright, Miller claims that both she and other historians mistakenly attributed Cartwright a founding role in the Hampden Club, which he did not join until 1813, after which time he did become a leading figure. She attributes the founding role to Cartwright's friend Thomas Northmore.
19 *The Times*, 24 January 1817.

insisted that 'there was not, if it were possible to describe them, a body of the dirtiest scavengers in England that he could more sincerely despise than that very society in its collective capacity'.[20] Despite these obvious hostilities (which others at the meeting shared with Cobbett), the key point in this episode is that the Hampden Club sought approval for its reform bill first within the Crown and Anchor meeting. The Hampden Club clearly considered that the sanction of those gathered at the tavern was crucial to the endorsement of the club as a leading exponent of reform in the country and a way of legitimising the submission of the Bill to Parliament. The people's parliament, however, would have none of it unless the moderates in the Hampden Club embraced more sweeping and much deeper political change.

The meeting produced a swift reaction from *The Times*. 'Ill friends are they to parliamentary reform', they chastised, 'who adopt such a course as this'.[21] The newspaper was most concerned that it was 'not aware till after the event had taken place' that the group had assembled. Taking issue with the 'secrecy' of the event, they questioned the representative nature of a group who met in that same 'dark, suspicious, and irresponsible manner' by which they had proposed parliamentary members be chosen—'that is, by ballot'. Significantly, then, even *The Times* now expected the Crown and Anchor to operate as an open and accessible part of the public sphere. They viewed amended resolutions as too extreme for the good of the country, charging the group with 'endeavouring, so far as in them lies, not only to overthrow the constitution directly and openly, but to subvert the very nature and habits of Englishmen'.

Although the use of the tavern in this fashion might point to, as Habermas contends, plebeian activity as mere mimicry of the bourgeois sphere, the events themselves, and the response to them from the mainstream public press, suggest otherwise. The strength of *The Times*' opposition suggests that the meeting's resolutions were out of step with what might be expected at the venue, and perhaps that the extreme views of the group might have gained some credibility from the venue itself—making it a dangerous, though powerful force in the testing political climate of the early nineteenth century. Though the Crown and Anchor's new plebeian tenants were in many ways conforming to the established cultural conventions of the venue, they evidently were prepared to challenge its politics and refashion the space for their own political purposes.

Domestic parliamentary reform was the central goal of Britain's radicals in the early decades of the nineteenth century, but a survey of Crown and Anchor meetings reveals that the focus of its tenants was not entirely insular. Many meetings convened at the tavern at this time had a strong international

---

20   Ibid.
21   Ibid.

perspective, and many gatherings were held in support of revolutionary activity abroad. In October 1820, for example, '300 persons of respectability' met at the tavern for the purpose of 'celebrating the revolutions in Naples, Spain and Portugal'.[22] Large meetings were held in 1823 to discuss ways to assist the independence movement in Greece, and during the 1840s thousands gathered to voice their support for the revolutionaries in Poland.[23]

The adoption of the Crown and Anchor as an alternative parliamentary space and outlet for the plebeian voice in the foreign affairs of the nation is perhaps most clearly evident in a meeting convened in early June 1823. Hunt organised the meeting to voice support of the 'brave Spaniards in the glorious struggle against the united tyrants of Europe'.[24] He advised the tavern delegates of his wish to invite the Spanish Ambassador, for, 'as the aristocracy of the country had assembled to express its opinion on the unprincipled invasion of Spain by France', he considered it 'expedient' that the people should also assemble 'for the same purpose'. Hunt clearly stamped the Parliament, as presently constituted, as an outlet for the voice of the aristocracy. It was the Crown and Anchor that provided a channel for the voice of the people.

As this episode reveals, proceedings at the tavern did not occur in isolation to those operating nearby at Whitehall. As Leslie Mitchell notes in her biography of Charles James Fox, 'geography allowed Westminster to press on the nerve of politics'; so too, the Crown and Anchor.[25] The two political spaces intersected on many occasions throughout the period. With the return of a number of more radical MPs to Parliament, the inflammatory content of the speeches and conduct of the radical members at the Crown and Anchor often found their way into the parliamentary record, when members were called upon to explain their actions or were castigated for their participation in tavern events. One case in point is the furore that stemmed from a dinner in May 1810, held to celebrate the release of Burdett from the Tower, following his vocal opposition to John Gale Jones's own imprisonment in the Coldbath Fields House of Correction. Samuel Whitbread, a Whig MP, attended the dinner but was sharply criticised by fellow Whig J. C. Curwen for his participation:

---

22 *Morning Chronicle*, 3 October 1820.
23 *Leeds Mercury*, 17 May 1823; *Morning Chronicle*, 16 May 1823. The tavern also hosted meetings of the Peoples' International League in the late 1840s. See the pamphlets: *The Report of the 14th Anniversary of the Polish Revolution: Celebrated at the Crown and Anchor tavern, on 29th November 1844* (London, 1845); *Report of a Public Meeting, held at the Crown and Anchor Tavern, Strand, on Monday, November 15, 1847, 'to explain the principles and objects of the Peoples' International League'* (London, 1847).
24 *The Times*, 3 June 1823.
25 Leslie G. Mitchell, *Charles James Fox* (Oxford: Oxford University Press, 1992), p. 34.

It was not to the inflammatory proceedings of a drunken meeting in a tavern that he looked for the opinion of the people. He abhorred such meetings, and lamented that men of character, talents and respectability should be found to countenance them.[26]

Although Whitbread defended the venue as a legitimate outlet of the voice of the people, the censure clearly had effect.[27] With the tantalising (though momentary) promise of the Whigs' return to government in 1811, Whitbread is reported to have distanced himself from the venue in preparation for a possible ascendancy to the Whig leadership.[28] As it was, the Whigs were to wait almost two decades for the opportunity.

The intersection of Crown and Anchor politics with events at Whitehall is further illustrated during the volatile events of October 1831. The early years of the 1830s were potent times throughout Britain and with the election of the Whigs to office came the tantalising promise of political change with the proposed *Reform Act*, based in no small measure on the original resolution of the Hampden Club. Like that proposal, the Whigs' *Reform Act* fell well short of universal male suffrage and caused deep divisions among radicals.[29] The refusal of the House of Lords to concede even partial reform, however, inflamed the disenfranchised. On news of the rejection, *The Times* despaired, 'What have the Lords *done*?'[30] The country convulsed with resentment and widespread rioting and unrest followed. Several of the Lords who voted against the Act had their homes attacked by incensed Londoners.

Lest there be no reform at all, many disparate radical voices united in support of a bill that promised to extend the franchise to only a limited number of the adult male population. As news of the rejection of the Act spread, the Crown and Anchor tavern became the focal point of metropolitan anger. 'Immense numbers' gathered in the Strand and the building was bursting with people,

---

26 *Parliamentary Debates*, 4 May 1809, p. 379, quoted in Michael Roberts, *The Whig Party 1807–1812* (London: Macmillan, 1939), p. 249. See also Baer, 'Political Dinners in Whig, Radical and Tory Westminster', p. 194. On Curwen, see J. V. Beckett, 'Curwen, John Christian (1756–1828)', *Oxford Dictionary of National Biography*, <http://www.oxforddnb.com/view/article/37334> (hereafter *ODNB*).

27 Roberts, *The Whig Party 1807–1812*, p. 249.

28 Ibid., p. 324. It was not the first time that Whitbread avoided a Crown and Anchor meeting for fear of political retribution. He reportedly approved of the motions of the Great Reform Dinner meeting in May 1809, but declined to attend as he considered it would be held against him. See *Morning Chronicle*, 6 May 1809. See also Roger Fulford, *Samuel Whitbread, 1764–1815: A study in opposition* (London: Macmillan, 1967), p. 252.

29 There are many works that focus on the radical involvement with the agitation over the *Reform Act*. Take, for example, Philip Harling, 'Parliament, the State, and "Old Corruption"', in Arthur Burns and Joanne Innes (eds), *Rethinking the Age of Reform, Britain 1780–1850* (Cambridge: Cambridge University Press, 2003), pp. 98–113; Nancy LoPatin, *Political Unions, Popular Politics and the Great* Reform Act *of 1832* (Basingstoke: Macmillan, 1999); Belchem, *'Orator' Hunt*, pp. 221–69; D. J. Rowe, 'Class and Political Radicalism in London, 1831–2', *Historical Journal*, vol. 13, no. 1 (1970), pp. 31–47; Prothero, *Artisans and Politics in Early Nineteenth-Century London*, pp. 268–99.

30 *The Times*, 10 October 1831.

with one observer noting that the ground floor was so full that a 'stranger would have supposed the meeting was there'.[31] The same was true on the next floor, 'all the way up the staircase to the great room'. Those unable to bear the pressure of the overcrowding were forced to leave the building so that 'two streams—one of ingress, the other of egress—were constantly flowing' from the building.

As those excluded from political power rallied at the Crown and Anchor, the Prime Minister, Earl Grey, held crisis talks with his Whig parliamentary colleagues.[32] The events of the evening of 12 October 1831 illustrate the connections between the two spaces of political power. After dining at the home of a fellow Whig MP, the Prime Minister returned in his carriage to Downing Street about 11 pm. Shortly before Earl Grey's arrival, a group of 13 men led by radical stalwart Francis Place confronted the Prime Minister's doorman. Place demanded that his delegation from the tavern receive an audience with the Prime Minister to discuss the state of unrest in the metropolis and the stalled reform agenda. With images of the French Revolution still so vivid in the collective memory of Britain's ruling elite and with domestic discontent percolating, Place's entourage would surely have caused some trepidation at Downing Street. Nevertheless, Grey agreed to meet with the delegation that evening.

The attention that Place's group received in the conservative press at the time illustrates the importance of exploring the connections between the physical structures of the public sphere and popular radical culture. Even though its editor had little regard for the politics of the reforming Prime Minister, the conservative *Courier* newspaper saluted Grey for his courage and poise in meeting with the group at such a late hour and on such short notice. For all the Prime Minister knew, the *Courier* columnist censured, the Crown and Anchor entourage could have been 'a deputation from the Rotunda revolutionists…and reserve, or even rudeness, on the part of the noble Earl would hardly have warranted surprise'.[33]

The term 'Rotunda revolutionists' emanated from the Blackfriars Road Rotunda—a building that became another locus of popular political activity in the early 1830s (and to which we will return later in the book). Under the control of indomitable radical Richard Carlile, the building became home to a diverse array of radical voices. It was the first time London radicals had a building *controlled* by members of the radical movement; it was a space of and for their own.[34] Despite reports of many respectable attendees at Carlile's seditious

---

31 See *Morning Chronicle*, 9 October 1831.
32 On Earl Grey, see E. A. Smith, 'Charles, Second Earl Grey and the House of Lords', in R. W. Davis (ed.), *Lords of Parliament Studies, 1714–1914* (Stanford: Stanford University Press, 1995), p. 79; John W. Derry, *Charles, Earl Grey: Aristocratic reformer* (Oxford: Blackwell, 1992).
33 *Courier*, 14 October 1831.
34 For further analysis of the role of the Rotunda in radical culture, see Chapters 6–8 of this study.

and blasphemous Rotunda events, the use of the building as the headquarters of the National Union of the Working Classes (NUWC) saw the site become synonymous with working-class radicalism: the unstable, unpredictable 'other', Edmund Burke's 'swinish multitude'. The *Courier* columnist was drawing on the collective understanding of the two venues when he chose to juxtapose Place's group from the Crown and Anchor with the potential threat had the delegation indeed emanated from the Rotunda. While it had operated for only a brief period as a radical venue, the Rotunda quickly established an identity as a space seething with revolutionary possibility. The powerful imagery associated with the venue allowed radicals drawn to the Rotunda to define themselves and their politics with their space and many wore the term 'Rotundanist' as a badge of honour. Space was again being employed as political shorthand.

For others, including Francis Place, the Rotunda men smacked of the unrestrained, unrespectable 'mob' elements of popular radicalism. 'Most of these men were loud and long talkers', wrote Place, and were 'vehement, resolute reckless rascals whose purpose was riot as providing an opportunity for plunder'.[35] Radical politics at this time was racked by what a contemporary observer described as 'the everlasting splittings and factions of the Londoners'.[36] So when Place could not badge his group with an organisational or an ideological tag because of these differences, the institutional label of the Crown and Anchor, like that of the Rotunda, provided the unifying and codifying banner for the delegation.

The throngs who assembled at the Crown and Anchor the evening before Place's mission to Downing Street were not the unruly mobs Place generally associated with the threat of riot and revolution at the Rotunda. *The Times* considered the meeting on 11 October as the 'most remarkable' of 'all the great political meetings held at the Crown and Anchor for these 40 years past'.[37] This was due not only to the sheer number who turned out, but primarily to the respectable appearance and conduct of the crowd. The more extreme tenets of radicalism that emanated from the Rotunda were a direct affront to a newly evolving moral code—from which a radical movement struggling for a place in the hegemonic order was not immune. For these radicals, the Crown and Anchor allowed for a safer public expression of their political dissent. In adopting the tavern nomenclature, the members of Place's delegation clearly and firmly located themselves within the radical political spectrum. They were at once distancing themselves from the unrespectable milieu of the Rotunda while at the same time drawing upon the collective cultural understanding and political legacy of the tavern. Despite sustained attempts to blacken those associated with the venue in both visual and text-based print culture, it nevertheless retained an identity as

---

35 Francis Place Papers, Add. Ms. 27791, ff. 47–57.
36 *White Hat*, 16 October 1819.
37 *The Times*, 11 October 1831.

a venue for respectable political dissent and the promulgation of reform through established means and processes. In this light, the willingness of the 'noble Earl' to meet with the delegation is clearer: by presenting the group as a Crown and Anchor delegation, Place had signalled to Earl Grey that his group did not pose a physical threat.[38] The tavern was, after all, familiar ground for the Earl from his early political life.[39]

From this episode it is evident that in adopting the Crown and Anchor as an alternative parliamentary space, more moderate and middling radicals could unite under its banner. Like the official seat of power, however, it also offered an outlet for an array of political voices. That Place's group unified more moderate voices under the Crown and Anchor nomenclature is not to suggest that the tavern itself was always a site of radical harmony and unity. Certainly, by the time Francis Place led his delegation to Downing Street in October 1831, the Crown and Anchor had become a locus for 'respectable' popular radicalism. But the Rotunda had opened as a radical venue only a year earlier and before this the Crown and Anchor often witnessed dissenting voices of rival radical groups—divisions based both on personality and on class and ideological lines.

If we return momentarily to the earlier decades of the century, we can see the seeds of class discontent in radical London's response to the turbulent events at Peterloo. The deaths and injuries occasioned by the attempt of the yeomanry to disperse the reform meeting caused outrage in many quarters of Britain. Radical groups sought to harness the popular fury by raising funds to support those injured or imprisoned, and focused largely on Hunt as the leading orator at Peterloo. In early September 1819, *The Times* reported a meeting of a group calling themselves the 'Westminster Committee of 200' who had met at the Crown and Anchor to determine the best way to distribute the funds that had been raised for those injured or arrested at Peterloo.[40] Those assembled included prominent metropolitan radicals such as Richard Carlile, Thomas Evans and his son, Thomas John Evans.[41] Arriving late to the meeting, Alexander Galloway

---

38   Place was not always concerned with ensuring the authorities recognised the radicals' peaceful agenda. As Paul Pickering notes, Place and other early nineteenth-century reformers, drawing on the philosophies of Utilitarian James Mill, invoked the threat of violence as a means of realising political reform. See Paul A. Pickering, '"Peaceably if We Can, Forcibly if We Must": Political violence and insurrection in early-Victorian Britain', in B. Bowden (ed.), *Terror: From tyrannicide to terrorism in Europe, 1605–2005* (St Lucia: University of Queensland Press, 2008), pp. 114–33. For a detailed account of Mill and the 'language of menace', see Joseph Hamburger, *James Mill and the Art of Revolution* (New Haven, Conn.: Yale University Press, 1963), especially pp. 48–96.
39   As an example, see his speech at the Crown and Anchor in Thomas Erskine, *Declaration of the Friends of the Liberty of the Press, Assembled at the Crown and Anchor Tavern, Saturday, January 19, 1793* (London, 1793), pp. 14–15.
40   *The Times*, 9 September 1819.
41   On the Evanses' participation in early nineteenth-century radicalism, and specifically the ultra-radical Spencean set, see Iain McCalman, *Radical Underworld: Prophets, revolutionaries and pornographers in London, 1795–1840* (Cambridge: Cambridge University Press, 1988), passim; Thompson, *The Making of the English Working Class*, especially pp. 177–91.

apologised for his tardiness, explaining that he had found that another radical committee, including Dr Watson, John Gale Jones, Arthur Thistlewood, Samuel Waddington and Thomas Preston, had assembled 'under the same roof' to take into consideration the 'self same question'.[42]

The meeting agreed to adjourn to enable Galloway to consult with the rival group over the best means to defray the funds that had been raised. The 'Westminster Committee of 200' met again on 8 September to discuss the outcome. A letter from the rival group, who had since removed themselves from the Crown and Anchor to the White Lion Tavern, was read to the meeting. It was clear that despite Galloway's endeavours, they continued to advance their plans alone. While the White Lion group acknowledged that the Westminster Committee of 200 had met for 'similar purposes', it went on to document arrangements already in place for a 'triumphal procession' to welcome Hunt back to London, including consigning flags of silk to the painter for 'suitable inscriptions' to be placed on them. The booking of the Great Room of the Crown and Anchor for the reception provided a sharp sting in the tail. 'The effects which were produced upon different members of the Committee', *The Times* jeered, 'convinced us there were some shades of difference in the political views of the Reformers assembled'.[43]

Resolution after resolution followed, as Galloway's Crown and Anchor group scrambled to regain control of radical London's response to this seminal event. After much discussion on the propriety of organising a mass procession, it was decided that a deputation be sent to meet with the White Lion group. After half an hour, they returned to the Crown and Anchor and, according to *The Times*, reported favourably on the plans that Thistlewood's group had in place.[44] *The Times* recorded that the Crown and Anchor group then passed a resolution declaring their intention of 'co-operating with Messrs. Watson and Co'. Sardonically, the editor continued that

---

42 On Alexander Galloway, veteran of the 1790s radical movement, machine-maker and engineer, see McCalman, *Radical Underworld*, esp. pp. 9–21, 108–12, 125–35; Hone, *For the Cause of Truth*. On Dr James Watson, veteran ultra-radical and surgeon, see McCalman, *Radical Underworld*, pp. 104–40; T. M. Parssinen, 'The Revolutionary Party in London, 1816–20', *Bulletin of the Institute of Historical Research*, vol. 45 (1972), pp. 266–82. On Thistlewood, ultra-radical and future leader of the Cato Street conspirators, see Prothero, *Artisans and Politics in Early Nineteenth-Century London*, esp. pp. 89–133; John Milsome, 'Arthur Thistlewood and the Cato Street Conspiracy', *Contemporary Review*, vol. 217 (1970), pp. 151–4; David Johnson, *Regency Revolution: The case of Arthur Thistlewood* (Compton Chamberlayne, UK: Compton Russell, 1974). On Thomas Preston, London-born shoemaker and member of the Spencean underground, see Prothero, *Artisans and Politics in Early Nineteenth-Century London*, esp. pp. 90–127; McCalman, *Radical Underworld*, pp. 19–20, 43–6, 106–32.
43 *The Times*, 9 September 1819.
44 Ibid.

[s]o eager were they to show that they were in earnest, they absolutely adjourned from the place in which they were sitting to the White Lion, in order to extend their fraternal embrace to their brothers in reform who were there assembled.[45]

The happiest member of the group was undoubtedly the landlord of the White Lion Tavern.

Despite the derision of *The Times*, the rival groups never really achieved this level of cooperation. While the *Examiner* referred to the events of the next evening as a 'foolish dispute' between the two radical parties, *The Times* offered a detailed report with the headline 'Rupture Among the Radicals', following a joint meeting of the two groups at the Crown and Anchor.[46] The 'Ultras' from the White Lion, it reported, took the chair of the meeting, offending Galloway and his party, who 'considered it no less than a usurpation of the very post they themselves occupied the former evening'. The *Morning Chronicle* reported that the White Lion 'junto' were 'far more formidable' and declined to report the meeting in detail as 'to describe what followed would be impossible'.[47] *The Times*, however, delighted in recounting the events. A great fracas ensued; the White Lion members determined to proceed with the procession and the Crown and Anchor radicals equally determined to oppose the plan. They feared that such a crowd assembled, so soon after Peterloo, might arm 'their foes with weapons furnished by imprudence or misconduct'. According to *The Times*, the meeting descended into disarray. It reported the surprise of the Crown and Anchor group 'that a deputation of 5 persons from an unknown body, should presume to dictate to, or alter the fixed determination of a recognized Committee, acting under the known confidence of Mr Hunt'.[48]

The editor advised readers that they were unable to report the outcome of the meeting, for

> at about one o'clock, we left the party contending who should pay for the room…Mr Waddington swore he'd be d——d if they should pay, for 'they *v*ere in*w*ited'. Others said they had elected their own Chairman, and proceeding in their own way, had made themselves responsible. In this way they fought on.

Despite concluding that 'want of rest compelled us to retire from the contest', the 'trifling, squabbling, penniless boobies' at the centre of the fray would continue to entertain the readers of the press for the rest of the week.

---

45   *Morning Chronicle*, 10 September 1819.
46   *Examiner*, 12 September 1819; *The Times*, 11 September 1819.
47   *Morning Chronicle*, 11 September 1819.
48   *The Times*, 11 September 1819. See also *Morning Chronicle*, 11 September 1819.

Notwithstanding the condescension of the mainstream press, the divisions and rivalry between the two groups had a strong ideological basis. The White Lion group represented the more extreme elements of radicalism, some of whom considered physical force a legitimate means to reform the political system. Just eight months after these meetings, Thistlewood would be executed alongside his fellow Cato Street conspirators.[49] There was also, however, a class element to the division. When Carlile, Evans and Galloway were deputed to meet with the White Lion group, they discovered 'men of intelligent minds, but evidently and unfortunately depressed by poverty'.[50] When *The Times* taunted, on 13 September, that the scene had become a case of '"White Lion versus Crown and Anchor" or "Fast versus feast"', they were referring to a dispute between the price of the planned dinner at the Crown and Anchor—the White Lion group opting for a cheaper dinner in order to allow Hunt's less wealthy supporters to join the occasion. Galloway reported going 'below stairs' to find the rival committee—a fitting architectural metaphor for the hierarchical class divisions that dogged the popular radical movement as much as wider British society in this period.[51]

What both this episode and the events surrounding the rejection of the *Reform Act* in 1831 reveal is that different radical groups and their disenfranchised supporters aligned their ideology and identity strongly with physical spaces. Despite a week of mocking the rival radical groups vying for Hunt's procession honours, even *The Times* was forced to concede the immense success of Hunt's procession: 'there was never an assembly of persons…conducted in so peaceable a manner; and we never before saw any where the proportion of the middling, and we might add the upper classes of society was so great.'[52] In the face of a potential overthrow by the more threatening White Lion milieu, the sigh of relief from *The Times* is almost palpable. The established cultural and political conventions of operation at the Crown and Anchor had been upheld.

In the case of the 1831 Reform crisis, radical leaders could use the Crown and Anchor to entice 'respectable' working-class radicals away from the maelstrom

---

49   The Cato Street conspiracy involved an attempt in 1820 to assassinate British cabinet ministers and overthrow the government by ultra-radicals, led by Arthur Thistlewood and guided by agent provocateur, the Home Office spy George Edwards. See G. T. Wilkinson, *An Authentic History of the Cato Street Conspiracy* (London, 1820); Robert Shaw, *Cato Street* (London: Chatto and Windus, 1972); Iain McCalman, 'Ultra-Radicalism and Convivial Debating-Clubs in London, 1795–1838', *English Historical Review*, vol. 102, no. 403 (1987), pp. 309–33; Milsome, 'Arthur Thistlewood and the Cato Street Conspiracy'; Johnson, *Regency Revolution*.
50   *The Times*, 11 September 1819.
51   This is not to suggest that radicalism was divided along strict class demarcations. Many radicals saw a benefit of eliminating distinctions between the working classes or middle classes, preferring a coalition of the 'useful' or 'productive' classes in their campaign for social and political reform.
52   *The Times*, 14 September 1819. The *Morning Chronicle*, 14 September 1819, reported that 'such a crowd was never before seen in London'.

of the Blackfriars Road Rotunda. Following the rejection of the *Reform Act*, Burdett and Place moved quickly to establish a National Political Union with its headquarters at the Crown and Anchor.[53] It was to be a union that would break

> through the trammels of caste to associate for the common interest in a common cause'; a union 'not of the working classes, nor of the middle classes, nor of any other class; but of all reformers,—of the masses, and the millions.[54]

The National Political Union endeavoured to encourage the establishment of branch unions in the various wards and parishes of London with the Crown and Anchor providing the central office.

Although the National Political Union was reported to have signed some 'respectable "working" men' to its ranks, it failed to convince the Rotunda stalwarts to unite with them. The failure of the short-lived National Political Union is due in large part to the deep suspicion and resentment of working-class radicals at their exclusion from the extension of the franchise proposed in the *Reform Act*. If class tensions had been simmering within the tavern environment throughout the first three decades of the century, the passage of the *Reform Act* in 1832 would bring the issue of class even further to the fore.[55]

* * *

The strong association of the Crown and Anchor radicals with support of the *Reform Act* as an interim measure did not signal the end of the tavern's radical political associations. There was a discernible lull in political activity at the tavern in the wake of the tumultuous events of 1832, as many of the Crown and Anchor's middling population retired from public political agitation, content with their own political success. The few meetings held over the ensuing 18 months, however, reveal a radical movement regrouping. The tavern soon became, once again, a key metropolitan venue for the disenfranchised. In December 1832, a meeting of Middlesex electors was held in the Great Room of the tavern to discuss the best means to ensure the return of Joseph Hume to Parliament. Hume, who had begun his parliamentary life as a Tory, was now

---

53 For a discussion of the National Political Union, see Rowe, 'Class and Political Radicalism in London', pp. 31–47; Prothero, *Artisans and Politics in Early Nineteenth-Century London*, pp. 287–311; Hamburger, *James Mill and the Art of Revolution*, pp. 77–87, 126–31; Dudley Miles, *Francis Place, The Life of a Remarkable Radical 1771–1854* (Brighton: Harvester, 1988), pp. 184–234.
54 *The Times*, 5 November 1831. See also *Poor Man's Guardian*, 5 November 1831; *Examiner*, 6 November 1831.
55 Thousands of men were now newly enfranchised, but the property qualifications of the Act ensured that vast numbers of the working class remained excluded from the franchise. E. P. Thompson's remains one of the best accounts of working-class reaction to the passing of the Reform Bill. Thompson, *The Making of the English Working Class*, pp. 888–909.

one of the staunchest advocates of universal male suffrage in the Parliament.[56] In the crowded Crown and Anchor meeting, he vowed to continue the fight to see the extension of the franchise, to realise vote by ballot and 'every measure to secure and extend civil and religious liberty'. His pledge was met with rapturous applause.[57] With only limited enfranchisement eventually delivered by the *Reform Act*, the tavern remained, as the lunar man in the moon envisaged 20 years earlier, a venue dedicated to seeing the 'people righted'.

As Hume was enthusiastically greeted on the tavern platform, former Crown and Anchor personalities began to fade from the venue. Hunt, who lost favour at the tavern during 1830–31 with his vocal opposition to the *Reform Act*, remained an impassioned supporter of universal male suffrage, but lost his seat of Preston in the 1833 election, and died of a stroke just two years after retiring to private life.[58] Hobhouse's involvement with the Crown and Anchor was cut short with his sudden shift away from radical reform. He was quickly ostracised by his old radical colleagues as he refused to pledge his support for the further extension of the franchise. Reform had consolidated the Whigs in power, and Hobhouse moved from outsider to political insider. Even as late as 1847, Hobhouse's betrayal had not been forgotten by a new generation of Crown and Anchor radicals. That year, celebrating the return of radical members to Parliament, Irish Chartist MP Feargus O'Connor revelled in his electoral victory over the old Crown and Anchor luminary. Hobhouse's only chance to remain in politics, O'Connor maintained, would be a seat in the House of Lords:

> If asked what Chartism could do, he answered it could do as much as the Queen, for it had made a peer of Sir J. C. Hobhouse. (Laughter) Thus it appeared that to lose the confidence of the people was to acquire fitness for companionship with the pantalooned old women of the House of Lords.[59]

The tavern's most prominent sage of the nineteenth century, Sir Francis Burdett, was also fast losing favour. Despite being imprisoned twice for his support of other radicals, gaining kudos for initiating the public agitation against the cruelties of Coldbath Fields House of Correction and generally championing the radical cause for three decades, his support of the *Reform Act* as a final settlement saw him denigrated in the working-class radical press as 'Sir Francis the Apostate'.[60]

---

56   On Joseph Hume, radical and politician, see Valerie E. Chancellor, *The Political Life of Joseph Hume, 1777–1855* (London: V. Chancellor, c. 1986); Ronald K. Huch and Paul R. Ziegler, *Joseph Hume, the People's MP* (Philadelphia: Diane Publishing, 1985).
57   *The Times*, 9 December 1832.
58   On Hunt's later years, see Belchem, *'Orator' Hunt*, pp. 270–5.
59   *Douglas Jerrold's Weekly Newspaper*, 30 October 1847.
60   *Working Man's Friend*, 9 March 1833.

As Baer observes, the numbers attending Burdett's political dinners had begun to decline during the late 1820s.⁶¹ The events were interrupted occasionally by the likes of Hunt and Cobbett, who chose to chastise Burdett on home turf for abandoning his radical principles.⁶² The decision to end his annual election dinners in 1832 signalled the beginning of the end of his long reign at the tavern. Though Burdett maintained sporadic involvement with the venue for a few years after 1832, by 1838, it was clear that the relationship had come to an end. Despite some supporters hoping that Burdett would receive 'as hearty a welcome at the Crown and Anchor as [he] ever did at any former period',⁶³ at a meeting of 'tradesmen' convened in the tavern on 22 May, Burdett was received with much hostility, with the crowd angrily calling for the 'turn-coat' to appear and asking 'where is Judas Burdett?'.⁶⁴ Emulating the theatrics of Parliament, a 'radical spouter' quickly 'dragged' working-class radical publisher Henry Hetherington to the chair to prevent Burdett taking control of the meeting. 'It is impossible to describe the uproar which continued throughout the whole of the proceedings', *The Times* reported, and it was 'with great difficulty that the hon. baronet...was able to force his way out of the room'.⁶⁵ The *Morning Chronicle* reported that Burdett was forced to hide in one room of the tavern before being accompanied down the Strand by the police.⁶⁶ Although Burdett, as Samuel Bamford recalled, was 'one of our idols, and we were loathe to give him up', the old tavern stalwarts simply had too strong an association with the *Reform Act* as a final political settlement for the new Crown and Anchor milieu.⁶⁷

Burdett's 'unseating' (both literally and metaphorically) from the Crown and Anchor did not mean an end to the tavern's prominence as a radical parliamentary stronghold. The *Reform Act* had motivated a new generation of radicals who were now more aware than ever of their exclusion from the political process. It also left them in possession of the extra-parliamentary venue. The 'elite of the Crown and Anchor spouters' now included the great 'Irish Agitator' Daniel O'Connell, Sir William Molesworth, Henry Brougham and John Roebuck.⁶⁸

---

61 Baer, 'Political Dinners in Whig, Radical and Tory Westminster', p. 198.
62 See, for example, the reports in *Poor Man's Guardian*, 1 December 1832; *Examiner*, 2 December 1832.
63 Letter from Stephen Dann, *The Times*, 9 April 1838.
64 *Morning Chronicle*, 22 May 1838. See also *Leeds Mercury*, 25 May 1838.
65 *The Times*, 22 May 1838.
66 *Morning Chronicle*, 22 May 1838.
67 Bamford, *Passages in the Life of a Radical*, p. 24.
68 The reference to the Crown and Anchor elite is from *The Times*, 21 July 1835. On Daniel O'Connell, see Oliver MacDonagh, *O'Connell: The life of Daniel O'Connell, 1775–1847* (London: Weidenfeld and Nicolson, 1991); Paul A. Pickering, '"Irish First": Daniel O'Connell, the native manufacture campaign, and economic nationalism, 1840–44', *Albion*, vol. 32, no. 4 (2000), pp. 598–616; Kevin B. Nowlan and Maurice R. O'Connell (eds), *Daniel O'Connell: Portrait of a radical* (Belfast: Appletree Press, 1984). On Sir William Molesworth, see Alison Adburgham, *A Radical Aristocrat: The Rt Hon. Sir William Molesworth, Bart., PC, MP of Pencarrow and his wife Andalusia* (Cornwall: Tabb House, 1990). On Henry Brougham, see Robert Stewart, *Henry Brougham, 1778–1868: His public career* (London: Bodley Head, 1986); William A. Hay, 'Henry Brougham and the 1818 Westmorland Election: A study in provincial opinion and the opening of constituency politics', *Albion*, vol.

O'Connell, a magnificent orator, delighted Crown and Anchor audiences with his impassioned and often mocking speeches slamming the Tory and Whig collusion over the *Reform Act*.[69] But it was to be Joseph Hume whom *The Times* conferred with highest Crown and Anchor honours; he, they claimed, occupied the 'professors chair of what many persons consider high treason, but the most charitable call misprision of treason, at the far-famed Crown and Anchor'.[70]

The Times had often chided the more radical of the earlier Crown and Anchor leaders, and the tone of their editorials sharpened depending on the threat posed by its new inhabitants to the long-established cultural conventions of the tavern. Following 1832, however, there is a discernible shift in the way the newspaper chose to describe the disenfranchised crowds attracted to events at the tavern. In June 1836, it reported on a meeting convened by O'Connell at which they described the audience as 'several members of the House of Commons who are distinguished for their ultra-radical principles, a considerable proportion of the printers and publishers of unstamped publications, and a tolerable sprinkling of unwashed artisans, Radical pothouse spouters, and Irish hod-men'.[71] Two years later, the reports continued in a similar vein. On reporting a meeting held in May 1838 to 'consider petitioning parliament' regarding the timing of the new Queen's coronation, *The Times* observer noted that the room was densely crowded by 'those who are in the daily habit of the almost endless meetings of the Radicals'.[72] It was therefore 'natural', they concluded, 'to anticipate that an outrage on the common principle of good manners would be committed'.

One of their most biting indictments of the Crown and Anchor assembly occurred in 1837 when a meeting was held to again assert a voice in the foreign affairs of the nation by protesting the 'unjust and oppressive' colonial policy of the British government towards the Canadian people, who had begun to agitate for greater self-governance. *The Times* editor lamented: 'Incredible as it may sound, these "working-men" are said to have actually wasted their time, spent their money, and worn their shoes the worse, in order that they might assemble at the Crown and Anchor.'[73]

36, no. 1 (2004), pp. 28–51; Michael Lobban, 'Henry Brougham and Law Reform', *English Historical Review*, vol. 115 (2000), pp. 1184–215. On John Roebuck, see S. A. Beaver, 'Roebuck, John Arthur (1802–1879)', *ODNB*, <http://www.oxforddnb.com/view/article/23945>

69 *Working Man's Friend*, 9 March 1833.
70 *The Times*, 6 January 1838.
71 *The Times*, 2 June 1836. For other reports on the meeting, see *Examiner*, 5 June 1836; *Preston Chronicle*, 4 June 1836.
72 *The Times*, 22 May 1838.
73 *The Times*, 5 April 1837.

The fear of the unstable and unpredictable mob evident in the reporting of Rotunda radicals in 1831 found a new target with the post-1832 Crown and Anchor tenants.[74]

The disparaging reports of *The Times*, however, do not appear to have dented the enthusiasm of the new Crown and Anchor milieu. On 4 March 1837, the *London Mercury* reported the ecstatic response of early Chartist leader Bronterre O'Brien to a meeting at the tavern to petition Parliament for more extensive political reform:

> I have been present at all sorts of political meetings…but never was it my good fortune to witness so brilliant a display of democracy as that which shone forth at the Crown and Anchor on Tuesday night. I often despaired of Radicalism before; I will never despair again after what I witnessed on that occasion…Four thousand democrats, at least, were at the meeting. The immense room of the Crown and Anchor was crowded to overflowing, several hundreds stood outside on the corridor and stairs or went away for want of accommodation.[75]

The meeting was convened to consider the most famous political petition of the early nineteenth century. When the London Working Men's Association, founded by William Lovett and Henry Hetherington, met at the tavern to petition for social and political rights for the working classes, they compiled the six points for a petition that would later become the People's Charter.[76] In this sense, the Crown and Anchor can lay claim as the birthplace of Chartism— the first mass working-class movement in Britain. The resistance of an earlier generation of radicals to the moderate reform measures espoused by the Hampden Club reveals how long these ideas had been percolating at the Crown and Anchor.

It would be misleading, however, to suggest that the middling classes no longer took an interest in political reform and political opposition at the tavern after 1832. When they again found reason to oppose the government of the day, they turned once more to the Crown and Anchor as the site for their public

---

74   These tenants included the 3000 people who assembled at the Crown and Anchor in 1834 to petition the King on behalf of the persecuted Dorchester unionists led by George Loveless (the Tolpuddle Martyrs). The meeting was addressed by Feargus O'Connor and Daniel O'Connell. See Joyce Marlow, *The Tolpuddle Martyrs* (St Albans, Herts: Panther, 1974), pp. 127–8.

75   *London Mercury*, 4 March 1837, reprinted in Dorothy Thompson, *The Early Chartists* (London: Macmillan, 1971), pp. 57–61.

76   For an account of the meeting, see *The People's Charter; With the address to the radical reformers of Great Britain and Ireland and a brief sketch of its origin* (London, 1848), p. 4. For more on William Lovett, prominent London radical, Owenite and Chartist, and Henry Hetherington, radical publisher (including of the *Poor Man's Guardian*) and journalist, see Chapter 7 of this study.

campaigns.⁷⁷ In the same year that the People's Charter was born, a group united by different political persuasion came together to agitate for the repeal of the *New Poor Law Act*.⁷⁸ The chair of the meeting, Earl Stanhope, was pleased that despite their 'differing in political opinions', they assembled in the large room of the tavern '[n]ot for the purpose of any party politics, but to exercise their constitutional rights, and in fulfilment of their public duty, to deliberate upon one of the most important subjects that could engage their attention'.⁷⁹ The tavern remained a central site of public debate of most important political questions of the period.

The use of the tavern by another powerful political group of the period, the Anti-Corn Law League, reveals the continuity of language, protocols and practices in relation to the Crown and Anchor, which had developed incrementally since the 1790s.⁸⁰ In 1842, the League employed a strategy reminiscent of that adopted by Francis Place's delegation to Prime Minister Grey in 1831. Rather than present unannounced on the doorstep of Downing Street, however, the Anti-Corn Law League politely gave advance warning to new Tory Prime Minister, Sir Robert Peel. Addressed from the tavern, and signed by John Brookes, chairman of a 'preliminary meeting of deputies from associations and religious congregations from various parts of the kingdom', the letter requested: 'That you will favour the deputation with an interview on the subject of the repeal of the corn laws… previous to the announcements of the intentions in Parliament on Wednesday next.'⁸¹

Despite attempting to avoid offending respectable sensibilities by issuing a written request, it nevertheless elicited a sharp response by *The Times*—remarkably similar to the rebuke of the effrontery of Place and his delegation by the *Courier*. *The Times* chided the League for its audacity, suggesting the futility of their efforts to throw Peel 'on his haunches in a single interview' to 'defer or modify his own well-considered plans till they accord with these fresh

---

77   'Old Corruption', as E. P. Thompson noted, still 'had vitality as the protracted struggle for the repeal of the corn laws was to show'. Thompson, *The Making of the English Working Class*, p. 905.
78   *Morning Chronicle*, 28 February 1837. For a discussion of the plebeian reaction to the 1834 Poor Law, see John Knott, *Popular Opposition to the 1834 Poor Law* (London: Croom Helm, 1986). See also Nicholas Edsall, *The Anti-Poor Law Movement 1834–44* (Manchester: Manchester University Press, 1971); Anthony Brundage, *The English Poor Laws 1700–1930* (New York: Palgrave, 2002).
79   *Morning Chronicle*, 28 February 1837. See also *London Dispatch and People's Political and Social Reformer*, 5 March 1837; *Examiner*, 5 March 1837. The speech was also published in full the same year. See *Earl Stanhope's Speech, on the New Poor Law, at a meeting held at the Crown and Anchor tavern* (London, 1837). A full account of the meeting, taken from the *Champion Newspaper* of 5 March 1837, was also circulated as a pamphlet: *Great Meeting at the Crown and Anchor on the Inhuman Poor-Law Act* (London, 1837).
80   On the Anti-Corn Law League, see Paul A. Pickering and Alex Tyrrell, *The People's Bread: A history of the Anti-Corn Law League* (London: Leicester University Press, 2000); Archibald Prentice, *A History of the Anti-Corn Law League* (London, 1853).
81   *The Times*, 9 February 1842. See also *Morning Chronicle*, 10 February 1842.

Crown and Anchor sentiments'.[82] The insouciant use of the phrase is telling. It was not necessary for *The Times* to expand on these 'fresh sentiments'. Political shorthand had again come into play.

The continued use of the tavern by moderate and middling rank reformers assisted with maintaining the association of the venue with moderate political opposition. Ironically, it also assisted with access to the site for the plebeian political milieu. The difficulties faced by Thistlewood and friends in paying for the room in 1819 were, in the early Chartist years, overcome with some ingenuity. When a meeting was convened at the tavern in March 1841 to remonstrate Parliament against the continuation of the New Poor Law, *The Times* reported that it was disturbed by a 'large body of Chartists' whose avowed object was 'to take possession of rooms for which other people pay, and thus to gain a platform for their own purposes for free'.[83] *The Times* correspondent was indignant at the intrusion of the respectable gathering as he lamented the 'avowed *tactique* of those misguided persons…to convert every public assembly to which they can gain admittance into an arena for some riotous exhibition of their own'. Like the newspaper's outrage over the secrecy of the 1817 Hampden Club meeting, the actions of the Chartists interrupted more than simply a meeting in progress. They threatened the long-established Crown and Anchor protocols and the established cultural understanding of the venue as a moderate and legitimate venue of the public sphere.

Just as radicals of the 1790s responded to the threat posed by John Reeves' loyalist Crown and Anchor society, the tavern's new radical milieu of the 1840s also raged against the involvement of more moderate middling groups at the venue. Indeed, Feargus O'Connor's radical newspaper, the *Northern Star*, saw the relationship between the Chartists and the Anti-Corn Law League as a confrontation between enemy camps. Although by this time there were many other choices for meeting places in the capital, the Crown and Anchor remained a central site in the machinations of political opposition. The *Northern Star* announced the 'total defeat of the Combined Armies of the League' by the 'Advance of the Royal Chartist Army of Observation' in what it dubbed the 'Great Battle of the Crown and Anchor'.[84] O'Connor launched a viperous and sustained campaign against the League, whom he considered 'Malthusian beggars', who expected workers to join in bettering the condition of the 'masters' yet who had never shown any disposition to do the same for the worker. The question of the Corn Laws paled to insignificance, according to O'Connor, compared with the failure to adopt the Charter.

---

82   *The Times*, 9 February 1842.
83   *The Times*, 12 March 1841. See also the report of an earlier meeting in *Examiner*, 7 March 1841. The tactic was Chartist policy and not restricted to meetings at the Crown and Anchor. See Paul A. Pickering, *Chartism and the Chartists in Manchester and Salford* (London: Macmillan, 1995), p. 4.
84   *Northern Star*, 13 March 1841.

The continuities between the pre and post-1832 years at the tavern are further evident in the relationship between the venue and Whitehall. Radical Members of Parliament continued to be censured within the House of Commons for their participation in Crown and Anchor meetings. In March 1838, Lord Maidstone took O'Connell to task for his public accusations of corruption against Tory House of Commons Committees, raising the allegations, he maintained, in order that O'Connell might contradict them. 'I am exceedingly obliged to the Noble Lord', countered O'Connell, 'for giving this publicity to the sentiments I entertain on the subject of Committees'. He confirmed that he had said 'every word of that' and, further, that he believed 'it to be perfectly true'.[85] A fracas then ensued with threat and counter-threat between Whig and Tory members over whether O'Connell's Crown and Anchor sentiments might result in a prosecution. The matter was eventually dropped, though not before O'Connell's parting shot that rather than retire from public censorship, he indeed courted it—not within the halls of Parliament, but at the Crown and Anchor. There, he pledged, he would appear 'from day to day and hour to hour, singly and alone, to answer any charge'. O'Connell was clearly signalling that in order to uphold his mandate to the people, he was to be held accountable not to the Parliament, but in the venue consecrated as the 'Real House of Commons'.

Remarkably, the connections between O'Connell, the Crown and Anchor and the House of Commons committee system were anticipated, in the form of a graphic satire, a decade earlier, at the time of the struggle for Catholic emancipation. The print *To Be...or...Not To Be The Clare MP: O'Connell and the Minister at the Bar of the (Crown) and (Anchor)*[86] (Figure 5.1) was produced by Charles Williams in 1828 in response to the election of O'Connell as the member for County Clare. Many Tory MPs, including Robert Peel, opposed the election, which they deemed illegal because of O'Connell's Catholicism. The matter was referred in the first instance to a House of Commons Election Committee. The print provides a clever double play on the term 'the Bar' as Prime Minister Wellington and O'Connell stand within the one 'bar' in which O'Connell was a legitimate member. At the same time, Peel thumbs his nose to O'Connell as he enters the door marked 'Committee Room', which bears the sign 'No Admittance but to True Blues', in reference to the Tory stranglehold on the committee process. The print reminds us that the Crown and Anchor had become a political symbol in its own right (as was reminiscent of the early nineteenth-century graphic satires surveyed in Chapter 4), identifying the tavern only in symbolic form. It also sharply illustrates the status of the venue as an analogue to Parliament.

---

85 *Northern Star*, 3 March 1838. See also J. A. Hamilton, *The Life of Daniel O'Connell* (London: W. H. Allen, 1888), pp. 142–4.
86 BM 15538.

Figure 5.1 *To Be…or…Not To Be the Clare MP: O'Connell and the Minister at the Bar of the (Crown) and (Anchor).*

Charles Williams, 1828. Copyright Trustees of the British Museum.

A meeting of the Anti-Corn Law League in the tavern in early February 1842 provides another potent example of the continued use of the Crown and Anchor as an alternative parliament.[87] After spending the day debating the morality of the Corn Laws, delegates from around the country marched in file to the House of Commons, in time for the arrival of the Members of Parliament and in anticipation of a rumoured announcement from Peel on the Corn Laws. The timing suggests that Brookes' approach to the Prime Minister the week earlier was only one part of their strategy. Upon their arrival at the House of Commons, the delegates were met by a line of policemen, who closed the gates, preventing their access to the Parliament. Undeterred, they launched a chorus of abuse towards MPs as they arrived for the sitting, with 'No Corn Law' and 'Down with the Monopoly' chanted throughout the afternoon. Sympathetic newspapers reported the events as a stand-off between the Leaguers—'those who represented the nation's wants'—and those in the seat of power who were

---

87 For a more detailed account of the events surrounding the meeting, see Pickering and Tyrrell, *The People's Bread*, pp. 166–9.

acting to protect the moneyed interests.[88] The content of Peel's speech did little to allay the League's hostility. They quickly issued their 'emphatic condemnation' of Peel's refusal to repeal the laws.

As Paul Pickering and Alex Tyrrell observe, even before the march to the House of Commons, the League viewed the Parliament with 'scepticism and contempt'.[89] They could 'point to a national constituency that far exceeded the parliamentary one'.[90] And as the League presented itself as a rival body to those occupying the seat of power, the Crown and Anchor provided an essential component of this challenge. As Clifford Geertz argues, all political authority requires a 'cultural frame' and, as other scholars have noted, every cultural frame requires a 'centre' that has a 'sacred status'.[91] As Lynn Hunt offers, such a 'centre' is 'the heart of things, the place where culture, society and politics come together'.[92] Clearly, such extra-parliamentary action of the League, and of other more plebeian groups excluded from the formal centre of political power, also required a rival 'centre'. The Crown and Anchor provided the physical 'heart' and the 'centre' for Britain's expanding political nation.

Reports in the mainstream press during this period also suggest that Crown and Anchor radicalism continued to have a strong influence on those occupying official seats of power at Westminster. Though *The Times* had long opposed the radical call for the introduction of a ballot system for voting, it conceded that there were merits in the 'secret system' in the face of the continuing power of the Crown and Anchor milieu to influence the parliamentary process:

> Where is the conscientious member who, being required to give an *open vote* in Parliament, can dare to exercise his honest convictions with any feeling of freedom or independence? Let him dare to do so, and forthwith he is pounced upon by the tribunals of the Crown and Anchor…the poor creatures who sit for these little metropolitan despotisms must vote, if they vote openly, under the goad and the lash.[93]

The Times was clearly still coming to terms with the demands of the public sphere and the extra-parliamentary political forces that coursed through it. Crucially, their reporting suggests that the Crown and Anchor had assumed a remarkable place on the political landscape of early nineteenth-century London—a space inhabited by those generally excluded from formal political

---

88   *Morning Chronicle*, 10 February 1842.
89   Pickering and Tyrrell, *The People's Bread*, p. 166.
90   Ibid., p. 167.
91   Lynn Hunt, *Politics, Culture and Class in the French Revolution* (Berkeley: University of California Press, 1984), p. 87. See also Epstein, *Radical Expression*, p. 76.
92   Hunt, *Politics, Culture and Class in the French Revolution*, p. 87.
93   *The Times*, 13 January 1838.

power but who collectively had an impact on the stronghold of power. It also suggests a more integrated and interlinked public sphere than the notion of a plebeian counter-sphere allows.

* * *

Given the vehemence of political discourse and the heterodox sentiments often expressed at the Crown and Anchor, we must consider why, despite successive waves of imprisonments for sedition and treason, the tavern remained a 'safe' outlet for political expression. As early as 1794, *The Times* reported that it witnessed toasts 'of the most seditious tendency', which 'ought to have sent the speakers to Botany Bay'.[94] Referring to the United Irishmen in 1797, Edmund Burke also complained that 'nor was the club at the Crown and Anchor one jot less treasonable than the Committee at Belfast; and what is worse the names are higher and members of parliament openly show themselves there'.[95] The long legacy of institutions such as the tavern with freedom of speech that Habermas linked so strongly with the emergence of the public sphere goes some way to explaining this protection, although as Barrell and Epstein remind us with the case of John Frost, such legacies were never assured.[96] The Home Office could not legislate to attack the function of a radical forum without encroaching on the rights of innocent recreational ale-house clubs.[97] True, individual speakers could still be prosecuted for libel, but the relatively close environment of the ale house meant that spies and shorthand recorders—the Home Office's main weapons in the prosecution of individuals—were easily detected.

Further, as Brett argues, political meetings guised as election or other celebratory dinners curiously escaped the definition of the public meeting or public speaking outlawed in both the Seditious Meetings Bill of 1795 and its offspring, the *Seditious Meetings Prevention Act* of 1819.[98] It is little wonder they quickly became such a popular form of political assembly during this period. The cultural understanding of the venue—as a parliamentary stronghold and political dining establishment—allowed the popular radical groups (whose meetings did not always involve dining) to exploit this wider legacy of tavern-based dissent and the political safety afforded by the Crown and Anchor's large parliamentary membership.

---

94   *The Times*, 5 May 1794.
95   Edmund Burke to Mrs Crewe, Correspondence, vol. iv, p. 448, quoted in H. P. Wheatley, *London Past and Present* (London, 1891), p. 480.
96   Barrell, 'Coffee-House Politicians'; James Epstein, '"Equality and No King": Sociability and sedition: the case of John Frost', in Gillian Russell and Clara Tuite (eds), *Romantic Sociability: Social networks and literary culture in Britain, 1770–1840* (Cambridge: Cambridge University Press, 2002), pp. 43–61.
97   Iain McCalman, 'Ultra-Radicalism and Convivial Debating Clubs in London 1795–1838', *English Historical Review*, vol. 102, no. 403 (1987), p. 311.
98   Brett, 'Political Dinners in Early Nineteenth-Century Britain', p. 539.

The absence of prosecutions emanating from the tavern is not to suggest that it was immune to the surveillance measures of the authorities.[99] When Hunt addressed his supporters there following his 'triumphal return' from Peterloo in 1819, he alerted the assembly to the presence of a magistrate, Mr Birnie, 'who had made his appearance that evening more than once in the gallery'.[100] Hunt directed the meeting 'to abstain from all invidious and inflammatory language' to prevent the police magistrate taking 'any advantage'. John Gale Jones was defiantly indignant that 'the presence of a magistrate at such a moment was a direct insult on all the company'. It is not clear from the public record how long Birnie tried his luck; while the presence of the magistrate undoubtedly made for good theatre for Hunt, the interference of the authorities in a public meeting so soon after Peterloo risked the wrath of a populace enraged by the callous response from the authorities both in Manchester and in London.

The relative political safety of the tavern as an outlet for public political dissent also raises the issue of women's involvement in Crown and Anchor radicalism. We know that despite the high possibility of public chastisement, some women in this period nevertheless chose to avow their radicalism in the public sphere. Unsurprisingly perhaps, the public record contains scant reference to the participation of women in Crown and Anchor meetings. The gendered nature of Crown and Anchor radicalism is starkly evident in both the visual culture surveyed in the previous chapter and in the public print culture mined for this chapter. Epstein and Baer both note the paucity of female involvement in public political dinners either in the metropolis or in regional England.[101] Epstein argues that such dinners not only allowed the formation of politically motivated clubs and associations, they were essentially masculine stomping grounds providing 'arenas for testing the courage of men's political convictions'. The 'challenges and counter-challenges to drink particular toasts or to stand by one's words and allegiances were', according to Epstein, 'in certain important respects analogous to the code of the duel'.[102] Elaine Chalus agrees that taverns supplied 'important, and uniquely male, venues for politicized socialising', though she maintains that this should not obscure the fact that '"Society" itself was charged with

---

99   The only prosecution I have been able to identify with the tavern involved activity just outside its walls. In 1819, one of Richard Carlile's young shopmen was arrested on the steps of the tavern for holding a placard that informed passers-by of a meeting to protest against the Peterloo massacre, though he was later acquitted in court.
100   *The Times*, 14 September 1819. There are other records of surveillance of Home Office spies at the tavern such as those reports submitted in the early 1830s monitoring the meetings at the tavern of the National Political Union. See, for example, Home Office Papers, HO64/13, fo. 105; HO64/13, fo. 124; HO64/14, fo. 138.
101   Baer, 'Political Dinners in Whig, Radical and Tory Westminster', p. 201; Epstein, *Radical Expression*, pp. 159–60. See also Jonathon Fulcher, 'Gender, Politics and Class in the Early Nineteenth-Century English Reform Movement', *Historical Research*, vol. LXVII (1994), p. 68.
102   Epstein, '"Equality and No King"', pp. 47–8.

politics' and that women's participation in parliamentary politics occurred within other settings, such as the private dinners, which while held within the home, nevertheless had strong political agendas.[103]

Although the deeply masculine milieu of the tavern (as well as societal pressure on women to abstain more generally from public politics) acted to curtail the participation of women, it would be misleading to suggest that women were entirely absent from Crown and Anchor functions. They were certainly present at the tavern for the many cultural activities that took place outside the venue's political functions, including balls and soirees held in the tavern's great assembly room.[104] Former actress and later Owenite preacher Miss Eliza Macauley provided lectures at the tavern on music, elocution and literature.[105] Women were also present at meetings with a clear political focus. As early as 1789, an advertisement for a dinner to debate the review of the characters of Pitt and Fox declared that 'admittance to Ladies and Gentlemen' was 'half a crown'.[106] The furore over the King's treatment of Queen Caroline also saw women assemble at the tavern in great numbers in September 1820.[107] Joyce Marlow reports that in a meeting at the tavern to petition the King on behalf of the Tolpuddle Martyrs, attended by up to 3000 people, the 'preliminaries' involved a 'lady who had travelled from Dorchester putting 2s. 6d. on the table to defray the expenses of the meeting'.[108] Furthermore, issues in which women were seen to have a legitimate involvement, such as the temperance movement, also saw women participate in large numbers. When Hunt and Cobbett discovered the presence of women at a meeting they convened to advocate temperance among the working classes (ironically in a tavern), they stopped the meeting and cleared a central space in the room for women to take their seats.[109] The incongruity between place and function also did not deter the organisers of the 1837 Great Temperance Festival where many women, who were 'remarkable for their superiority of dress and their attractive countenances', were among the 800 who assembled in the Great Room.[110] *The Times* clearly took no issue with female involvement in such a respectable cause.

---

103 Elaine Chalus, 'Elite Women, Social Politics, and the Political World of Late Eighteenth-Century England', *Historical Journal*, vol. 43, no. 3 (2000), p. 675.
104 See, for example, a ball held in 1803 at which there was a 'numerous and highly respectable assemblage of both sexes'. *The Times*, 21 February 1803.
105 See the broadsheet *Miss Macauley's Literary and Musical Regalio at the Crown and Anchor*, NS1069 B137, fo. 38, City of Westminster Archives, London.
106 *The Times*, 21 April 1789.
107 *The Times*, 8 September 1820.
108 Marlow, *The Tolpuddle Martyrs*, p. 127.
109 *A Full Report of the Proceedings of a Public Meeting Held at the Crown and Anchor Tavern, the Strand, on Monday, Dec. 13, 1819, to consider the propriety of adopting a plan for abstaining from the use of wine, spirits, beer, tea, coffee &c.*(London, 1819).
110 *The Times*, 27 December 1837.

Though the *Northern Star* observed only one woman amongst a crowd of almost 2000 assembled to consider the question of postponing the coronation in May 1838[111] (yet another example of quasi-parliamentary activity at the Crown and Anchor), by November 1842, they reported that women were present in large numbers in a meeting convened in honour of the 'political victims' imprisoned during the government's renewed assault on political dissent during the early Chartist years.[112] On that occasion, the paper noted, the tavern was 'crammed to suffocation' and it was not only the number of women who fainted from the congestion that most startled the editor, but the number of men who followed suit. Later again, in a meeting convened in March 1846 in order to evince 'sympathy with the Poles in their present struggle', the *Northern Star* noted that the large room of the tavern was densely crowded and contained a 'sprinkling of the fair sex'.[113]

From what we know of the participation of women in mass street demonstrations, it is likely that the big political events at the tavern, which attracted thousands to the Strand site, might well have included many women. What is clear is that when women did participate, they did so from the floor or the gallery, but never, it seems, from the platform. A thorough survey of private records of Crown and Anchor associates lies beyond the scope of this study, but the issue of female participation in this archetypal space of the public sphere nevertheless warrants further investigation. What is clear is the prominence of women from 1848 when the Crown and Anchor made way for a new institution at the Strand premises, the Whittington Club. The brainchild of Douglas Jerrold, the Whittington was a unique example of mid-century urban sociability (Figure 5.2).[114] It was one of the first such clubs to be aimed at the lower middle class and, most remarkably, full membership was open to women. Rejecting the sites of sociability in which the 'form of woman was always banished', not only was membership open to women, they also participated from the platform, not only from the floor.[115]

---

111 *Northern Star*, 26 May 1838.
112 *Northern Star*, 26 November 1842.
113 *Northern Star*, 28 March 1846.
114 For more on the fascinating Whittington Club, see Christopher Kent, 'The Whittington Club: A bohemian experiment in middle class social reform', *Victorian Studies*, vol. 18, no. 1 (1974), pp. 31–55; and Kathryn Gleadle, *The Early Feminists: Radical Unitarians and the emergence of the women's rights movement, 1831–51* (New York: St Martin's Press, 1995), pp. 140–70.
115 See, for example, *Douglas Jerrold's Weekly Newspaper*, 23 January and 16 October 1847; *Whittington Club Gazette*, 4 May 1850. Harriet Martineau lectured there, as well as a Mrs Balfour, on 'celebrated women'.

Figure 5.2 Great Room, Crown and Anchor Tavern, Whittington Club Soiree. This image is one of the very few surviving images of the Great Room in the historical record.

Illustrated London News, 19 February 1848.

***

Despite prolific accounts of the thousands of political assemblies held at the Crown and Anchor over the course of half a century, there are very few descriptions of the physical space itself in the public record. The account of the interior of the building that leads the preceding chapter is drawn largely from the architectural plans and title deeds, which remain in the possession of the original owner, the Duke of Norfolk. For the social historian, few contemporary works describe the building in any detail or record the response of visitors to it, other than the frequent astonishment at the size of the Great Assembly Room or acknowledgement of its notoriety in the late eighteenth and early nineteenth centuries. Samuel Bamford's fleeting reference to the venue is one of the few responses from a radical perspective. His account belies a simple physical evaluation; there is a reverential tone to the recountal as he describes 'gazing around a large hall', which 'seemed wonderfully grand and silent for a tavern'.[116] This is in sharp contrast with the 'conflicting emotions' he reported

---

116   Bamford, *Passages in the Life of a Radical*, p. 23.

on entering the 'dimly lighted' 'den' of the House of Commons.[117] By the time of Bamford's visit, of course, the Crown and Anchor had become an integral part of a national political culture. That so few descriptions exist in the public record suggests the ultimate form of political shorthand. Perhaps no descriptions were necessary, as to write or speak of the Crown and Anchor was to know it.

Despite Baer's 'deep reading' of the Westminster political dinners, and the multitude of other scholars who detail events occurring on the site, the space of the tavern itself plays little role in any analysis. By so doing, the importance of the venue itself to the development of such rituals and formalities, and to their wider dissemination throughout Britain, has been overlooked. For example, Baer's assessment that the Crown and Anchor was chosen by Burdett and his radical supporters for geographical purposes, rather than adopting the ideological mantle of Charles James Fox, presupposes that the mere location of the venue was the deciding factor. Although the location undoubtedly allowed Burdett 'mastery over the borough',[118] the appropriation of the tavern space provided much more. It was clearly more than just a physical structure within which political groups could assemble. It took on far deeper meaning both within radical culture and in the wider public sphere. The accommodation of a new generation of radicals at the Crown and Anchor attests to the venue's longevity as both a political icon and an outlet for political opposition. It also attests to the vitality and doggedness of those who remained excluded from the franchise after 1832. By providing a 'legitimate' public space for dissenting political expression, the venue enticed many newly (mostly male) politicised followers into the public sphere. It also gave these new followers a radical identity—a rubric under which to associate. In the decades before the encompassing umbrella of 'Chartism', the Crown and Anchor provided a credible public identity to a vast array of (often conflicting) political ideologies and groups in London. Despite its increasingly plebeian patrons and, in particular, its use by more militant Chartist followers, the tavern retained its status as an alternative or rival political forum for those excluded from the formal channels of political power.

As we will see in the following chapters, not all radical spaces had the cultural traditions or political kudos that radicals drew on when assembling at the Crown and Anchor. Nor, however, did they necessarily have the restrictions that such cultural conventions implied. On one hand, the opening of Richard Carlile's Blackfriars Road Rotunda allowed radical London a spatial and ideological demarcation in opposition to the image of moderate and 'respectable' radicalism of the Crown and Anchor in the early 1830s. Yet as we will also see, the Rotunda offered radical London much more than the rough and unrespectable mantle implied by Francis Place.

---

117   Ibid., p. 26.
118   Baer, 'Political Dinners in Whig, Radical and Tory Westminster', p. 189.

6. 'Temple of Knowledge and Reason': culture and politics at 3 Blackfriars Road, Surrey

As we have seen in the previous chapters, by the early nineteenth century the very name of the Crown and Anchor tavern clearly signposted its political associations and identity. The tavern's longstanding presence on the metropolitan landscape, combined with its early liberal-aristocratic connections, helped to secure its place as a bastion for London's politicised middling classes. If the Crown and Anchor tavern had come to symbolise the moderate and measured opposition to the political landscape during the Reform agitation of late 1830, events south of the Thames signalled that plebeian radicals with more pressing intent had found a new home. On the evening of 8 November, a crowd of almost 2000 assembled at the Rotunda, Richard Carlile's newly leased premises in Blackfriars Road, Surrey, during a period of intense unrest in the Reform crisis. The magistrates of the city, wrote one contemporary observer, were 'all of the opinion' that the 'heated harangues' at the Rotunda were the source of the rioting that gripped the city.[1] Their attention on the building was also fuelled by rumoured plans of riots during the King's expected visit to the city, and of assassination plots against Prime Minister, Lord Wellington, and Home Secretary, Robert Peel.

Carlile was also well aware of the focus of the authorities on his new building. Anticipating a riot on 8 November, he reportedly instructed the cleaner at the Rotunda to make six staves out of the rails of some staircases to 'imitate those of Constables', paint them tricoloured and inscribe them with the word 'Rotunda'.[2] Whether Carlile really intended the staves to be used in defending the premises or whether they served a purely provocative symbolic purpose is unclear. The mood of the crowds who gathered at the venue that evening suggests that Carlile could have had both purposes in mind. By early evening, an angry crowd of about 1500 people proceeded in unison from the Rotunda, over Blackfriars Bridge and into the city, shouting 'Down with the police' and 'No Peel'—a hostile affront to both the new metropolitan police and the man responsible for their inception, Home Secretary, Robert Peel. At the head of the cavalcade marched a flag-bearer—proudly and provocatively raising a tricolour flag emblazoned with the word 'Reform'. It was a call to march. Joined by others along the route through the Strand, including many women, they proceeded

---

1 *Bell's Weekly Messenger*, 14 November 1830.
2 Home Office Papers, HO64/11, November 1830, fo. 249.

to Downing Street, where several scuffles ensued. The A-Division of the new police force was quickly summoned from Scotland Yard. With a police line formed several men deep across King Street, a 'general fight ensued' and, in the skirmish, it was reported that 'many received broken heads'. The police line held strong and prevented the crowd from menacing the House of Commons. Moreover, the police gained a crucial symbolic victory—the triumph of the evening reported by *The Times* was that the tricolour flag was successfully captured by police.[3] As James Vernon notes, symbolic icons such as the tricolour flags were often targeted by rival groups, 'as if destroying a flag would destroy the resolve of their opponent'.[4] The triumph with which the police captured the flag shows the authorities understood its significance as a potentially powerful impetus to action.

Characteristically, Carlile's public pronouncements did little to allay the authorities' fears. By eight o'clock on 9 November, the theatre was filled to capacity. With magistrates in attendance, and police numbers bolstered by many 'respectable' householders in the area invested as special constables, Carlile barricaded the doors to the theatre, but went ahead with his planned lecture.[5] Military officers were stationed at Blackfriars Bridge in case of riot—rumoured to begin at the Rotunda at 11 o'clock that evening. Yet by midnight all remained relatively quiet. Some stone throwing and scuffles with police were reported, but fears of assassination attempts proved unfounded. The tricolour flags remained intact, the staves remained concealed and the Rotunda's doors were not breached.

Despite the anticlimax of the evening, the incidents of early November reveal that, by 1830, London's plebeian radicals (and the tricolour flag) had found a new rallying point. Between 1830 and 1832, the Rotunda became the pre-eminent arena of London radical activity featuring such luminaries as Richard Carlile, William Cobbett, Henry Hunt, John Gale Jones and Daniel O'Connell, as well as providing the headquarters for the highly influential National Union of the Working Classes (NUWC).[6] The Rotunda also provided the platform for a new generation of less orthodox, freethinking radicals such as the Reverend Robert Taylor, Eliza Sharples and an eccentric duo, John 'Zion' Ward and Charles Twort. London's diverse radical groups and ideologies assembled under the Rotunda's roof during the two years of Carlile's lease in vocal opposition to 'Old Corruption'.

---

3   *The Times*, 9 November 1830. See also *Jackson's Oxford Journal*, 10 November 1830.
4   James Vernon, *Politics and the People: A study in English political culture c.1815–1867* (Cambridge: Cambridge University Press, 1993), p. 115.
5   *The Times*, 11 November 1830. See also Theophila Campbell Carlile, *The Battle for the Freedom of the Press, as Told in the Story of the Life of Richard Carlile* (London, 1899), p. 122.
6   For more on the National Union of the Working Classes, see Chapters 7 and 8 of this study.

The Rotunda was among the new venues that had transformed London's urban cultural and political landscape at the beginning of the nineteenth century, and which offered new possibilities for meetings and assemblies. As Thomas Markus contends, towns in this period were configured in entirely different ways, and not only did they appear different, they also 'felt' different because of the changed composition of the built environment and altered relationships between old and new spaces.[7] Where patrons of the Crown and Anchor could draw on the cultural understanding of the space that had developed over decades, the expanding public sphere provided unprecedented opportunities for new radical spaces with a new 'feel' and new modes of operating. James Epstein has argued that a marked feature of popular radicalism in this period was the search to gain access to and control sites of assembly.[8] Plebeian radicals tried hard to make the Crown and Anchor their own, but they were never more than one of a multitude of constituencies using its ample facilities, and their attentions did little to shift the place of the Crown and Anchor in the popular imagining or in political language. In the metropolis, the struggle for access and control was arguably, albeit briefly, most successful at Carlile's Blackfriars Road Rotunda.

With the Rotunda as a new institution on the political landscape, Carlile needed to move quickly to establish its radical credentials. In so doing, he turned to the very symbols that had once been used so effectively by caricaturists to denigrate the radical cause. He invoked political shorthand, not only with the tricoloured painted staves, but by adorning the facade of the Blackfriars Road Rotunda with two enormous tricolour flags—the effect intensified by the backdrop of an otherwise uniform terrace-house streetscape. Inside the venue, smaller tricoloured flags, framed by sprigs of laurel (the radical symbol for victory), lined the passages of the building. The layered meaning of agency and threat embodied in the tricolour allowed Carlile a potent insignia under which to open the Rotunda; he publicly pledged 'a brave and glorious struggle and a successful war under its tri-colored banner against aristocratic or clerical despotism [and] corruption'.[9]

There could be no mistaking the cultural understanding Carlile intended to create at his new premises. The tricoloured flag had long carried a potent message of dissent in Britain and the 1830 French Revolution saw British radicals embrace a renewed pride in the ideals embodied in the tricolour. After a hiatus of some years, it re-emerged in Britain alongside the cap of liberty as political

---

[7] Thomas Markus, *Order and Space in Society: Architectural form and its context in the Scottish Enlightenment* (Edinburgh: Mainstream, 1982), p. 1.
[8] James Epstein, *In Practice: Studies in the language and culture of popular politics in modern Britain* (Stanford: Stanford University Press, 2003), p. 113.
[9] *Prompter*, 12 November 1830.

shorthand for plebeian agency and action.[10] The tricolour represented a potent unifying motif of liberty, with a pernicious twist: it provided an unequivocal indication of menace and revolution. As Henry Vizetelly was to recall years later, the tricoloured flags were as 'irritating to the peeler [police] of those days as a red rag is to an infuriated bull'.[11] Moreover, as one report to the Home Office maintained, it also represented for many a 'symbol of treason'.[12]

Many of the leading historians of early nineteenth-century radicalism, from E. P. Thompson and Iain McCalman to James Epstein, Iorwerth Prothero, Joel Wiener and David Worrall, have noted the presence of the Rotunda on the radical landscape of the period. This body of work has tended to focus on specific Rotunda identities, rather than looking at the impact of the Rotunda on the nature of radicalism during this period. E. P. Thompson, for instance, resurrected the sober and industrious members of the NUWC,[13] whom Prothero also considered synonymous with Rotunda radicalism.[14] McCalman and Epstein have focused on Richard Carlile and flamboyant Rotunda orator and entertainer the Reverend Robert Taylor as examples of the less orthodox elements evident in radical culture at that time.[15] Worrall has examined the theatrical aspects of Rotunda radicalism, specifically the performance of the *Captain Swing* play by Taylor.[16] Wiener's account of the Rotunda remains one of the most extensive to date.[17] His chronological and descriptive account of the building, however, is limited in its scope by his interest in the institution first and foremost as an episode in the life of Richard Carlile. Further, work in other scholarly disciplines such as sociology, science, literature and natural history has also explored the earlier cultural institutions that inhabited the premises in the decades before

---

10 On the reintroduction of radical symbolism in the early nineteenth century, particularly the cap of liberty, see James Epstein, *Radical Expression: Political language, ritual and symbol in England, 1790–1850* (Oxford: Oxford University Press, 1994), pp. 80–1.
11 Henry Vizetelly, *Glances Back Through Seventy Years: Autobiographical and other reminiscences* (London 1893), vol. 1, p. 63.
12 Home Office Papers, HO40/21/25, November 1830, fo. 260.
13 E. P. Thompson, *The Making of the English Working Class* (London: Penguin, 1968), pp. 891–2.
14 See also Joseph Hamburger, *James Mill and the Art of Revolution* (New Haven, Conn.: Yale University Press, 1963), p. 288, who conflates the National Union of the Working Classes with 'Rotundaites' in the index.
15 Iain McCalman, 'Popular Irreligion in Early Victorian England: Infidel preachers and radical theatricality in 1830s London', in R. W. Davis and R. J. Helmstadter (eds), *Religion and Irreligion in Victorian Society* (London: Routledge, 1992), pp. 51–67; Epstein, *Radical Expression*, pp. 138–40.
16 David Worrall, *Theatric Revolution: Drama, censorship and Romantic period subcultures 1773–1832* (Oxford: Oxford University Press, 2006), pp. 340–60.
17 Joel Wiener, *Radicalism and Freethought in Nineteenth-Century Britain: The life of Richard Carlile* (Westport, Conn.: Greenwood Press, 1983), pp. 165–90.

Carlile's lease.[18] These earlier tenants—namely, the Leverian Museum and the Surrey Institution—were important public institutions in their own right.

This study builds on this body of scholarship to explore the influence and impact of the premises at 3 Blackfriars Road from a broader perspective, with particular focus on the layers of identity associated with the site between 1798 and the early 1840s, how this influenced and impacted upon radical culture, and what it tells us of the nature of the public sphere in this period. The remaining three chapters explore how, and why, the Rotunda engendered such passions as displayed by the hundreds who answered Carlile's call to protect the building and its tricolour flags.

This chapter introduces the site itself and its varied inhabitants. With few traces of architectural evidence remaining in the historical record, it will begin, as far as is possible, by 'reconstructing' the building, for an understanding of the physical structure of the space itself is necessary to understand the nature of Rotunda radicalism. It surveys the venue's 'prehistory' as the Leverian Museum and the Surrey Institution before turning to the period of Carlile's tenancy. Its identity as a venue of knowledge and learning for the working classes, in the context of other outlets for working-class education, is then examined. The intellectual and educative legacies of the site neatly articulated with Carlile's key ambition for the Rotunda: to provide a 'general lecturing and discussion establishment' dedicated to the principles of 'freethought and free discussion'. This, he believed, would usher in a new era of radicalism, lead to total reform of the social, political and economic systems and realise the emancipation of the British working classes.[19] To properly understand the history of the building, therefore, we have to take a longer view, for this approach also tells us more about the tumultuous period of its most notorious tenant.

* * *

Located on the Surrey side of Blackfriars Bridge, the Rotunda was built in 1788–89 for James Parkinson by the eminent London builder James Burton (alias James Haliburton) to house the significant natural history collection of Sir Ashton Lever.[20] The collection, originally housed in Lever's famous

---

18   See the sociologist Charles Tilly, 'Spaces of Contention', *Mobilization: An International Quarterly*, vol. 5, no. 2 (2000), pp. 135–59, who uses the Rotunda example of early November 1830 to illustrate 'spatial patterns in contentious politics'. Scholarship from the other disciplinary fields will be evident in the following references.
19   *Prompter*, 13 November 1830.
20   For a brief account of the Leverian Museum, see Richard D. Altick, *The Shows of London* (Cambridge, Mass.: Belknap Press, 1978), pp. 28–32. On Lever, see P. E. Kell, 'Lever, Sir Ashton (1729–1788)', in *Oxford Dictionary of National Biography*, <http://www.oxforddnb.com/view/article/16530> (hereafter *ODNB*). On

Holophusikon museum in Leicester Square, comprised a tremendous assembly of natural curiosities, antiquities and artefacts sourced from around the world, many from the South Pacific expeditions of James Cook. Amassed over a 12-year period, the 26 000 items in the collection were initially displayed at Leicester House in 1775.[21] It was hailed as one of the finest natural history collections ever exhibited in Britain, rivalling any similar collection on the Continent.[22] Lever marketed his new London enterprise aggressively and, like others controlling many of the public cultural institutions that bloomed in this period, he sought to define its status by boasting the patronage of many aristocratic supporters including the 'Royal Highnesses the Dukes of Cumberland and Brunswick'.[23]

Lever's collection came at great financial cost. The collection reportedly amounted to a colossal £50 000. The opening of the Leicester Square museum to public admission failed to offset the cost of the investment. In the nine years of its operation, Lever maintained that he raised only £13 500 from admissions.[24] Facing increasing debt, by 1784, he was forced to dispose of the collection. Lever nevertheless remained convinced that the collection was worthy of being the 'Object of National Attention' and he, alongside other natural history collectors, lobbied hard to see it remain in the hands of the British public.[25] Lever, determined that the collection was too rare and valuable to be dispersed by 'common sale', successfully petitioned Parliament to dispose of the contents of the museum by lottery. The scheme ultimately proved another financial failure. The lottery was drawn in March 1786 after selling only 8000 of the 36 000 tickets available. Land agent James Parkinson secured the collection after his wife, Sarah, purchased the winning ticket for him.[26] Without the means to house the massive collection, Parkinson immediately sought to dispose of his winnings by sale. When the collection again failed to attract any significant interest, Parkinson decided to construct a purpose-built facility for it. Despite an uncertain beginning, it was to be an institution that could have easily been cited by Habermas as an example of the public sphere in action.

James Parkinson (not to be confused with the surgeon and radical associated with the Newgate circle), see H. S. Torrens, 'Parkinson, James (bap. 1730, d. 1813)', *ODNB*, <http://www.oxforddnb.com/view/article/21370>. On James Burton, see H. M. Colvin, *A Biographical Dictionary of British Architects* [hereafter *BDBA*], fourth edn (New Haven, Conn.: Yale University Press, 2008), pp. 203–4.

21 'Lever's museum consisting of natural curiosities and productions of art. Petition of Sir Ashton Lever', *Journal of the House of Commons* (1803 reprint), 1784/06/07, vol. 40, <http://www.bopcris.ac.uk/bop1688/ref1572.html> (hereafter 'Petition of Sir Ashton Lever').

22 See reports of witnesses called to attest to the significance of the collection to the House of Commons committee in 'Petition of Sir Ashton Lever'.

23 *Now Open, Patronised by their Royal Highnesses the Dukes of Cumberland and Brunswick, the Leverian Museum…Leverian Museum broadside*(London, n.d.)

24 'Petition of Sir Ashton Lever'.

25 Ibid.

26 Torrens, 'Parkinson, James'.

6. 'Temple of Knowledge and Reason'

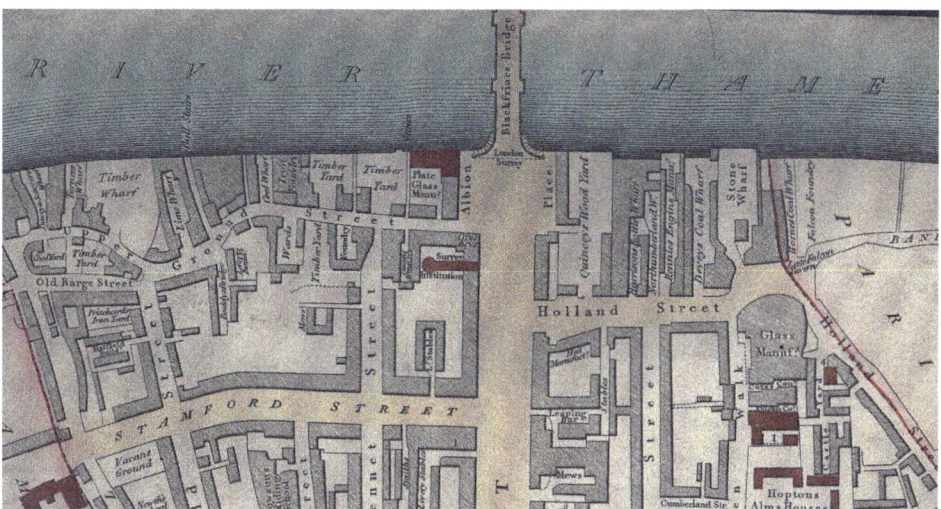

Figure 6.1 Map of Blackfriars Road, Parish of Christchurch, Surrey, c. 1820. Note the Surrey Institution shaded red, centre left.

Copyright Southwark Local History Library.

The site at 3 Blackfriars Road offered considerable scope for Parkinson's venture, occupying an ample 1000 square yards (1.4 ha) on the Surrey side of the Thames, just a few doors down from the entrance to Blackfriars Bridge (Figure 6.1). Construction of the building, designed jointly by Parkinson and Burton, began in 1787 and by December the doors of the Leverian Museum opened.[27] Guarding over the humble exterior of the 'four-storey yellow stock brickwork' terrace house was an 'elegant portico of the Ionic order', which was adorned with a female Romanesque statue of Contemplation (Figure 6.2).[28] Upon entering the premises, visitors were met by the 'beautifully romantic appearance' of two columns of hexagonal stone extracted from the Giant's Causeway in the north of Ireland. The entrance hall also featured a flat ceiling from which rose an oval-shaped dome with skylights to help illuminate four glass cases displaying arrows, daggers, tomahawks and other 'different curious weapons' placed (somewhat incongruously) alongside the skeleton head of an elephant and the stuffed 'Favourite Dog, of a particular friend of Sir Ashton Lever's'.[29] It was, after all, early days in the history of public museums and the arrangement of exhibits.

---

27 Burton's legacy survives today in the Bloomsbury area of London, which he was largely responsible for developing in the late eighteenth century.
28 Akermann is quoted in Sir Howard Roberts and W. H. Godfrey (eds), *Survey of London* (Bankside: London County Council, 1950), vol. xxii, pp. 115–17.
29 These descriptions of the collection, and those that follow, are taken from *A Companion to the Museum (Late Sir Ashton Lever's)* (London, 1790), pp. 4–5.

Figure 6.2 Front facade of the Leverian Museum, 3 Blackfriars Road.

V. Davis, 1805. Copyright Wellcome Library, London.

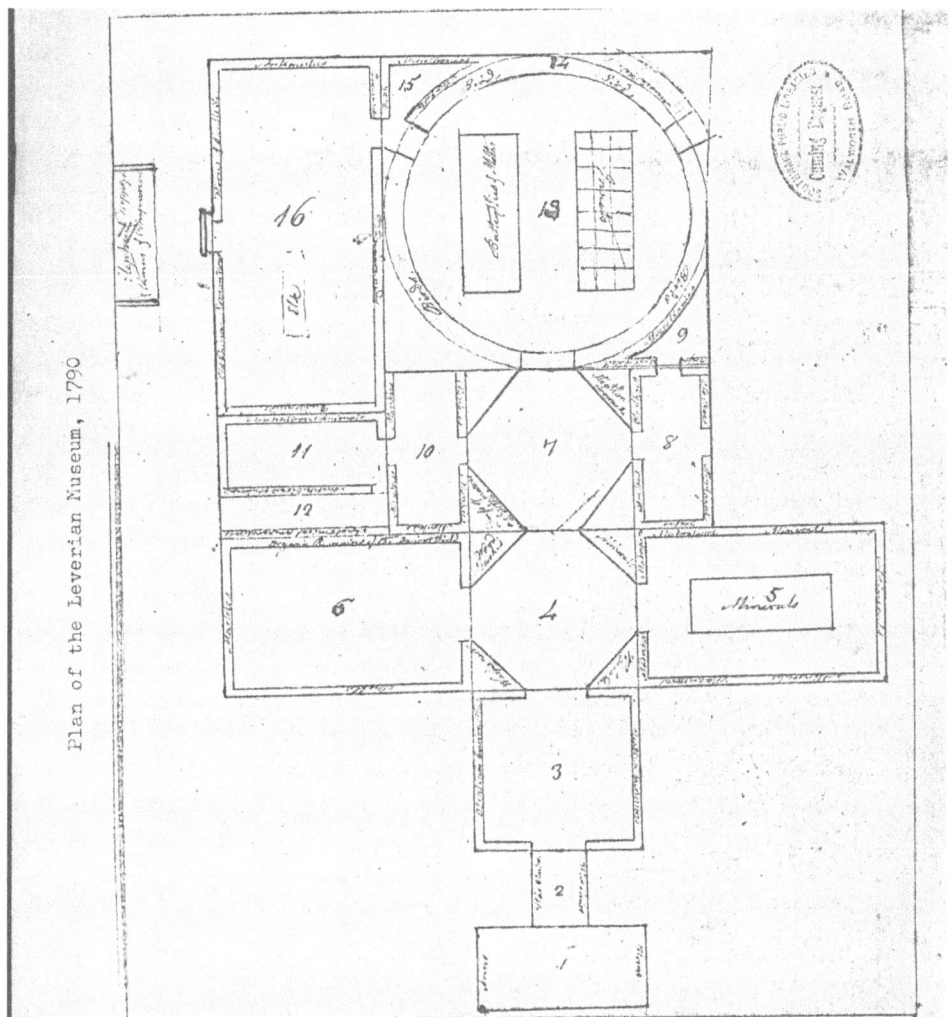

Figure 6.3 Floorplan of the Leverian Museum, prepared by a visitor, c. 1807. This appears to be the only plan for the premises at 3 Blackfriars Road to have survived in the historical record.

Possibly drawn by Richard Cuming. Copyright Southwark Local History Library.

Moving along the passage, visitors entered the first of the main exhibition rooms (Figure 6.3). Further examples of weaponry and garments collected from the Sandwich Islands adorned the vestibule—an arched passage leading into a spacious anteroom with arched ceiling. Dedicated with the inscription 'To the Immortal Memory of Captain Cook', the room was again lighted by 'central openings in a domed ceiling' and housed hundreds of curiosities and artefacts from Cook's South Pacific expeditions. From there, visitors moved through to the Saloon. The Saloon was outfitted with four 'elegant deep mahogany glass cases' containing 'curious exotic plants' from around the globe, including filigree moss from Lapland and 'curious unknown plants' from Botany Bay, New South Wales.[30] To the right and left of this room were the North Room and South Room respectively, both of 'handsome proportions' lighted by skylights and housing similar ephemera and, not surprisingly, hundreds more 'curiosities'.

Visitors to the museum then progressed through to the Fish Room, which provided access to three smaller rooms to the right and one room to the left.[31] The arrangement of the displays channelled visitors from the rooms in the wings back to the central Saloon and Fish Room, which, in turn, provided a passage through to the Leverian's most elegant and commodious apartment: the Rotunda. Decorated in the style of a 'Grecian temple', the room (later to become known as the Rotunda's small theatre) was captured in perpetuity by the magnificent drawings of celebrated nature artist Sarah Stone (Figure 6.4). The dome, entablature and an upper viewing gallery were supported by 'eight Doric columns, of Derbyshire marble, whose entablature [was] crowned by a balustrade of the same materials', as is clearly visible in Stone's illustration.

Early public museums such as the Leverian played an important role in the formation of the bourgeois public sphere, reflecting the changing nature of urban society and culture as it sought to separate 'culture' from the sphere of the state and the court. Before the late eighteenth century, collections of such material remained in the hands of private aristocratic or noble collectors and were open only to private audiences.[32] Recently, scholars of the history of the museum have begun to question the simple dichotomy between the transition from private collections to public forms of display, recognising that the evolution of museums is 'as much a story of continuity as it is of change'.[33]

In the eighteenth century, the rising middling classes were keen aspirants to what were formerly aristocratic cultural realms such as art and other cultural collections. Their enthusiasm provided opportunities for private entrepreneurs such as Lever and Parkinson with an eye for commercial ventures. As cultural scholar Tony Bennett notes, such venues allowed another public outlet for reasoned critique, rational exchange and debate. Moreover, in providing an outlet for genteel urban sociability, they also allowed the formative bourgeois public to develop a 'corporate self-consciousness'.[34]

---

30 For a detailed description of the collection, see ibid. The companion includes a drawing by Sarah Stone of the 'Grand saloon and Gallery' (small theatre) of the building. See also J. C. H. King, 'New Evidence for the Contents of the Leverian Museum', *Journal of the History of Collections*, vol. 8 (1996), pp. 167–86.
31 The description of the floorplan is taken from Anthony Ella, *Visits to the Leverian Museum* (London, 1805).
32 Andrew McClellan, 'A Brief History of the Art Museum Public', in Andrew McClellan (ed.), *Art and its Publics: Museum studies at the millennium* (Cornwall: Blackwell, 2003), p. 4.
33 Samuel J. M. Alberti, 'Owning and Collecting Natural Objects in Nineteenth-Century Britain', in Marco Beretta (ed.), *From Private to Public: Natural collections and museums* (Sagamore Beach, Mass.: Science History Publications, 2005), p. 141.
34 Tony Bennett, *The Birth of the Museum: History, theory, politics* (London: Routledge, 1995), pp. 25–6.

6. 'Temple of Knowledge and Reason'

Figure 6.4 Rotunda, Leverian Museum, drawn by Sarah Stone. This room would later be known as the small theatre of the Rotunda.

From *A Companion to the Museum Late Sir Ashton's*, 1790. Copyright City of London, London Metropolitan Archives.

The development of this 'corporate self-consciousness' required distinctions between those who belonged and those who did not. Many private collections were open to the public, but retained an exclusivity based on social class. According to Samuel Alberti:

> [A]s in other aspects of the public sphere, civic and metropolitan elites retained control of museums throughout, and although admission criteria of these various groups became ostensibly more inclusive, privileged access continued to be granted to expert and esteemed visitors—exclusively middle-class, and usually men.[35]

---

35 Ibid., p. 153.

In the case of the Leverian, the gender exclusions are less clear-cut than Alberti suggests. Stone's drawings of the Leverian Museum provide evidence that women (and children) were part of the museum's clientele.[36] Nevertheless, the social exclusivity based on class that Alberti refers to is certainly evident in the history of the Leverian. Before Lever moved his collection to London, the sheer numbers attending his public openings in Manchester saw him exclude those who came by foot.[37]

By allowing public entry, both Lever's and Parkinson's museums saw a blurring of the boundaries between not only public and private, but between high and low culture.[38] The cost of admission, however, was clearly another means of defining those who were eligible to be admitted to the venue; a fee for entry potentially excluded the majority of the population. Such tangible measures were only part of the system that defined the eligible inhabitants of the space; the higher status individuals associated with the venture (including aristocratic patronage) also defined who could be part of the 'corporate consciousness'.

Another means by which a venue could help define itself (and its clientele) was location. This was particularly relevant to London with its intense population growth of the eighteenth and early nineteenth centuries and its new opportunities for sociability, class-based geographical division and urban cultural institutions. The location of such a new institution was vital to attracting the 'right' clientele. Ironically, Lever's original move from Manchester to Leicester Square proved disastrous, and Parkinson also took a gamble in relocating the collection to the purpose-built facility in nearby Surrey away from the centre of the metropolis. Although only a short a distance from the centre of London, it was located on the southern side of the Thames—an area not normally frequented by the literati 'Fashionables of the West End'.[39] As John Barrell contends, for the 'politest classes'—the aristocrats and Members of Parliament—London 'east of the still notional line of Regent Street must have been, if not terra incognita, then still much of it largely unexplored'.[40]

---

36 See Figure 6.4. *A Companion to the Museum (Late Sir Ashton Lever's)*. See also King, 'New Evidence for the Contents of the Leverian Museum', pp. 167–86. Tony Bennett considers that museums provided women with an opportunity to participate in the public sphere. See Bennett, *The Birth of the Museum*, pp. 29–33.
37 Kell, 'Lever, Sir Ashton'. Richard Altick notes that one keen visitor who was turned away circumvented Lever's rule by returning atop a cow. Altick, *The Shows of London*, p. 29.
38 Ibid., p. 5.
39 David Hadley, 'Public Lectures and Private Societies: Expounding literature and the arts in Romantic London', in Donald Schoonmaker and John A. Alford (eds), *English Romanticism: Preludes and postludes* (Michigan: East Lansing Colleagues, 1993), p. 45. My thanks to Gillian Russell for providing me with this reference.
40 John Barrell, 'London and the London Corresponding Society', in James Chandler and Kevin Gilmartin (eds), *Romantic Metropolis: The urban scene of British culture, 1780–1840* (Cambridge: Cambridge University Press, 2005), p. 100.

Those thirsting for urban sociability, however, could be fickle. As Richard Altick contends, purely commercial museums, even in the centre of London, tended to have a short lifespan in the early nineteenth century.[41] It is difficult to gauge the extent to which the South London location contributed to the Leverian's failure. Parkinson's venture never entirely succeeded as a commercial operation and, by 1806, Parkinson already had several failed attempts to sell the collection to successive government administrations. When his application was finally referred to Sir Joseph Banks for a decision, Banks refused to recommend that the government purchase the collection.[42] Infuriated by the decision, Parkinson was forced to offer the collection for public auction. Despite attracting great public interest in both Britain and on the Continent, it took two months to clear almost 8000 lots. At final calculations, the auction had raised a disappointing £6600.[43]

With the contents of the Leverian finally disposed of, it took Parkinson almost two years to find new tenants for the premises. By 1808, his wait was over when proprietors of a new public venture, a scientific and literary institution, took up the lease. The Surrey Institution—another archetypal space of Habermas's bourgeois public sphere—had its genesis in the success of the Royal Institution, which, as historian Jon Klancher notes, was founded in 1799 by a 'consortium of aristocratic landowners with the intention of amalgamating science to commerce, philosophy to technology, and literary traditions to the newest conditions of modernity'.[44] The success of the Royal Institution spawned many imitators, including the Surrey, and these scientific and literary institutions became an important part of the new assembly of public cultural arenas for rational exchange and debate.[45] For almost 15 years, the Surrey Institution became a haven for the knowledge-thirsty rising middling classes, offering scientific and literary lectures and discourses each week, along with reading and 'conversation' rooms. Many of Britain's most notable scientists, engineers, authors, artists and architects appeared at the Rotunda theatre during the Surrey's heyday.[46]

---

41   Altick, *The Shows of London*, p. 4.
42   Parkinson believed this was because Banks hated Lever and 'therefore hate[d] the collection'. See Torrens, 'Parkinson, James'.
43   Ibid.
44   Jon Klancher, 'Transmission Failure', in David Perkins (ed.), *Theoretical Issues in Literary Study*, Harvard English Studies, vol. XVI (Cambridge, Mass.: Harvard University Press, 1991), pp. 173–95, quoted in Peter J. Manning, 'Manufacturing the Romantic Image: Hazlitt and Coleridge lecturing', in Chandler and Gilmartin, *Romantic Metropolis*, p. 229.
45   For a detailed history of the Surrey Institution, see Frederick Kurzer, 'A History of the Surrey Institution', *Annals of Science*, vol. 57 (2000), pp. 109–41; Geoffrey Carnell, 'The Surrey Institution and its Successor', *Adult Education*, vol. 26 (1953), pp. 197–208. See also Gillian Russell, 'Spouters or Washerwomen: The sociability of Romantic lecturing', in Gillian Russell and Clara Tuite (eds), *Romantic Sociability: Social networks and literary culture in Britain, 1770–1840* (Cambridge: Cambridge University Press, 2002), pp. 128–32. David Hadley calculates that about 30–32 such literary and scientific institutions operated around London between 1798 and 1837. See Hadley, 'Public Lectures and Private Societies', p. 46.
46   Kurzer, 'A History of the Surrey Institution', p. 121.

Prior to opening the new institution, James Parkinson's architect son, Joseph T. Parkinson, was engaged to undertake considerable renovations to ensure the premises were fit for purpose. According to science historian Sophie Forgan, a scientific society needed to embrace a number of different functions including operating as a museum and providing in addition a library, an observatory or laboratory and rooms for lectures, classes, meetings and for the officers.[47] How those functions were 'embodied into rooms and articulated within the building', argues Forgan, 'had implications for the structure of scientific discourse'.[48] When Joseph Parkinson planned his modifications to the Surrey premises, he was able to draw on the model of the Royal Institution. With the building already accommodating the museum and meeting room requirements, he added a 60 ft (18 m) library with galleries on three sides, and a new chemical laboratory.[49]

The laboratory was promoted as one of the Surrey's most valued assets and patrons of the Institution attended lectures and demonstrations on subjects such as the 'elements of Chemical Science' and 'Pneumatics and Electricity'.[50] The room was hailed as one of the finest examples of an experimental laboratory in the country, though science historian Frederick Kurzer contends that, like much of the Surrey, it was employed predominantly for supporting the 'performance of lecture experiments rather than in the pursuit of specific research projects'.[51] It is clear though (as Kurzer himself acknowledges) that some research from the Surrey's science programme did lead to important discoveries. As an example, the public experiments of Sir Goldsworthy Gurney at the Surrey laboratory led to new developments in gas illumination and he was subsequently invited to design the new lighting for the House of Commons chamber.[52]

Joseph Parkinson also modified the building's prime asset, the Rotunda room, into a circular theatre capable of seating up to 500 people. The new space was described by London chronicler Rudolph Ackermann as 'one of the most elegant rooms in the metropolis' and was captured in a Rowlandson aquatint, which featured a Frederich Christian Accum chemical lecture (Figure 6.5).[53] Along with the upper gallery, a lower gallery was added by the younger Parkinson and was described as 'curiously constructed, being sustained by iron columns

---

47 Ibid., p. 95.
48 Sophie Forgan, 'Context, Image and Function: A preliminary enquiry into the architecture of scientific societies', *British Journal for the History of Science*, vol. 19 (1986), p. 91.
49 On Joseph Parkinson and the renovations to the building, see Colvin, *BDBA*, pp. 736–7. See also Kurzer, 'A History of the Surrey Institution', p. 118. It is difficult to discern from the available descriptions and plans whether Joseph Parkinson converted the room numbered 16 on the 1790 plan as the library or constructed an entirely new room to the right of the Rotunda. See Figure 6.3.
50 Rendle Collection (Southwark File), n.d., fo. 288, London Metropolitan Archives Library.
51 Kurzer, 'A History of the Surrey Institution', p. 120.
52 G. B. Smith, 'Gurney, Sir Goldsworthy (1793–1875)', rev. Anita McConnell, *ODNB*, <http://www.oxforddnb.com/view/article/11764>
53 Akermann is quoted in Roberts and Godfrey, *Survey of London*, p. 116.

and their projecting cantilevers or trusses'.[54] The Rotunda was 36 ft (11 m) in diameter; the ground section contained nine rows of seats, which rose above each other in 'commodious gradation'.[55] The first gallery contained two rows of seats and the upper gallery three rows. Light filled the room from the ceiling dome and warmth was provided in the winter through flues containing heated air, which were concealed in the walls, making the building a comfortable all-season venue.

Figure 6.5 'Surrey Institution', Thomas Rowlandson.

From Rudolph Ackermann's *Microcosm of London*, 1809. Copyright Wellcome Library, London.

The scientific lecture theatre, as Forgan notes, began to develop a particular form by the early nineteenth century. They often assumed the shape of an 'amphitheatre or hemisphere' modelled not on the stage theatre, but on the anatomical theatre that originated in Padua and that featured raked seating upwards from the floor in a circular pattern.[56] The premises at Blackfriars Road proved ideal for this purpose; the Surrey inherited the circular gallery and Joseph Parkinson's seating modifications allowed for an imitation of the style

---

54 Ibid.
55 Ibid.
56 Forgan, 'Context, Image and Function', p. 101.

adopted in the Royal Institution.⁵⁷ The shape of the theatre certainly added to the performance of the lectures. From the lecturer's perspective, observes Forgan, all eyes 'gazed down upon him'.⁵⁸ Parkinson's modifications, which won him a place in the annual exhibition of the Royal Academy of Arts, also clearly impressed Ackermann, who described the premises as an 'academic mansion'.⁵⁹

Alongside rational scientific instruction, the Surrey's literature and cultural program was equally lauded by the Institution's management.⁶⁰ The proprietors assembled a rich array of arts and cultural programs presented by some of the leading humanities figures of the day. Among the most prominent and esteemed presenters of the Surrey's cultural programs was the literary luminary Samuel Taylor Coleridge, who, according to his contemporaries, delivered magnificent lectures on the writings of Shakespeare and provided critical analysis of classical poetry and literature.⁶¹ Music instruction was also catered for with esteemed composer and organist Samuel Wesley delivering lectures on music for almost two years at the Surrey.⁶² Wesley was subsequently replaced by Dr William Crotch, former professor of music at Oxford University and Principal of the Royal Academy of Music, who oversaw the Surrey's music program for 12 years.⁶³ The field of architecture was also well represented at the Surrey, with London architect James Elmes providing instruction on architectural history, as well as a critique of the design and function of the new urban architecture.⁶⁴

Kurzer notes that while the managers of the Surrey insisted on a high intellectual standard for the lectures, they also recognised the importance of the performance as an element of instruction, directing that the presentations at the Institution should also 'blend instruction with rational amusement'.⁶⁵ This directive allowed for the engagement of such flamboyant figures as Gregor von Feinaigle (formerly Gregor Feinoegl). A mnemonist and educator, Feinaigle gave a series of lectures at the Surrey in 1811.⁶⁶ A former German monk, he anglicised his surname and adopted the prefix 'von' as a pretence to aristocratic heritage.⁶⁷ Feinaigle's show involved teaching orphans to remember complex sequences of dates, poetry or mathematical equations, which he demonstrated to audiences before

---

57 Ibid., p. 102.
58 Ibid.
59 Quoted in Roberts and Godfrey, *Survey of London*, pp. 115–17.
60 On lectures at the Surrey, see Gillian Russell, 'Spouters or Washerwomen', pp. 128–32.
61 Kurzer, 'A History of the Surrey Institution', pp. 134–5.
62 Philip Olleson, 'Wesley, Samuel (1766–1837)', *ODNB*, <http://www.oxforddnb.com/view/article/ 29072>
63 Ibid.
64 Kurzer, 'A History of the Surrey Institution', p. 133.
65 Ibid., p. 121.
66 Feinaigle would later start an institution in his own name in Dublin. The Feinaigle Institution would establish schools that operated on his system of regular examinations and free of corporal punishment. See Terence Richardson, 'Feinaigle, Gregor von (1760–1819)', *ODNB*, <http://www.oxforddnb.com/view/article/9252>
67 Ibid.

signing many of them to a series of lessons to learn the memory techniques.[68] Feinaigle's biographer, Terence Richardson, admits Feinaigle did cultivate an 'air of mystery' from both his past as a monk and the 'sources of his arcane techniques', but maintains he was 'no charlatan'.

The directive for 'rational amusement' alongside instruction from the Surrey proprietors was also fulfilled by celebrated writer and critic William Hazlitt who was said to have delighted his audiences for three successive seasons with lectures on the 'English Poets from Chaucer', the 'English Comic Writers' and 'Drama of the Elizabethan Age'.[69] Hazlitt's lectures, as Peter Manning notes, provided much more than simply an outlet for knowledge and information; observers applauded them as performances, 'intense, immediate theatre', as testified by the repeatedly large audiences.[70] The Secretary of the Surrey Institution, P. G. Patmore, had a long association with London's literary elite (even in less celebratory times such as during John Hunt's imprisonment in Coldbath Fields prison) and it was he who convinced Hazlitt to undertake the series of lectures in 1818.[71] Hazlitt received 200 guineas for the work, which he considered 'very well for ten weeks work', which included the royalties for the printed editions of the lectures.[72] Hazlitt attracted a wide range of London cultural and political literati to his lectures at the Surrey including William Godwin, John Keats and Henry Crabb Robinson as well as artists Benjamin Robert Haydon and William Bewick, and radical writers John Hunt and William Hone.[73]

The new lecturing institutions tapped into the emerging middling-class drive for respectability through education and self-improvement.[74] Although lecturing was a well-established form of entertainment and instruction at multipurpose venues such as the Crown and Anchor tavern, the emergence of scientific and literary societies provided a new stage for the practice.[75] Such

---

68 Ibid.
69 *Surrey Institution Circular*, 1 October 1822, Guildhall Library Collection, London. For Hazlitt's account of his 'Comic Writers' lectures, see his letter to Macvey Napier, 26 August 1818, reproduced in Hershel Moreland Sikes (ed.), *The Letters of William Hazlitt* (London: Macmillan, 1979), p. 185. Gillian Russell notes that in any regard, 'in analyzing lectures, it is important not to overestimate the "rational" at the expense of the "entertainment"', as the more serious scientific instruction was 'bound up with its status as a social event'. See Russell, 'Spouters or Washerwomen', p. 125.
70 Manning, 'Manufacturing the Romantic Image', p. 230.
71 Patmore and Hazlitt became close friends following Hazlitt's lectures at the Surrey. In 1854, Patmore published a detailed account of his relationship with Hazlitt and other friends of London's literary circles in *My Friends and Acquaintances: Being memorials, mind-portraits, and personal recollections of deceased celebrities of the nineteenth century: with selections from their unpublished letters* (London: Saunders and Otley, 1854). See Sikes, *The Letters of William Hazlitt*, p. 181n.
72 William Hazlitt to Francis Jeffrey, 12 May 1818, reprinted in Sikes, *The Letters of William Hazlitt*, p. 182.
73 Manning, 'Manufacturing the Romantic Image', p. 230. The lectures were so successful that Hazlitt repeated them at the Crown and Anchor tavern during 1818.
74 Hadley, 'Public Lectures and Private Societies', p. 45.
75 Forgan, 'Context, Image and Function', p. 96. See also Ian Inkster, *Scientific Culture and Urbanisation in Industrialising Britain* (Aldershot: Ashgate, 1997), pp. 80–107. For a discussion of public lecturing in this period, see Russell, 'Spouters or Washerwomen', pp. 123–44.

institutions helped establish a new middling-class identity, providing a forum for intellectual exchange, collectivity and association.[76] Although the Surrey was modelled on the Royal Institution, and therefore drew on the cultural conventions of the 'parent' institution, it soon established its own feel and a distinct identity. Despite the Surrey's geographic isolation from the 'fashionable West End' (or perhaps because of the intellectual freedom of expression it allowed), as David Hadley notes, the 'Romantic era's most significant [literary] criticism...was offered in the least pretentious of London's literary institutes'.[77] This, he argues, 'may testify eloquently to the impulse and aspirations which had led professionals, bankers, shopkeepers, writers, and some highly skilled artisans, to found a Surrey Institution'.[78]

Despite the relative silence in Habermas's original work of the role of such institutions in the formation of the public sphere, it is evident, as Roy Porter argues, that the nature and practice of the scientific and literary institutions made them key outlets for rational exchange and discussion.[79] As Paul Elliott adds, such institutions allowed members of the public to 'buy into' the 'Enlightenment rationality and advertise their membership of the club of public rational discourse'.[80] The explicit rule against political or theological discussion at such institutions could account for Habermas's oversight, though radical political ideas, while not officially on the lecture calendar of the Surrey Institution, certainly circulated at the site. The Surrey's membership, argues Hadley, was 'more down-market, more Dissenter, and even more earnest' than some of the 'Fashionables of the West End' who declined to travel there to hear their friend Coleridge lecture.[81] He describes the Surrey's political influences as 'catholic', as evidenced by the catalogue contents of the library: 'Beccaria, Burke, Letters of Junius, Leveller pamphlets, Locke, Milton, Montesquieu.'[82] Manning concludes that there were many Quakers and Dissenters in the Surrey audience, who, Crabb Robinson recalled in his diary, were served an 'indiscreet and reckless' reading of Voltaire, 'the modern infidel'.[83] The Surrey was also not

---

76 Jonathan Barry, 'Bourgeois Collectivism? Urban association and the middling sort', in Jonathan Barry and Christopher Brooks (eds), *The Middling Sort of People* (London: Macmillan, 1994), p. 95. For a useful analysis and overview of the scholarship in this field, see Paul Elliott, 'The Origins of the "Creative Class": Provincial urban society and socio-political marginality in Britain in the eighteenth and nineteenth centuries', *Social History*, vol. 28, no. 3 (2003), pp. 361–87.
77 Hadley, 'Public Lectures and Private Societies', p. 58.
78 Ibid.
79 Roy Porter, 'Science, Provincial Culture and Public Opinion', *British Journal for Eighteenth Century Studies*, vol. 3 (1980), pp. 20–46.
80 Elliott, 'The Origins of the "Creative Class"', p. 366.
81 Hadley, 'Public Lectures and Private Societies', p. 45.
82 Ibid., p. 57.
83 Crabb Robinson, quoted in Manning, 'Manufacturing the Romantic Image', p. 231.

unique in this more marginal political milieu; Ian Inkster's study of scientific culture in Britain argues that Dissenters and other marginal groups were often a dominant force in other such institutions.[84]

Hazlitt's literary lectures in particular often came with biting political commentary. At the core of his political beliefs were the 'revolutionary principles of 1688 and 1789',[85] and Hazlitt's friend, the painter William Bewick, recorded that when members of the audience disagreed with his political sentiments, Hazlitt would 'calmly turn back the leaf of his copy and deliberately repeat the sentiments with great energy and a voice more determined than before'.[86] It appears Hazlitt's detractors were fewer in number than those who revelled in his lectures for he became a favourite Surrey Institution orator. One correspondent to *The Times* regretted Hazlitt's frequent but 'unfortunate and irrelevant political allusion', contending that he was wrong in venting them before a mixed audience assembled for amusement and instruction in science and literature.[87] More disturbing for the correspondent, however, was the audience reaction: 'so well dressed and respectable an audience emulating the uproar of one-shilling gallery behaviour.' Whether it was the liberal political views of the Surrey patrons or the commercial imperatives of the venture, the proprietors could not ignore that the theatre was filled with 'most respectable audiences' even during Hazlitt's most notorious performances.[88]

The audience reaction to Hazlitt's lectures suggests that the prevailing image of the sober intellectual climate of the Surrey and other such institutions of the bourgeois public sphere should be reconsidered. Forgan also notes that until the mid-nineteenth century, even audiences of the serious educational instruction utilised their voices to indicate their approval or disapproval with 'boos and cheers "hear-hear" and such'.[89] Such reaction indicates the continuities between more traditional popular modes of entertainment and the new forums for rational-critical discourse and debate. The Surrey was clearly operating as an institution of the bourgeois public sphere, adopting many of the official rules and the informal conventions of the parent institution. It is evident, however, that by populating the venue with both audience and orators, the demarcation lines between such ventures and those of a more plebeian nature were more fluid than a simple bourgeois–plebeian binary allows.

---

84 Inkster, *Scientific Culture and Urbanization in Industrialising Britain*.
85 Hadley, 'Public Lectures and Private Societies', p. 45.
86 T. Landseer (ed.), *Life and Letters of William Bewick*, 2 vols (London, 1871), quoted in Kurzer, 'A History of the Surrey Institution', p. 135. The correspondent was undoubtedly unaware of the involvement of Mr Alsager, commercial editor of *The Times*, on the Committee of the Surrey Institution. It was Alsager who proposed that Hazlitt be engaged to deliver the course of lectures on the English poets. See Augustine Birrell, *William Hazlitt* (London: Macmillan and Co., 1922).
87 *The Times*, 12 November 1818.
88 The observation comes from the *Morning Chronicle*, 23 February 1818.
89 Forgan, 'Context, Image and Function', p. 102.

Despite the initial strong appeal to the middling classes, institutions such as the Surrey came under heavy financial pressure to maintain their activities. For the Surrey's proprietors, the end came in 1823, after many years of expenditure 'exceed[ing] its investment income by some £700 per annum'.[90] In a final bid to rescue the venture, the managers proposed levying the proprietors with an additional annual subscription. It was summarily rejected by the majority of proprietors, 450 of whom together had initially provided the significant sum of £22 500 to establish the Institution. And it appears that the location of the venue could, once again, have played a role in its demise. At least one contemporary observer blamed the failure of the Institution on the site itself, which he considered 'most injudicious, since it was completely out of the mighty stream of human beings which never ceases to its flow through the centre of the metropolis'.[91] The demise of the Surrey, however, just like the Leverian before it, could also have been due to the voracious appetite for new forms of urban sociability. As Richard Altick notes, this period was marked not only by the instability of popular taste, but also by its 'restless demand for innovation'.[92]

Having decided to close the Institution, the Surrey proprietors now sought to recoup some funds from the defunct venture. The premises were stripped of their 'entire substance' starting with the library's collection of journals and books—successfully auctioned above its valued price—along with the shelves, furniture and clocks that once adorned the room. The circular theatre was 'dismantled to its walls and foundations', with the iron rails, seats, staircases and mahogany handrails, iron pillars and front railings sold for £28; the three rows of circular seats round the upper gallery sold for £7 each.[93] Cultural appendages, such as the bronze statues of the 'different fathers of science and literature, such as Homer, Bacon, Locke and Newton', were also removed.[94] There remained little tangible trace of the once-celebrated 'academic mansion'.

Following the Surrey's demise, the premises were used intermittently by a variety of inhabitants and exhibitors, including some reportedly less reputable penny gaff productions and a wax works.[95] By 1826, it was reported that the exterior of the building was now inscribed 'Rotunda Wine and Concert Rooms' and was frequented by 'lovers of a good glass of wine' who were entertained every Tuesday and Thursday evening with professional singing and music.[96]

---

90 Kurzer, 'A History of the Surrey Institution', p. 136. Hadley notes the initial set-up cost borne by the 450 proprietors. Hadley, 'Public Lectures and Private Societies', p. 56.
91 W. Swainson, *Taxidermy: With the biography of zoologists* (1840), quoted in Torrens, 'Parkinson, James', *ODNB*.
92 Altick, *The Shows of London*, p. 3.
93 Kurzer, 'A History of the Surrey Institution', p. 138.
94 Akermann is quoted in Roberts and Godfrey, *Survey of London*, p. 116.
95 Altick, *The Shows of London*, p. 32.
96 *Every Day Book*, 18 July 1826, held in the collection of printed ephemera catalogued as the 'Surrey Rotunda' and held in the Wellcome Institute Library, London (hereafter Wellcome Collection).

Entry was free as patrons were expected to buy their refreshments and the venue was said to have attracted large numbers, including women. The wine and concert rooms continued to operate through the following year and were joined in 1827 by a new spectacle, Cooke's Amphitheatre. During this time, a larger circular theatre was constructed at the rear of the premises for equestrian purposes, much to the dismay of local residents who protested against the 'horse performances'.[97] In 1828, the Rotunda expanded further its reputation for innovative public entertainment, becoming home to a revolving dioramic panorama illustrating 'all the principle events that have occurred between the Turks and the Greeks' painted on almost '20,000 square feet of canvas'.[98] Though the venue in this period appears to have had an entirely commercial outlook, there was a patina of plebeian political association when the new proprietors, a Mr and Mrs Ford, held a benefit concert in 1827 to aid those 'suffering and distressed' in the manufacturing districts of the country.[99]

In that same year, Richard Carlile, now released from his long prison term at Dorchester, also had provincial England on his mind as he undertook a tour of the districts that provided such strong moral and financial support to himself, his family and his shop workers during the decade. During Carlile's 1827 tour, he suffered first hand the impact of the government's restrictive legislation on the spatial logistics of the radical movement. Carlile was repeatedly frustrated by the efforts of established clergymen and local magistrates to prevent the staging of his lectures by either restricting his access to lecture halls or closing down his meetings as they got under way. During the 1829 tour of the north of England, which he undertook with the infamous Reverend Robert Taylor, the 'infidel missionaries' were again frustrated by the efforts of the authorities and clergy in Nottingham and Leeds to prevent their discourses. They were evicted from five different lecturing halls.[100]

Both Carlile and Taylor were acutely aware of the need for a new radical forum. Even before undertaking the 1829 tour, Taylor had identified the importance of feeling a 'tangibility of our great cause about us'.[101] What radicalism needed, he felt, was a 'substance and a nucleus' in the form of a dedicated space from which to operate. Taylor had long recognised the benefits of obtaining a permanent lecturing establishment. In 1826, with the aid of several financial backers, he purchased the 'Areopagus' or Salter's Hall Chapel.[102] Taylor offered £5 shares in the venture and it became the headquarters for his Christian Evidence Society.

---

97 *Prompter*, 13 November 1830. For local resident dissent, see 'Surrey Rotunda', fo. 61, Wellcome Collection.
98 *Description of the Historical, Peristrephic or Revolving Dioramic Panorama, Now Exhibiting in Great Surrey Street, Blackfriars Road*(London, 1828). See also the report of the panorama in *Morning Chronicle*, 14 October 1828.
99 On the Rotunda Wine Rooms and the benefit concert, see 'Surrey Rotunda', ff. 73–4, Wellcome Collection.
100 See Wiener, *Radicalism and Freethought in Nineteenth-Century Britain*, pp. 155–60.
101 *Lion*, 23 January 1829.
102 *Devil's Pulpit*, vol. 2, 1832, 'Memoir of the Reverend Robert Taylor'.

His imprisonment in 1827 for a blasphemous discourse, however, forced the sale of the premises; Taylor's 'fine theatre of free discussion' was thus 'sacrificed to the manes of despotism'.[103] The difficulties Carlile encountered with venues while on his provincial tours were mirrored in the capital. Although many landlords could have been sympathetic to Carlile's political aims, his freethinking tenets and infidel ideals (which attracted much publicity during the 1820s trials) were entirely another matter. Carlile had attempted to turn his premises at 62 Fleet Street into a makeshift lecturing hall, but the inadequacy of these plans was quickly realised when Taylor began lecturing and commanded audiences far in excess of the 100 people the seating allowed.

The Blackfriars Road Rotunda secured for Carlile the capacity for large crowds as well as the 'substance' and the 'nucleus' that Taylor had dreamt of for the radical movement. By the time Carlile entered the premises in May 1830, however, the once 'noble apartments' had suffered from use by multiple tenants and neglect, and the building was in a dilapidated state. His straitened financial position following his lengthy prison term through the 1820s could hardly have allowed him to take on either the refurbishment costs or even the rent alone, which amounted to a heavy £400 a year.[104] With the assistance of wealthy freethinking allies, William Devonshire Saull and Julian Hibbert, as well as anonymous donations to the cause of 'rational debate', Carlile undertook refurbishments to make the building fit for public use at the considerable sum of £1300.[105]

For Carlile, it was an investment with the promise of incalculable dividends; the Rotunda was to provide the catalyst for a new era of English radicalism. Carlile publicly declared that the Rotunda would help launch a 'war' against political and religious despotism, which he held responsible for the ills of British society. He anticipated that it would become a shrine for reform. In the opening issue of the *Prompter*, Carlile exalted at the birth of a new radical space, announcing that the Rotunda was

> a capitol of public virtue, the nucleus for a reformation of abuses,— the real House of Commons, in the absence of a better—the palladium of what liberty we have…the birth-place of mind, and the focus of virtuous public excitement.[106]

---

103 Ibid.
104 *Prompter*, 2 July 1831; Home Office Papers, HO64/11, June 1830, fo. 46.
105 Home Office Papers, HO64/11, June 1830, fo. 46, 29 November 1831. William Saull, radical philanthropist, freethinker and wine merchant, also lectured at the Rotunda in early 1832. See Wiener, *Radicalism and Freethought in Nineteenth-Century Britain*, pp. 164, 252; Iowerth Prothero, *Artisans and Politics in Early Nineteenth Century London, John Gast and his Times* (Folkestone: Dawson, 1979), pp. 260–3, 308–11. On Julian Hibbert, radical and long-time financial supporter of plebeian radicals, see Campbell, *The Battle for the Freedom of the Press*, pp. 245–50; Joel Wiener, 'Hibbert, Julian', in Joseph Baylen and Norbert Gossman (eds), *Biographical Dictionary of Modern British Radicals* [hereafter *BDMBR*] (Sussex: Harvester Press, 1979), vol. 1, pp. 221–2.
106 *Prompter*, 13 November 1830.

Importantly, it was to be a public place where the disenfranchised and the disaffected would not only be heard, but where their collective discontent would be seen. No longer would the radical community be at the whim of landlords who controlled who spoke and what was uttered. Moreover, Carlile envisaged that, like the relationship between the Anti-Corn Law League and the Crown and Anchor, the Rotunda too could provide the 'centre' and a 'heart' for the real representatives of working people.

Carlile's primary intention for the Rotunda was to institutionalise the popular dissemination of knowledge. Carlile not only vowed to wage 'a war against despotism' at the Rotunda; a 'war' against the 'ignorance of the whole country' was central to his aims for the venture.[107] He believed that working people needed, and wanted, a venue for 'free, open and fair discussion', which would serve as a place of general instruction and learning for themselves and their children. Through free discussion—intellectual exchange unhindered by religious dogma or political orthodoxies—the 'necessary purgation and purification of the public mind' would be achieved to clear the way for the inevitable new order of society.[108] In a period marked by the competing claims over the British Constitution, Carlile maintained that it was free discussion that was the 'only necessary Constitution—the only necessary Law to the Constitution'.[109]

The Rotunda offered an ideal setting for the lecturing function Carlile envisaged. The statue of Contemplation that adorned the front entrance of the building both symbolised its function as an educational institution and triggered public memory of the learned history of the site itself, at least in its Leverian and Surrey heydays. Carlile declared that in establishing the Rotunda as a forum of free speech, he was seeking to rekindle the 'character' of the Surrey Institution, which, along with the Leverian Museum, he described as 'an honour to the neighbourhood'.[110] Carlile saw the Rotunda as an advancement on these institutions by allowing for 'freedom of speech and discussion in political and theological matters'.[111] Clearly, continuity existed between the various outlets of the public sphere that occupied the site over time.

By invoking the legacy of both the Surrey and the Leverian for a working-class audience, Carlile and Taylor could tap into a flourishing popular and radical culture during the 1820s and early 1830s. Over these decades radicalism frequently took the form of an 'intellectual culture', adapting to and influencing the working-class thirst for self-improvement and knowledge.[112] E. P. Thompson

---

107 Ibid.
108 *Prompter*, 4 December 1830.
109 Carlile quoted in Thompson, *The Making of the English Working Class*, p. 844.
110 *Prompter*, 13 November 1830.
111 Ibid.
112 On the drive for self-improvement in radical culture, see Patricia Hollis, *The Pauper Press: A study in working-class radicalism of the 1830s* (Oxford: Oxford University Press, 1970); Thompson, *The Making of*

has argued that during this period of 'silent instruction', a specifically working-class consciousness began to evolve and manifest itself, which rejected middle and ruling-class control of working-class culture—particularly in the field of education. Ruling-class views on the education of the lower classes were dominated by concerns over the effect on the ranks and status quo of English society. Established clergymen frequently expressed the view that to give a workingman more education than was necessary to read the Bible would 'do him an injury'.[113] They argued that the acquisition of political knowledge by those outside the political nation would 'confound the ranks of society' and thereby threaten the stability of that society.

When it became evident that working people were acquiring knowledge independently, E. P. Thompson and Patricia Hollis argue, the ruling-class strategy moved to control and direct the kind of knowledge that could be obtained.[114] Although conservative Methodist ministers insisted that unmonitored literacy was the 'snare of the devil', the acquisition of 'useful knowledge' was thought godly and full of merit.[115] Groups such as the Society for the Diffusion of Useful Knowledge (SDUK) provided an educational outlet for working people that centred on science, botany, mathematics and especially the applied sciences.[116] The discussion of politics, however, was strictly forbidden. These groups were supported by radicals as diverse in social standing as the artisan Francis Place and the lawyer and Whig parliamentarian Henry Brougham, who believed that if working people were determined to acquire knowledge, it was essential that they should have access only to 'suitable' knowledge.[117]

Many working-class radicals regarded Brougham's useful knowledge societies as 'props to decaying superstition' and ridiculed the SDUK as 'education mongers' who offered useless knowledge.[118] These radicals, buoyed by the re-emergence

---

the *English Working Class*, pp. 781–820; Richard Johnson, '"Really Useful Knowledge": Radical education and working-class culture, 1790–1848', in John Clarke, C. Critcher and Richard Johnson (eds), *Working Class Culture: Studies in history and theory* (London: Hutchison, 1979), pp. 75–102; Iain McCalman, *Radical Underworld: Prophets, revolutionaries and pornographers in London, 1795–1840* (Cambridge: Cambridge University Press, 1988), pp. 181–5. For a recent analysis of the phenomenon of self-improvement, as well as the debates in the historiography, see Anne Rodrick, *Self-help and Civic Culture: Citizenship in Victorian Britain* (Aldershot: Ashgate, 2004), especially ch. 1.

113 Hollis, *The Pauper Press*, p. 9.
114 Ibid., pp. 6–18.
115 For a discussion of 'useful knowledge', see Philip Connell, *Romanticism, Economics and the Question of 'Culture'* (Oxford: Oxford University Press, 2005), especially pp. 76–92; Johnson, '"Really Useful Knowledge"', pp. 75–102; Thompson, *The Making of the English Working Class*, p. 811.
116 For a recent study of the SDUK, see Rebecca Brookfield Kinraide, The Society for the Diffusion of Useful Knowledge and the Democratization of Learning in Early Nineteenth-Century Britain, Unpublished PhD dissertation (Madison: University of Wisconsin, 2006). See also Ian Haywood, *The Revolution in Popular Literature: Print, politics and the people, 1790–1860* (Cambridge: Cambridge University Press, 2004), pp. 101–24.
117 Philip O'Connell, *Romanticism, Economics and the Question of Culture* (Oxford: Oxford University Press, 2001), pp. 76–92; Hollis, *The Pauper Press*, p. 8.
118 Johnson, '"Really Useful Knowledge"', p. 79.

of the printed works of Thomas Paine (thanks largely to Carlile), held that as man was essentially a rational being, he therefore had an inalienable right to knowledge.[119] They questioned the right of any one class to monopolise the power and benefits of knowledge and education, and believed the education of the poor was limited in the interests of the rich, the ignorance of the people being purposely perpetuated by 'Old Corruption' to secure their privileged position in society.[120]

The dissemination of 'really useful' knowledge and the removal of ignorance therefore became principle objectives in radical reform. Working-class radicals sought social, moral and political improvement in society and insisted that it was through the acquisition of knowledge by working people that the radical struggle against the establishment would succeed. In this sense, radicals saw Rotunda education as a means of power and a weapon with which to bring down the ruling elite and established order. As John Gale Jones noted, knowledge would 'make the people bid defiance to any tyranny attempted to be put on them by their oppressors'.[121] They recognised that the articulate consciousness of the autodidact was readily transformed into political consciousness.[122]

The drive for respectable self-improvement amongst the working classes in the early nineteenth century revealed itself in a number of formal popular educational institutions.[123] Mutual improvement societies were a response to the working-class tradition of mutual and communal study. These societies sought primarily to promote efficiency in reading and writing, but also operated as reading and discussion groups, using the proceeds of a weekly contribution of one or twopence to fund the establishment of small libraries for their members' use.[124] This period also saw the rise of the mechanics' institutes, which, as the name suggests, began as educational clubs for mechanics, offering their members lectures and classes in the various fields of science.[125] They were, however, generally controlled by middle-class patrons and, like the SDUK, they came under fire from radicals for perpetuating the knowledge systems of the

---

119 O'Connell, *Romanticism, Economics and the Question of Culture*, p. 80; Hollis, *The Pauper Press*, p. 19.
120 Johnson, '"Really Useful Knowledge"', p. 78.
121 Home Office Papers, HO64/11, 1831, fo. 309.
122 Thompson, *The Making of the English Working Class*, p. 781.
123 For more on working-class education, see Jonathon Rose, *The Intellectual Life of the British Working Classes* (New Haven, Conn.: Yale University Press, 2001); Michael Sanderson, *Education, Economic Change and Society in England 1780–1870*, second edn (Basingstoke: Macmillan, 1991).
124 For a discussion of mutual improvement societies, see Rose, *The Intellectual Life of the British Working Classes*, pp. 58–91.
125 On the mechanics institutes, see Gregory Claeys, 'Political Economy and Popular Education: Thomas Hodgskin and the London Mechanics Institute, 1823–8', in Michael T. Davis (ed.), *Radicalism and Revolution in Britain, 1775–1848* (London: Macmillan Press, 2000), pp. 157–75; Edward Royle, 'Mechanics Institutes and the Working Classes, 1840–1860', *Historical Journal*, vol. 14 (1971), pp. 305–21; Michael Stephens and Gordon Roderick, 'The Working Classes and Mechanics' Institutes', *Annals of Science*, vol. 29, no. 4 (1973), pp. 349–60; Rose, *The Intellectual Life of the British Working Classes*, pp. 63–76.

dominant culture.¹²⁶ The exclusion of political and religious topics from the institutes' agendas particularly riled working-class radicals. Denying the people knowledge of their true political rights was seen as conserving the existence of the corrupt social order.

An extract from Francis Place's correspondence regarding the SDUK underscores this point:

> My experience which is extensive in time, as well as over a considerable space, convinces me that if the project can be established it must be by workmen themselves, and conducted wholly by them. I am certain that it is impossible if attempted in any other way.

He attributed this recalcitrance directly to what E. P. Thompson later recognised as an emerging working-class consciousness:

> In their present state they are too suspicious of evil intentions in those called their betters to consent to be led by them, or to conform to any plan which is not placed wholly under their control. Were it not for this feeling, the Mechanics' Institution would probably have three times as many members of the working classes as it has now.¹²⁷

Place was clearly no longer entirely satisfied to stand among a crowd of radical grandees at the Crown and Anchor. He recognised that knowledge directed by the middle classes would simply find no favour with class-conscious working families.

The 'Zetetic Societies', which arose directly out of Carlile's struggle with the government for freedom of publication during the 1820s, provide another example of working-class educational forums that flourished in this period. Originally acting as support groups during Carlile's long incarceration in Dorchester prison, these societies sprang up across Britain during the mid-1820s and functioned also as reading circles to disseminate political and theological knowledge in the spirit of the period's radical intellectual culture.¹²⁸ 'Zetetic' signified the acquisition of useful knowledge, and their charter was to cater for

---

126   Prothero, *Artisans and Politics in Early Nineteenth Century London*, p. 79; Kinraide, The Society for the Diffusion of Useful Knowledge, p. 14.
127   SDUK In-letters, Francis Place to Thomas Coates, 22 December 1833, quoted in Kinraide, The Society for the Diffusion of Useful Knowledge, p. 14.
128   This section on the Zetetic movement is based on Iain McCalman's account of the societies, which remains the most extensive written to date. See Iain McCalman, Popular Radicalism and Freethought in Early Nineteenth Century England, Unpublished MA thesis (Canberra: The Australian National University, 1975), pp. 83–171. See also Epstein, *Radical Expression*, pp. 112–19; Thompson, *The Making of the English Working Class*, pp. 798–9; Edward Royle, *Victorian Infidels* (Manchester: University of Manchester Press, 1974), pp. 35–9; Gwyn Williams, *Rowland Detrosier; A working-class infidel 1800–34* (York: St Anthony's, 1965). On women's involvement in the Zetetic societies, see Iain McCalman, 'Females, Feminism and Free Love in an Early Nineteenth Century Radical Movement', *Labour History*, no. 38 (1980), pp. 1–25.

the 'mental, moral and social improvement' of their members.[129] A brief survey of the Zetetic educational principles reveals how indebted the Rotunda educators were to the earlier pedagogy. Zetetics rejected religious-based education because they considered that it perpetuated social privilege, 'stupefied the mind with dull and constant repetition' and was 'useless to society'.[130] Traditional classical education was also rejected for similar reasons. Zetetics believed that study of obsolete languages and biblical history caused 'intellectual sterility'. Instead, they offered members lectures on political theory, art, science and history, and devoted monthly subscriptions to the purchase of a library. Zetetic knowledge was therefore a means of freeing workingmen from the domination of their alleged social superiors and eliminating an 'oppressive social and political system'.[131] Carlile believed that Zetetic knowledge would enable people presently held down by ignorance or indoctrination to be elevated to their rightful place in society and to acquire enough social, moral and economic leverage to destroy the establishment, including the established church.

Carlile therefore tasked his Rotunda educators to spread knowledge where none had existed, or where ignorance had resulted in the indoctrination of people by superstition and Christianity. Some of his colleagues had impressive educational credentials. Robert Taylor, an ex-Anglican clergyman, had been a Fellow with the Royal College of Surgeons in 1807, and completed a Bachelor of Arts at Cambridge University in 1813. John Gale Jones had trained as a surgeon and apothecary. Carlile himself was educated in a village school before spending two years at a grammar school in Devon. As we saw in earlier chapters, he taunted authorities that his lengthy stint in prison enabled a deeper understanding of, and commitment to, the Enlightenment philosophers and radical political theorists. Eliza Sharples (who will we meet in greater detail in Chapter 8) attended a boarding school until her early twenties, where she described being 'educated in the prejudices' she now sought to remove from the minds of her audience. This, she believed, enabled her to sympathise with and understand the fears of her audience when renouncing Christianity.[132]

Crucially, it was not through direct political education that Carlile and his Rotunda allies initially envisaged effecting the necessary changes to society, but through science and reason. 'Every step taken', wrote Carlile in December 1830, 'will be founded upon scientific evidence'.[133] At the Rotunda, however, there would be a vital difference to other working-class educational institutions

---

129   Thompson, *The Making of the English Working Class*, p. 799. As Thompson notes, the theories of the Enlightenment 'came to them with the force of revelation'.
130   McCalman, Popular Radicalism and Freethought in Early Nineteenth Century England, p. 132.
131   Ibid., p. 122.
132   *Isis*, 11 February 1832.
133   *Prompter*, 4 December 1830. For the importance of science in early nineteenth-century radicalism, see also McCalman, Popular Radicalism and Freethought in Early Nineteenth Century England, pp. 130–4, 139–43; Epstein, *Radical Expression*, pp. 123–42; Johnson, '"Really Useful Knowledge"', p. 88.

offering scientific instruction: for 'reason' to prevail, Carlile pledged that there would be 'no priestcraft, no disposition to deceive the people'.[134] He regarded science as the means by which to 'disburden the mind of superstitious fears' and the scientific basis of rational knowledge was stressed for its iconoclastic effect on superstition and Christianity; it opened people's eyes to the absurdities of religion and revealed the material foundations of man's nature.[135] Rational discourse and discussion would provide a basis for universal enlightenment, as well as the end of oppression and exploitation of working people. In this respect, the very conditions that Habermas identified as necessary for the development of the bourgeois public sphere were recognised by Carlile a century and a half earlier as crucial for the emancipation of working people. Moreover, in his repeated emphasis on the Rotunda as the first and only venue dedicated to free discussion, he clearly considered that the existing venues of the public sphere—of either bourgeois or plebeian origin—were less open to rational debate and discussion than Habermas would subsequently allow.[136]

Carlile believed the dissemination of radical principles among the people could best be achieved by providing an outlet for as many variants of radicalism as possible. Both veteran radicals and newcomers alike assembled under the Rotunda's roof during the turbulent political times of the early 1830s to castigate political and religious authority as bastions of an unjust, unequal and immoral society—from the veteran Jacobin debater John Gale Jones to the eccentric millenary duo John 'Zion' Ward and Charles Twort, and to Eliza Sharples, billed as the first Englishwoman to speak publicly on political and religious issues.[137] The most vehement and stinging attacks on religion and the clergy, however, came from Reverend Robert Taylor, whose showmanship and ridicule of the church and its practices continually delighted packed Rotunda audiences.

Of all the radicals associated with the Rotunda, the most organised and militant political activists belonged to the National Union of the Working Classes (NUWC). The NUWC was a purely political group and its members generally distanced themselves from Carlile's and Taylor's often scandalous attacks on established religion. The group conducted its meetings at the Rotunda from mid-1831 to early 1832, espousing a political agenda concerned primarily with reforming the corrupt parliamentary electoral system in favour of universal

---

134 *Prompter*, 4 December 1830.
135 G. D. H Cole, *Richard Carlile, 1790–1843* (London: Fabian Society Pamphlets, 1942), p. 17.
136 Ibid.
137 On John 'Zion' Ward and Charles Twort, followers of Joanna Southcott and founders of the Shilohites, see W. H. Oliver, 'John Ward—The messiah as agitator', *Prophets and Millennialists: The uses of biblical prophecy in England from the 1790s to the 1840s* (Auckland: Auckland University Press, 1978); J. F. C. Harrison, *The Second Coming: Popular millenarianism, 1780–1850* (New Brunswick, NJ: Rutgers University Press, 1979), pp. 152–60, 228–30; Jackie Latham, *Search for A New Eden, James Pierrepont Greaves (1777–1842): The sacred socialist and his followers* (Madison, NJ: Fairleigh Dickinson University Press, 1999), pp. 71–6, 111–21.

manhood suffrage.[138] In addition, some of the most noted radicals of the period graced the stages of the Rotunda. William Cobbett delivered a series of lectures on the French Revolution and, in late 1830, the Irish 'Liberator' Daniel O'Connell chaired several NUWC meetings on the situation in Ireland. Purely political groups, such as Henry Hunt's Radical Reform Association, a forerunner of the NUWC, as well as those radical propagandists such as Cobbett and Jones who eschewed Carlile's freethinking tenets, could feel equally at home in the Rotunda with infidels such as Taylor and Ward.

Carlile's willingness to accommodate a diverse array of radical expressions could also have had less altruistic motivations, for commercial imperatives required him to attract as wide a patronage as possible. They also saw Carlile attempt to recoup some of the operating costs by offering £5 shares in the venture (a system employed for the establishment of the scientific and literary institutions such as the Surrey). He also offered the Rotunda's rooms for hire, with the fee for the large theatre ranging between one and two guineas a night. Faced with the significant sum of £1000 per annum to keep the building open, Carlile also charged admission to the lectures and performances. He aimed to attract Londoners from all levels of society by offering a binary pricing system similar to that employed in the traditional theatres of the day.[139] For instance, during his, Taylor's and later Sharples' lectures, patrons had the choice of admission to the boxes for fourpence, the pit for threepence or the gallery for twopence. Sharples offered half-price admission for Monday evening lectures and staged several gratuitous lectures on Fridays. Jones offered slightly cheaper lectures at one penny and at sixpence, while the NUWC charged their members one penny and non-members twopence to attend their meetings and debates to offset the cost of the hire of the large theatre.

The building itself was ideal as a space intended to cater for a diverse and often disparate plebeian radical movement. With the addition of the large equestrian enclosure during the late 1820s, the premises now consisted of two large circular theatres suitable for lecturing, the smaller of which (featured in Rowlandson and Pugin's print of a Surrey Institution lecture) seated about 500 people and was intended to be Robert Taylor's own venue. Carlile's description of the room rekindled the feel of its Surrey heyday, promoting it as an extravagantly outfitted room with marble pillars and balustrades, and a stage. A statue of Contemplation (possibly that which previously guarded the exterior of the building) also adorned the room, in keeping with its educative function. The

---

138   Henry Hetherington's radical newspaper, *Poor Man's Guardian*, records many details and advertisements of the NUWC meetings at the Rotunda, and elsewhere in London. For the 'Constitution' and the 'Objects of the National Union', see *Prompter*, 28 May 1831. A more detailed account of the NUWC is provided in Chapters 7 and 8 of this study.
139   For further detail on how the Rotunda operated according to theatrical modes, see Chapter 7 of this study.

dome, however, had a new feature. It was now decoratively painted with the 12 signs of the zodiac—the images employed by Taylor to demonstrate his astronomical theological theses.

The larger theatre was less decorative than the smaller but had the benefit of catering for much larger crowds, with capacity for about 2000 people. Carlile recognised the need for refurbishing and repair work: 'It is but roughly fitted up', he wrote in November 1830, 'yet well suited to such meetings as are held in it'. Carlile envisaged hiring it out primarily for 'political usage'.[140] His description suggests that a spatial hierarchy soon evolved at the premises and the various spaces within the Rotunda became coded with meaning: the rough and nondescript space of the large theatre for the purely political offerings of the NUWC, while the decorative, respectable and more intimate environs of the smaller theatre would be kept for Carlile's showmen (and woman)—the infidel orators Taylor, Sharples and Ward. Different cultural conventions could operate, it appears, within one venue. Even so, Carlile's plans were sometimes thwarted by logistical imperatives. Though the small theatre had 'communication' with both the entrance passage and the library room, the subsequent popularity of Robert Taylor's lectures and extravaganzas often meant having to rely on the generous seating capacity of the larger theatre. Carlile was forced to promise that when funds allowed the 'general appearance' of the space would 'correspond with its already general celebrity'.[141]

* * *

Before examining the Rotunda's radical education curriculum in more detail in the following chapters, it is worth reflecting on the impact of the venue on the early nineteenth-century 'march of mind'. The fierce battles for the freedom of the press during the 1820s and 1830s have tended to focus many scholars on the flourishing print medium and a crediting of the printed word with providing the main impetus for the 'march of mind'. Radical printers continued, despite a sustained campaign of intimidation and prosecution, to produce cheap papers defying the four-penny stamp tax. Carlile was arguably the key player in the struggle for freedom of the press during the 1820s and early 1830s. In 1821, he proclaimed that the printing press was 'the best weapon a man can yield against tyrants'; it had arrived like a 'true messiah to emancipate the great family of mankind'.[142] In the *Republican*, Carlile claimed that if given the 'free exercise of the press for seven years' he would 'annihilate Christianity'.[143] After the immense initial success of the Rotunda, however, Carlile considered that rapid expansion of infidel ideology among the populace was due more to

---

140   *Prompter*, 13 November 1830.
141   Ibid.
142   McCalman, Popular Radicalism and Freethought in Early Nineteenth Century England, pp. 89–91.
143   *Republican*, 8 December 1820.

preaching and discussion than to the reading of books. Carlile believed that by incorporating the principles of free speech into a theatre of learning (rather than relying solely on the printed word), he was providing the best form of political and theological instruction for the working people of England.

Such a change in opinion from one of the central figures in the battle for press freedom in the early nineteenth century warns against overstating the centrality of print as a radical weapon in combating ignorance and educating the masses. McCalman's detailed and extensive account of plebeian radicalism in his study of the radical underworld reminds us that much knowledge dissemination took place informally in multipurpose radical venues; it was closely related to, or incorporated within, other radical activities. As historians dealing with traditional methods of communication know too well, oral communication leaves few records; printed material leaves many. Historian David Vincent has argued that the oral transmission of knowledge—previously an intrinsic element of popular culture—declined sharply in the early nineteenth century as a direct consequence of the proliferation of print: 'the pursuit of useful knowledge inevitably involved a withdrawal from the essentially communal process of oral transmission, set the literate apart from the illiterate, and created new lines of demarcation within the working class.'[144]

E. P. Thompson's image of a literate reading public, who absorbed radical knowledge through written ideological tracts and journals, similarly oversimplifies the processes and factors that shaped this 'intellectual culture'. The picture of autodidacts rising at five o'clock to read radical texts, though undoubtedly accurate, conveys a somewhat abstract and mechanical process and tends to obscure other forms of communication that contributed to this culture.

Associating the oral transmission of knowledge exclusively with the illiterate, or emphasising that an exclusively literate reading public was recruited during the 'march of mind', distorts the picture of early nineteenth-century radical culture. The new passion for knowledge was undoubtedly fed by the burgeoning political press, but the importance of additional, alternative or supplementary means of radical communication based on oral communication is clearly evident in the historical record. The scholarship of historians such as McCalman, Epstein and David Worrall (and for the later Chartist years that of Paul Pickering and Alex Tyrrell) confirms that oratory, visual demonstration, revivalism and theatricality were also essential to the communication of radical knowledge.[145]

---

144 David Vincent, 'The Decline of the Oral Tradition in Popular Culture', in Robert Storch (ed.), *Popular Culture and Custom in Nineteenth Century England* (London: Croom Helm, 1982), p. 42.
145 On the continuing importance of oral traditions in the early to mid-nineteenth-century radicalism, see Paul A. Pickering, 'Class Without Words: Symbolic communication in the Chartist movement', *Past & Present*, no. 112 (1986), pp. 144–62; Paul A. Pickering and Alex Tyrrell, *The People's Bread: A history of the Anti-Corn*

Furthermore, as Peter Bailey argues, in wider society in the early nineteenth century there remained 'still a vigorously oral culture whose psychodynamics remain close to those of primarily oral societies'.[146] More recent scholarship from Jonathon Rose on literacy and the British working class, and from David Vincent himself, views the acquisition of knowledge from oral and written sources as a symbiotic relationship.[147]

It is clear that the reading habit itself could be a public act in the institutions of the public sphere and was often supported by some kind of fellowship and mutuality. Discussion and debate helped new radical followers digest often abstract and difficult texts. The continued popularity of debating clubs in taverns and coffee houses and the sermons of the dissenting chapels underscores the importance of public venues in both oral and visual education during this period, and for sating the need of working people for fellowship and community. The oral dissemination of knowledge continued to flourish in the semi-literate society of the early 1830s and remained a dominant educational medium often complementary to, rather than in conflict with, printed propaganda.

The enormous initial popularity of the Rotunda is perhaps the best indication of the importance of oral communication of knowledge in the early 1830s. While people had access to the ideologies of the Rotunda radicals in journals such as the *Prompter*, Sharples' *Isis* and Taylor's *Devil's Pulpit*, hundreds still flocked to the Rotunda to hear and see the explanation and demonstration of those theories. Moreover, the example of the Rotunda shows the symbiotic relationship between all these modes of radical communication. Along with other radical coffee houses, the Rotunda provided an outlet for the sale of illegal radical 'unstamped' newspapers. Hawkers traversed the passages and surroundings of the building supplying copies of Carlile's new publishing endeavour, the *Prompter*, and later the *Devil's Pulpit*, *Isis* and the NUWC's *Poor Man's Guardian*. In turn, these papers recorded and publicised the respective lectures, meetings and performances at the Rotunda, though Carlile intended to make the *Prompter* the true mouthpiece of the venue.

The increase in literacy levels in this period, the emphasis in early radical historiography on the role of the press in the 'march of mind', as well as the prominence of the battle for the freedom of the press in the story of the 1820s have tended to overshadow both the continuation of traditional modes of

---

Law League (London: Leicester University Press, 2000), especially ch. 9. On the continuing oral tradition more generally, see Adam Fox and Daniel Wolfe (eds), *The Spoken Word: Oral culture in Britain, 1500–1850* (Manchester: Manchester University Press, 2002).
146 Peter Bailey, 'Conspiracies of Meaning: Music-hall and the knowingness of popular culture', *Past & Present*, vol. 144 (1994), p. 147n.21.
147 See David Vincent, *The Rise of Mass Literacy: Reading and writing in modern Europe* (Cambridge: Polity Press, 2000), pp. 89–102; Rose, *The Intellectual Life of the British Working Classes*, pp. 83–4.

communication and new forums for working-class rational discourse and debate. It also perhaps obscured Habermas's view of Britain's expanding political nation when he sought to define the nature of the public sphere.

By the end of its first year of operation, the Rotunda had already developed multiple identities. By drawing on the cultural conventions of the previous inhabitants of the site, Carlile established a venue known for working-class instruction and education. The scenes that opened this chapter from October 1830, as well as the continuing involvement in Rotunda radicalism of London's more militant and plebeian radicals, also established the venue's reputation as an outlet for more extreme political expression. The following chapter narrows the lens on Rotunda radicalism to examine the substance of Rotunda pedagogy and, crucially, the means by which it was communicated to its audience. It explores how the dissemination of the message was as important as the message itself. In so doing, it demonstrates how another layer of identity—as a venue for popular entertainment—evolved. It also charts a further phase in the venue's development, which cemented the most enduring of its identities, that of the space that proudly and vehemently defended its tricolour flags and one that remained seething with revolutionary possibility.

7. 'Bitten with the Rotunda notions': audience, identity and communication 1830–1832

The opening of the Rotunda in 1830 marked a new phase for London's radical culture. For a combination of geographical, temporal and social reasons, the venue provided a much needed rallying point for plebeian metropolitan radicalism in the early 1830s and catered for a whole spectrum of London's diverse radical ideology under one roof. For a period in 1830–32, the radical community found a venue open almost every night of the week, offering a rich array of heterodox political and theological thought communicated in a variety of ways. Working-class London, to Francis Place's chagrin, had been 'bitten with the Rotunda notions'.[1]

By way of illustration, the programme at the Rotunda in the final week of November 1830 proceeded as follows: on Sunday mornings and evenings, patrons attended 'the best theological service that has yet to be presented to a congregation'.[2] They listened as Richard Carlile read from the 'sublime pages' of Volney's *Ruins of Empire* before they were enlightened by the Reverend Robert Taylor's elucidation of all the 'mysteries of religion' through his explanation of 'zodiacal transits' and astronomical principles. The Radical Reform Association (RRA), a purely political group, met under the tricolour flag on Monday evenings to discuss the new Whig administration and the merits of vote by ballot. Carlile himself directed the political discussions on Tuesday evening reviewing the parliamentary speeches of the previous week along with a justification of the conduct of the agricultural labourers in the Swing disturbances of the period. On Thursday, veteran radical orator John Gale Jones lectured on the necessity of political reform, doubting the resolve of the new Whig government to effect any real change. Friday evening saw Taylor repeat the Sunday lecture, such was the popularity of his ribald and absorbing performances.

The great attraction of the Rotunda to the radical community can better be understood by briefly examining the range of other venues available to London's plebeian radicals for meetings and debate. Prior to the Rotunda's opening, several different public forums for radical debate had prevailed in London's radical culture, including (as we have seen with the Crown and Anchor) taverns and ale houses, dissenting chapels and coffee houses. Though Habermas countenanced

---

1 Francis Place [Add. MS 27790, ff. 39–47], reprinted in D. J. Rowe, *London Radicalism 1830–1843: A selection from the papers of Francis Place* (London: London Record Society, 1970), p. 42.
2 *Prompter*, 27 November 1830.

such venues as crucial avenues for the rational debate of the bourgeois public sphere, the rich body of radical scholarship initiated by E. P. Thompson and Iain McCalman clearly reveals the plebeian connections of such venues overlooked by Habermas. As radical forums, ale houses and taverns (including those less ostentatious than the Crown and Anchor) held many advantages; they had long been pivotal institutions in popular culture, providing entertainment and a feeling of community and solidarity for workers.[3] Patrons could smoke, drink and socialise with their fellow workers whilst debating the merits of old and new political ideas and programmes.

By the 1820s, coffee shops and houses were also becoming popular centres of radical activity, assuming many of the traditional social and recreational functions of ale houses. As we saw earlier, Habermas declared the coffee house to be the archetypal space of the public sphere. Coffee houses were relatively cheap and easy to establish, and proprietors could operate without the surveillance of licensing justices or brewers. They therefore had the advantage of being able to stock radical journals and tracts, which patrons could buy or read in the premises. The coffee house embodied the notion of free speech and, from the early eighteenth century, particularly in the metropolis, they provided fertile ground for discussion and promulgation of political radicalism, atheism and free thought.[4]

Both tavern and coffee-house radicalism adapted to the surveillance and suppression of radical activities in the period following the Six Acts by adopting the format of radical debating clubs.[5] Although the informal and often opaque character of such clubs offered some advantages for evading prosecution, their informal nature also held serious disadvantages for radicalism. Their amorphous character produced organisational difficulties and affected the wider dissemination of radical ideology. By advertising meetings, radicals risked identifying their premises and groups as centres of sedition.[6] This in turn limited their ability to attract new followers to the radical cause. In this sense they were limited forums, appealing only to those already converted to radical thinking. Most taverns and coffee houses came nowhere near the capacity of the Crown and Anchor so the numbers they could accommodate precluded radical meetings on a large scale. The actual environment of the tavern and the coffee house also restricted the recruitment of new followers. As we saw in the

---

3 For general references on ale houses, taverns and coffee houses, see Chapter 5 of this study.
4 Brian Cowan, 'What was Masculine about the Public Sphere? Gender and the coffeehouse milieu in post-Restoration England', *History Workshop Journal*, vol. 51 (2001), p. 140.
5 Iain McCalman, 'Ultra-Radicalism and Convivial Debating Clubs in London 1795–1838', *English Historical Review*, vol. 102, no. 403 1987, pp. 312–15.
6 Ibid.

case of the Crown and Anchor, the masculine culture that emanated from these premises acted to exclude many possible followers in women, as well as those who were already active participants in the radical movement.[7]

Dissenting chapels redressed some of these disadvantages. Within the chapels, political dissent could be cloaked in religious terms and licences for dissenting ministers and their chapels were notoriously easy to obtain, as Carlile was to discover when he successfully obtained one for the Rotunda.[8] Ministers could advertise the proceedings openly and were able to cater to much larger audiences—some of the popular chapels attracting congregations of several hundred.[9] Chapels also provided a more congenial atmosphere for women; spy reports attest to their regular attendance.[10] At the same time, however, radical chapels catered for only one branch of radicalism, excluding political groups that eschewed the use of religious language, or those for whom religion was not the driving social and political issue.

The Rotunda overcame the major disadvantage of both taverns and chapels as radical debating forums by accommodating an astonishing diversity of organisations and outlooks. It was unique as a radical venue in its ability to combine many of the positive elements of other radical forums under one roof. Apart from the two theatres that accommodated the larger meetings, the Rotunda's coffee room also served as a meeting and debating place for radicals. The ex-Cato Street radical turned Home Office spy Abel Hall regularly met his radical colleagues in the coffee room before the main lectures, and again afterwards to discuss the lecture, or simply to socialise.[11] The coffee room assumed many of the characteristics of traditional taverns and coffee houses—Carlile having engaged a vintner to supply refreshments to patrons, including wines, coffee, tea, chops, steaks and fruit.[12] Several subcommittees of the National Union of the Working Classes (NUWC) used it as their regular

---

7   Catherine Hall, 'Private Persons Versus Public Someones: Class, gender and politics in England, 1780–1850', in Carolyn Steedman, Cathy Urwin and Valerie Walkerdine (eds), *Language, Gender and Childhood* (London: Routledge & Kegan Paul, 1985), p. 18.
8   McCalman, 'Ultra-Radicalism and Convivial Debating Clubs in London', p. 315.
9   Iain McCalman notes that the tavern clubs could have appealed at a 'deeper level' by 'satisfying religious longing'. Ibid., p. 318.
10 Home Office spy Abel Hall provides many accounts of women in chapels throughout his reports of 1827–32, at Home Office Papers, HO64/11. On Abel Hall, tailor and Home Office informer, see Iain McCalman, *Radical Underworld: Prophets, revolutionaries and pornographers in London, 1795–1840* (Cambridge: Cambridge University Press, 1988), pp. 133, 181–2, 195–8, 232–3. For women's involvement in Dissenting churches and rational religion, see Anna Clark, *Struggle for the Breeches: Gender and the making of the British working class* (Berkeley: University of California Press, 1995), pp. 92–118; Barbara Taylor, *Eve and the New Jerusalem: Socialism and feminism in the nineteenth century* (London: Virago, 1983); Linda Wilson, '"Constrained by Zeal": Women in mid-nineteenth century nonconformist churches', *Journal of Religious History*, vol. 23, no. 2 (1999), pp. 185–202.
11 See his many detailed reports about the Rotunda at Home Office Papers, HO64/11, HO64/12.
12 *Prompter*, 13 November 1830; Home Office Papers, HO64/11, n.d., fo. 249.

meeting place during 1831.[13] Along with the coffee room, the many other rooms adjoining the theatres, including two large billiard rooms with apartments, an extensive bar and the 'long' room—previously the Surrey's library—could also be hired for meetings. A 'dwelling house' that occupied the top three floors at the front of the premises allowed Carlile to engage the services of a housekeeper—one with whom Taylor would later become embroiled in a sordid and very public affair.[14]

The facilities at the Rotunda even enabled open-air meetings to be conducted from the premises. Radicals used the portico during the agitation of November 1830 and later during the Reform Crisis in October 1831 to communicate with thousands of people rallying outside who were unable to gain entry to the building. On that occasion, Taylor, Carlile and Henry Hunt addressed the 2000 inside the Rotunda, while working-class radicals William Carpenter, John Cleave and John Hunter relayed the message to the estimated 3000 people assembled outside.[15] Later in the evening they were addressed by Hunt and Irish radical William Thompson from the portico. Police officer William Chambers complained that

> [n]ot only are the morals and sentiments of the poorer classes corrupted by the Inflammatory and Blasphemous language of the...orators within, but...the great crowds...on the outside are also addressed from the top of the portico with seditious speeches.[16]

The location and physical structure of the Rotunda allowed a blurring of the traditional outdoor radical space with that of the indoor. Much to the alarm of its resident neighbours, the Rotunda had a capacity for large crowds to overflow onto Blackfriars Road either towards the bridge or down the main thoroughfare (Figure 7.1).[17] Such capacity helped to fulfil Carlile's aim to disseminate the radical message to as many people as possible, particularly at times of heightened social unrest. Importantly, it provided a public arena for political activity far larger than those available in chapels, clubs and (most) taverns.

---

13 Home Office Papers, HO64/11, 12 August 1831, fo. 410.
14 For more on this episode, see Chapter 8 of this study.
15 Joel Wiener, *Radicalism and Freethought in Nineteenth-Century Britain: The life of Richard Carlile* (Westport, Conn.: Greenwood Press, 1983), p. 278.
16 Home Office Papers, HO40/25, 10 November 1830, fo. 214
17 The Home Office received many complaints from neighbours. See, for example, Home Office Papers, HO40/020/25, fo. 213, complaining of the nuisance created by the large and noisy crowds, and of the blasphemy of the lectures in early November 1830. See also HO44/21, ff. 408–9; HO44/22, ff. 97–8; HO44/23, ff. 76–7, 154–5, 172–3.

7. 'Bitten with the Rotunda notions'

Figure 7.1 Architectural view of the Surrey Rotunda, Sir Ashton Lever's Museum in Blackfriars Road, London.

Artist and date unknown. Copyright Wellcome Library, London.

In many ways, the dissenting chapel licence Carlile obtained for the Rotunda was in keeping with its modes of operation. The sport of exposing inconsistencies and historical absurdities in the Christian faith became a Rotunda forte, due largely to the oratorical brilliance of the Reverend Robert Taylor.[18] The essence of Taylor's critique was simple enough. He argued that the first priests were actually astronomers who gave 'ingenious' names to the celestial bodies for the purpose of assisting memory recall; however, 'religious blockheads' took these as names of real people whose actions and sufferings were founded in history.

---

18 I am indebted to Iain McCalman, who, in the late 1980s, first introduced me to the figure of Robert Taylor. Iain encouraged me to explore his fascinating contribution to Rotunda culture in my Honours thesis, *Radicalism as Theatre: The Blackfriars Road Rotunda 1830–32* (Canberra: The Australian National University, 1989). See also Iain McCalman, 'Popular Irreligion in Early Victorian England: Infidel preachers and radical theatricality in 1830s London', in R. W. Davis and R. J. Helmstadter (eds), *Religion and Irreligion in Victorian Society* (London: Routledge, 1992), pp. 51–67; James Epstein, *Radical Expression: Political language, ritual and symbol in England, 1790–1850* (Oxford: Oxford University Press, 1994), pp. 138–40; Edward Royle, 'Taylor, Robert', in Joseph Baylen and Norbert Gossman (eds), *Biographical Dictionary of Modern British Radicals* [hereafter *BDMBR*] (Sussex: Harvester Press, 1979), vol. 1, pp. 467–70.

This had since become the basis of Christianity.[19] Thus, Taylor believed that while the sacred Scriptures had been written in an allegorical and mystical way, they could be understood and explained by reason.

Drawing on the example of scientific institutions such as the Surrey, Taylor fortified his critiques of Christian evidence with 'experiments and facts' to illustrate his ideas and give 'vigour to the mind'. Visual demonstration played a crucial role in Rotunda education; tangible scientific demonstration and observation were seen as vital means of countering religious superstition. Lectures were always accompanied by impressive props and contemporaries noted that the theatres were equipped with 'all the apparatus necessary for the explanation and elucidation of his subject'.[20] One regular prop was an orrery, a clockwork assemblage of the planets used to explain his solar myths. He claimed to be awaiting funds to purchase an 'eidouranian', which was superior to the orrery in that it imitated the 'motions of heavenly bodies'.[21] The zodiacal images that Carlile had painted around the dome of the small theatre were central to Taylor's performance. By way of example, Taylor pointed to the sign of Virgo to explain the astronomical origin of the birth of Christ to the Virgin Mary, scandalously suggesting that 'they would find a young woman who had not been quite so prudent as she ought to have been'.[22] By his rationalist interpretation of the Gospels, the 12 apostles of Christ were similarly allegories of the 12 signs of the zodiac. The use of such props underscores the value Rotunda radicals placed on observation as a means of learning. 'Observation', Eliza Sharples argued, was 'the very element of experience; a profound knowledge of things is the consequence of perseverance and just observation'.[23]

Paradoxically, the emphasis on free thought in Rotunda education went hand in hand with intense religiosity. From the outset, religious overtones pervaded Rotunda proceedings. Taylor's notoriety as an 'El Dorado of science' was matched only by his cachet as a man of the cloth; his background as a member of the Anglican Church enabled him to employ the romantic and emotive devices of the established church to attract and captivate his audiences. He emulated its ritual and ceremony in most of his Rotunda performances, deriving his 'Canticles, Creed, Lessons, Thanksgiving and Collect' from the Anglican service—a format he adopted because of its 'majestic rhythms...and declamatory grandeur'.[24]

---

19 Home Office Papers, HO64/13, 27 March 1831, fo. 37.
20 Parolin, Radicalism as Theatre, pp. 25–6. Home Office Papers, HO64/13, 13 November 1830, fo. 2. Other preaching infidels of the day also employed devices to explain their subject. After Rowland Detrosier died in 1834, Carlile advertised his 'philosophical apparatus' for sale. These included magic lanterns, astronomical slides, a globe receiver and a large transparent circle. See *Scourge For the Littleness of Great Men*, 11 December 1834.
21 Home Office Papers, HO64/11, 13 November 1830, fo. 119.
22 Home Office Papers, HO64/13, 13 November 1830, fo. 5.
23 *Isis*, 19 May 1832.
24 McCalman, *Radical Underworld*, p. 188.

The announcement of Taylor and Carlile's 'joint apostleship', the promotion of Sunday lectures as divine services and the observance of Taylor's title of 'Reverend', all accentuated the image of the Rotunda as a church.

In addition to borrowing from the church service, Taylor donned the full pontificals of the Anglican clergymen for all his Rotunda discourses. His theatre was also carefully outfitted for such 'services'. According to contemporary descriptions, it sported a raised altar complete with a 6 ft crucifix and a communion table laden with bread and wine 'similar to those prepared in the Established Church for the Administration of the Sacrament'.[25] The infidel service commenced with Carlile or Taylor's young assistant, Harrison, reading the first lesson—generally a chapter of Volney's evocative and sonorous *Ruins of Empire*—followed by a second reading of a chapter from the Bible relevant to Taylor's lecture. Each sermon delivered by Taylor was read from a 'written document in black covers similar to the sermon books of the Established Clergy'.[26] A 'prayer' was often also read by Taylor or Carlile during the service. The 'New Lord's Prayer', which Home Office recorders confirm was 'commonly used at the Rotunda', played upon the language of the Lord's Prayer: 'May that peace which virtue gives possess your heart and minds that you may hear and understand and may the reward of knowledge and virtue be with you and remain with you for ever and ever.'[27]

Taylor's performances indicate that radical free thought and religiosity were not necessarily incompatible.[28] In many respects, religion and irreligion drew on the same set of conventions for public communication. Rotunda radicals and other infidel preachers of the period recognised the romantic and emotive appeal of religion to the imaginations of working people. This religiosity was not exclusive to the Rotunda. As Prothero notes, 'many radicals clearly felt the need to clothe their activities in a religious garb' to cater for the interest and attraction in 'rational religion'.[29] The Dissenting chapels of the 1820s had also represented themselves as places of deist religious worship. Their preachers issued liturgies outlining forms of public worship and made use of a variety of religious rituals and ceremonies. Josiah Fitch, an eccentric radical preacher who operated from the aptly named Grub Street Chapel, recognised the importance of religious qualifications in being accepted as a radical educator.[30] He was compelled to complement his qualifications as a schoolmaster with a licence for preaching.

---

25 Home Office Papers, HO64/11 n.d., fo. 293; and HO64/13, 3 April 1831, fo. 50.
26 Home Office Papers, HO64/11, n.d., fo. 293; HO64/13, 3 April 1831, fo. 50.
27 Home Office Papers, HO64/13, 13 November 1830, fo. 3.
28 Parolin, Radicalism as Theatre, pp. 26–7.
29 Iowerth Prothero, *Artisans and Politics in Early Nineteenth Century London, John Gast and his Times* (Folkestone: Dawson, 1979), p. 263.
30 On Josiah Fitch, schoolteacher and freethinker, see McCalman, *Radical Underworld*, pp. 190–2. Fitch was not unique in this respect. See the account of the Reverend Scholefield in Paul Pickering and Alex Tyrrell, '"In the Thickest of the Fight": The Reverend James Scholefield and the Bible Christians of Manchester and

Religion was deeply rooted in early nineteenth-century popular culture; ceremonies of folk life such as births, deaths and marriages were saturated with religious associations.[31] The Bible was an integral part of literate working people's lives and of folk culture generally. Abel Hall's reports of the increase in numbers of attendances at the Rotunda on Sundays, while perhaps to be expected given the tempo of the working week, also suggest that the venue met a need for those disillusioned with mainstream religion.[32]

The romanticism of Volney and the intense ceremony and rich theatricality of Taylor's discourses, coupled with his extravagant scientific displays, could induce feelings of intellectual intoxication for some of the observing audience. The discovery of radical knowledge, especially the recognition of the endless possibilities of free thought, could engender an intense emotional experience—something akin to religious conversion.[33] After attending one of Taylor's performances in 1830, a young architect's clerk, William Knight, filled several manuscript pages with his newfound inspiration:

> [I]n vain my pen attempts to express the throbbing joys which fill my heart, no tongue can utter and no Christian's mind can imagine the pleasures which fill my soul...Be still my heart for thou art free! thou cans't reach the Heavens.[34]

Although Rotunda radicalism could have offered psychological satisfactions akin to religious belief, Carlile never intended to deceive his patrons into the 'deist public worship' he claimed was a feature of Fitch's chapel and which merely mimicked Christian superstition.[35] Given the history of Carlile's enmity towards the established church, there is little doubt that the religiosity of the Rotunda performances was utilised primarily as a means to mock and thereby debunk and demystify the central tenets of orthodox religion. Taylor adopted the church rituals in blasphemous mockery of the religious service; lampooning the practices of the established church particularly delighted Rotunda audiences. On entering the stage, Taylor would make three low bows to the

---

Salford', *Albion*, vol. 26, no. 3 (1994), pp. 461–82.
31 Edward Royle, *Radical Politics 1790–1900: Religion and unbelief* (London: Longman, 1971), p. 9.
32 Home Office Papers, HO64/11, 4 December 1831, fo. 202.
33 McCalman, 'Popular Irreligion in Early Victorian England', p. 55.
34 See Knight's letter printed in the *Examiner*, 14 November 1830. See also McCalman, *Radical Underworld*, p. 189. On the intense emotional connections often made between the audience and the performer, see Peter Bailey, 'Conspiracies of Meaning: Music-hall and the knowingness of popular culture, *Past & Present*, vol. 144 (1994), pp. 138–70. See also Lynn M. Voskuil, 'Feeling Public: Sensation theater, commodity culture and the Victorian public sphere', *Victorian Studies*, vol. 44, no. 2 (2002), p. 246. Gillian Russell argues that performances by Thomas Erskine, barrister and Whig MP, in the courtroom engendered similar emotions from his audience. See Gillian Russell, 'The Theatre of Crim. Con.: Thomas Erskine, adultery and radical politics in the 1790s', in Michael T. Davis and Paul A. Pickering (eds), *Unrespectable Radicals? Popular politics in the age of reform* (Aldershot: Ashgate, 2008), pp. 57–70.
35 McCalman, 'Popular Irreligion in Early Victorian England', p. 53.

communion table and to the 6 ft crucifix. Hall regarded this extravagant use of gesture and motion as 'mockery of the clergy' and viewed Taylor's burlesque of the sacrament as particularly blasphemous. With the aid of his water and wine, which were placed on a communion table, Taylor imitated the clergy's practice of administering the communion sacrament. After repeating 'this is Christ's blood', he drank the wine and exclaimed, 'O Blessed Jesus your blood is good indeed'. Following the drinking of the wine, he rested his head on a desk as 'if in liqor [sic]' and imitated church prayer.[36] Hall's reports clearly testify to the fact that Taylor's audiences recognised his 'mock solemnity'. He reported that throughout the performance there was abundant applause and great laughter for the antics of the 'Devil's Chaplain'.

Taylor's penchant for theatricality was particularly evident in his flair for melodrama. The rise in the number of melodramatic performances in all theatrical spheres coincided with the emerging Romantic movement in England. Like Romanticism, melodrama became an avenue through which to express direct and powerful emotions.[37] Taylor's 'Devil Raising' derived much of its popularity from its use of melodramatic principles of intense emotion, moral dichotomies of 'good' and 'bad' and flamboyant special effects.[38] With the theatre in darkness and Taylor dressed in full clerical regalia, he would begin by chanting: 'Satan, Beezlebub, Baal, Peor, Belial, Lucifier, Abbaddon, Appolyon, thou King of the Bottomless Pit, thou King of Scorpions…to whom it is given to hurt the earth… Appear.' A large globe on the stage promptly lit up and a hideous caricature of Lucifer appeared. With a flick of the wrist, Satan became an 'angel of light' as the reverse side of the globe revealed a zodiacal symbol of the sun.[39] Not surprisingly, the 'Devil Raising' regularly attracted crowds of between 700 and 1000, and on some occasions hundreds assembled outside were unable to obtain admission.

Carlile promoted Taylor as his star attraction and Rotunda placards all over London projected both a glamorous and a mysterious image of the radical performer. Describing Taylor as 'His Satan Majesty's chaplain' was clearly calculated to capture the attention of the London populace. Taylor's eccentricity, both public and private, accentuated his image as an entertainer to the extent that one contemporary compared his 'fine voice' with that of Charles Kemble,

---

36   Home Office Papers, HO64/13, 3 April 1831, fo. 54.
37   One of the most useful surveys of the genre remains Michael R. Booth, *English Melodrama* (London: Herbert Jenkins, 1965). See also Martha Vicinus, '"Helpless and Unfriended": Nineteenth-century domestic melodrama', *New Literary History*, vol. 13 (1981), pp. 127–43; Louis James, 'Taking Melodrama Seriously: Theatre, and nineteenth-century studies', *History Workshop Journal*, no. 3 (1977), pp. 151–8; Jane Moody, *Illegitimate Theatre in London, 1770–1840* (Cambridge: Cambridge University Press, 2000).
38   Parolin, Radicalism as Theatre, p. 38. See also David Worrall, *Theatric Revolution: Drama, censorship and Romantic period subcultures, 1773–1832* (Oxford: Oxford University Press, 2006), p. 357.
39   See the description of this 'Devil Raising' in *Devil's Pulpit*, 27 November 1830.

the most famous actor of the day.⁴⁰ Taylor's choice of clerical dress and other flamboyant attire helped in his manufacture as a star performer. Aside from the clergy's pontificals, he regularly wore white kid gloves, posed with an eyeglass and had his hair arranged in curls over his forehead according to the dandy fashion. Whilst preaching, he made a point of 'flourishing a scented cambric handkerchief, trimmed with a deep lace border, at every pause in his discourse'.⁴¹ He delighted in his various diabolical nicknames: the 'Devil's Chaplain', the 'Archbishop of Pandemonium', 'Primate of all Hell' and 'Apostle to the Church of the Rotunda'.⁴² All were played upon by Taylor to create an image of iconoclasm and notoriety.

It was then, perhaps, a natural progression that Taylor should extend his theatrical endeavour and pen his own full-length melodrama for the Rotunda stage. *Swing! Or who are the Incendiaries?* saw a sharp shift towards political instruction for the Devil's Chaplain. Promoted by Carlile as a 'politico-tragedy', *Swing!* defended the agricultural labourers of several southern counties who were rioting during 1830–31 in response to falling wages, tithes and the introduction of automatic threshing machines.⁴³ The *Prompter* boasted to its readers of the literary and theatrical excellence of the tragedy, reporting that the 'language is worthy of Otway, and the denouement of the plot beats that of any other popular tragedy'.⁴⁴ The play, described as an 'admirable tragedy' in which the audience could 'alternately cry and laugh', was standing entertainment for two nights a week at the Rotunda and ran for several weeks.

That Carlile should embrace such a theatrical production at first seems incongruous given his earlier disdain for the theatre. In 1828, he declared he was 'no great admirer' of the 'theatrical profession', viewing it as 'a corresponding principle with that mass of fiction, of which all theology is a part, by which man is so much degraded'.⁴⁵ These sentiments were also expressed by Carlile's ideological paladin, Thomas Paine, as well as by the 1790s radical intelligentsia of the Godwin circle.⁴⁶ To understand Carlile's about-face, and his decision to

---

40 Iain McCalman, Popular Radicalism and Freethought in Early Nineteenth Century England, Unpublished MA thesis (Canberra: The Australian National University, 1975), p. 186.
41 H. Vizetelly, *Glances Back Through Seventy Years* (London, 1893), vol. 1, pp. 98–9.
42 *Prompter*, 4 December 1830.
43 For a more detailed account of the *Swing!* play, see McCalman, 'Popular Irreligion in Early Victorian England', p. 57; Worrall, *Theatric Revolution*, pp. 340–60. Jane Moody offers a brief account of the play, and the Rotunda, in her study of 'illegitimate theatre' of the period. As Gillian Russell notes in her review of Moody's book, the Rotunda represented the 'far end of the spectrum of illegitimacy', and its relegation to the 'very margins' of Moody's book weakens its claim to be a 'definitive account' of theatre's 'illegitimacy'. See Gillian Russell, 'Recent Studies in Late Georgian Theater and Drama', Book review, *Journal of British Studies*, vol. 42, no. 3 (2003), pp. 396–405.
44 *Prompter*, 5 February 1831. Carlile is here referring to Thomas Otway (1616–93), celebrated poet and playwright.
45 *Lion*, 14 March 1828.
46 David Karr, '"Thoughts that Flash like Lightning": Thomas Holcroft, radical theater, and the production of meaning in 1790s London', *Journal of British Studies*, vol. 40, no. 3 (2001), p. 327.

market the Rotunda as a theatre, we must consider the political context of the theatrical trade in this period. In 1737, the government of the day established the position of Examiner of Plays to preside over the moral and political health of the stage, a role that continued well into the next century. At the same time, a system was introduced so that the authorities could close theatres operating without a licence.[47] Such official regulation meant the government dictated what material was deemed appropriate for London audiences. Moreover, the Patent Theatres—Drury Lane, Covent Garden and the Haymarket—were alone licensed to perform dramatic forms of tragedy and comedy.

The vigorous political life of the early nineteenth century was therefore kept out of the licensed Patent Theatres of London through direct government intervention. Although David Karr's fascinating study of Thomas Holcroft and radical theatre in the 1790s reveals ways in which both performers and audiences could circumvent these official constraints in mainstream theatres, by 1833, one contemporary observer considered that at a time when the 'public mind' was 'so absorbed in politics' the stage, commonly supposed to 'represent the times', was devoid of politics.[48] The association of the Patents with 'Old Corruption'—thought to be responsible for the theatre monopolies—was anathema to a whole class of people growing conscious of their strength and culture, and of their exclusion from political and social power.[49] Their truculence had been manifested in 1809, when a price rise at the Drury Lane theatre led to the notorious 'OP' (Old Price) riots, which rocked central London for several weeks.[50]

A mounting resentment of the monopolies of the Patent Houses was also reflected in the proliferation of popular theatricals in saloon theatres, penny gaffs and other illegal theatre venues during the 1820s. It also led to greater support of the more formal 'minor theatres' that flourished in response to a growing market for sites of urban sociability among middling and plebeian classes. These were licensed only to produce what theatre historian Jane Moody

---

47   On the regulation of theatres, see Leonard Conolly, *The Censorship of English Drama, 1737–1824* (San Marino, Calif.: Huntington Library, 1976); Worrall, *Theatric Revolution*, pp. 1–32.

48   Michael Booth, *Nineteenth Century Plays* (Oxford: Clarendon Press, 1969), vol. 1, p. 7. On political theatre in the 1790s, see John Barrell, '"An Entire Change of Performances?" The politicisation of theatre and the theatricalisation of politics in the mid-1790s', *Lumen*, vol. 17 (1998), pp. 11–50; Karr, '"Thoughts that Flash like Lightning"'; Gillian Russell, '"Burke's Dagger": Theatricality, politics and print culture in the 1790s', *British Journal for Eighteenth Century Studies*, vol. 20 (1997), pp. 1–16. For a recent study of the intersections of politics and theatre in the 1830s, see Katherine Newey, 'Reform on the London Stage', in Arthur Burns and Joanna Innes (eds), *Rethinking the Age of Reform, Britain 1780–1850* (Cambridge: Cambridge University Press, 2003), pp. 238–53. For an overview of political theatre for the working classes during the Chartist years, see Marc Brodie, 'Free Trade and Cheap Theatre: Sources of politics for the nineteenth-century London poor', *Social History*, vol. 28, no. 3 (2003), pp. 346–60.

49   C. Barker, 'A Theatre for the People', in Kenneth Richards and Peter Thompson (eds), *Nineteenth Century British Theatre* (London: Metheun, 1971), p. 11.

50   E. P. Thompson, *The Making of the English Working Class* (London: Penguin, 1968), p. 806.

describes as 'illegitimate forms such as melodrama, pantomime, burletta and spectacle', though they soon challenged their exclusion from the 'legitimate' dramatic forms of the Patents.[51]

These venues flourished outside the City of Westminster, as the 1737 Act specifically limited the power of the Lord Chamberlain to scrutinise theatrical texts to be performed in the borough. Minor theatres, while still requiring licences from local magistrates, were clustered in East London and, to the great advantage of Carlile, south of the Thames, in Surrey. The Surrey Theatre (originally the Royal Circus) was also located on Blackfriars Road and became a noted working-class theatre during the early 1830s.[52] In addition to the Surrey, a short distance away could be found the Coburg and the Bower theatres.[53] The poet and literary critic Leigh Hunt considered in 1831 that the 'trade of a theatrical critic' would now take place in the 'classical ground of Southwark', rather than the 'once witty neighbourhood of Covent Garden' and, by 1840, the social observer Henry Mayhew also identified many theatres on the 'Surrey side' that were renowned for catering to a working-class audience.[54] As Moody suggests, Hunt's observation reflected the 'disintegration of old hierarchies and the emergence of new forms and places of dramatic performance'.[55] The 'new feel' that Thomas Markus identified of towns and cities of this period was also reflected in sites of urban sociability. Paradoxically, while the location in Surrey played a role in the demise of the Leverian and the Surrey Institution, the cultural development of the environs surrounding the Rotunda helped in establishing another layer of identity as a theatre. The cultural topography of London had been refigured.

Carlile's reticence about the theatre as a mode of popular entertainment therefore centred on the restriction of free speech, which he so lauded at the Rotunda, and the dearth of political critique in the formal theatres of the period. The Rotunda was unique in offering entertainment that reflected the uneasy political climate of the day. Even the minor theatres generally avoided politically charged theatrical productions in order to protect their own licences. This ultimately meant the exclusion of 'dangerous' political material such as Taylor's politico-tragedy, *Swing!*, from licensed theatres of the day.

Although Rotunda performers such as Taylor were great entertainers, the purpose of the theatricals was the reverse of frivolous. Serious political

---

51 Moody, *Illegitimate Theatre in London*, p. 5.
52 As David Worrall notes, audiences sometimes confused the Surrey Theatre with the Rotunda. A 'competitive spin-off' of Taylor's play, written by Charles Barnett and titled *Swing! A Farce*, opened at the Surrey Theatre only a few weeks after Taylor's opening night at the Rotunda. See Worrall, *Theatric Revolution*, p. 359. See also Moody, *Illegitimate Theatre in London*, pp. 35–7.
53 Worrall, *Theatric Revolution*, p. 341.
54 Barker, 'A Theatre for the People', p. 22.
55 Moody, *Illegitimate Theatre*, p. 33.

assertions were being made throughout. Taylor's dramas aimed to infuse anti-establishment propaganda with entertainment value. In *Swing!*, he employed overtly political dialogue:

> Our proud and haughty lords
> That make the laws only to serve themselves,
> and hire the clergy, like the gospel dogs
> That lickt the beggars sores, to slobber us
> Into patience, would, if they could
> Make air and water theirs, and not suffer us
> To breathe or drink of the stream, but by their
> Allowance.[56]

The enormous popularity of *Swing!* and Taylor's other Rotunda performances also convinced Carlile that theatre was an effective mode of communication, particularly as he believed that the majority of English people were unwilling to 'listen to what may be termed the philosophy of politics'.[57] He claimed that a 'great adroitness, with some finesse' was necessary to gain their continued attention and he believed that political theatre could achieve this. If this meant drawing on the modes of communication of the formal theatres, so be it. There seems little doubt that Rotunda radicals recognised that the method of delivering a political message was as important as the message itself.

In adopting theatrical modes, however, Carlile was also capturing the nuances of a much more traditional form of plebeian entertainment that remained outside the institutional setting of either the Patent or the minor theatres, but in another older, more plebeian tradition of folk theatre, or 'countertheatre'.[58] The ballad singers and 'patterers' with their pavement farces, street-corner parodies and satirical monologues, all represented forms of counter, or folk, theatre.[59] Those re-enacting the cruelties of Coldbath Fields House of Correction during the election parades of Sir Francis Burdett (outlined in Chapter 2) belonged to this tradition, and much of the entertainment in pubs and coffee houses also took the form of countertheatre. Free-and-easies provided radicals with entertainment where they could relax and gossip in a convivial atmosphere and be stimulated by 'dramatic, fantastic, and humorous performances', as well as participating in the ritual 'hullabaloo of singing, toasting and chanting'.[60] Although less overtly theatrical than formal popular theatre, countertheatre still incorporated the underlying principles of burlesque, satire and drama.

---

56   Robert Taylor, *Swing! Or who are the incendiaries* (London, 1831), p. 31.
57   *Prompter*, 20 November 1830.
58   The term 'countertheatre' was first coined by E. P. Thompson, 'Patrician Society, Plebeian Culture', *Journal of Social History*, no. 4 (1974), pp. 382–405.
59   Thompson, *The Making of the English Working Class*, p. 782.
60   McCalman, *Radical Underworld*, p. 121.

Characterised by a mocking or lampooning of the texts, offices and ceremonies of the establishment, it was performed to undermine traditional authority by ridiculing its roles, functions and symbols of distinction.[61] In countertheatre, play and event were used as indirect means of conveying a political message that could be interpreted and understood by rich and poor, literate and illiterate. Many of these performances took the form of lampooning the establishment and its officers. Ordinary men could become 'kings or heroes of the night'.[62] This form of social inversion was an intrinsic part of the tradition of countertheatre.

This mode of political communication had a long tradition in popular radical culture as a means of sparking and sustaining interest in the radical cause. Such was the popularity of countertheatre in plebeian culture that some radicals explicitly adopted its modes in an effort to gain popular support. John Wilkes' use of countertheatrical devices in the latter half of the eighteenth century contributed enormously to his popular appeal.[63] His public manner—epitomised by flamboyant gestures, dress, theatricality, wit and irreverence—won him the immediate admiration of all those who would have loved to flout authority. Much of Taylor's popular support was similarly derived from his 'countertheatricality'. Aside from his flamboyant dress and eccentricity, his propensity for low burlesque and his mocking of authority were vital elements in his appeal. For plebeian audiences, the Rotunda tapped into traditional modes of communication and conviviality in popular culture but also provided the more formal setting of a theatre, which allowed patrons to enjoy the trappings of new modes of urban sociability.

Carlile's pricing format also catered for working-class audiences. He priced his theatrical entertainment well below that of the formal theatres in order to disseminate the radical message as widely as possible. He boasted that the Rotunda provided the 'cheapest theatrical entertainment to be found' in London and the relatively low cost of admittance to performances found a receptive audience among the working classes of the metropolis. Though the minor theatres provided a more affordable option for plebeian theatregoers than the Patents, there remains some contention among scholars as to the affordability of such theatres for the majority of the population. Marc Brodie notes that prior to the 1830s the admission prices for the Coburg remained relatively out of reach of many—the boxes, four shillings; the pit, two shillings; and the

---

61 John Brewer, 'Theatre and Counter-Theatre in Georgian Politics: The mock elections at Garrat', *History Today*, vol. 33 (1983), p. 22.
62 McCalman, *Radical Underworld*, p. 121.
63 John Brewer, *Party Ideology and Popular Politics at the Accession of George III* (Cambridge: Cambridge University Press, 1982), pp. 163–200.

gallery one shilling—compared with the much lower cost of the penny gaffs.[64] The comparative affordability of the Rotunda tickets at sixpence or one penny provided an attractive alternative for working-class audiences.

The working-class recognition of the Rotunda as a forum for popular theatre was perhaps most evident in the audience reaction to, and involvement in, the performances. Traditionally, melodrama accorded an opportunity for audiences to participate in their entertainment through cries of 'shame' for the arch villain or 'bravo' for the hero. It provided a communal theatrical interaction between actors and audience, which was also evident at the Rotunda theatre. Home Office spy Abel Hall reported that Rotunda performers received 'theatrical applause' in great quantities, suggesting that audiences reacted to the performances as if in a traditional theatre house.[65] Another Home Office recorder testifies similarly that cries of 'bravo' and long and loud applause became familiar accompaniments to Taylor's lectures and extravaganzas.[66]

This audience reaction suggests Carlile may have underestimated the degree of political awareness and political engagement of Rotunda patrons. Cries of 'shame' or 'bravo' and extra applause during seditious or blasphemous acts were two of the ways Rotunda audiences expressed their disgruntlement with authority. For a people who lacked the political voice or strength to express their disapproval formally, the communal interaction between radical leader and followers provided an opportunity to register disaffection with the injustices of Old Corruption. As Marc Baer contends in relation to mainstream plebeian theatre, 'a place in the audience was also a voice'.[67] The more explicit political content of Rotunda performances provided audiences an opportunity for a more potent expression of their discontent.

By offering political instruction in the guise of theatre, the Rotunda also provided sanctuary for what we might term 'closet radicals'—people who might otherwise have been repelled by the more formal or clandestine political groups that met in taverns and coffee houses. People could voice their political will and independence by attending political theatre. Patrons could not be arrested for attending the theatrical performances, although their presence automatically acted to register their political discontent. The Rotunda also offered a powerful alternative for those working people who wanted access to radical theory but who were concerned about the illegality of unstamped papers and journals. The repressive legislation levelled at the unstamped press, and the severe punishments surrounding its distribution, meant that alternative, less provocative means of obtaining radical knowledge were particularly valuable.

---

64 Brodie, 'Free Trade and Cheap Theatre', p. 350.
65 Home Office Papers, HO64/11, 25 September 1830, fo. 167; HO64/12, 27 February 1832, fo. 47.
66 Home Office Papers, HO64/13, 3 April 1831, fo. 50.
67 Marc Baer, *Theatre and Disorder in Late Georgian London* (Oxford: Clarendon Press, 1992), p. 177.

Recent scholarship has argued for the centrality of the theatre—both plebeian and bourgeois forms—in urban sociability in early nineteenth-century Britain.[68] Lynn Voskuil links audience involvement in theatrical performances with a voice in the public sphere: 'while hisses, catcalls, and shouts cannot be equated with rational discourse, such accounts of audience behaviour bespeak a conception of the public sphere grounded in verbal exchange, specifically in the articulation and public debate of fiercely held opinions.'[69]

This is a crucial point. Participation in, and an impact on, the public sphere cannot alone be limited to the sober, rational discourse of middle-class institutions such as the Surrey Institution. Public opinion was clearly reflected in, and generated by, voices within such middle-class institutions, but also in spaces such as the Rotunda, which, for Habermas, sat outside the bourgeois public sphere. The example of the Rotunda poses a serious challenge to the dichotomous approach of thinking towards the two separate spheres.[70]

* * *

The device of theatricality was not the only form of radical communication employed at the Rotunda; other modes of radical discourse and exchange also found an outlet within its walls. The Rotunda accommodated purely political radical groups and identities, even those who eschewed Carlile's assaults on Christianity. In July 1830, Henry Hunt's Radical Reform Association (RRA) found a home at the Rotunda. The new Metropolitan Political Union (MPU) formed by Irish and English radicals under the chairmanship of Daniel O'Connell (and later Hunt) also found in the Rotunda a perfect venue for their lofty ambition to unite the whole of London's radical opinion in one organisation.[71] Despite early disputes between Carlile and the MPU over its direction, the July Revolution in France injected a new urgency to consolidate and

---

68 See, for example, the work by Gillian Russell, *Women, Sociability and Theatre in Georgian London* (Cambridge: Cambridge University Press, 2007); idem, *The Theatres of War: Performance, politics, and society, 1793–1815* (Oxford: Clarendon Press, 1995); Voskuil, 'Feeling Public'; Julie A. Carlson, 'Hazlitt and the Sociability of Theatre', in Gillian Russell and Clara Tuite (eds), *Romantic Sociability: Social networks and literary culture in Britain, 1770–1840* (Cambridge: Cambridge University Press, 2002), pp. 145–65; Simon During, '"The Temple Lives": The Lyceum and Romantic show business', in James Chandler and Kevin Gilmartin (eds), *Romantic Metropolis: The urban scene of British culture, 1780–1840* (Cambridge: Cambridge University Press, 2005), pp. 204–26; Moody, *Illegitimate Theatre*.
69 Voskuil, 'Feeling Public', p. 248. Julie Carlson argues that although Habermas paid little attention to theatre as an institution of the public sphere, it was nevertheless 'instrumental in negotiating changes in forms of representation and representability'. Carlson, 'Hazlitt and the Sociability of Theatre', p. 147.
70 Gillian Russell also argues that the 'potent space' of the Beaufort buildings (in the Strand) was less a counter-public than a space that extended 'the limits of inclusivity encoded in notions of the commercialized public sphere in its classic Habermasian formulation'. Gillian Russell, 'Spouters or Washerwomen: The sociability of Romantic lecturing', in Russell and Tuite, *Romantic Sociability*, p. 129.
71 For an RRA meeting that attracted more than 1000 people, see *Morning Chronicle*, 15 August 1830. For more on the RRA and the MPU, see Prothero, *Artisans and Politics in Early Nineteenth Century London*, pp. 25–281, 386ns17–18; D. J. Rowe, 'Class and Political Radicalism in London, 1831–2', *Historical Journal*, vol. 13, no. 1 (1970), pp. 31–47; John Belchem, *'Orator' Hunt: Henry Hunt and English working-class radicalism* (Oxford: Clarendon Press, 1985), pp. 194–213.

centralise metropolitan radicalism. William Cobbett used the occasion to deliver a series of 11 immensely successful lectures at the Rotunda on the French example and on 'the English boroughmongers', which energised the political meetings at the Rotunda for the remainder of the year.[72]

It was not long, however, before the divisions that had destabilised London's radicalism for decades emerged at the Rotunda. Despite Carlile's public aim to establish a venue of free discussion for all tenets of radicalism, his polemics against many of London's leading radicals, as well as his criticism of the strategy to make universal suffrage the key demand of reform, soon impacted on relationships within the Rotunda. The tumultuous events of early November 1830 revealed the first rifts, and again centred on the personalities of Hunt and Carlile. The opening of the Rotunda saw a truce (albeit tenuous) in the bitter feud between the two men, which originated in their respective prison cells and continued into the late 1820s. In the year before Carlile assumed the tenancy of the Rotunda, he caustically asserted that he had never known a political association 'more contemptibly devoid of intellect and useful purpose' than Hunt's Radical Reform Association.[73] That they came together under the roof of the Rotunda suggests that both men recognised the potential of the venue for driving London radicalism in this period. The veiled harmony was to be short-lived. Ultimately, it was the threat of prosecution that again brought the two radical leaders to blows.

Although Carlile frequently claimed that his numerous prosecutions were 'heaven' to him, others such as Hunt and Cobbett were less enthusiastic about a return to prison life. Cobbett, for instance, was due to deliver a lecture to a packed Rotunda audience in early November after thousands assembled the previous evening to hear him speak. At the last moment, he had an emissary deliver Carlile a message advising that he was too ill to proceed with the next lecture. Many of the Rotunda fraternity suspected cowardice in the face of possible prosecution.[74] A greater schism in Rotunda solidarity was to follow. On 11 November 1830, following the heady events caused by the anticipated visit of the King to the city, Hunt pre-empted the rumours of state warrants being issued for his arrest for his role at the Rotunda meetings and presented himself to the magistrates. During this meeting, Hunt was reported to have disavowed any connection with the Rotunda leaders.[75] The denial led to a public row after the incident was reported in *The Times*, which Hunt subsequently maintained misrepresented his statement to the magistrates. Acknowledging that he had 'disclaimed any connexion' with the leaders of the Rotunda after being

---

72 See Cobbett's *Weekly Political Register*, 2 October 1830; George Spater, *William Cobbett: The poor man's friend* (Cambridge: Cambridge University Press, 1982), vol. 2, pp. 493–5.
73 *Lion*, 9 October 1829.
74 Prothero, *Artisans and Politics in Early Nineteenth Century London*, p. 280; Home Office Papers, HO40/21, 8 November 1830, fo. 262.
75 Belchem, *'Orator' Hunt*, p. 214.

accused of being the 'sole cause of holding nightly meetings', he offered that he never disputed their 'propriety of doing so'.[76] The minor concession went little way towards placating other Rotunda stalwarts.

Hunt was clearly rattled by the threat of prosecution and proceeded carefully at the next meeting of the RRA. On 15 November 1830, he interrupted his address to object to the tricolour flag that one audience member had raised over his head. Hunt requested its removal, seeing no reason for its display unless they were assembled specifically to discuss the revolution in France. Further antagonising some members of his audience, he questioned why they wanted any flag at all. Some 'well-dressed persons', *The Times* reported, had retorted that 'the tri-colour flag is no humbug; let it stand as the badge of liberty'.[77] *The Times* reported that despite several of the audience showing 'a very marked dislike of [Hunt's] sentiments', the removal of the flag was put to the vote, and accordingly it was removed from the meeting.[78] Abel Hall's correspondence to the Home Office, however, suggested that Hunt was forced to proceed with the meeting with the flag in place. Whatever the actual outcome on the night, the incident added further fuel to the tense relationships at the venue. Other Rotunda leaders moved quickly to re-establish the centrality of the tricolour. Taylor responded with his now familiar theatrical wit; spy reports attest that he appeared the following week with his eyeglass suspended from a huge tricolour ribbon draped around his shoulders.[79]

If Hunt's objection to the tricolour flag was not enough to alienate him from his fellow radicals at Blackfriars Road, his denunciation of Carlile as a coward at Peterloo and a government spy sealed his expulsion from London's new leading radical forum. It also effectively signalled the end of the RRA; Rotunda radicals split over their support for either Carlile or Hunt and, as Prothero notes, the group 'rapidly declined amidst these quarrels'.[80] Leading Rotunda radicals such as John Gale Jones were frustrated that once again 'party feeling and disunion had broken in upon the professed advocates of reform'.[81] Despite Carlile's wish to provide a venue under which London radicals could unite, he simply could not ignore Hunt's bitter accusation of him being a government spy. Carlile's decision in late November to raise the price of the theatre hire to five guineas for the large theatre and two guineas for the small theatre helped to 'do away with the Radical Association from meeting there'.[82] By December, Carlile's decision to no longer allow the RRA to use the Rotunda was the 'death blow'.[83]

---

76 *The Times*, 13 November 1830.
77 Ibid.
78 *The Times*, 16 November 1830.
79 Home Office Papers, HO64/11, 30 November 1830, fo. 148.
80 Prothero, *Artisans and Politics in Early Nineteenth Century London*, p. 280.
81 *The Times*, 22 November 1830.
82 Home Office Papers, HO64/11, 22 November 1830, fo. 143.
83 Prothero, *Artisans and Politics in Early Nineteenth Century London*, p. 281. For the end of the RRA, see *Prompter*, 20 November 1830, 4 December 1830. See also *The Times*, 12 November 1830.

With the RRA now defunct (the MPU having followed a similar fate earlier that year), Carlile, Taylor and Jones provided the political instruction at the Rotunda with lectures on political economy and republicanism. Although Jones was an accomplished veteran radical orator, Carlile was a poor public speaker and lacked the charisma, showmanship and oratorical skills to sustain Rotunda audiences. Though prison had developed him as a scholar, he never learned the skills of effective public speaking and Rotunda audiences at his political meetings began to fall.[84]

The formation of the National Union of the Working Classes (NUWC) in April 1831 helped revive the Rotunda's political credentials among the radical community.[85] Although Carlile had long objected to the effectiveness of and need for political associations, the NUWC provided Carlile with not only a much needed injection of rental income from the Rotunda, but also a boost to his claim to provide a radical forum for all reformers. The NUWC grew out of the disillusionment of plebeian radicals with the middle-class leaders of the Reform movement, including the Crown and Anchor stalwarts encountered in an earlier chapter, and the impending likelihood of some measure of reform with the election of the new Whig administration. The group would become the most effective working-class radical organisation of the early 1830s.[86] Its mandate—universal male suffrage, annual parliaments, vote by ballot and the removal of property qualifications for MPs—would provide the blueprint for that crucible of working-class radicalism, the People's Charter. The NUWC combined the talents of radical artisans William Lovett, Henry Hetherington, James Watson, John Cleave, William Carpenter, John Gast and the veteran ultra William Benbow, with Rotunda financier and radical strategist Julian Hibbert.[87] As Prothero notes, by July, 'the new union had absorbed all the ultra-radical groups in London'.[88]

---

84 Wiener, *Radicalism and Freethought in Nineteenth-Century Britain*, p. 167.
85 On the NUWC, see Rowe, 'Class and Political Radicalism in London'; Prothero, *Artisans and Politics in Early Nineteenth Century London*, esp. pp. 281–99; William Lovett, *The Life and Struggles of William Lovett, In his pursuit of bread, knowledge and freedom* (London: Trübner & Co., 1876), pp. 68–89; Patricia Hollis, *The Pauper Press: A study in working-class radicalism of the 1830s* (Oxford: Oxford University Press, 1970), pp. 40–5, 198–204, ch. 8, passim.
86 McCalman, *Radical Underworld*, p. 198.
87 On William Lovett, see Joel Wiener, *William Lovett* (Manchester: Manchester University Press, 1989); David Large, 'William Lovett', in Patricia Hollis (ed.), *Pressure from Without in Early Victorian England* (London: E. Arnold, 1974), pp. 105–30; Eileen Janes Yeo, 'Will the Real Mary Lovett Please Stand Up?: Chartism, gender and autobiography', in Malcolm Chase and Ian Dyck (eds), *Living and Learning, Essays in Honour of J. F. C. Harrison* (Brookfield, Vt: Scholar Press, 1996), pp. 163–81. On Henry Hetherington, radical publisher (including of the *Poor Man's Guardian*) and journalist, see George J. Holyoake, *The Life and Character of Henry Hetherington* (London, 1849); Prothero, *Artisans and Politics in Early Nineteenth Century London*, pp. 268–99; Joel H. Wiener, 'Hetherington, Henry (1792–1849)', in *Oxford Dictionary of National Biography* [hereafter *ODNB*], <http://www.oxforddnb.com/view/article/13136>. On John Cleave, see Henry Weisser, 'Cleave, John', *BDMBR*, vol. 2, pp. 138–41; Hollis, *The Pauper Press*, esp. pp. 77–80, 149–64, 198–202, 281–3. On John Gast, see Prothero, *Artisans and Politics in Early Nineteenth Century London*. On William Carpenter, see Chapter 6, Note 7. On William Benbow, see Iowerth Prothero, 'William Benbow and the Concept of the "General Strike"', *Past & Present*, vol. 63 (1974), pp. 132–71.
88 Prothero, *Artisans and Politics in Early Nineteenth Century London*, p. 285.

The NUWC met in the large theatre of the Rotunda every Wednesday, with attendances of up to 1000 during 1831.[89] The Rotunda became the organisational headquarters of the new Union as committee members were encouraged to establish smaller parish or regional 'classes' of 25 members each. The class leaders would then meet back at the Rotunda each week to discuss the members' concerns, lead discussions and debate the Reform crisis and other logistical measures. By late 1831, discussion over the direction of the Reform Bill took precedence at NUWC meetings with 'other topics having lost their interest pending the National Question'.[90] The NUWC was far from projecting a united voice for either support or rejection of the limited measures proposed in the Act. John Gale Jones argued for the ballot and universal suffrage while Taylor advocated excluding the '"Soldiery" from the franchise given their abjectstate [sic] of servitude rendering them incapable of the proper exercise of that privilege'.[91] Whether the Rotunda radicals were, as D. J. Rowe suggests, 'endeavouring to make the best of both worlds' in continuing to demand universal suffrage while 'still offering tacit support to the Whig measure', or whether the use of Francis Place's memoirs to draw this conclusion has perhaps muddied the waters, the Rotunda nevertheless played a key role in plebeian response to the Reform Bill crisis.[92] As Francis Place led his delegation from the Crown and Anchor to Downing Street, the Rotunda provided the major metropolitan rallying point for working-class reaction to the Reform Bill.

One of the key Rotunda figures of the NUWC was the Manchester radical William Benbow. It was from the Rotunda that Benbow first launched his notorious proposal for a 'Grand National Holiday', or a month's general strike, as well as a national convention.[93] As Prothero notes, the idea of a national convention was not new in British radicalism. The success of the American and French examples of the late eighteenth century energised British radicals. They recognised the opportunity such a convention provided for a revolutionary change of guard and there were sporadic attempts to organise such a gathering throughout the early nineteenth century, culminating with the Chartist Convention of 1839. It was, however, Benbow's call for the 'people' to unite, amass provisions for a week and withdraw their labour from the economy for a month that was to capture the attention of radicals throughout Britain and, no doubt, that of the

---

89 Ibid. Prothero estimates an average attendance of 500 during this time. Although Carlile initially charged the group the three guineas hire fee for the large theatre, by July, he offered it for the proceeds of the entry charge (one penny for members, twopence for non-members).
90 *Republican*, 26 March 1831.
91 Ibid. See also Home Office Papers, HO64/11, 20 August 1831, fo. 412.
92 Rowe, 'Class and Political Radicalism in London'. See also E. P. Thompson, who noted the 'unscrupulous manoeuvres' of Place and his attempts to 'limit the influence of the Rotunda men'. Thompson, *The Making of the English Working Class*, p. 894.
93 Prothero, 'William Benbow and the Concept of the "General Strike"'.

authorities.⁹⁴ Though the 'holiday' nomenclature helped temper the concept, the plan remained revolutionary at heart. Benbow had long been, as Prothero argues, an advocate of physical-force tactics and his intention for the 'holiday' was to provide the kindling to ignite a political revolution. Although Benbow's plan excited great interest (the first edition of the published plan sold out and a second edition was produced), the NUWC simply did not yet have consensus among its ranks, the national reach or organisational structure to engender support, let alone coordinate a mass general strike. It was to remain a work in progress that Benbow would revisit and amend over the following two decades.

Regardless of whether the plan ever came to fruition, the promulgation of such views from the ultra-radical organisation of London whose headquarters was at the Rotunda saw the development of yet another layer of identity at the venue as a centre for radical militancy and revolutionary intent. George J. Holyoake would later recall in his memoir of Carlile that the 'prophecy of the day was, that the Rotunda would cause a Revolution in England'.⁹⁵ As we saw in Chapter 5, the *Courier* clearly considered the Rotunda milieu as a threat when it sought to distinguish Francis Place's Crown and Anchor delegation group from that of the danger posed by the 'Rotunda revolutionists'.⁹⁶

The venue's identity as a haven for extreme radicalism is evident in other examples of print culture from the period. Although the Rotunda never featured in the graphic satire to the scale of the Crown and Anchor prints, it nevertheless appeared in one of the most popular prints of the day titled *John Gilpin!!!*, by leading caricaturist John Doyle (pseudonym 'HB').⁹⁷ Published in 1831, the print is based upon the famous poem of the same name by William Cowper. In the poem, John Gilpin, out with his family to celebrate his wedding anniversary, loses control of his horse, which charges, taking him 10 miles beyond his original destination of Edmonton and then back again.⁹⁸ In the print, William IV is shown as the errant and misfortunate horse rider, satirising the Monarch's impotency during the Reform Bill crisis.⁹⁹ The beer bottles depicted on the King's waist are labelled 'Rotunda Pop' and 'Birmingham Froth' (the latter in reference to Thomas Attwood's Birmingham Political Union) and are beginning

---

94 As Prothero notes, historians have afforded Benbow credit as the first person to have publicly advocated a general strike.
95 George J. Holyoake, *The Life of Richard Carlile* (London, 1849), pp. 14–15.
96 *Courier*, 14 October 1831.
97 This is possible because, unlike the 1790s, most prints of this period were reformist by nature and the enemy was seen as the aristocrats opposing reform—not the divided voice of the working class. See M. D. George, *Catalogue of Political and Personal Satires Preserved in the Department of Prints and Drawings in the British Museum* (London: The Trustees of the British Museum, 1978), vol. 11, p. xxxiii.
98 William Cowper's poem *The Diverting History of John Gilpin* was written in 1782 and, according to Cowper's biographer, John Baird, became the most popular poem of the decade. John D. Baird, 'Cowper, William (1731–1800)', *ODNB*, <http://www.oxforddnb.com/view/article/6513>
99 George, *Catalogue of Political and Personal Satires*, vol. 11, p. 483. William IV dissolved Parliament and pressured Grey to modify the Bill to conciliate its opponents in the House of Lords.

to explode. M. D. George, the celebrated British Museum print surveyor, notes—as evidence of the enduring subversive image of Rotunda radicalism—in her description of the print that '"Rotunda pop" stands for sedition and profanity: the revolutionary ultra-Radicals at the Rotunda (Rotundanists) in Blackfriars Road were anti-Whig'.[100] She might have said so much more.

One of the more ominous and perhaps most publicised warnings concerning the Rotunda milieu came from an alarmist pamphlet penned by Edward Gibbon Wakefield.[101] In *Householders in Danger of the Populace*, thought to have been published in late 1831, Wakefield classifies the dangerous elements of London society as 'the populace', whom he divides into three distinct categories: the 'common thieves'; 'the rabble' (those led into crime by circumstance and poverty); and 'the Desperadoes', the men of the Rotunda.[102] The Rotunda men he further divided into two groups: the supporters of Henry Hunt and those men who had formerly been associated with the Owenites, though he pointed to universal suffrage as the unifying mandate under the Rotunda banner. All members of the populace, Wakefield warned, were 'bent on a state of anarchy'.

Of the Rotunda revolutionaries, he described Hunt's supporters as 'loose single men, living here and there in lodgings, who might set fire to London'. These men, of whom Wakefield counted about 1000, were 'not less dangerous on account of their number' for though they were 'poor creatures', 'careless and inert' workmen, they had a 'naturally weak intellect; having deficient foreheads and a sinister expression'. The Owenites, however, he found 'worthy of respect on public grounds', but though 'sober men', they were of 'scanty knowledge and utterly impracticable'. Their danger lay in the fact they were fanatics and idealists; these men would become the leaders if 'the populace' as a whole began to revolt. While the extent of circulation of the pamphlet is unclear, it is likely to have aroused particular interest given Wakefield's own, unwelcome notoriety. His infamous abduction of, and forced marriage to, fifteen-year-old heiress Ellen Turner resulted in three years' imprisonment in Newgate.[103] The Rotunda radicals were certainly aware of the pamphlet. It became the source of great hilarity and derision at one NUWC meeting at which Wakefield's criminal past and the pamphlet itself were mocked mercilessly by Julian Hibbert.[104]

Reports in the mainstream press also conflated Rotunda radicalism with criminality. Within months of the venue opening, *The Times* reported:

---

100   Ibid., p. 484.
101   Wakefield would become one of the leading proponents of colonisation. See David J. Moss, 'Wakefield, Edward Gibbon (1796–1862)', *ODNB*, <http://www.oxforddnb.com/view/article/28415>
102   Edward Gibbon Wakefield, *Householders in Danger of the Populace* (London, 1831). The quotations that follow are taken from the pamphlet.
103   Wakefield's brother, who acted as an accomplice, was also imprisoned in Newgate.
104   *Poor Man's Guardian*, 3 December 1831.

> The nightly meetings which have for some time past been held at the Rotunda...were known to have collected together great multitudes of persons, the majority of whom were composed of thieves and other ill-disposed persons, who were ready to join with others in the commission of any illegal acts, to disturb the peace of the metropolis.[105]

Similar reports continued throughout 1831, citing the large crowds assembling each evening as targets for an 'organized gang of thieves and ruffians' who had 'assaulted, robbed and hustled' many of those milling near the venue.[106] Inside or outside the prison walls it seems that the opponents of radicalism had made up their minds: radicals were dangerous criminals. This blanket typification of radicals in the public sphere (incarcerated or otherwise) makes the persistence of radical culture all the more heroic.

London's radical community themselves also promulgated the notion of revolutionary threat emanating from the Rotunda and played some role in cultivating the image of the dangerous and unpredictable mob. As Ian Haywood notes, in the Swing tragedy, 'Swing's success is attributed to the Rotunda'.[107] David Worrall also notes that the play was a 'continuous celebration of Carlile's Rotunda and its place in working-class radical rationalist politics':[108] 'And has old Swing turned rational at last/Has he been at that horrible Rotunda,/Where nothing is going on but REASON?'[109]

Though the Rotunda radicals celebrated the venue's revolutionary possibilities and wore the term Rotundanist as a badge of honour, they also were forced to contend with hostility from within the London reform movement itself. The most enduring criticism of the Rotundanists has come from the memoirs of Francis Place. As we will recall from an earlier chapter, Place described the Rotunda men as 'vehement, resolute reckless rascals whose purpose was riot as providing an opportunity for plunder'.[110] His mistrust of the Rotunda's ultra-radicals was particularly evident in the attempt to form the National Political Union as an alliance between middling and plebeian reformers. He and other organisers were determined to ensure that the new council of the Union consisted of 'respectable working men untainted with Rotunda heresy'.[111]

Yet even Carlile, who allowed the NUWC access to the Rotunda, remained publicly critical of the group's objectives. Acknowledging in the *Prompter* that

---

105 *The Times*, 11 November 1830.
106 *The Times*, 31 March 1831, 12 October 1831.
107 Ian Haywood, *The Revolution in Popular Literature: Print, politics and the people, 1790–1860* (Cambridge: Cambridge University Press, 2004), p. 109.
108 Worrall, *Theatric Revolution*, p. 351.
109 Taylor, *Swing! Or who are the incendaries?*, p. 13, quoted in ibid., p. 353.
110 Francis Place Papers (Add. MS 27791, ff. 47–57).
111 Francis Place quoted in Rowe, 'Class and Political Radicalism in London', p. 40.

it was the 'best effort at the formation of a political society that has yet been made, and contains more stability of principle than has been essayed in any former scheme of the kind', he nevertheless concluded that it remained 'very defective...the high flown style and title assumed is quite aristocratical and ludicrous'.[112] The public attacks must have infuriated the leaders of the nascent association. Nevertheless, in the Rotunda, the ultras of the NUWC found a place where they controlled who could assemble and what could be uttered. Such freedom to operate must have gone some way to compensate for Carlile's churlish behaviour.

Although the NUWC also met at more traditional radical meeting places such as public houses, coffee shops (including Benbow's own) and radical chapels, the importance of the Rotunda to the group, despite Carlile's animosity, is clearly evident in the following extract from radical ultra John Cleave. To a packed Rotunda audience, he relayed his hope that 'they would in one short year be able to build themselves a Rotunda to meet at and debate in, and enable them to laugh at their enemies, as well as to establish the liberties of their country. (Tremendous cheering).'[113] Place certainly feared that 'the influence of the Union [NUWC] had become extensive, and was increasing' because of its ability to disseminate an image of an organised, structured and united London working class to the provinces. The Rotunda played a crucial role in cultivating this image.[114]

For Henry Hetherington, the Rotunda promised even more. Along with Carlile, he also considered that the venue provided a voice for the people who remained disenfranchised from the formal political channels; the Rotunda was their 'centre', the 'House of the Unrepresented'. Prothero's contention that the NUWC's Rotunda meetings 'were mainly for publicity' clearly underestimates the importance of the site to the group.[115] There, unlike the other radical spaces we have so far explored, radicals found a venue where the radical community themselves determined what Stallybrass and White refer to as the 'cultural conditions' that act to regulate behaviour and how people experience a particular space.[116] We should not underestimate the significance to the radical movement of a space controlled by their own. This was a period when property and political power were inextricably linked. The struggle for the freedom of the press was accompanied by another, albeit less recognised struggle for access

---

112   *Prompter*, 28 May 1831.
113   *Poor Man's Guardian*, 29 October 1831.
114   Rowe, 'Class and Political Radicalism in London', p. 43. Place's involvement in the formation of the National Political Union was a direct response to the threat posed by the Rotunda milieu. See Joseph Hamburger, *James Mill and the Art of Revolution* (New Haven, Conn.: Yale University Press, 1963), pp. 77–90.
115   Prothero, *Artisans and Politics in Early Nineteenth Century London*, p. 285.
116   Peter Stallybrass and Allon White, *The Politics and Poetics of Transgression* (Ithaca, NY: Cornell University Press, 1986), quoted in James Epstein, *In Practice: Studies in the language and culture of popular politics in modern Britain* (Stanford: Stanford University Press, 2003), p. 113.

to spaces in which to organise. Epstein has argued that a marked feature of popular radicalism in this period was the search to gain access to and control sites of assembly.[117] The Rotunda was such a space.

The Home Office also recognised the Rotunda as a key centre of radical sedition; both the Tory Home Secretary, Robert Peel, and his Whig replacement, Lord Melbourne, employed spies and informers to keep constant vigilance over the proceedings and to report on any possible 'mischief' emanating from the lectures and meetings.[118] During the November 1830 agitation, letters from surrounding residents and government officials poured into the Home Office, warning of the dire consequences of the moral corruption of the values of working-class people through the 'lawless and abandoned proceedings' at the Rotunda.[119] The concern over the possible threat posed by the Rotunda went all the way to the top. According to E. P. Thompson, then Prime Minister and former army commander, the Duke of Wellington, saw the contest as

> one between the Establishment and the Rotunda, which he compared to two armies *'en présence'*. It confused his military mind very much to reflect that he could place no river between armies, with adequate sentinels and posts on the bridges. The enemy was installed at sensitive points within his own camp.[120]

Wellington's military training had prepared him for engaging with enemies from without, not for confronting an 'enemy' marshalling just across the Thames.

There is no doubt that the Home Office actively sought legal means to close the building, which had long been a menace to the authorities. In a letter dated 9 November 1830, a senior police official named Chambers wrote to Peel expressing his belief that the Rotunda constituted a 'disorderly house' and advised Peel that under existing legislation a magistrate could be called upon to close the building. Yet despite precedents of successful closures on these grounds from the earlier *Seditious Meetings Act* of 1795, Chambers advised Peel that in the case of the Rotunda, he 'entertained considerable doubt of the power of convicting in a summary manner'.[121] Peel then made inquiries as to the validity of the dissenting chapel licence issued to the Rotunda given the types of meetings

---

117 Ibid.
118 See *Home Office Reports* concerning the activities at the Rotunda in Home Office Papers, HO64/11, HO40/25.
119 See, for example, Home Office Papers, HO40/25, 4 November 1830, fo. 33.
120 Thompson, *The Making of the English Working Class*, p. 894.
121 Home Office Papers, HO40/25, 9 November 1830, fo. 179. On the closures of premises under the 1795 Act, see Clive Emsley, 'Repression, "Terror" and the Rule of Law in England During the Decade of the French Revolution', *English Historical Review*, vol. 100, no. 397 (1985), p. 812.

being conducted there. Despite receiving an answer apparently favourable to the authorities, evidently neither avenue was strong enough to force a legal closure.[122]

What, then, accounts for the apparent inability of the authorities to close the Rotunda at a time when all radical activity was under the sustained threat of prosecution? Carlile's ability to secure a dissenting chapel licence goes part of the way in explaining the continuing operation of the premises. Within the chapels, political dissent could be cloaked in religious terms.[123] Radicals were conscious that scriptural language carried weight in society, especially with London juries.[124] This is not to say that non-conformist ministers could evade prosecution but political dissent voiced within the confines of a dissenting chapel proved harder to suppress than other forms of radical political expression. Further, the dissenting chapel licence also helped Carlile avoid the necessity of a theatre licence, which would likely have been revoked by local magistrates following the production of the politically charged *Swing!* play.[125]

The diversity of the Rotunda offerings could have itself helped facilitate the premises' immunity from prosecution. The impressive, scholarly credentials of performers such as Taylor and Sharples assisted in promoting the Rotunda as a reputable learning establishment. The theatricality of Rotunda performances also provided some legal protection. By employing the often satirical yet non-verbal symbols associated with countertheatre to convey their radical messages, Rotunda orators deployed an effective means of dodging the wrath of the prosecuting societies. Burlesque or satirical performances were technically difficult to prosecute because much of the 'sedition' was implicit. It lay in the use of excessive gesture, motion, dress and expression.

Moreover, the brilliantly successful defence of radical publisher William Hone in his three libel trials of 1817 set a legal precedent concerning the prosecution of satires, which assisted the radical movement for more than a decade.[126] Hone, a poor bookseller and radical, was indicted for publishing blasphemous libels in the form of parodies on the Catechism, Litany and Creed. He conducted his own defence, and his introduction of ludicrous parodies as evidence in his defence caused such amusement in the courtroom that the Sheriff threatened to arrest 'the first man I see laugh'.[127] Despite Chief Justice Ellenborough's instruction to the jury that the work was the 'most impious and profane libel', it nevertheless returned 'not guilty' verdicts in all three trials. For more than a decade, all

---

122 Home Office Papers, HO64/11, 10 November 1830, fo. 114.
123 McCalman, 'Ultra-Radicalism and Convivial Debating Clubs in London', p. 315.
124 Ibid., p. 319.
125 Moody, *Illegitimate Theatre*, p. 103.
126 Thompson, *The Making of the English Working Class*, p. 792.
127 Ibid., p. 793.

parodies, burlesques and satires were immune from prosecution. The authorities dared not risk repeat embarrassments with juries who could not be relied upon to convict such entertaining personalities as Hone; their flouting of authority and irreverence all too easily won the people's affections.

Such diversity of Rotunda meetings might also have acted to dilute the purely political aspirations, and perceived threat, of the NUWC. Furthermore, the adoption of the 'Union' nomenclature, in line with the flourishing number of political unions based on Thomas Attwood's model from Birmingham, also assisted the NUWC to operate without the threat of prosecution.[128] With the majority of political unions supporting the Whig measure of reform, to target the opposition voices from the NUWC might have been perceived as engaging in class warfare. The extent to which the use of the term 'union' by all these groups was calculated to ensure some protection under the new *Combination Act*, which, although severely curtailing the rights of union organisation, nevertheless legalised their existence, also warrants further investigation.[129]

Though all of these factors could have provided a veil of protection, the answer must surely lie in the inability, or unwillingness, of the government of the day to enact the powers they evidently held under the Six Acts, even given the expiration of the *Seditious Meetings Act* in 1824.[130] Legal historians have highlighted the limits of the 'repressive' measures of successive governments throughout both the 1790s and the early nineteenth century and of governments who grappled with the rights of the people to meet, discuss and petition under peaceful conditions with the perceived threat of riot and public disorder arising from the spread of popular radicalism. Clive Emsley argues that the legislative acts of the 1790s were formulated in the tradition of eighteenth-century law and, rather than mandating that all offenders would be punished, 'held out the threat of punishment'. 'No subsequent legislation', he continues, 'set out to ensure that they would be enforced to the letter. Only the *Seditious Meetings Act* was ever used, and this was rarely.'[131]

Philip Harling similarly makes an important distinction between 'the readiness to use the mailed fist' and the 'frequency of its use' in his study of the law of

---

128 For an in-depth study of the rise of political unions and their influence on the passing of the *Reform Act*, see Nancy LoPatin, *Political Unions, Popular Politics and the Great Reform Act of 1832* (London: Macmillan, 1999).
129 Prothero considers that, regardless of the nomenclature, the NUWC displayed 'expressions of trade union consciousness' in the early 1830s. Prothero, *Artisans and Politics in Early Nineteenth Century London*, p. 275.
130 See J. Ann Hone, *For the Cause of Truth: Radicalism in London 1796–1821* (Oxford: Clarendon, 1982), p. 286.
131 Emsley, 'Repression, "Terror", and the Rule of Law', p. 813. See also Philip Harling, 'The Law of Libel and the Limits of Repression, 1790–1832', *Historical Journal*, vol. 44, no. 1 (2001), pp. 107–34; Michael Lobban, 'From Seditious Libel to Unlawful Assembly: Peterloo and the changing face of political crime, c.1770–1820', *Oxford Journal of Legal Studies*, vol. 10, no. 3 (1990), pp. 307–52.

seditious and blasphemous libel in the period 1790–1832.[132] Though Harling argues that these laws were sporadically enforced because the Home Office lacked the 'institutional means to embark on a policy of wholesale prosecution', the very possibility of prosecution under the laws provided the government with a 'formidable instrument of oppression'.[133] It was the arbitrariness of the government's approach to prosecution, coupled with the vague legal definitions of sedition and blasphemy, as well as the often harrowing experiences of defendants when they did choose to prosecute, that in effect provided a 'formidable instrument of harassment, if ultimately not an efficient instrument of repression'.[134] These were particularly uncertain times for those engaging in political dissent, for as legal historian Michael Lobban notes, 'the limits of acceptable political debate had broadened' and in so doing, the definition of political crime also shifted.[135]

Significantly, it was one of Carlile's written protests rather than a Rotunda oratory that eventually landed him in trouble with the law after a hiatus of five years. In the third issue of the *Prompter*, dated 27 November 1830, he addressed a letter '[t]o the Insurgent Agricultural Labourers'—a fairly minor article placed on an inside page. His intention was to extend a 'feeling heart' to the rural poor, who had begun rioting and destroying food and property as a response to starvation and harsh working conditions. Carlile's advice to the labourers to 'go on as you have done' was interpreted by the authorities as a seditious call to arms. He later claimed that 'neither in deed, nor in word, nor in idea, did I ever encourage, or wish to encourage…acts of arson or machine breaking'.[136] In January 1831, however, Carlile was sentenced to two further years' imprisonment, in Giltspur Street Compter.[137]

The prosecution took Carlile and other radicals by surprise. Many of his past publications had been far more seditious and blasphemous than the *Prompter* letter. Indeed, Taylor's performance of the *Swing!* tragedy contained far more seditious and provocative material than Carlile's letter. Carlile had also publicised his dislike of 'mobs' and 'mob action', and his assertion that a 'few bullets' be distributed among the heads of rioters in Bristol matched the most callous middle-class reactions.[138] Carlile's assertion that the prosecution was planned as a means to close the Rotunda was thus probably correct.

---

132   Harling, 'The Law of Libel and the Limits of Repression', p. 107.
133   Ibid., p. 120.
134   Ibid., p. 111.
135   Lobban, 'From Seditious Libel to Unlawful Assembly', p. 327.
136   *Prompter*, 14 May 1831. For a more detailed account of Carlile's arrest, see Wiener, *Radicalism and Freethought in Nineteenth-Century Britain*, pp. 174–7.
137   As Wiener notes, unlike his previous imprisonments, this time, Carlile received little support from the radical community. He had so alienated himself from other working-class reformers that few 'were prepared to embrace him in his hour of need'. Wiener, *Radicalism and Freethought in Nineteenth-Century Britain*, p. 177.
138   McCalman, Popular Radicalism and Freethought in Early Nineteenth Century England, p. 205.

Carlile's claim gained even greater credence with Taylor's arrest and subsequent conviction in July 1831 for blasphemous libel.[139] By this stage, the authorities must have considered that curbing Taylor's growing popularity and reach was worth risking defeat in the courtroom, for in April the authorities filed a suit against Taylor for two provocative lectures delivered on Good Friday and Palm Sunday. In the lectures, he described God as a 'GOUTY OLD MAN IN AN ARMCHAIR', who had a proclivity to 'A DROP OF crater' and who had not really been crucified but rather some other 'blaspheming infidel'.[140] The risk paid off for the authorities: Taylor's prosecution for blasphemous libel was successful, led to a conviction of two years' imprisonment in Horsemonger-Lane Gaol and meant the end of a 14-year spell of immunity from libels cast in the form of burlesque and satire.

The strategy of prosecuting the key Rotunda individuals would strike a major blow to Carlile's 'Palladium of Liberty'. Yet the relative proximity to the Rotunda of his new prison quarters at the Giltspur Street Compter, as Wiener notes, allowed him to keep a close watch on the affairs of the premises and, like his previous period of incarceration, to continue managing the production of a key publication, the *Prompter*.[141] A year after the doors of the Rotunda first opened to the radical community, Carlile could still delight that he had created

> the best school that was ever open among the human race. Oxford, Cambridge, the London University, the King's College are Folly's seats, contrasted with the Rotunda. There has been more expansion of mind generated at the Rotunda, in the last year, than in all the world beside.[142]

Despite quarrelling with most of the leading metropolitan radicals during the time, Carlile created a space that fused the positive elements of other working-class centres of learning and conviviality to effect a new and unique venue on the London landscape. The promotion of the Rotunda as a popular theatre enhanced its appeal within popular culture. It was an attractive option for a newly urbanised working population who valued the escapism, relaxation and pure fun of theatre. The theatricals presented at the Rotunda embodied elements of folk, or countertheatre, which was indigenous to working-class culture and valued by working people as part of a vernacular political tradition. The Rotunda's patina of scholarship, its use of non-verbal symbols, as well as drama, burlesque and satire to convey its political message all combined to make it a haven for metropolitan working-class radicalism.

---

139 *Morning Chronicle*, 31 May 1831. For a more detailed account of the arrest and conviction, as well as Taylor's split with Carlile and his post-prison career, see McCalman, 'Popular Irreligion in Early Victorian England', pp. 59–64.
140 Quoted in Wiener, *Radicalism and Freethought in Nineteenth-Century Britain*, p. 179.
141 Ibid., p. 178.
142 *Prompter*, 12 November 1831.

The significance of the Rotunda as a public space and its layers of identity have been overlooked largely because of the piecemeal approach to its history. The emphasis on the NUWC in traditional radical historiography, for instance, has obscured the rich material in Rotunda sources that illuminates the presence and involvement of women in Rotunda radicalism—at a time when some historians contend that the masculine temper of early nineteenth-century radicalism, and importantly its type of venues, acted to exclude a whole nation of possible followers in women.[143] The relationship between female radical activity and the Rotunda—from orators to audience—and its implication for debates on gender and the public sphere will be explored in the next chapter. There is yet more to say about how London was 'bitten with the Rotunda notions'.

---

143   Hall, 'Private Persons Versus Public Someones', p. 18.

8. 'Pythoness of the Temple': Eliza Sharples and the gendered public of the Rotunda

With Robert Taylor and Richard Carlile now ensconced in their separate prisons, and numbers declining nightly at the Rotunda, the 'Palladium of Liberty' was in dire financial straights. The entry of the National Union of the Working Classes (NUWC) to the repertoire of Rotunda radicalism provided a much needed boost to the finances of the institution and, importantly, its radical credentials. The NUWC, however, was purely a political group whose organisation and structure were modelled on traditional forms, and forums, of radical male sociability. With the imprisonment of the flamboyant Taylor, Rotunda radicalism had all but lost its theatrical element, which had so captivated its male and, by the accounts of Home Office spy Abel Hall, its female audiences. Carlile worked desperately from within his prison cell to keep the venture alive. In the late months of 1831, he took the pragmatic step to rent the theatres (when not used by the NUWC) to a circus, a concert company and, on one occasion, a man exhibiting a 'Phenomena of Nature': a horse with seven legs. Given Carlile's previous barbs regarding the flippant nature of popular entertainment, it must have stung deeply to see his prized venue reduced to a forum of trivial spectacle. Nevertheless, such performances kept the Rotunda open. Abel Hall testified that the equine show was 'very well attended'.[1]

Although the freak shows provided momentary financial relief, Carlile eagerly sought to re-energise the Rotunda's radical agenda. In September 1831, he announced the arrival of a 'new Jesus Christ' who was to lecture at the Rotunda on Thursday evenings under various titles of 'Shiloh', 'messiah' and 'Sion'. John 'Zion' Ward, a fifty-year-old crippled former shoemaker of Irish descent, had progressed through popular sectarianism, having been a Calvinist, Methodist, Baptist, Sandemonian and Southcottian before obtaining the revelation that he was the new Shiloh, or Joanna Southcott's spiritual offspring.[2] Ward believed that he was Jesus Christ and had formerly been Satan, and his millenarian Rotunda sermons, with titles such as the 'Judgement Seat of God', 'Balaam's Ass' and 'Fall of Man', enthralled Rotunda audiences. Charles Twort, a former

---

1 Home Office Papers, HO64/12, 17 January 1832, fo. 12.
2 On Ward, see Chapter 6, Note 137. On Southcott, see James Hopkins, *A Woman to Deliver Her People: Joanna Southcott and English millenarianism in an era of revolution* (Austin: University of Texas Press, 1982); Frances Brown, *Joanna Southcott: The woman clothed with the Sun* (Cambridge: Lutterworth, 2002); J. F. C. Harrison, *The Second Coming: Popular millenarianism 1780–1850* (New Brunswick, NJ: Rutgers University Press, 1979), pp. 16–18, chs 5 and 6; Anna Clark, *Struggle for the Breeches: Gender and the making of the English working class* (Berkeley: University of California Press, 1995), pp. 107–11.

warehouse labourer, assisted Ward at all his lectures. The immense popularity of the two men was due both to their eccentricity and to the popular appeal of their millenarianism. During the early decades of the nineteenth century, revivalism gripped Britain on an enormous scale and the preoccupation with prophecies of the second coming of Christ extended through every level of society.[3] Carlile initially offered Ward the Rotunda thinking his brand of infidelism and millenarianism might appeal to the 'bible-besotted multitude', but the enormous success of the prophet's dazzling harangues soon caused Carlile to take the duo seriously.[4] Ward wore the mantle of Taylor with ease; his performances, also drawing upon principles of countertheatre and his ideology, were an eccentric blend of 'rationalism, republicanism and chiliastic mysticism'.[5] Despite attracting crowds of up to 2000 at the Rotunda, the duo left London to continue on their roving lecture circuit and Carlile was again left without a major drawcard.[6]

By January 1832, large placards were seen around London announcing a 'new occupation of the building'.[7] Carlile again tantalised patrons with a return to Taylor and Ward's brand of Rotunda radicalism, only this time, sensationally, in female form. Perhaps buoyed by the popularity of the 'Phenomena of Nature', and prompted by the need for immediate financial returns, Carlile promoted his new star attraction as a virtual freak show. Dubbed 'Lady of the Rotunda' and 'Isis' (derived from the romantic myth of the Egyptian Goddess of Reason), Eliza Sharples was billed as the first Englishwoman to speak publicly on matters of politics and religion in a 'style unparalleled in this country' (Figure 8.1).[8] Her identity was concealed for many months to protect her family and the resultant mystery aided her image as a curiosity. The appearance of 'Isis' at the Rotunda was promoted as intensely as an opening night at the theatre—the publicity not unlike that which aroused the contemporary notoriety surrounding the display of the semi-naked body of the African woman Saartjie Baartman, dubbed the 'Hottentot Venus'.[9]

---

3   E. P. Thompson describes the impact on the working class as 'millennial instability'. E. P. Thompson, *The Making of the English Working Class* (Harmondsworth: Penguin, 1968), p. 878. See also Iain McCalman, *Radical Underworld: Prophets, revolutionaries and pornographers in London, 1795–1840* (Cambridge: Cambridge University Press, 1988), for the influence of millenarian principles on early Spencean radicals (pp. 50–72), and on the 1830s revival (p. 202).
4   *Prompter*, 3 September 1831. For a brief account of the type of followers attracted to Ward's chiliasm, see Jackie Latham, 'The Bradleys of Birmingham: The unorthodox family of "Michael Field"', *History Workshop Journal*, vol. 55 (2003), pp. 189–91.
5   Iain McCalman, Popular Radicalism and Freethought in Early Nineteenth Century England, Unpublished MA thesis (Canberra: The Australian National University, 1975), p. 200. As E. P. Thompson noted, Ward 'directed his messianic appeal towards the dynamic of Radicalism'. Thompson, *The Making of the English Working Class*, p. 879.
6   Their lecturing tour did not last long, however, for in early 1832 the pair was found guilty of blasphemy in Derby and imprisoned for two years. Thompson, *The Making of the English Working Class*, p. 880.
7   *The Times*, 30 January 1832.
8   Report from *Christian Advocate*, reproduced in *The Times*, 30 January 1832.
9   On Saartjie Baartman, see Rachel Holmes, *The Hottentot Venus: The life and death of Saartjie Baartman: born 1789—buried 2002* (London: Bloomsbury, 2007); Sadiah Qureshi, 'Displaying Sara Baartman, the "Hottentot

The promise of a reinvigorated Rotunda even stirred Taylor from the malaise of his prison cell. 'The spirit of the Rotunda lives', he wrote, 'and will live for ever in this country. The steps gained in the last two years cannot be retraced. It opens with new spirit, with new attraction, with all that is lovely and virtuous in woman to grace it.'[10] Sharples' opening night was a promotional dream for Carlile; it was timed to coincide with a date auspicious to all radicals: the anniversary of the birth of Thomas Paine.

Figure 8.1 Eliza Sharples with a copy of *Isis*, c. 1832.

From Theophila Carlile Campbell, *The Battle for the Freedom of the Press*, London, 1899. Courtesy of the Barr Smith Library, Adelaide.

If Carlile's fervid promotion of the Lady of the Rotunda was designed to rouse radical followers, it also sparked the interest of conservative groups. The editor of the *Christian Advocate* feared that the claims of a new occupation of the building were merely a ruse, believing that 'the change of performers will only

---

Venus''', *History of Science*, vol. 42 (2004), pp. 233–57; Richard D. Altick, *The Shows of London* (Cambridge, Mass.: Belknap Press, 1978), pp. 268–72. A similar promotional strategy to that of Sharples was later employed for the female lecturers of the Owenite movement. See Barbara Taylor, *Eve and the New Jerusalem: Socialism and feminism in the nineteenth century* (London: Virago, 1983), p. 140.
10 'Memoir of the Reverend Robert Taylor', *Devil's Pulpit* (London, 1832), vol. 2, p. xii.

occasion a reiteration of those scenes of blasphemy and immorality which have so long been a disgrace to the metropolis'.[11] His prediction was soon proved correct. In the tradition of Taylor, Ward and Carlile, Sharples used the Rotunda platform to castigate the priesthood, expose religious superstition and denigrate established authority. She promised 'sweet revenge' on those responsible for the incarceration of Carlile and Taylor. She accused the government of complicity in the devastating outbreak of cholera. They had 'laid such burdens on the people that they could not exist and thus created pestilence among them while they "Rolled in Luxury"'.[12] Hall reported that Sharples' lectures were committed and energetic, containing some of the strongest abuse of church and state that he had witnessed.[13]

The theatrical success of Taylor's popular performances was drawn upon when Sharples appeared wearing a 'showy' dress for her lectures, stepping onto a stage strewn with the radical symbols of white thorn and laurel leaves.[14] It is worth dwelling for a moment on this image; a simple description of such accoutrements belies the underlying tensions in the scene. Here, on a stage previously occupied only by men, in a venue that was otherwise publicly associated with the rough, unrespectable elements of radicalism, appeared a woman in respectable dress. Standing amidst the politically charged symbols of radicalism, Sharples delivered some of the most fervent castigations against church and state. Here was the inversion of familiar binaries: the respectable infidel, the feminine radical.

Eliza Sharples has long been recognised in radical historiography as having entered a 'moral marriage' with Richard Carlile after the collapse of his cheerless marriage to Jane.[15] She is also noted for providing a home to the young Charles Bradlaugh, later to become a leading member of the British secularist movement and a Radical MP, after his commitment to free thought led to alienation from his family.[16] Most accounts of radicalism in this period have recognised her role as editor of *Isis* and her appearance as the Lady of the Rotunda, though many such analyses have been coloured by her daughter's claim that Carlile had written most of her lectures for her. The emergence of studies focusing on

---

11   *Christian Advocate*, reproduced in *The Times*, 30 January 1832.
12   Home Office Papers, HO64/12, 27 February 1832, fo. 47.
13   Ibid.
14   Home Office Papers, HO64/12, 14 February 1832, fo. 38; HO64/12, 27 February 1832, fo. 47.
15   See, for example, Joel Wiener, *Radicalism and Freethought in Nineteenth-Century Britain: The life of Richard Carlile* (Westport, Conn.: Greenwood Press, 1983), pp. 191–216; Guy Aldred, *Richard Carlile, Agitator: His life and times* (London: Pioneer Press, 1923), pp. 152–8; James Epstein, *Radical Expression: Political language, ritual and symbol in England, 1790–1850* (Oxford: Oxford University Press, 1994), pp. 133, 144–5; Iowerth Prothero, *Artisans and Politics in Early Nineteenth-Century London, John Gast and his Times* (Kent: Dawson, 1979), pp. 262, 290; R. S. Neale, *Class in English History, 1680–1850* (Oxford: Blackwell, 1981), pp. 205–14.
16   Edward Royle, *Victorian Infidels* (Manchester: University of Manchester Press, 1974), pp. 193, 210.

women's involvement in early nineteenth-century radicalism have gone some way to recognising Sharples' own contribution to the movement, though many works contain only fleeting reference to her.[17]

The recent study of Sharples by Helen Rogers is the most comprehensive to date.[18] It is an important contribution to radical historiography though it has, perhaps, been driven too forcefully by an attempt to exorcise Carlile from Sharples' story. Ostensibly, such a criticism might appear contradictory in a study that seeks to extricate another female radical, Susannah Wright, from the shadow of Richard Carlile. In an attempt to see Sharples in her own light, or to acknowledge her independent contribution to early nineteenth-century radicalism, however, we need not deny the influence of Carlile in shaping her principles, or even his role in penning her Rotunda lectures, or the words for *Isis*. Just as the relationship between Carlile and Susannah Wright involved collective authorship, the evidence of Sharples' intellectual commitment to radical principles both before her Rotunda appearance and in her later years suggests that she and Carlile shared an intellectual partnership, as well as a romantic one. As Rogers herself notes, Sharples' own interpretation of Christianity had a striking influence on Carlile, resulting in what Sharples claimed as the 'Christian conversion' of one of the most committed, influential and strident infidels in British history.[19]

Although Sharples' appearance at Blackfriars Road lasted only a matter of months, her experience provides an opportunity to focus on her in the wider context of Rotunda radicalism. While this chapter engages with Sharples' nascent public political involvement, it does not attempt a biographical approach or aim to examine her life beyond the Rotunda, but rather uses her story to examine how radical women engaged with the space and helps illustrate the gendered nature of Rotunda radicalism. Despite the masculine image that dominated both the print culture of the period and the subsequent historiography of the venue, Carlile established a space that both catered for and attracted a significant number of women at a time when other radical venues were less inclusive. Sharples' experience provides a platform from which to view other women involved in the Rotunda—notably, the anonymous female audience members whose attendance was recorded by Home Office spies and reporters. It allows the exploration of the feminist continuities of the site both prior to and following Carlile's occupation of the premises. The significance of female involvement at the Rotunda is examined in light of other venues open

---

17 See, for example, Clark, *Struggle for the Breeches*, pp. 183, 186; Barbara Taylor, *Eve and the New Jerusalem*, pp. 82, 128–9. A brief biography is provided in Ruth Frow and Edmund Frow, *Political Women, 1800–1850* (London: Pluto Press, 1989), pp. 35–9, 50, 63, 66, 85. Similarly, studies focusing on religious dissent also make mention of Sharples. See, for example, Martin Priestman, *Romantic Atheism: Poetry and freethought, 1780–1830* (Cambridge: Cambridge University Press, 1999), pp. 212–18.
18 Helen Rogers, *Women and the People: Authority, authorship and the radical tradition in nineteenth-century England* (Aldershot: Ashgate, 2000), pp. 48–79.
19 Ibid., p. 53.

to women in this period, providing an important opportunity for this chapter to survey the gendered terrain both of Rotunda radicalism and of the early nineteenth-century public sphere.

* * *

Eliza Sharples was born into a prosperous middle-class manufacturing family in Bolton, Lancashire, in 1804. Educated at a ladies college until the relatively late age of twenty, both home and school instilled a strong commitment to Christian principles. Sharples first met Carlile and Taylor in her hometown during the Lancashire leg of their 1829 'Infidel Mission'.[20] Her daughter's memoirs provide some insight into how a respectable middle-class woman with a staunch Evangelical upbringing came to cross paths with the most notorious infidels of the day. Theophila Carlile Campbell, one of the four children to be born of the eventual union between Sharples and Carlile, suggests that her mother first became aware of her father in the years before 1829 when he dined at the home of a Liverpool banker, the father of a school friend of Sharples.[21] Although Sharples claims not to have met Carlile on that occasion, it nevertheless sparked her interest, which was soon further heightened when she encountered a relative reading one of his early publications. Offered the use of her cousin's library, which contained some of Carlile's works, she thereafter sought more publications through a free-thought bookseller in Bolton, known only as Mr Hardie. Carlile's philosophies, Sharples later wrote, prompted a deep transformation. She described herself as a 'brand snatched from the fire'; she experienced a 'new birth…unto righteousness'—an intense emotional conversion not unlike that felt by William Knight from his seat in the Rotunda audience.[22]

Upon learning of Carlile's imprisonment, Sharples sought an interview with him through Hardie, the bookseller. Like Susannah Wright in the decade before her, she was determined to champion the cause of the imprisoned infidels.[23] Sharples began a written correspondence with Carlile and, with her dedication to his philosophies determined, she decided to travel to London to meet her new radical mentor. Her first visit with him also cemented her dedication to the man himself. Her daily visits to his prison quarters at the Compter soon saw an intimate relationship develop. After many years of (apparently mutual) unhappiness with Jane, whom Carlile claimed did not share his unyielding

---

20   Theophila Carlile Campbell, *The Battle for the Freedom of the Press as Told in the Story of the Life of Richard Carlile* (London, 1899), pp. 148–9.
21   Ibid., p. 149.
22   *Isis*, 27 October 1832.
23   During this prison term, Carlile was no longer supported by Jane, from whom he formally separated in the early 1830s. After the death of a wealthy supporter, Carlile provided an annuity of £50 a year for life for her and his children, which enabled her and her sons to establish their own radical bookshop. Campbell, *The Battle for the Freedom of the Press*, p. 150; Wiener, *Radicalism and Freethought in Nineteenth-Century Britain*, p. 196.

dedication to the radical cause, Carlile was bewitched by the possibility of a true infidel as a soul mate. Even before meeting Sharples in person, he anticipated that she would become 'my daughter, my sister, my friend, my companion, my wife, my sweetheart, my everything'.[24]

Convinced that Sharples would also invigorate Rotunda radicalism (and thereby his financial fortunes), Carlile took the bold step of evicting the NUWC from their headquarters in the larger theatre. His 'Goddess of Reason' was now the sole attraction and manager of the premises.[25] Only two months after first meeting with Carlile in his prison cell, at age twenty-eight and with no previous experience in the public world of politics, Sharples became editor of a new radical weekly publication, *Isis*, and was promoted as the first woman in England to lecture publicly on politics on the stage of the Rotunda.[26] Sharples was initially billed to give two lectures every Sunday (at sixpence for the pit and boxes, one shilling for the gallery), on Monday evenings (for half-price admission) and each Wednesday (at full price). She also provided a gratuitous lecture on Friday evenings to accommodate those unable to meet the modest entry charges.

Under Sharples' guide, the Rotunda was to be a place of 'sound political, moral and philosophical instruction'.[27] Her lectures, Hall noted, became a 'regular strain of abuse of Religion, Priests and all institutions'.[28] She argued that man and his language, thought and manners were perfectible on Earth and therefore the only sin was the absence or denial of knowledge and free discussion to all people.[29] Christianity, she held, was the chief barrier to the dissemination of knowledge; by denying the people education, priests were denying man's liberty. Nor was knowledge espoused merely for intellectual fulfilment. Sharples urged her audience to think and act upon their new thoughts. Passive submission and non-resistance were seen as the 'doctrine of priesthood'.[30]

Carlile's shrewd marketing of his celebrated recruit initially paid dividends. Sharples' lectures were received with much interest. Hall reported that 'no interruptions took place in her proceedings', which were 'listened to with great attention and much applause'.[31] Certain elements of Sharples' performances at the Rotunda drew on the theatrical. She was led ceremoniously onto the

---

24 Quoted in Rogers, *Women and the People*, p. 51.
25 Home Office Papers, HO64/12, 26 January 1832, fo. 19. Carlile advised the NUWC that they may not have use of the venue for some weeks to make way for Sharples and the group was forced to move their meetings to James Watson's Chapel in Finsbury.
26 The first edition of *Isis* appeared on 11 February 1832, and it ran until 15 December that year.
27 *Isis*, 11 February 1832.
28 Home Office Papers, HO64/12, 27 February 1832, fo. 47.
29 Neale, *Class in English History*, p. 209.
30 *Isis*, 11 February 1832.
31 Home Office Papers, HO64/12, 3 March 1832, fo. 52.

stage by Julian Hibbert and surrounded by radical symbols as stage props. They never came close, however, to the melodramatic and histrionic displays of Taylor. Sharples presented a more measured and structured production, reflecting perhaps that it was early days in her infidel conversion, as well as Carlile's growing dislike of Taylor's drama and jest, which, he considered, had begun to cloud the radical message itself.

Sharples' first lectures were calculated to establish her as an independent voice. She was an unknown in either London circles or the wider radical community, and the success of her public campaign depended partly on convincing the audience that she was delivering her own message, and not simply providing a mouthpiece for Carlile and Taylor from beyond the prison walls. On opening night, she declared that she was

> neither of Taylor nor Carlile; neither of Owen or Saint Simon…I will be the little busy bee extracting the honey from all their doctrines…I stand here, not to be an organ of their sentiments, I have formed a mind and found a soul of my own, and I stand here unpersuaded by anyone, a free and independent woman…I will use no argument until I understand it, and adopt no maxim until I have studied it.[32]

Yet Sharples was nevertheless dismissed as a puppet of Carlile and Taylor. Her inexperience and image as a stooge were reinforced when Hibbert immediately led her from the stage following her lectures.[33] Unlike the other Rotunda orators, she refused to field questions from the audience, demanding instead that they be put in writing to her. Had Carlile not been in desperate need to revive the Rotunda's fortunes, or presented with the delicious possibility of her inauguration on the anniversary of Paine's birth, he might have allowed Sharples more time to develop her political acumen before launching her into the public sphere.

Despite her daughter's claims, the prevailing image of Sharples in this early period of her radical career is not entirely supported by the Home Office reports of Abel Hall.[34] Hall observed that much of the handwriting on her early lecture notes accorded with that of Carlile or Taylor. Importantly though, only a month after Sharples' first lecture, Hall observed by 'the character of the handwriting' that the first few pages of her lecture were written by herself, with the latter section most probably by Carlile, as witnessed by her making several stumbles in the reading.[35]

---

32   *Isis*, 11 February 1832.
33   Home Office Papers, HO64/12, 14 February 1832, fo. 38.
34   From a close reading of *Isis*, Helen Rogers also considers that Sharples 'brought her own political theology to its pages' and that the publication is 'best seen as the product of an unequal collaboration'. Rogers, *Women and the People*, p. 53.
35   Home Office Papers, HO64/12, 14 February 1832, fo. 38, 27 February, fo. 47.

8. 'Pythoness of the Temple'

Once again, it is necessary to also look beyond the printed word when assessing the impact of Sharples' lectures at the Rotunda. Just as Susannah Wright's performance in the courtroom adds another dimension to our understanding of her story, so too Sharples' performance of her lectures provides a richer picture of her contribution to Rotunda radicalism. While she did stumble and mispronounce words on occasion, Hall attests to the strength of her convictions: 'I never saw or heard a more abusive or inflammatory language made of in any assembly and in which she takes a most Vulgar Pride in delivering.'[36] On another occasion, he wrote that 'her lecture throughout was more than before a very strong and mixed abuse of all Religions and Governments'.[37] Only a month after first stepping onto the Rotunda stage, she was beginning to find her own voice. Hall reports Sharples presenting a lecture written by Taylor (again observing the handwriting), but he reports that Sharples had altered it, erasing much of the astronomical interpretation of the Scriptures, which she was beginning to question in favour of her growing commitment to what she described as 'rational Christianity'.[38] On this particular occasion, Hall reports, she substituted Taylor's astronomical passages with 'her opinions on Drs Gall and Spurzheim Phrenology'—the theory of brain function and skull size that was to become another area of keen interest in Sharples' radical philosophy.[39] If she was ever a cipher, she soon began to think for herself. In this way, she was surely not unlike many younger radicals—men as well as women—who learned their craft from veterans of the public sphere.

* * *

Sharples was the first woman to take to the Rotunda stage, but she was not the first woman to be involved with the Rotunda—in its former guise as a museum, scientific and literary society or even under its radical tenure. Tracing the history of its occupation from the late eighteenth century through the early nineteenth century allows us to track the gendered nature of these public sphere institutions and reveals a continuity of female patronage. As we saw in Chapter 6, the Sarah Stone prints of the Leverian depict women among the paying visitors to the museum. Similarly, the Rowlandson print of

---

36 Home Office Papers, HO64/12, 3 March 1832, fo. 52.
37 Home Office Papers, HO64/12, 27 February 1832, fo. 47.
38 For the appeal of rational religion to women, see Ruth Watts, 'Rational Religion and Feminism: The challenge of Unitarianism in the nineteenth century', in Sue Morgan (ed.), *Women, Religion and Feminism in Britain, 1750–1900* (New York: Palgrave Macmillan, 2002), pp. 39–52; Kathryn Gleadle, 'British Women and Radical Politics in the Late Nonconformist Enlightenment, c.1780–1830', in Amanda Vickery (ed.), *Women, Privilege, and Power: British politics, 1750 to the present* (Stanford: Stanford University Press, 2001), pp. 123–51; Clark, *Struggle for the Breeches*, pp. 92–118; Taylor, *Eve and the New Jerusalem*.
39 Home Office Papers, HO64/12, 12 March 1832, fo. 58. Dr Franz Joseph Gall was a Viennese physician who devised theories of brain size and function and related its development to skull structure so as to allow a character reading from the shape of the skull. For a brief time, he joined with J. G. Spurzheim to advance his system, which was later coined 'phrenology'. On Gall and Spurzheim, and the development of phrenology, see John Van Wyhe, *Phrenology and the Origins of Victorian Scientific Naturalism* (Aldershot: Ashgate, 2004).

Accum's lecture at the Surrey Institution attests to the considerable numbers of women who attended the Surrey's scientific lecture programme.[40] Further, we know that women were invited to apply for (limited) membership of the Surrey: membership of £2 2 s per annum allowed admittance to the lectures and to the Surrey's library. The Institution, however, remained demarcated along gendered and spatial lines: male members alone could access the full benefits of membership, which provided some areas for an exclusively male sociability—to read the morning and evening papers in the 'News Room' and to the 'Reading Room', where 'new books and pamphlets of present interest' could be found.[41]

Despite the limits on membership, the Surrey's attitude to women was modelled, like much of its organisation and philosophy, on the prestigious Royal Institution. Thomas Young, Professor of the Royal Institution from 1801, had lofty ambitions for his organisation, hoping that it might 'in some degree supply the place of a subordinate university to those whose sex or situation in life has denied them the advantage of an academical education in the national seminaries of learning'.[42] Though it is unclear whether the institutions ever provided this level of fulfilment for their female members, this mandate clearly demonstrates that the thirst for knowledge and instruction in this period was not confined to any one particular class or gender.

The aims of Professor Young and that of Carlile were not entirely dissimilar. When Carlile took up the lease of the Rotunda in 1830, the participation of women was crucial to his agenda. For Carlile, ignorance was responsible for sexual inequality and discrimination. 'There is no kind of equality more desirably advantageous for the welfare of the human race, than equality with the sexes', he argued, and the only way to achieve such equality was for women to acquire knowledge.[43] Not only did Carlile philosophically reject the 'doctrine of woman as domestic agent', he institutionalised its opposite in the Rotunda itself. When Sharples joined the Rotunda milieu, it already had a strong female following. Hall's extensive reports to the Home Office reveal the presence of large numbers of women, as well as some youths and children, at Rotunda lectures throughout the period 1830–32. Sharples emphasised that there was to be 'no

---

40   Gillian Russell argues that the presence of women at institutions such as the Surrey 'was essential to the legitimation of their claims to politeness and civility as well as to their financial survival'. Gillian Russell, 'Spouters or Washerwomen: The sociability of Romantic lecturing', in Gillian Russell and Clara Tuite (eds), *Romantic Sociability: Social networks and literary culture in Britain, 1770–1840* (Cambridge: Cambridge University Press, 2002), p. 133.
41   *The Times*, 1 October 1813.
42   From Bence Jones, *The Royal Institution* (London, 1871), quoted in Peter J. Manning, 'Manufacturing the Romantic Image: Hazlitt and Coleridge lecturing', in James Chandler and Kevin Gilmartin (eds), *Romantic Metropolis: The urban scene of British culture, 1780–1840* (Cambridge: Cambridge University Press, 2005), p. 242n. Women were admitted to upper circles in the days of the Surrey Rotunda Wine and Concert Rooms. See folio 58 in the collection of printed ephemera on the 'Surrey Rotunda' held in the Wellcome Institute Library, London (hereafter Wellcome Collection).
43   *Lion*, 4 April 1828.

distinction between the sexes' at the venue under her leadership.[44] Her opening lectures paid particular attention to her female audience members. She made impassioned appeals for them to follow as she led them to a state of equality:

> I will set before my sex the example of asserting an equality for them with their present lords and masters, and strive to teach them all, yes, all, that the undue submission, which constitutes slavery, is honorable to none.[45]

Sharples' most important task, she declared, was to see the rebirth of the Rotunda as the 'Temple of Knowledge and Reason' for the radical community as a whole. By welcoming women and children to the Rotunda, Carlile and Sharples overcame one of the genuine impediments to women's public political participation.

The significance of the Rotunda as a forum for working-class women in this period can be better appreciated by considering the opportunities available for their participation in other radical venues. One key outlet for discussion and intellectual exchange for women was within the radical family itself. Radical networks and discussion groups had long operated within private homes. Those women, including Susannah Wright, who attended the home of B. B. Jones and his wife, for instance, enjoyed the safety, familiarity and flexibility of intellectual exchange in a private setting, which more easily accommodated the domestic and childrearing roles generally ascribed to women. This private radical space also acted to protect those women who did not wish to expose their adherence to radicalism to the public gaze. It was, however, also a restrictive space, separating women from the psychological benefits of citizenship and participation in the public sphere.

In terms of public engagement, however, some historians of the radical movement contend that the increasingly institutionalised form of radical sociability posed new challenges for women wishing to participate in wider radical culture. Dorothy Thompson and Catherine Hall, for example, note that during the late eighteenth century, the traditional site of protest of the street, which once saw the communal participation of men, women and children, was increasingly replaced with a move to indoor spaces with more formal and organised movements of the nineteenth century.[46] Although the 'institutional framework' of the radical movement—the clubs and societies—was 'central to the task of building a common culture', it nevertheless resulted in the increasing marginalisation

---

44 *Isis*, 3 March 1832.
45 *Isis*, 11 February 1832.
46 Dorothy Thompson, 'Women and Nineteenth-Century Radical Politics', in Juliet Mitchell and Ann Oakley (eds), *The Rights and Wrongs of Women* (London: Penguin Books, 1976), pp. 112–38; Catherine Hall, *White, Male and Middle Class: Explorations in feminism and history* (Oxford: Polity Press, 1992), pp. 134–5.

of women who found such venues harder to negotiate than men.[47] Such sites of 'homosociality' developed both formal and informal means of excluding women. The deterrents to female inclusion ranged from the times the meetings operated to the tavern milieu: 'pubs were coming to be seen as unsuitable places for respectable women'.[48] Hall does not suggest that women were absent from the radical movement—indeed plebeian women were in 'considerable numbers' and with 'considerable strength' in organisations such as the Female Reform Associations, in the Owenite communities and later among the Chartists—but rather from the key institutional structures through which that culture was experienced. Therefore men and women were confronted by a gendered radical culture, which they increasingly experienced in 'very different ways' from one another.[49]

That early nineteenth-century radical culture was gendered in the way Hall describes is of little doubt. Her brief analysis of working-class women is, however, set within a study focusing predominantly on middle-class women in the public sphere, and as such offers an overview of the radical scene rather than attempting to differentiate how different sites engaged or appealed to women of different social rank. If we repopulate the institutions of the public sphere with their historical actors, however, we do see some women in the venues typically associated with radical male sociability. As Anna Clark astutely argued in *Struggle for the Breeches* (now an essential companion to E. P. Thompson's *The Making of the English Working Class*), while the separate sphere model may have restricted the public involvement of middling and upper-class women in early nineteenth-century Britain, for working-class women (and men), the demarcation between the two spheres was never as rigid. She argues that such a division between the public and the private was a 'class privilege denied to working men and women. Working men were denied political power, and working women could not take shelter in the home, but had to earn wages.'[50]

Surveying the scholarship of authors such as Hans Medick, John Gillis, David Gilmour and Dorothy George on forms and practices of plebeian sociability, Clark argues that plebeian men and women continued to socialise together in public until the mid-nineteenth century, in venues including 'workshops, pubs, and streets'. Moreover, women were able to create organisational forms that 'transcended the boundaries between work and home'.[51] The milieu of the tavern or the pub was not as alien to plebeian women as Hall suggests was the case for middling-class women. As Clark notes, when plebeian women organised and met, it was often in a pub, as evidenced, to take one example, by

---

47   Hall, *White, Male and Middle Class*, p. 134.
48   Ibid.
49   Ibid., pp. 138–9.
50   Clark, *Struggle for the Breeches*, p. 2.
51   Ibid., p. 26.

the Female Radical Reformers of Manchester, who assembled for their meetings in the Forresters' Arms tavern.[52] The historical record is littered with evidence of such groups throughout the period from the 1820s to the 1840s.

Nevertheless, as Clark herself notes, many plebeian women also had serious misgivings about the tavern as a venue for male sociability; the detrimental effect of such outlets on family finances and the engendering of violence were ignored in later scholarship, which promulgated the 'nostalgic vision of artisan communities'.[53] Radical men themselves recognised the spatial dimension of female participation in the political realm. The *Poor Man's Guardian* attributed women's dislike of political associations because

> they are apt to abstract husbands from the scene of their domestic duties, and to make them neglect their wives for the club-room and public-house. Women very naturally like their husbands to stay at home in the evening, and not to spend their money to get drunk at the public-house...Let us therefore, my friends, when we meet to discuss politics, avoid the public-house, and make our sittings as short as possible.[54]

The emphasis remained on keeping their wives happy with their absence, rather than inviting them into public participation.

As discussed in Chapter 6, the tavern, coffee house and pub were not the only forums available for radical assembly in this period. Dissenting chapels provided another outlet for plebeian radicalism and, as the performances of Reverend Robert Taylor and John 'Zion' Ward attest, elements of radical religion also became part of the Rotunda's appeal. Women were particularly numerous and prominent in the millenarian movements.[55] Dissenting chapels also held considerable appeal for women. At the very least, they catered for more communal involvement than the coffee shop or the tavern allowed. More importantly, Clark notes, radical religion 'imbued the common people, especially women, with a sense of spiritual equality'; it provided 'an intellectual outlet denied them in politics'.[56] Further, the institutionalised structure of dissenting chapels allowed women to learn the organisational skills, the 'language of protest' and 'knowledge of the precedent of female heroines which later aided them to join in radical political organisations'.[57]

---

52 *Poor Man's Guardian*, 21 January 1832.
53 Clark, *Struggle for the Breeches*, pp. 25, 30.
54 *Poor Man's Guardian*, 14 September 1833.
55 J. F. C. Harrison notes that 'whether in the role of prophetess or wealthy patroness or adoring disciple', women appear 'prominently in millenarian movements'. Harrison, *The Second Coming*, p. 31.
56 Clark, *Struggle for the Breeches*, p. 93.
57 See ibid., p. 117; Taylor, *Eve and the New Jerusalem*, p. 173. On the relationship between Robert Owen and the wider radical movement, see Eileen Yeo, 'Robert Owen and Radical Culture', in Sidney Pollard and John Salt (eds), *Robert Owen: Prophet of the poor* (London: Macmillan, 1971), pp. 84–114.

The Owenite movement provided another alternative for women disenchanted with established religion to engage not only in religious heterodoxy but also to agitate against social and political orthodoxies. This cooperative movement, initiated by celebrated reformer Robert Owen, envisaged a 'New Moral World' in which all classes and both genders lived harmoniously and equitably in a system based on communal property and family life.[58] Barbara Taylor's seminal work on the movement, *Eve and the New Jerusalem*, recovered the crucial gender aspects of Owenism, which had been largely forgotten in earlier histories of the movement and in the practice of socialism itself. Taylor argues that the vision for the New Moral World was motivated primarily by equality in both sexual and labour relations before the feminist ideals were subsumed by class as the dominant factor in the economics of labour relations. Working women could find a place within Owenite cooperative communities and engage in trade unionism, which allowed them not only to access feminist and radical political theory but also to practice social, political and sexual equality and liberation. Ironically, it was the issue of gender that critically divided the movement in the mid-1830s over the question of women's labour and it would take several years to recover in force. By 1840, the movement had again strengthened, although in a markedly different structure and with a strategy shaped more upon rational religion and freethinking tenets but with cooperative organisation and collectivity still paramount.[59]

The parallels between the Owenite feminist philosophy and Carlile's vision for the Rotunda are evident. Many of the early male Rotunda leaders were also identified as Owenites. If we recall Gibbon Wakefield's alarmist pamphlet warning of the dangers of the London populace, he separated the Rotunda men into the supporters of Henry Hunt and the disciples of Robert Owen. Though we cannot identify the many women who joined Rotunda audiences, we can speculate that if Owenite men were attracted to Rotunda radicalism, and a vision of women's rights was publicly projected by Carlile, Owenite women could have been part of the earlier Rotunda milieu as well.

There is little doubt, as Clark maintains, that the Owenite movement constituted a minority group (albeit an important one) amidst working-class radicalism in this period, largely because of the extreme nature of their agenda. By the 1830s, there was mounting pressure on women of all ranks to adopt the codes of respectability, and the radical Owenite agenda of marital and sexual equality was a direct affront to such codes. The popularity of dissenting chapels and other outlets for 'rational religion' can also be better understood in this light. Removed from the unseemly association with drink in the pub or tavern, dissenting chapels 'provided an institutional infrastructure for the "respectable"

---

58   Taylor, *Eve and the New Jerusalem*, p. 62.
59   Ibid., pp. 118–19.

elements of plebeian culture'.[60] Carlile also recognised the need to address the issue of respectability, though he had long argued that the social and sexual subjection of women under established religion had nothing to do with morality or respectability. Nevertheless, even before the doors of the Rotunda opened, Taylor noted the benefits of presenting a respectable facade for the success of infidelism. 'All that infidelity wants for its general triumph', he claimed in 1829, 'is the dress that can put on an equality with the best appearance of other principles, the enough of money that is called respectability'.[61]

The trappings of respectability were particularly important to the Rotunda proprietors.[62] Despite their infidel affinities, Sharples and many other Rotunda performers cultivated an air of respectability. Sharples herself originated from the ranks of the middle classes and, in her opening lecture, she presented herself as an educated and genteel woman who sought endorsement of her respectability from her female followers: 'Will you gather round me and give me that countenance in virtuous society which we all seek and need, and without which life to us is wretchedness.'[63] For all his 'roughness', Taylor's credentials as a member of the Royal College of Surgeons and his associations with the Anglican Church helped the Rotunda's presentation as a respectable premise.[64] The status of the Rotunda's financial backers also assisted the reputable image of the establishment. Hibbert and Saull were described by Abel Hall as 'men of property' and their direct involvement in the lectures and debates at the Rotunda helped enhance the image of the Rotunda as a respectable venue.[65] Further, the adoption of a binary pricing system for admission also suggests that Carlile intended to cater for the desire for respectability; patrons could define their status by purchasing better seats for a higher price. There are parallels

---

60   Clark, *Struggle for the Breeches*, p. 99. Participation in the chapels perhaps assisted with the 'attainment of personal and collective respect and dignity', which Neville Kirk contends were features of working-class respectability in the mid-nineteenth century, as well as providing a 'practical safeguard against recurrent threats of insecurity, poverty and unemployment'. Neville Kirk, *Change, Continuity and Class: Labour in British society, 1850–1920* (Manchester: Manchester University Press, 1998). See also Peter Bailey, 'Will the Real Bill Banks Please Stand Up? Towards a role analysis of mid-Victorian working class respectability', *Journal of Social History*, vol. 12 (1977), pp. 337–8. For an overview of the debates about working-class respectability among historians, see Neville Kirk, *The Growth of Working Class Reformism in Mid-Victorian England* (Beckenham: Croom Helm, 1985), pp. 174–82.
61   *Lion*, 3 April 1829.
62   See, for example, the report to the Home Office that recorded Carlile imploring his Rotunda audience of the need for respectability and for 'orderly behaviour'. Home Office Papers, HO40/20-25, n.d., ff. 238, 250.
63   *Isis*, 11 February 1832.
64   It appears that Taylor played the role of the respectable gent convincingly, for after his release from prison in 1833 he left his Rotunda companion, Miss Richards (who sued him for breach of promise), to marry an older, wealthy and 'respectable' woman. Iain McCalman, 'Popular Irreligion in Early Victorian England: Infidel preachers and radical theatricality in 1830s London', in R. W. Davis and R. J. Helmstadter (eds), *Religion and Irreligion in Victorian Society* (London: Routledge, 1992), p. 60.
65   See Chapter 6, Note 106.

here with the demands of radical prisoners for a separate space to that occupied by ordinary felons—an attempt to define one's identity according to a spatial hierarchy within a venue.

Carlile hoped the Rotunda would be viewed as a finishing school of moral and intellectual culture, and claimed that infidelism created a body of sober men, 'much respected in their neighbourhoods'.[66] Sharples agreed with the sobering effect of infidelism on members of the working class and refuted allegations that the Rotunda was breeding 'thieves and prostitutes':

> We do not wish to deal with criminals here. I am sure we do not make any; for they who come here, men, women, or children, will have their minds so exercised on matters of useful knowledge, that six months acquaintance with us shall make them sober, rational, honest, and generous, in all their dealings with society. We have no consideration for miserable sinners.[67]

Even the poorer patrons attending the half-price or gratuitous lectures were urged to cultivate the manners and appearance of respectability for the sake of their standing in the community and the infidel cause.[68] By developing a respectable venue, Taylor and Carlile considered that Rotunda radicals could move one step closer to the general acceptance of infidelism as a serious alternative to established religion.

Preoccupations with respectability began to influence both the working and the middling classes in the pre-Victorian period. Crucially, as Clark notes, the definitions of respectability were not rigid; they shifted between the plebeian and middle classes, and over time, much as the demarcations between classes themselves remained fluid.[69] Hall's reports attest to the presence of working-class women and men in Rotunda audiences, but was it only plebeian women who were attracted to the diverse range of offerings at the venue? We know that Carlile had female supporters in the upper ranks of society—notably, the wealthy Chichester sisters from Ebworth Park, Gloucestershire, who supported him financially for many years, but it is unknown whether they ever attended Rotunda performances.[70] Hall's reports suggest that women from different ranks were attracted to the venue, and he categorised the women of the Rotunda

---

66 *Prompter*, 2 July 1831.
67 *Isis*, 11 February 1832.
68 Home Office Papers, HO40/20-25, n.d., ff. 238, 250.
69 Clark, *Struggle for the Breeches*, pp. 43, 54.
70 Campbell, *The Battle for the Freedom of the Press*, pp. 252–4. Campbell reports that the ladies were 'advanced thinkers' and great friends to both Richard and Eliza. On the Chichester sisters, see Jackie Latham, *Search for A New Eden, James Pierrepont Greaves (1777–1842): The sacred socialist and his followers* (Madison, NJ: Fairleigh Dickinson University Press, 1999), pp. 89–149, especially pp. 121–38; idem, 'The Political and the Personal: The radicalism of Sophia Chichester and Georgiana Fletcher Welch', *Women's History Review*, vol. 8, no. 3 (1999), pp. 469–87.

as either 'respectable' or 'decent' and noted them in the various levels of the Rotunda's spatial hierarchy—in both the 'pit and boxes' and in the gallery seats.[71] It is difficult to ascertain precisely on what basis Hall considered one woman 'respectable', while another 'decent', but we can surmise that Hall's differentiation between the two descriptors was based on accoutrements. For men, rank could be determined not only be dress, but by occupation. In terms of the wider issue of class, Hall reported during 1830–31 that Taylor's audience consisted overwhelmingly of the 'middling sort' of ambitious artisans, small shopkeepers and lesser professionals. He also witnessed many 'gentlemen' donating considerable sums of money to Carlile's and Taylor's prison funds. Carlile also boasted about the select company attracted to Rotunda performances. They included, he stated, 'men and women most respectably-attired, officers in the army and navy, physicians, surgeons, astronomers, theologians, critics, [and] mechanics'.[72]

Carlile also identified a high number of respectable, 'well dressed' women who attended Taylor's lectures, believing they were attracted by his suave manners and good looks. It has been argued that they belonged to the same category of intellectually frustrated women as Eliza Sharples—those beginning to demand the right to intellectual inquiry and fulfilment and questioning their condemnation to a life of marriage and domesticity.[73] This position is supported by the strong showing of women at Sharples' lectures. Few details are known of these women, though Abel Hall observed that most were 'the same as attended in Taylor's time'.[74] He observed that even at Sharples' gratuitous and half-price evenings, she attracted a wide variety of interest from within different ranks of society. On one Friday evening in early March 1832, he recorded people of 'all ranks among whom was 59 Females, several youths and 11 children under 12 years'.[75] These observations caution against assuming that the availability of cheap or free seats meant the attendance solely of poorer members of the working class or led to a class-based demarcation within the venue. As Richard Altick notes, curiosity could be a great leveller and led to the 'cultural interplay'

---

71 See, for example, Home Office Papers, HO64/11, n.d., fo. 202.
72 *Prompter*, 12 November 1830. Carlile's claims are not without foundation. In 1834, the Rotunda coffee-shop proprietor, Georgiana Richards, filed for damages against Reverend Robert Taylor for breach of promise of marriage. During the trial, Joshua Fletcher, a surgeon from London Road, was called as a witness, acknowledging he had been to lectures at the Rotunda at least once a month and had seen *Swing!* performed. See *The Times*, 28 November 1834. In another report, a Mr Easley, 'retired stockbroker', advised that he and a friend, 'an indigo broker', attended a political lecture by Cobbett. See *The Times*, 1 July 1833.
73 Iain McCalman, 'Females, Feminism and Free Love in an Early Nineteenth Century Radical Movement', *Labour History*, no. 38 (1980), pp. 12–13.
74 Home Office Papers, HO64/12, 27 February 1832, fo. 47.
75 Home Office Papers, HO64/11, May 1831, fo. 302; HO64/12, 3 March 1832, fo. 52. See also the account of Dan Chatterton, the veteran communist and atheist of the late nineteenth century, who recalled attending the Rotunda lectures of Carlile and Taylor with his father. Andrew Whitehead, 'Dan Chatteron and his "Atheistic Communistic Scorcher"', *History Workshop Journal*, vol. 25, no. 1 (1988), pp. 83–99.

between the classes that was not always evident in other public institutions.[76] It is likely that the lack of cultural conventions at play in the Rotunda—a new type of space in the public sphere—as well as its multiple layers of identity provided a safer place for middling-class women to commit their patronage compared with other sites with more established (and masculine) conventions of political exchange and discussion.

Even though the modes of behaviour might still have been in the process of negotiation early in the Rotunda's radical life, we cannot ignore the fact that despite the concern and pretensions of respectability, visitors to the Rotunda were entering what was regarded as the most notorious den of blasphemy and sedition in London. Rotunda radicals continued to serve out some of the most blasphemous humour available in the city. For all their respectability, Rotunda audiences were subjected to, and apparently revelled in, outspoken and fierce denunciations of the establishment. The bawdy, ribald and often profane subculture of countertheatre provided radicals with an ideal medium through which to voice their message of dissent. Audiences participated in spectacles of outrageous sacrilege by Taylor, Ward and Sharples, and listened to assertions of female equality and sexual freedom—issues of great contention among middling and plebeian communities as the emerging 'respectable' image of women as confined to the domestic sphere and as sexless until marriage began to take hold.[77]

To find such outwardly respectable Englishmen and women at a venue that became renowned for its decidedly unrespectable modes and practices provided a dilemma for early scholars of the radical movement who relied on traditional historical models and theories of nineteenth-century working-class respectability. Many of these were drawn from the observations of contemporaries (among them Francis Place and later Henry Mayhew), who identified two distinct and exclusive constituencies in working-class life, imposing the dichotomy between 'respectables' and 'roughs'. These masculine definitions of working-class respectability, or otherwise, structured many early accounts of nineteenth-century radicalism.

Rather than viewing respectability as a fixed absolute, historians such as Peter Bailey and Neville Kirk examine it as a dynamic phenomenon. Kirk considers that the working classes could employ respectability for family or individual status, a 'mark of distinction and respect at work, a source of class pride, or a contradictory jumble of all of these significations and more besides'.[78] Bailey charged E. P. Thompson with presenting values such as moral sobriety,

---

76   Richard D. Altick, *The Shows of London* (Cambridge, Mass.: Belknap Press, 1978), p. 3.
77   For scholarship that discusses Carlile's philosophies regarding sex and birth control, see Chapter 3, Note 90.
78   Kirk, *Change, Continuity and Class*, pp. 112–13.

economic thrift, temperance and self-help, self-improvement and self-sufficiency as characteristic cultural absolutes.[79] Rather, Bailey considered that respectability constituted a more fluid set of roles, which could be deployed by working people in occasional ways or in different settings.[80] Seemingly contradictory modes of behaviour could therefore exist within a single working-class lifestyle. Although Bailey did not consider whether this fluidity was experienced equally by men and women, the case of the Rotunda and other studies of working-class women suggest that it also applied to women.

The Rotunda itself exhibited signs of the dualistic character of working-class respectability. In the same way that the audience could move in and out of respectable roles, so too Rotunda performers oscillated between blasphemous harangues denying the validity of Christianity and sermons espousing the benefits of self-improvement and self-help. Taylor's congregation might be instructed in blasphemy one week and on the 'laudableness of rational ambition' the next. His *Moral Catechisms* and *First to Thirteenth Moral Discourses* advocated virtues such as 'moral fortitude', 'government of temper', 'industry' and 'temperance', as well as free love and family planning.[81] Bailey's thesis helps explain how the decidedly unrespectable modes and forums of countertheatre were continuing to thrive as forms of working-class dissent in an age in which the values of respectability were beginning to permeate radical culture. While the trappings of respectability were readily apparent in working-class culture, it appears that they did not necessarily involve the displacement of older conformities. This ability of working people to combine respectable and unrespectable modes and pleasures without jeopardising their social standing or sense of inner consistency provides another explanation for the popularity of the Rotunda in working-class culture, particularly for women.

Although we cannot know for certain whether Abel Hall's description of 'respectable' women signalled participation by the ranks of middle-class women or 'respectable' working women, the earlier accounts of audience reaction to William Hazlitt's lectures at the Surrey Institution detailed in Chapter 6 suggest that middling-class respectability could be deployed in similarly calculated ways. Despite Catherine's Hall's general assessment that middle-class women were increasingly marginalised and excluded from the political public, the examples of the Surrey and the Rotunda suggest that at venues

---

79   Bailey, 'Will the Real Bill Banks Please Stand Up?', pp. 337–8.
80   Bailey considers that respectability was assumed as a role or a cluster of roles that were practised in certain situations rather than being a permanent code of values. As such, many men registered in the 'mental dossiers' of middle-class observers could have been known as such on the evidence of a single role performance. In a way, the role-playing of respectability was a new form and style of countertheatre. Ibid., pp. 336–53.
81   McCalman, *Radical Underworld*, p. 190.

traditionally outside those associated with political discussion and exchange, women of rank continued to defy this marginalisation by supporting those more gender-inclusive venues. Anna Clark and Dorothy Thompson regard postwar radicalism as the pinnacle of female participation in radical politics that the Chartists helped to destroy. In this respect, regardless of the rank of the women who were attracted to the venue, the Rotunda can be viewed as either the last gasp of gender inclusiveness in radical culture or a milieu well ahead of its time.

The enthusiasm with which Sharples promoted herself as a respectable woman was calculated partly to pre-empt the accusations of immorality and indecency from publicly engaging in the political arena. For radical women such as Sharples, Barbara Taylor reminds us, 'egalitarian principles tugged in one direction while the tightening claims of respectable femininity pulled in another'.[82] Inevitably, the accusations against Sharples of unrespectable behaviour were soon forthcoming. One correspondent's report to *The Times* considered her a

> female who exhibits herself in so unfeminine a manner…so utterly illiterate is the poor creature, that she cannot yet read what is set down for her with any degree of intelligibility…with her ignorance and unconquerable brogue…her 'lecturing'…is almost as ludicrous as it is painful to witness.[83]

Another report contemptuously described her as the 'Pythoness of the temple', branding her message as 'rubbish' and suggesting retirement from the public sphere back to a domestic role, where, they supposed, she would more fittingly be occupied as a 'housemaid, or servant of all work, in some decent family…She is strong enough for either, and neither of them are so laborious as the treadmill'.[84] Unfeminine, illiterate, working class, provincial and destined for criminality—such belittling and demoralising comments were designed to strip any 'pretence' of respectability Sharples might have hoped her accoutrements would have afforded her.

Rotunda orators seized on such vicious attacks. Quick to defend Sharples against such accusations, John Gale Jones sought the approbation of the Rotunda audience in support of Sharples:

---

82   Taylor, *Eve and the New Jerusalem*, p. 221.
83   *The Times*, 14 February 1832.
84   *The Times*, 30 January 1832.

He (Mr. Jones) had even been told that the Lady had delivered an indecent lecture (Shame). He would put it to the audience if such were the case (Cries of No). Was there one present that could countenance such an assertion (Loud cries of No).[85]

Members of the audience also censured *The Times* on their reporting of Sharples' lectures. Though the correspondence remained unpublished, they prompted *The Times* editor to send along his own reporter to the 'temple of infidelity' to 'satisfy ourselves of which of the conflicting statements of our correspondents was true'.[86] Although the subsequent report acknowledged that previous correspondents' claims that Sharples resembled a 'servant' or 'country actress' (substitute prostitute) were unjust, *The Times* continued to focus on her appearance, finding her 'figure is good, her appearance and manner rather genteel than otherwise, and she is much more like a pretty woman than an ugly one'. The content of her lecture drew more scorn: it was the 'sorriest rubbish' they had ever read or heard, 'an ill-conceived attack upon the Christian faith'. They dwelt on her Lancashire accent, attacking her pronunciation—'"hanimal" "for animal", "hignorance for ignorance"'.[87] Like Susannah Wright in the decade before, Sharples quickly discovered that taking her radicalism into the public sphere was a risky endeavour for a woman.

The cultivation of respectability at the Rotunda goes some way to explaining why, unlike the case of Susannah Wright's female supporters, the female members of the Rotunda audience appear to have evaded public mention and, by default, public scorn. It was also ironically assisted by the masculinisation of the public Rotunda identity in the print culture of the period surveyed in the previous chapter. The focus on the revolutionary male obfuscated women's involvement in the Rotunda by shielding them from the public eye and, thereby, from public censure.

If we turn to the historical record, we can see that Rotunda women faced other, more subtle, albeit less public, means of chastisement. During 1831, Robert Taylor frequently issued challenges to clergymen to debate the evidence of the Christian religion. Though few were foolish enough to accept his challenge, one ex-Canadian missionary, Reverend Osgood, did debate him on several occasions. It was during these debates that Taylor's theatricality, wit and brilliant oratorical skills particularly shone. As Hall noted, Osgood

---

85   *Isis*, 17 March 1832.
86   *The Times*, 18 February 1832.
87   Ibid.

was too old and inept to match wits with the 'Devil's Chaplain', and Taylor not only won all the debates convincingly, but Osgood was also made the 'subject of derision' by attendants.[88]

Though Taylor clearly trumped Osgood in the debates, the latter's intervention can be seen as an attempt to cleanse the infidel space on several levels. He was accompanied to the Rotunda by an entourage of genteel church ladies whose role was to place Bible passages and other reading material on the seats to enlighten the Rotunda heathens.[89] Though they listened intently to Osgood's presentation, they avoided any theological contamination by promptly leaving the theatre before Taylor began his rebuttal.[90] It is worth noting that Osgood chose to take only genteel, respectable female supporters. Such intervention is reminiscent of the Quaker Ladies entering the seething underworld of Newgate prison to redeem and reclaim the female prisoners. Like the 'unfortunate wretches' of Newgate who were faced with the morality, piety and respectability of the Visiting Ladies Committee, Rotunda women were also confronted with an alternative model of middling-class feminine moral virtue.

Circulation of rumours that a brothel was operating on the premises might also have acted to dissuade female patrons wishing to be seen to be adhering to the codes of respectability. Abel Hall reported to the Home Office the concern of some of his Rotunda associates that the coffee shop and sleeping apartments were being used for illicit purposes after Carlile engaged the services of Miss Georgiana Richards and her 'maid-servant', Margaret Beauchamp, to operate the coffee shop. Hall reported the 'very loose appearance' of the two women, suggesting that their involvement at the Rotunda extended beyond the supply of refreshments. Hall reported that, where once the NUWC radicals would retire to the coffee shop after lectures for refreshments, this was no longer the case with the new coffee-shop proprietors. 'The opinion formed of them', he wrote after observing that they had hung red curtains over the glass doors and windows, was that 'they either do or intend to keep it as a Brothel'.[91]

The association of female coffee-shop proprietors with prostitution was not altogether new in early nineteenth-century London. As historian Brian Cowan

---

88 Home Office Papers, HO64/11, n.d., fo. 191; HO64/11, n.d., fo. 200. Carlile invited such exchanges because he recognised the power of observation; what better way to defuse the 'superstitions' of Christianity than for his audiences to witness Taylor counter every assertion made by the Christian ministers and dismantle the Christian doctrine with his oratorical brilliance.
89 David Worrall, *Theatric Revolution: Drama, censorship and Romantic period subcultures, 1773–1832* (Oxford: Oxford University Press, 2006), p. 356.
90 Osgood himself, however, was tainted with the Rotunda stain when he was mentioned in *The Times* as one of the Rotunda speakers. Defending his reputation in a letter to the newspaper, he likened his 12 visits to the building with the 'same view as a physician would visit a hospital', wishing that 'more ministers of the gospel' would follow his lead and 'give medicine to the sick instead of employing most of their time in giving cordials to those who are in health'. *The Times*, 22 November 1830.
91 Home Office Papers, HO64/11, n.d., fo. 249.

shows, coffee-house proprietors had long been associated with a more illicit enterprise: 'The low social status of the coffee-house keeper only served to accentuate the coffee-woman's vulnerability to the solicitations of her customers.'[92] Abel Hall's testimony could have been influenced both by the growing personal relationship between the coffee-shop proprietor and Robert Taylor at the Rotunda and by his increasing antagonism towards Carlile. In Hall's report to the Home Office, he expressed his doubt that, even if Carlile were aware of the operation, he would object to the brothel plan. Carlile's more marginal advocacies—such as the promotion of equality and freedom in sexual relations as a means of liberating women—often overshadowed many of his more political beliefs, not only among hostile radicals turned informants, but even among many in the plebeian radical community.[93]

* * *

By the end of April 1832, facing deepening financial burden, Carlile and Sharples took what must have been the wrenching decision to end their tenure at the Rotunda. Although some of the responsibility for the demise of the Rotunda has been attributed to Sharples' lack of business acumen (particularly compared with Carlile's previous wife, Jane), in reality, the Rotunda had teetered on the brink of closure ever since the imprisonment of Taylor.[94] By February 1832, Sharples reported that no less than £1000 was needed to keep the venture open, to cover rent, taxes, lights, repairs, servants and to keep it in 'good order'.[95] If that mammoth task was not enough, she inherited an impossibly heavy debt of £300 amassed since the imprisonment of Taylor and Carlile.[96]

Aside from these dire financial difficulties, it is clear that Sharples failed to capture the imagination of radical London. By the end of March 1832, she could not sustain the initial interest in her performances. Facing dwindling audiences of both men and women, she despaired that women of the radical community had not embraced her cause:

---

92   Brian Cowan, 'What was Masculine about the Public Sphere? Gender and the coffeehouse milieu in post-Restoration England', *History Workshop Journal*, vol. 51 (2001), p. 147.
93   For the reception of Carlile's ideas on birth control, see Clark, *Struggle for the Breeches*, pp. 181–5; Hera Cook, *The Long Sexual Revolution: English women, sex and contraception 1800–1975* (Oxford: Oxford University Press, 2005), pp. 70–6; Angus McLaren, 'Contraception and the Working Class: The social ideology of the English birth control movement in its early years', *Comparative Studies in Society and History*, vol. 18 (1976), pp. 238–45.
94   In private correspondence, Carlile declared that 'the present Mrs C is not a good business woman'. Richard Carlile to Thomas Turton, 3 January 1842, Carlile Papers, Henry E. Huntington Library, San Marino, California (hereafter Carlile Papers).
95   *Isis*, 11 February 1832.
96   Ibid.

> I verily believe that I stand alone in this country, as a modern Eve, daring to pluck the fruit of this tree, and to give it to timid, sheepish man. I have received kindnesses and encouragements from a few ladies since my appearance in the metropolis, but how few![97]

The passage bears striking resemblance to the despair of Susannah Wright's supporters a decade earlier. Neither woman enjoyed sustained support from the women of the radical community. Helen Rogers considers that her failure resulted partly from her 'presentation as a goddess [which] was in tension with her democratic principles and with the collective and egalitarian spirit of contemporary reform movements'.[98] Perhaps Sharples' vision for a new social order for both working-class men and for women of all ranks was so outlandish that it smacked of the more bizarre prophecies of Joanna Southcott. As Anna Clark notes, 'the role of female prophetesses was anchored in visionary proclamations and in other-worldly spiritual context...their influence was evanescent and could not translate into female authority in the wider society'.[99]

Given the parallels with Wright's experience of participation in the public sphere, Sharples' intimate connection with Carlile cannot be overlooked when assessing the reasons for her inability to forge a stronger leadership role in London radicalism. Where Wright embraced Carlile's most marginal of advocacies, including birth control and sexual freedom, Sharples embodied them, bearing him four children outside a legal marriage. As Clark notes, 'issues of morality had always divided plebeian society, with some rejecting libertinism in favor of religion'.[100] Moreover, the expectation that she could have achieved a prominent place among leading male radicals is perhaps misplaced. In a period when few radicals of any rank advocated equal social or political rights for women, it is perhaps not surprising that Sharples' aim to be a 'leader of the people' would not come to fruition.

This is not to say, however, that her brief participation on the Rotunda stage did not produce a lasting legacy. Sharples helped create an enduring tradition of female participation on the site. Edward Royle first noted the 'tenuous continuities' of secularism at the Rotunda and the wider environs of South London in his book *Victorian Infidels*.[101] The significance of the female dimension of this continuity, however, was overlooked. Evidence of the Rotunda's occupation after the departure of Carlile and Sharples is fragmentary, but it is possible to trace a succession of females involved at the site of 3 Blackfriars Road, not only as audience but as orators.[102]

---

97 *Isis*, 31 March 1832.
98 Rogers, *Women and the People*, p. 64.
99 Clark, *Struggle for the Breeches*, p. 117.
100 Ibid., p. 179.
101 Royle, *Victorian Infidels*, p. 192.
102 For an account of Sharples' life post-1832, as well as her death amidst poverty in 1852, see Rogers, *Women and the People*, pp. 66–71.

Figure 8.2 Eliza Macauley, 1819.

Copyright Wellcome Library, London.

Shortly after the departure of Sharples, the Rotunda again came under female management with the arrival of Eliza Macauley, a former actress and Christian turned Owenite preacher (Figure 8.2).[103] In August 1832, Macauley established the Surrey and Southwark Equitable Exchange Bank on the model of Owen's own National Equitable Labour Exchange. The Exchange operated a system whereby workers deposited their goods, which were then valued by a committee according to the amount of labour invested in them.[104] An exchange note was then issued, allowing the member to purchase goods in return. Macauley's Exchange also allowed women to 'add their industry to that of their husbands' by issuing exchange vouchers for women's labour.[105] Drawing on the model of Carlile's

---

103   See Taylor, *Eve and the New Jerusalem*, p. 71. On Macauley, see also Frow and Frow, *Political Women*, pp. 83–92; *Lancashire and Yorkshire Co-operator*, May 1832; *The Crisis*, 7 July and 25 August 1832; *Isis*, 3 November 1832; *Poor Man's Guardian*, 11 January 1834; Eliza Macauley, *Autobiographical Memoir of Miss Macauley* (London: Charles Fox, 1834 and 1835); Frow and Frow, *Political Women*, pp. 82–92. As one of the first autobiographies by a working-class woman, Macauley's has come to the attention of scholars interested in women's life writing. See, for example, Jane Rendall, '"A Short Account of My Unprofitable Life": Autobiographies of working class women in Britain c.1775–1845', in Trev Lynn Broughton and Linda Anderson (eds), *Women's Lives/Women's Times: New essays on auto/biography* (New York: State University of New York Press, 1997), pp. 31–50.
104   Taylor, *Eve and the New Jerusalem*, p. 86.
105   See the pamphlet outlining the scheme: *Surrey and Southwark Equitable Exchange Bank, Commercial Reform Surrey and Southwark Institution (late the Rotunda) Equitable Exchange Bank and Bazaar, near the*

operation of the Rotunda, Macauley also used the premises to deliver lectures on gender equality, financial reform and the superstition of established churches. The lectures were conducted every Sunday and Wednesday evenings; Macauley defended her decision to lecture on a Sunday despite protestations in the local community determining that 'the true spirit of Christianity is to do good on the Sabbath'.[106] 'Ladies', she advertised, were 'admitted free'. She also promoted her plans to open a school of education and science for adults and an infant school in the Rotunda. Despite her efforts, the venture did not succeed and, in 1835, Macauley penned her memoirs from the Marshalsea Debtors' Prison.[107]

The demise of Macauley's endeavour saw the Rotunda again return to an outlet of popular entertainment. In 1835, a magician advertising 'conjuring tricks' was said to be performing there.[108] In 1837, the *London Dispatch and People's Social Reformer* reported that a licence to operate the premises as a concert room had been rejected, though, by 1839, it was operating as the 'Surrey Grand Café and Musical Saloon', featuring billiard tables and tavern facilities.[109]

Thereafter follows a gap in the historical record in terms of political use and female involvement in the Rotunda until the early 1840s. The period 1842–43 saw a brief return to the premises' heyday as a focal point for multifarious radical identities. There was again an Owenite connection with strong female presence among the new tenants. Harriet Martineau, radical-liberal, and another unnamed 'lady speaker' were reported lecturing at the Rotunda in November 1842.[110] The Rotunda's identity as a gender-inclusive venue for knowledge and instruction was also rekindled with the opening of the Hall of Science—the term for an Owenite institution that provided classes to boys and girls without differentiation of subject matter based on gender (Figure 8.3).[111]

---

bridge, Black-friars Road (London, 1832).
106   Ibid. Unlike Sharples, Macauley was not new to the lecturing scene when she appeared at the Rotunda. She was earlier involved in the Dissenting chapel run by Josiah Fitch. See Prothero, *Artisans and Politics in Early Nineteenth-Century London*, p. 260. During her career as an actress, Macauley also provided lectures for entertainment at the Crown and Anchor tavern on elocution, music, comedy and literature. See the broadsheet *Miss Macauley's Literary and Musical Regalio at the Crown and Anchor*, Acc. NS1069 B137 (38), City of Westminster Archives, London.
107   Taylor, *Eve and the New Jerusalem*, p. 71.
108   *Jackson's Oxford Journal*, 17 January 1835.
109   *London Dispatch and People's Social Reformer*, 22 October 1837; *The Charter*, 3 February 1839.
110   *Morning Chronicle*, 2 November 1842, 18 November 1842; *The Times*, 2 November 1842, 17 November 1842.
111   See the prospectus of the South London Hall of Science in which they announced their aim to 'render the Institution an efficient and powerful instrument in forwarding the cause of Popular Reform'. They also announced the opening of the South London Rational School where boys and girls were to be instructed in 'all branches of knowledge', as they were 'fully convinced the present system of female education is lamentably defective'. See the 'Surrey Rotunda' collection, 1842, fo. 129, Wellcome Collection.

Figure 8.3 South London Rational School meeting in the Large Theatre of the Rotunda. This illustration provides a rare glimpse of the Large Theatre, which housed the performances of the Reverend Robert Taylor's play *Swing! Or who are the incendiaries?*, as well as meetings of the National Union of the Working Classes. The image is from the mid-1840s when the South London Rational School used the premises.

Copyright Wellcome Library, London.

In his private correspondence from July 1842, Carlile quipped that the 'Socialists' had taken over his Rotunda. 'The Social Thieves of Lambeth', he despaired, 'have possessed themselves of my Rotunda! How I envied the rogues of Sunday!'[112] Carlile found some solace that the Rotunda was again working for 'public purposes', noting that his friend George Holyoake, secretary to the Lambeth Branch of the Rational Society, was due to lecture there the following day. Holyoake wrote to Carlile thereafter, advising he had 'elicited some warm cheers for you this morning at the Rotunda'.[113]

In the tradition of the NUWC, the South London branch of Chartists also held meetings throughout 1843, with the 'largest gathering' since they 'obtained

---

112   Richard Carlile to Thomas Turton, 12 July 1842, Carlile Papers.
113   George Jacob Holyoake to Richard Carlile, 24 July 1824, reprinted in Campbell, *The Battle for the Freedom of the Press*, p. 258.

possession of the Rotunda' occurring in July that year.[114] In late 1843, leading Chartist Bronterre O'Brien was reported to be lecturing there, and a soiree was held in his honour in the Rotunda's large theatre in January the following year.[115] In January 1843, the *Examiner* reported a meeting to appeal for the Repeal of the Corn Laws, which attracted a gathering of some 1500 people.[116]

After reportedly spending 'several hundred pounds' on the premises, by 1844, Holyoake's branch of the Rationalists was also forced from the Rotunda for want of funds and due to the lack of a 'Resident Director' to manage and invigorate the site.[117] Not wanting 'so important an arena for philosophical investigation' to be lost to the 'cause of philanthropy and reason', Holyoake proposed a subscription plan to allow the premises to be turned into a 'Philosophical Institute' for the magnificent Owenite lecturer Emma Martin.[118] Holyoake reported that Martin, though 'not the advocate exclusively of any party', was 'precisely fitted for the management of the Rotunda, eminently calculated to adorn it by her talents, give it efficiency by her energy, and conduct it with that nice propriety which would merit for it great support'.[119] Holyoake believed under her tutelage, the Rotunda would again realise a 'Reign of Reason'. Despite his reticence about the socialists and his Rotunda, Carlile might well have approved. As Barbara Taylor mused, the funeral sermon Martin penned upon learning of Carlile's death in 1843, which contained caustic attacks about the established clergy and Old Corruption, would have 'warmed his own heart'.[120] Though the subscription effort raised the required amount of £250, the landlord intervened in the plan, refusing to lease the building for 'atheistical purposes'.[121] The power of the landlord to exclude Martin and other rationalist groups again points to the inextricable link between political power and property in the early nineteenth century and the continuing struggle for access to sites of assembly. It further highlights the significance of Carlile's success during 1830–32 in providing the radical movement with a unique space of their own.

The feminist continuities at the site into the 1840s also reveal that there were other, more inclusive outlets for women's political participation than the radical scholarship of the period suggests. The dominance of Chartism in these years,

---

114 See *Northern Star*, 22 October 1842, 29 October 1842, 4 March 1843, 15 July 1843, 29 July 1843, 30 September 1843.
115 *The Movement*, 30 December 1843.
116 *Examiner*, 21 January 1843.
117 *The Movement*, 3 February 1844, 20 April 1844.
118 On Emma Martin, see Taylor, *Eve and the New Jerusalem*, especially pp. 68–73, 130–55; George Jacob Holyoake, *The Last Days of Mrs Emma Martin* (London, 1851); Frow and Frow, *Political Women*, pp. 83–5, 104–6, 110–15. Martin also published several tracts herself, including a work dedicated to Richard Carlile upon his death in 1843. See Emma Martin, *A Funeral Sermon Occasioned by the Death of Richard Carlile* (London, 1843).
119 *The Movement*, 3 February 1844; Royle, *Victorian Infidels*, pp. 192–3.
120 Taylor, *Eve and the New Jerusalem*, p. 142.
121 Royle, *Victorian Infidels*, pp. 192–3.

both in terms of its mass support and in the subsequent historiography, has led to an emphasis on the separation and segregation of women from the radical movement. As Barbara Taylor's study reminds us, the early Chartist years also saw a reinvigoration of the Owenite movement. The marginalisation of women in the Chartist movement has tended to overshadow the continuation of the liberating and inclusive traditions of Owenism and those from Carlile's legacy.

* * *

By way of conclusion, I wish to return to late 1831 (even before Sharples' entry onto the Rotunda stage) to show how the feminising of the space impacted on even the most masculine of the Rotunda identities: the NUWC. Despite some dissenting voices, the NUWC took an early position in respect to women's rights, firmly excluding women from their vision of political reform; 'why talk of restoring them to their social rights until we have first obtained our own?', questioned Henry Hetherington, ironically, a leading London advocate of Owenism.[122] The prevailing mandate of the NUWC remained universal male suffrage and membership was open only to men. Yet on 29 October 1831, John Cleave, a leading NUWC figure, moved a resolution that wives of members be admitted to Rotunda meetings free of charge. In his supporting arguments for the resolution, Cleave considered that

> the meetings would be ornamented by the women and [he] was satisfied that there would be more peace and happiness at home. He was aware that women in general were Tories (a laugh); but if they could be induced to attend there, they would shortly become republicans, (cheers) and they would then rear up the next generation not like the slaves of the present age. (Great cheering).[123]

Though the resolution met with resounding cheers from the meeting and was passed unanimously, it is clear from Cleave's justification for their newfound inclusiveness that there would be a long way to go before the NUWC would see women as equal radical compatriots. It was surely no coincidence that the veiled concession occurred within the confines of the Rotunda where the NUWC witnessed firsthand the successful participation of women in other radical forums and which tempered the otherwise segregational tendencies of this most masculine of Rotunda affiliates.

Following the adoption of the resolution, it appears that some wives embraced the opportunity to participate in the Rotunda meetings. One Home Office report noted 32 wives of members were among the 500 attendees at a meeting in late

---

122   Quoted in Taylor, *Eve and the New Jerusalem*, p. 82. Taylor notes that Hetherington would soon alter these opinions and become a close friend and ally to leading Owenite proponent Emma Martin.
123   *Poor Man's Guardian*, 29 October 1831.

November.[124] Just as women were beginning to find a seat alongside their husbands at NUWC meetings, however, in January 1832, Carlile evicted the NUWC to make way for Sharples. Though the NUWC continued to operate out of other meeting venues (and returned sporadically to the Rotunda), the timing appears critical for the participation of women. By mid-1832, women aligned with the NUWC began to form separate groups. The gender separation was institutionalised in the Female Reform Societies, and public notices of NUWC meetings no longer extended an invitation to women.[125] There is a certain irony that the radical leader most vocal in promoting women's rights and equal participation might have played even a small role in encouraging a separate model of organisation.

The gender relationships gleaned from this brief episode suggest that the anointing of the NUWC as a forerunner of the Chartists is merited in more ways than its approach to reform of the political system. The role ascribed for women as auxiliary radicals was to find increasingly strong favour in the Chartist years. My intention here is not to oversimplify what Anna Clark has shown to be the complex negotiation of gender roles throughout the nineteenth century. As she argues, the

> working-class movement did not simply reject the 'feminine' in favor of the 'masculine' version of class and a middle-class notion of domesticity; rather, radicals struggled for decades to define masculinity and to solve a persistent sexual crisis.[126]

This episode at the Rotunda highlights the tensions inherent in the gender struggle within early nineteenth-century radicalism. That an organisation as gender-defined as the NUWC could be tempted to include women testifies to the fact that other Rotunda radicals not only considered women as radical equals but also created a venue to accommodate their participation. This suggests further that the gender-inclusive public of the Rotunda deserves greater recognition in radical and feminist historiography for its key role in shaping the social and political aspirations of a generation of radical men and women.

---

124 Home Office Papers, HO64/11, 23 November 1831, fo. 441.
125 See *Poor Man's Guardian*, 21 July 1832. Many meetings of the Female Society were held at William Benbow's Theobalds Road Institution—another important radical venue in this period.
126 Clark, *Struggle for the Breeches*, p. 264.

9. Conclusion

Despite the importance of the venues examined in this book to Britain's political history, none remains standing on London's urban landscape. Newgate continued to operate as a prison throughout the nineteenth century, and although it underwent further renovation and extension during the century, it failed to shake its loathed reputation for squalor and harshness. Newgate's continued resistance to prison reform and the apparent inability to effect either reform or redemption of its prisoners were lamented throughout the century. By 1902, pending another wave of reform measures, the authorities evidently considered this resistance was intractable; a decision was made to demolish the prison and to build a new central criminal court, which continues to occupy the site today. Architectural historian Harold Kalman regrets the demise of Newgate: 'With it was lost a testament to the genius of George Dance the Younger, as well as an important milestone in prison design.'[1]

Few Londoners at the turn of the century might have shared Kalman's nostalgia for the architectural significance of the building. In 1900, the *Sphere* wrote that Newgate's demise was 'not to be regretted', for 'its history is of the most unsavoury order'.[2] Public hangings continued on the street outside Newgate until 1868 when Victorian sensibilities saw executions removed from the public gaze and to a site inside the prison.[3] That few traces remain of the prison, save an original cell door and some signage now placed in the London Museum, suggests that despite its historical and architectural significance, it remained a site of loathing and awe for much of the London populace. Its demolition provided an opportunity to erase not only its physical presence from the metropolitan landscape but also its horrors from public memory.

George Laval Chesterton's appointment as Governor of Coldbath Fields House of Correction in 1834 saw the prison move closer to the conditions that inspired Michael Ignatieff's study of the site. Chesterton sought to introduce the separate and silent system into Coldbath Fields, as well as the relentless, and infamous, hard-labour system that subjected prisoners to the inane task of picking oakum or hours of exhausting and unrelenting work on the treadmill.[4] The prison was substantially enlarged according to the radial design during the 1830s and, by

---

1 Harold D. Kalman, 'Newgate Prison', *Architectural History*, vol. 12 (1969), p. 58.
2 Quoted in Anthony Babington, *The English Bastille: A history of Newgate gaol and prison conditions in Britain 1188–1902* (London: Macdonald & Co., 1971), p. 235.
3 Nevertheless, the prison continued to be a site of intrigue for Londoners. According to Anthony Babington, it remained a 'sort of penal museum' throughout the nineteenth century, regularly visited by throngs of interested sightseers. Ibid., p. 231.
4 On developments at the prison under Governor Chesteron's management, see his memoirs: George Chesteron, *Revelations of Prison Life; With an enquiry into prison discipline and secondary punishments* (London:

the 1860s, more closely resembled the 'latest example of prison architecture at Pentonville'.⁵ The prison's existence was, however, relatively short-lived compared with the venerable site of Newgate. The *Prison Act* of 1877 resulted in a swathe of prison closures and Coldbath Fields was one county prison considered superfluous by the newly appointed Prison Commissioners, who now oversaw the management and operation of Britain's gaols.⁶ Shortly after its closure, the site was officially granted to the Post Office, which occupies it to this day. The current British Postal Museum and Archive web site maintains that postal workers of the late nineteenth century objected so vocally to working at 'Coldbath Fields'—a 'name long associated with the feared gaol'—that postal management was forced to revert to a former name for the area, Mount Pleasant, from 1888.⁷ Though the physical structure of the prison remained intact for some time, the change in nomenclature helped in some way to erase Coldbath Fields House of Correction also from public memory.

Although the Crown and Anchor was renamed the Whittington Club after Douglas Jerrold successfully gained the lease of the premises for his new experiment in urban sociability, it continued to be known as the 'ancient Temple of Freedom' well into the nineteenth century.⁸ As its Whig parliamentary patronage declined after 1832, so too it appears did the condition of the premises. Whittington Club members went to considerable effort during 1850 to raise funds to undertake substantial renovations, focusing particularly on a restoration of the Great Room. They eventually raised the considerable sum of £5000 deemed necessary to refashion the space, which included construction of a larger gallery for musicians, repainting the walls and providing extra gas lighting and cushioned seating around the room.⁹ A ball was held to mark the restoration, celebrating the transformation of 'our Great Room' from 'the grub to the butterfly'.¹⁰ How devastating for the tireless fundraisers that only four years later, in December 1854, the entire building was razed by fire.

When the blaze broke out in the tavern's kitchen at 5.30 am, fire engulfed the premises so rapidly that the 20 servants occupying the top floor of the premises were forced to make a 'rapid exit' in their nightdresses through one of the parapet windows, making a 'circuit of the stone coping round the building',

---

Hurst and Blackett, 1856); Henry Mayhew and John Binny, *The Criminal Prisons of London and Scenes of Prison Life* (London: Griffin, 1862), pp. 275, 280–8; Michael Ignatieff, *A Just Measure of Pain: The penitentiary in the Industrial Revolution, 1750–1850* (New York: Columbia University Press, 1980), pp. 189–96.
5   Thomas Archer, *The Pauper, the Thief and the Convict* (London, 1865; reprinted, New York: Garland, 1985), p. 152.
6   Babington, *The English Bastille*, p. 228.
7   The British Postal Museum and Archive, 'Mount Pleasant', <http://postalheritage.org.uk/history/places/mountpleasant>
8   D. Foster, *Inns, Tavern, Alehouses, Coffee Houses etc, In and Around London* (City of Westminster Archives, c. 1900), vol. 20, p. 301.
9   *Whittington Club Gazette*, 19 October 1850.
10 *Whittington Club Gazette*, 16 November 1850.

onto the roof and across to the adjacent premises occupied by the *Illustrated London News*.[11] In a matter of minutes, 'flames swept furiously through the great room' and burst through the large windows at its eastern end, creating an 'alarming appearance' for onlookers. Although the *Illustrated London News* considered that the 'building itself had little to recommend it', they nevertheless recognised it as a site of 'great historic interest', dedicating three broadsheet pages complete with illustrations to memorialise its significance in London's urban history (Figure 9.1).[12] With the premises now 'laid in ashes', and given the close proximity to the *Illustrated London News* offices, the editor offered an apology to his readers for the smudged paper used for the very edition that reported the Crown and Anchor fire. Thumbing through those pages more than a century and a half later, I was provided with a tangible, albeit brief, contact with a long lost radical space by those same smudges.

Figure 9.1 Fire at the Crown and Anchor

Illustrated London News, 9 December 1854

Following the fire, the premises were rebuilt on the same plan as the Crown and Anchor, and continued to operate under the name of the Whittington Club until the 1870s, although attracting a markedly different milieu than that

---

11 *Morning Chronicle*, 4 December 1854.
12 *Illustrated London News*, 9 December 1854.

which promised so much under the Whittington Club. Even before 1854, the gender inclusiveness that was the hallmark of the club had all but sunk 'into oblivion'.[13] According to historian Christopher Kent, it 'became a more or less ordinary city men's club' though it retained a 'mild radical tint'.[14] Whittington women, both he and fellow historian Kathryn Gleadle concur, 'ceased to find the club congenial'.[15] The Whittington finally closed in 1873, though the building reopened the same year as the Temple Club—yet another incarnation of the site as an outlet for male metropolitan sociability (Figure 9.2).[16] By 1888, it was used as a printing house, with the *World* newspaper remarking that its 'Corinthian columns' were all that remained as a reminder of the Crown and Anchor epoch.[17] At the turn of the twentieth century, London tavern and inn chronicler D. Foster referred to the tavern as an 'ancient Temple of Freedom' and anticipated that though 'the giants of democracy have passed away', the 'recollection of the Crown and Anchor will long live amongst the people of England'.[18] This book has sought to make a contribution to realising Foster's hope. For though the Crown and Anchor was a seminal site in British political and radical history, prior to this study, it occupied only an amorphous place in the rich body of historiography focused on this period. Lamentably, the current structure occupying the site now lives as a testament to the mediocrity and mendicity of mid-twentieth-century London architecture—a long way from its days as a leading cultural and political site of urban sociability.

Following George Holyoake's failed attempt to see the Rotunda restored to its former Carlilean glory under the tutelage of Emma Martin, the Rotunda passed to new owners. The new proprietors sought once again to draw upon one of the Rotunda's many layers of identity and applied for a licence to operate the premises as a minor theatre. The application was rejected in 1844 on the grounds that the Rotunda had been used 'for propagating infidel principles and socialism'.[19] The owners might have hoped time had erased these associations and they reapplied for the licence three years later. The application was again unsuccessful. By 1858, they surely envisaged that there was sufficient temporal distance between the notorious Devil's Chaplin, or the scandalous *Isis*, or indeed its later socialist connections, and applied for the theatre licence once more. On this occasion, the owners appealed to the licensing magistrates' sense

---

13 Kathryn Gleadle, *The Early Feminists: Radical Unitarians and the emergence of the women's rights movement, 1831–51* (New York: St Martin's Press, 1995), p. 170.
14 Christopher Kent, 'The Whittington Club: A bohemian experiment in middle class social reform', *Victorian Studies*, vol. 18, no. 1 (1974),p. 54n.
15 Gleadle, *The Early Feminists*, p. 169.
16 *Norman Collection of Taverns*, vol. 6, Guildhall Library, City of London, p. 74. See also Walter Thornbury, 'The Strand (Southern Tributaries)', *Old and New London*, vol. 3 (1878), pp. 63–84.
17 *World*, 26 December 1888.
18 Foster, *Inns, Tavern, Alehouses, Coffee Houses etc*, p. 301.
19 See the advice from Lord Chamberlain's office to John Parkinson (son of James), dated 9 May 1844, Southwark Local Studies Library, London.

of nationalism, claiming that as the two largest theatres in London at the time were in foreign hands, the Rotunda could become the home of 'National Drama'. According to theatre historian Tracy Davis, the new owners hoped 'that such a noble aim would erase any tendency to exercise ideological grudges on dead managers and inanimate real estate'.[20] Their aspirations were soon quashed, however, when the magistrates rejected the application for a third time. The stench of infidelism, it seems, would take many years to fade.

Figure 9.2 Front right corner of the Temple Club, following rebuilding on the same plan as the Crown and Anchor, c. 1880

Strand Estate Collection. Copyright His Grace the Duke of Norfolk (per the Archivist, Arundel Castle)

Less is known of the Rotunda's days beyond the successive failure of its owners to secure a theatre licence. It reportedly operated as a penny gaff at some time during the mid-century, before it operated as the Rotunda Auction and Sale Rooms for 'trade purposes'. By 1908, the building was known only to be operating as the 'London depot of an Edinburgh firm'.[21] Despite surviving

---

20   Tracy Davis, *The Economics of the British Stage, 1800–1914* (New York: Cambridge University Press, 2000), p. 35. See also David Worrall, *Theatric Revolution: Drama, censorship and Romantic period subcultures, 1773–1832* (Oxford: Oxford University Press, 2006), p. 349.
21   *Notes and Queries*, 19 September 1908.

Radical Spaces

the wrath of the authorities throughout the nineteenth century, the Rotunda did not escape the devastation of enemy bombers during World War II. The *Survey of London* of 1950 contains a description of what it calls the 'mutilated remains' of the Rotunda still standing at that date (Figure 9.3a/b). It has since been demolished for modern office space—a somewhat melancholy postscript for the once great radical theatre.

Figure 9.3a Demolition of the Rotunda site in January 1958. The circular roof of the small theatre of the Rotunda.

Copyright Southwark Local History Library.

9. Conclusion

Figure 9.3b The marble columns of the small theatre are visible in the remains.

Copyright Southwark Local History Library.

The struggle surrounding the acquisition of a theatre licence by the new owners neatly summarises the underlying theme of this study—that the radical spaces of the past are not merely 'inanimate real estate' in which radical culture unfolded. That the Surrey magistrates continued to invoke an 'ideological grudge' against the building more than two decades after Carlile's departure from his cherished Rotunda speaks to the complex associations between culture and space presented in this study. This study has argued that despite the diversity in the typology of radical spaces there is a dynamic, dialectical and symbiotic relationship between radical culture and the sites in which it operated.

This symbiotic relationship saw the sites themselves transformed into radical spaces; they became imbued with radicalism. Section one of the book demonstrated how the configuration of Newgate gaol and its separate quarters for state prisoners made it easier for radicals to resist prison reform. In the new prison, exemplified at the time by Coldbath Fields House of Correction, architectural changes were intended to allow for the implementation of the ideals of reform—separate and solitary confinement, prison labour, religious instruction and the promise of redemption—and new regulations surrounding the management and operation of prisons were intended to eradicate the corruption of keepers predicated on spatial and financial hierarchies. Here again radical culture adapted and prevailed. The radical resistance to the criminal identity ascribed by the prison, as well as to the authorities' concern about the danger of ideological contagion, meant that reform measures failed to silence radicals. The new spatial arrangements of the prison, which originally disregarded political status, were altered to accommodate radical prisoners separately to the remaining prison population.

In the Crown and Anchor tavern, the venue was also shaped to a significant extent by its radical associations. To view the inclusion of the Crown and Anchor in the prints surveyed in Chapter 4, for instance, as merely a contextual or spatial apparatus for the artist—a convenient aesthetic backdrop—would be underestimating both the adroitness of the artist and the power of the symbols they employed to create meaning. The Crown and Anchor itself became part of the artists' palette of symbols and signs used to communicate with their audience, giving their work both a spatial and an ideological grounding. The venue was so imbued with its ideological associations that its nomenclature became a form of metonymy—or political shorthand—in the language of the public sphere.

The Rotunda was also indelibly marked by its radical associations. Despite its early, and well-known, incarnations as the Leverian Museum and the Surrey Institution, the Rotunda's radical political connections under Richard Carlile, the Devil's Chaplain and *Isis* were what provided the model for its later socialist occupants. Moreover, it was Carlile's tenancy that fuelled the 'ideological grudge' exhibited by the Surrey magistrates and which provided the rationale for the authorities to prevent a resurgence of radical ideals in any future public use.

If the venues themselves were transformed into radical spaces by those who populated them, the effect clearly worked both ways. This study has documented the vital relationship between space and radical culture, demonstrated by the way in which the spaces impacted on, and interplayed with, the multifarious radical identities of the early nineteenth century. Even the prison space—designed to punish and silence heterodox political and religious expression—provided an opportunity for radical men, and women, to assert a new status and define a radical identity. Radical culture prevailed in the age of prison reform and resistance of the identity ascribed by the prison space played a central role

9. Conclusion

in shaping the culture. As *The Times* mused in 1835, John Arthur Roebuck MP would 'sink into insignificance' as a radical publisher 'unless anyone should be so senseless as to prosecute him once or twice and get him sent to rusticate in Coldbath Fields…[and] enter into the dietary by which radicals acquire strength and thrive'.[22] Radical prisoners resisted both the ideological and the spatial attempts to align them with other categories of prisoners and drew on the example of earlier (and less plebeian) generations of radical prisoners to assert their rights as political prisoners. Of particular significance in this regard is the case of Susannah Wright. In contesting her criminal identity, her gender became of secondary significance. She defined herself first and foremost as a radical—a status far more elusive for women outside the prison walls.

Such a paradox is also evident in the identity ascribed by the Crown and Anchor appellation. Despite the satanic and seditious associations of the tavern in the caricatures and satires featured in Chapter 4, as well as the often disparaging reports in the mainstream press, the representations of the venue in the print culture of the period helped establish the tavern as a legitimate space of political opposition. As a result of the venue's longstanding parliamentary and bourgeois connections, it became synonymous with political reform achieved through established means and processes. The sheer size of the hall meant that it could readily serve as a venue for national gatherings of men who, *inter alia*, believed that their interests were not represented or respected in the House of Commons. Not surprisingly, the Crown and Anchor came to be known as an alternative parliament, a place where the *real* representatives of the people could assemble. As we have seen, in 1842, the assembly of a national delegation of the Anti-Corn Law League at the tavern was reported *Hansard*-like in the public press. At the same time, MPs deliberated on repeal a stone's throw away. It was debatable where the real power lay.

This proximity to formal political power was reflected in the cultural conventions that developed at the site and which remained largely intact as middling, and later plebeian, radical groups vying for a place in the political nation began to appropriate the tavern space. The Crown and Anchor, both the site and the nomenclature, provided a political identity under which to associate, not only for the delegations led by respectable radicals, but for a new generation of radical men and women who demanded political reform but who shied away from the more militant milieu of other radical spaces such as the Rotunda.

As section three of this book reveals, however, the masculine and militant identity ascribed to the Rotunda was but one of many layers of identity

---

22 *The Times*, 19 June 1835. The newspaper here is referring to the series of unstamped weekly addresses edited by Roebuck entitled *Pamphlets for the People*. On Roebuck, see S. A. Beaver, 'Roebuck, John Arthur (1802–1879)', *Oxford Dictionary of National Biography*, <http://www.oxforddnb.com/view/article/23945>

developed at the Blackfriars Road site. By opening the premises to multivalent forms of radical expression, the Rotunda leaders responded to the needs of a whole class of people who were simultaneously becoming aware of their strength and culture and of their exclusion from political and social power. For those who ordinarily lacked the political voice or opportunity to express their discontent formally, attending Rotunda performances and interacting with radical leaders provided an opportunity to register disgruntlement with the injustices of 'Old Corruption' and to present a united stand against religious and political authority. It offered a politically muted section of the populace a chance to demonstrate their oppositional views and, more importantly, their political independence.

The Rotunda and its radical clientele exerted a significant impact and influence on the cultural and political environment of early nineteenth-century London. The immense, albeit short-lived, popularity of the Rotunda was due largely to its attraction as an agent of popular culture. It offered a congenial atmosphere for all members of the working class: men, women and children. It catered for a range of psychological needs, which included the powerful 1830s drive for knowledge and—to borrow from J. F. C. Harrison's account of popular culture—a 'craving for fellowship and community activity, love of ritual or ceremony, crusading for a cause, or even flirting with the forbidden'.[23] Crucially, it offered women an outlet for public political participation, both as orators and auditors, and marked an important moment of gender inclusiveness in radical culture, which was later largely lost during the Chartist years.

For radicals of the early nineteenth century, access to the spaces highlighted in this study also crucially meant a voice in the public sphere. Not only did removal from the public realm into the 'private' space of the prison fail to silence radical voices; it often amplified them. Susannah Wright's experience, and that of the many male radical prisoners in this study, suggests that prison failed to impede participation in the public sphere. The prison discourses of radicals—from the claim for the right to be treated better than other classifications of prisoners to use of their own prison publications to air their grievances—indicate that the radical public sphere did not operate in isolation from the mainstream. The ability of radicals in this period to initiate public debates over the status of political prisoners saw them influence public opinion, challenge the very notion of Britishness and alter the way the authorities responded to those imprisoned for political crimes. The concessions they won would have repercussions for the prison experiences of successive waves of political prisoners.

By crossing the threshold of an institution as prominent on the metropolitan landscape as the Crown and Anchor, we gain new insights into the development

---

23   J. F. C. Harrison, *The Early Victorians, 1832–51* (London: Weidenfeld and Nicholson, 1971), p. 132.

of the public sphere with the expansion of the political nation during the early nineteenth century. This study of the Crown and Anchor reveals that the bourgeois participants of Habermas's construct of the public sphere were not alone; this archetypal public venue catered to a much wider audience than Habermas allows.

Under Habermas's model of the public sphere, the Rotunda might be dismissed as a venue that merely attempted to imitate the cultural institutions of the middle classes. Although elements of the Surrey Institution are clearly evident in the operational conventions of the Rotunda, these melded with traditional plebeian forms of learning, political communication and sociability. By offering palatable politics in a venue with multiple attractions, Rotunda radicals introduced a new breed of Londoners to political and theological radicalism and to rational discourse and exchange—people who might otherwise have shied away from the rougher, more clandestine or masculine atmosphere of taverns and ale houses, or those averse to the formality of organised political groups. Such a plebeian space on the London cultural landscape challenges Habermas's dismissal of the plebeian sphere as mimicry. The fusion of traditional and nascent cultural forms evident at the Rotunda also disrupts the demarcation between the two spheres implicit at the heart of the counter-sphere thesis.

The view of radical culture as a counter-public sphere arose in response to Habermas's failure to recognise plebeian participation in his bourgeois construction of the public sphere. The criticisms of Craig Calhoun and Geoff Eley, to name just two, of Habermas's neglect in this regard are valid ones and their revisions have been crucial to placing the concept on the agenda of historians of popular politics. In chastising Habermas for his neglect of the plebeian public sphere, we have, perhaps, forgotten the key developments in British historiography. While English-speaking scholars are necessarily engaging with the 1989 translated edition of the book, we must remember that Habermas wrote the original German version in 1962. At this time, he did not have the benefit of the seminal work of E. P. Thompson, who was the first to comprehensively chart the public participation of England's plebeian radicals and reformers in forming public opinion and effecting political and social change.[24] Perhaps Habermas can be excused for not recognising the importance of this rational-critical discourse among the working classes when, at the time he wrote the book, most scholars of British history had also failed to do so.

---

24 Habermas himself notes the development in his contribution to Craig Calhoun's study, although 'confesses' that it was only upon reading 'Mikhail Bakhtin's great book *Rabelais and His World* have my eyes become really opened to the *inner* dynamics of a plebeian culture'. See Jürgen Habermas, 'Further Reflections on the Public Sphere', trans. Thomas Burger, in Craig Calhoun (ed.), *Habermas and the Public Sphere* (Cambridge, Mass.: MIT Press, 1992), pp. 421–61.

Despite the paucity of attention to the plebeian elements of the public sphere, Habermas's neglect has opened a new vein of inquiry and debate. Although historians such as Brian Cowan lament the overuse of the concept, conclusions drawn in this study suggest that further interrogation of the public sphere has much to offer scholars of early nineteenth-century culture and society. If nothing else, it provides a conceptual premise from which to examine the expanding political nation through the lens of the physical spaces in which the public sphere happened. Moreover, if, as E. P. Thompson famously suggested, 'class happens', it happened in buildings of brick and mortar such as prisons, taverns and theatres. The different nature of these spaces—ownership, control, purpose—and their histories have provided us with an invaluable index of cultural activity over time, and of change, in terms of both class and gender.

This study has inevitably raised further questions than its scope allowed room to pursue. Three immediately suggest themselves. Although Irish political prisoners have attracted the attention of historians, British political prisoners as a whole remain an understudied group in modern British history.[25] Yet, as this book has shown, their story has much to reveal beyond a narrative account of life within the prison walls. This is particularly true of a nation that defines itself in large part by its legal traditions and the rights encapsulated by them. More work is clearly warranted on charting the attitudes towards, and the treatment of, the political prisoner in England throughout the nineteenth century. The concept of the political prisoner as—to borrow from Sir Leon Radzinowicz and Roger Hood—a '*sui generis* species' speaks to the values of a nation.[26] How these attitudes and values were transported, both literally and metaphorically, around the Empire would also enrich our understanding of the wider British world.

So too, a detailed analysis of the Rotunda's National Union of the Working Classes (NUWC), is wanting in radical historiography. The NUWC played a vital role in pre-1832 reform agitation and was seen as the exponent of militant working-class consciousness and as the forerunner of Chartism. A more thorough understanding of the ideology and organisation of the NUWC would enrich our understanding of Chartism as the first mass working-class movement in British history. A closer study of the NUWC's often contradictory attitude towards women might further illuminate how women charted the gendered terrain of radical culture in the early nineteenth century.

The methodology of populating radical spaces has shed new light on the participation of women in radical culture and, more generally, in the wider public sphere. This approach is particularly fruitful given the 'extremely limited

---

25 For example, see the recent study by Sean McConville, *Irish Political Prisoners, 1848–1922: Theatres of war* (London: Routledge, 2003).
26 Sir Leon Radzinowicz and Roger Hood, 'The Status of Political Prisoner in England: The struggle for recognition', *Virginia Law Review*, vol. 65 (1979), p. 1421.

audibility of mid-Victorian working-women's voices'.²⁷ Women are evident in places previously considered as providing a less congenial atmosphere for women. And although radical culture centred on taverns and coffee houses (with their largely masculine milieu), there were places, such as the Rotunda, that provided a welcoming and inclusive environment for women. Wright's experience of the legal system signals the need for further investigation of the gendered politics of the courtroom in this period. A similar approach to other public spaces might also find women where none were thought to gather.

This book has surveyed three examples of radical spaces in early nineteenth-century London: the prison, as an example of an imposed radical space; the Crown and Anchor tavern, as an established cultural space appropriated and contested by successive generations of radicals; and the Rotunda, as one of the first spaces controlled and operated by radicals themselves. This study reveals that, despite the physical, operational, temporal and spatial differences between the sites, such spaces were both shaped by and helped to shape the social and political aspirations of the generation of radical men and women who populated them. By the end of his long radical life, John Gale Jones had traversed them all—and undoubtedly many more. Though neither he nor most of his contemporaries lived to see the fruits of their endeavours, we might speculate that they would attest to the importance of these radical spaces on the long path to realising a new, more inclusive social and political order for Britain.

---

27   Neville Kirk, *Change, Continuity and Class: Labour in British society, 1850–1920* (Manchester: Manchester University Press, 1998).

Bibliography

Primary sources

Archival sources

Arundel Castle Archives
ACC2 Strand Estate Papers

AC MSS, Howard Letters and Papers, 1636–1822, II

Bishopsgate Institute
Papers of George J. Holyoake

British Library
Francis Place Papers

Correspondence of Leigh Hunt

City of Westminster Archives
Foster, D. *Inns, Tavern, Alehouses, Coffee Houses etc, In and Around London*, vol. 20, c. 1900.

Guildhall Library Collection
Nobel Collection: Surrey Institution Papers.

Norman Collection: *Collection of newspaper and other cuttings related to London inns, taverns, coffeehouses, clubs, tea gardens, music halls, c.1885–1900*, 5 vols.

Henry E. Huntington Library, San Marino, California
Richard Carlile Papers

London Metropolitan Archives
Rendle Collection, Southwark File

Middlesex Sessions of the Peace Papers

Public Record Office

Home Office Papers

HO40/20-25	British Nineteenth Century Riots and Disturbances.
HO64	Discontent and Authority in England 1820–40.
HO64/11	Police and Secret Service Reports, 1827–1831, Police and Secret Service Reports, reports from Stafford of Seditious Meetings, Libellous Papers, 1830–33.
HO64/12	Police and Secret Service Reports, 1832.
HO64/13	Secret Service Miscellaneous Reports and Publications
HO64/15	Reports 1834–37.
HO64/16	Reports and Miscellaneous, 1827–33.
HO64/17	Police and Secret Service Reports, 1831.
HO64/18	Seditious Publications, 1830–36.

Southwark Local Studies Library

Surrey Institution/Rotunda Collection

Wellcome Library

'Surrey Rotunda' Collection, 1784–1858.

West Yorkshire Archive Service, Leeds

Humphrey Boyle Papers

Contemporary newspapers and periodicals

Bell's Life in London, 14 July 1822.

Bell's Weekly Messenger, 14 November 1830.

Black Dwarf, 1820–24, selected dates.

Cobbett's Weekly Political Register, 1816–30, selected dates.

Courier, 1798–1831, selected dates.

Daily Journal, 6 November 1723.

Devil's Pulpit, 2 vols, 1832.

Douglas Jerrold's Weekly Newspaper, January–October 1847.

Epicure's Almanack, London, 1815.

Examiner, 1808–43, selected dates.

Evening Mail, 1 July, 11 July, 12 July 1791; 25 July 1796.

Gauntlet, 1830–37, selected dates.

General Evening Post, 30 March 1790.

Hampshire Telegraph and Sussex Chronicle, 10 February 1823.

Illustrated London News, 1848–54.

Isis, 11 February 1832 – 15 December 1832.

Jackson's Oxford Journal, 1810–35, selected dates.

John Bull, 15 July 1822.

Lancashire and Yorkshire Co-operator, May 1832.

Leeds Mercury, 21 April 1810; 25 January 1817; 17 May 1823; 25 May 1838.

Lion, 4 January 1828 – 25 December 1829.

London Chronicle, 12 July 1791; 1 April 1797; 28 November 1789.

London Dispatch and People's Political and Social Reformer, 5 March, 22 October 1837.

Manchester Times and Gazette, 10 March 1838.

Morning Chronicle, 1800–54, selected dates.

Morning Herald, 6 February 1786; 15 July 1791; 24 December 1798.

Morning Post, 12 January, 24 December 1798.

Morning Post and Daily Advertiser, 15 July 1791.

Newgate Monthly Magazine, September 1824 – August 1826.

New Times, 27 March 1823.

Northern Star, 1840–46, selected dates.

Notes and Queries, 10 March 1866.

Nottingham Journal, 1824–26, selected dates.

Nottingham Review, 1820–30, selected dates.

Oracle and Daily Advertiser, 27 December 1798.

Poor Man's Guardian, 9 July 1831 – 26 December 1835.

Plymouth and Cornish Advertiser, 13 February 1823.

Preston Chronicle, 4 June 1836.

Reasoner, 1846–65, selected dates.

Republican, 27 August 1819 – 29 December 1826.

Republican, or Voice of the People, 1831–32.

Reynolds Miscellany, 14 August 1847.

Scourge For the Littleness of Great Men, 4 October 1834 – 21 January 1835.

Star, 15 July 1791.

Strand Magazine, 1891.

Sun, 27 December 1798.

The Charter, 3 February 1839.

The Crisis, 7 July, 25 August 1832.

The Movement, 30 December 1843; 3 February, 20 April 1844.

The Times, 1788–1860, selected dates.

Trewman's Exeter Flying Post or Plymouth and Cornish Advertiser, 25 January 1821.

True Briton, 28 July 1794.

White Hat, 16 October 1819.

Whitehall Evening Post, 12 July 1791; 26 July 1796; 1 February 1798.

Whittington Club Gazette, 30 March 1850 – 16 November 1850.

Working Man's Friend, 1833–34, selected dates.

Contemporary books, pamphlets, broadsides, autobiographies, and so on

Anonymous/unattributed pamphlets

A Companion to the Museum Late Sir Ashton Lever's. London: 1790.

A Concise View of the British Ladies Society for Promoting the Reformation of Female Prisoners. London: Hatchard and Son, 1839.

A Full Report of the Proceedings of a Public Meeting held at the Crown and Anchor Tavern, the Strand, on Monday, Dec. 13, 1819, to consider the propriety of adopting a plan for abstaining from the use of wine, spirits, beer, tea, coffee &c. London: Thomas Dolby, 1819.

A Letter to Both Sexes, on the Case of Mrs and Miss Carlile. London: W. Day, 1821.

Association for Preserving Liberty and Property Against Republicans and Levellers: Association papers, part 1. London, 1793.

Bridge-Street Banditti, versus The Press. Report of the trial of Mary-Anne Carlile, for publishing a New Year's address to the reformers of Great Britain. London: R. Carlile, 1821.

Considerations on the Late Elections for Westminster and Middlesex, Together with some facts relating to the House of Correction in Coldbath Fields. London: J. Hatchard, 1802.

Deed of the Arundel Buildings Estate, Middlesex, The property of His Grace the Duke of Norfolk. Surveyed and drawn by R. & H. R. Abraham architects. London, 1836.

Description of the Historical, Peristrephic or Revolving Dioramic Panorama, Now Exhibiting in Great Surrey Street, Blackfriars Road. London, 1828.

Great Meeting at the Crown and Anchor on the Inhuman Poor-Law Act. London: Mills and Sons, 1837.

Miss Macauley's Literary and Musical Regalio at the Crown and Anchor. London, [1820?].

Now Open, Patronised by their Royal Highnesses the Dukes of Cumberland and Brunswick, the Leverian Museum...Leverian Museum Broadside. London: D. Cartwright, n.d.

Objects and Rules of the National Political Union, instituted October 31st, 1831 with an address to the people of England, adopted at a general meeting of the National Political Union, held at the Crown and Anchor Tavern, Strand, Dec., 1st 1831. London: E. Wilson, 1831.

Report of a Public Meeting, Held at the Crown and Anchor Tavern, Strand, on Monday, November 15, 1847, 'to explain the principles and objects of the Peoples' International League'. London, 1847.

Report of the Trial of Mrs Carlile, on the Attorney General's Ex-Officio Information for the Protection of Tyrants: With the information and defence at large before Mr Justice Abbott and a special jury at the Guildhall. London: J. Carlile, 1821.

Report of the Trial of Mrs Susannah Wright. London: R. Carlile, 1822.

Some Account of the Parish of St Clement Danes. London: J. Wilkinson, [1796?].

Surrey and Southwark Equitable Exchange Bank, Commercial Reform Surrey and Southwark Institution late the Rotunda Equitable Exchange Bank and Bazaar, near the bridge, Black-friars Road. London, 1832.

The Abuse of Prisons, or, An Interesting and Impartial Account of the House of Correction in Cold-Bath-Fields, and the treatment of Mr Gale Jones founded upon a minute inspection of the prison and a personal interview with him. London: J. Gold, 1811.

The Case of the New House of Correction in Coldbath Fields, And that of the new prison in Clerkenwell, in the county of Middlesex, fairly and impartially stated. By a Brother Magistrate. London: P. Norbury, 1801.

The Debate in the House of Commons on March 26, 1823, on Mr Hume's presenting a petition from Mary Ann Carlile, a prisoner in Dorchester Gaol. London: T. Moses, 1823.

The Man in the Moon. London, 1820. Reprinted, Edgell Rickword. *Radical Squibs and Loyal Ripostes: Satirical pamphlets of the Regency period, 1819–1821.* Bath: Adams and Dart, 1971, pp. 83–106.

The People's Charter; With the address to the radical reformers of Great Britain and Ireland and a brief sketch of its origin. London: C. H. Elt, 1848.

The Report of the 14th Anniversary of the Polish Revolution: Celebrated at the Crown and Anchor tavern, on 29th November 1844. London: C. Fox, 1845.

The Real or Constitutional House that Jack Built. London, 1819. Reprinted, Edgell Rickword. *Radical Squibs and Loyal Ripostes: Satirical pamphlets of the Regency period, 1819–1821.* Bath: Adams and Dart, 1971, pp. 59–82.

The Secrets of the English Bastille Disclosed, To which is added a copy of the rules and orders by which the whole system is regulated, by a Middlesex magistrate. London: Rivington, 1799.

The Speech of John Gale Jones, Delivered at the British Forum, held at the Crown and Anchor in the Strand. London: R. Carlile, 1819.

The Triumphal Entry of Henry Hunt Esq. into London on Monday September 13, 1819...A full report of the speeches at the Crown and Anchor. London: Thomas Dolby, 1819.

Truth and Reason Against Place and Pension; Being a candid examination of the pretensions and assertions of the society held at the Crown and Anchor, and of similar associations in various parts of the metropolis. Addressed to John Reeves, Esq., and his associates. London: James Ridgway, 1793.

Ackermann, Rudolph. *Microcosm of London*. London: Ackermann, 1809.

Bamford, Samuel. *Passages in the Life of a Radical*. 1844. Reprinted. Oxford: Oxford University Press, 1984.

Bannantine, James. *Memoirs of Edward Marcus Despard*. London: James Ridgway, 1799.

Bennet, H. G. *A Letter to the Common Council and Livery of the City of London, On the abuses existing in Newgate*. Second edn. London, 1818.

Bentham, Jeremy. *Panopticon: Or, the Inspection House: Containing the idea of a new principle of construction applicable to any sort of establishment, in which persons of any description are to be kept under inspection: and in particular to penitentiary houses, prisons, houses of industry...and schools*. 1787. Reprinted. London: T. Payne, 1791.

Boyle, Humphrey. *Report of the Trial of Humphrey Boyle for Publishing an Alleged Blasphemous and Seditious Libel, As one of the shopmen of Mr Carlile*. London: R. Carlile, 1822.

Brayley, E. W. *Beauties of England and Wales, London and Middlesex*. Vol. 1. London: T. Maiden, for Vernor, Hood and Sharpe etc., 1810.

Burdett, Sir Francis. *An Impartial Statement of the Inhuman Cruelties Discovered! in the Coldbath Fields Prison*. Part 1. London: J. S. Jordan, 1800.

Burke, Edmund. *Philosophical Enquiry into the Origin of our Ideas of the Sublime and Beautiful*. 1756. Reprinted J. T. Bolton, ed. London: Routledge and Kegan Paul, 1958.

Burks, Joseph. *A Sworn Statement by J. Burks on the Severity of the Treatment of Prisoners in the House of Correction, Coldbath Fields, And a denial that he had expressed a regret for his statements on the subject. With an account of his imprisonment*. London, 1798.

Buxton, Thomas Fowell. *An Inquiry, Whether crime and misery are produced or prevented, by our present system of discipline: illustrated by descriptions of the Borough Compter, Tothill Fields and the proceedings of the Ladies Committee at Newgate*. London: John & Arthur Arch, 1818.

Carlile, Richard. *A New Year's Address to the Reformers of Great Britain*. London: R. Carlile, 1821.

Carlile, Richard. *Jail Jottings (1820–1825); With an introductory account of Carlile's mock trial for blasphemy and his speech from the dock*. Guy Aldred, ed. London: Bakunin Press, 1913.

Cartwright, F. D. (ed.). *The Life and Correspondence of Major Cartwright*. 2 vols. 1826. Reprinted. New York: A. M. Kelley, 1969.

Chesterton, George Laval. *Revelations of Prison Life*. 1856. Reprinted. New York: Garland, 1984.

Cobbett, William. *Eleven Lectures on the French and Belgic Revolutions, and English Boroughmongering: Delivered in the Theatre on the Rotunda, Blackfriars Bridge*. London: W. Strange, 1830.

Cobbett, William. *The Autobiography of William Cobbett: The progress of a plough-boy to a seat in Parliament*. 1833. Reprinted. William Reitzel (ed.). London: Faber, 1967.

Collingwood, Francis and John Woollams. *Universal Cook, and City and Country Housekeeper*. London: J. Scatchard & J. Whitaker, 1792.

Cunningham, Peter. *Hand Book of London*. London: Murray, 1850.

Davenport, Allen. *The Life and Literary Pursuits of Allen Davenport...Written by himself*. 1845. Reprinted. Malcolm Chase (ed.). Hants, UK: Scolar Press, 1994.

Dickens, Charles. 'A Visit to Newgate'. In *Sketches by Boz*. London: Chapman & Hall, 1877.

Dixon, Hepworth. *The London Prisons: With an account of the more distinguished persons who have been confined in them*. London, 1850. Reprinted. New York: Garland Publishing, 1995.

Eaton, Daniel Isaac. *Extortions and Abuses of Newgate*. London, 1813. Reprinted in *Newgate in Revolution: An anthology of radical prison literature in the age of revolution*. Michael Davis, Iain McCalman and Christina Parolin, eds. London: Continuum, 2005, pp. 145–66.

Ella, Anthony. *Visits to the Leverian Museum*. London: Tabart & Co., 1805.

Erskine, Thomas. *Declaration of the Friends of the Liberty of the Press, Assembled at the Crown and Anchor Tavern, Saturday, January 19, 1793.* London: J. Ridgway & H. D. Symonds, 1793.

Gillray, James. *The Works of James Gillray from the Original Plates, With the addition of many subjects not before collected.* London: H. G. Bohn, [1830?].

Gordon, Charles. *The Old Bailey and Newgate.* London: T. F. Unwin, 1902.

Grant, James. *The Great Metropolis.* Vol. 2. London: Saunders & Otley, 1837.

Griffiths, Arthur. *The Chronicles of Newgate.* London: Chapman and Hall, 1884.

Hamilton, J. A. *The Life of Daniel O'Connell.* London: W. H. Allen, 1888.

Holcroft, Thomas. *Memoirs of the Late Thomas Holcroft.* William Hazlitt (ed.), vol. 1. London: Longman, Hurst, Rees, Orme and Brown, 1816.

Holyoake, George J. *The Life and Character of Henry Hetherington.* London: J. Watson, 1849.

Holyoake, George J. *The Life and Character of Richard Carlile.* London: J. Watson, 1849.

Holyoake, George J. *The Last Days of Mrs Emma Martin.* London: J. Watson, 1851.

Holyoake, George J. *Life of Holyoake: Sixty years of an agitator's life.* London: T. Fisher Unwin, 1900.

Hone, William. *The Political House that Jack Built.* London, 1819. Reprinted, Edgell Rickword. *Radical Squibs and Loyal Ripostes: Satirical pamphlets of the Regency period, 1819–1821.* Bath: Adams and Dart, 1971, pp. 35–58.

Hone, William. *The Man in the Moon.* London, 1820. Reprinted, Edgell Rickword. *Radical Squibs and Loyal Ripostes: Satirical pamphlets of the Regency period, 1819–1821.* Bath: Adams and Dart, 1971, pp. 83–98.

Howard, John. *The State of the Prisons in England and Wales, With preliminary observations, and an account of some foreign prisons.* London: William Eyres, 1777.

Hudson, J. W. *A History of Adult Education.* 1851. Reprinted. New York: A. M. Kelley, 1969.

Hughes, Rev. Rice. *A Letter on the Meeting at the Crown and Anchor Tavern 14th July 1791; For the purpose of celebrating the anniversary of the Revolution in France, addressed to the patrons and stewards of that meeting*. London: W. Woodfall, 1791.

Hunt, Henry. *Memoirs of Henry Hunt, Esq., Written by himself in his majesty's jail at Ilchester*. 3 vols. London: Thomas Dolby, 1820.

Hunt, Leigh. *The Correspondence of Leigh Hunt, Edited by his Eldest Son*. Thornton Leigh Hunt (ed.), 2 vols. London: Smith, Elder and Co., 1862.

Jones, B. B. 'The Peoples' First Struggle for Free Speech and Writing'. *The Reasoner*. 5 June 1859, pp. 178–9.

Leeds, W. H. *Illustrations of the Public Buildings of London: With historical and descriptive accounts of each edifice*. Vol. 2. Second edn. London: John Weale, Architectural Library, 1838.

Linton, William J. *James Watson: A memoir of the days of the fight for a free press in England and of the agitation for the People's Charter*. 1879. Reprinted. New York: A. M. Kelley, 1971.

Lloyd, Thomas. 'Impositions and Abuses in the Management of the Jail of Newgate'. London, 1794. Reprinted in *Newgate in Revolution: An anthology of radical prison literature in the age of revolution*. Michael Davis, Iain McCalman and Christina Parolin, eds. London: Continuum, 2005, pp. 69–79.

Lovett, William. *The Life and Struggles of William Lovett, In his pursuit of bread, knowledge and freedom*. London: Trübner & Co., 1876.

Macauley, Eliza. *Autobiographical Memoir of Miss Macauley*. London: Charles Fox, 1834 and 1835.

Martin, Emma. *A Funeral Sermon Occasioned by the Death of Richard Carlile*. London: J. Watson, 1843.

Mayhew, Henry and John Binny. *The Criminal Prisons of London and Scenes of Prison Life*. London: Griffin, 1862.

Middleton, Charles. *Plans, Elevations and Sections of a House of Correction, for the Country of Middlesex; Intended to be erected in Cold Bath Fields, in the Parish of St James's, Clerkenwell*. London: John Rider, 1787.

Neild, James. *State of the Prisons in England, Scotland and Wales...Together with some useful documents, observations, and remarks, adapted to explain the conditions of prisoners in general*. London: John Nichols and Son, 1812.

Patmore, Peter George. *My Friends and Acquaintance: Being memorials, mind-portraits, and personal recollections of deceased celebrities of the nineteenth century: with selections from their unpublished letters*. London: Saunders and Otley, 1854.

Place, Francis. *The Autobiography of Francis Place, 1771–1854*. Mary Thale, ed. Cambridge: Cambridge University Press, 1972.

Porson, Professor [Southey and Coleridge]. *The Devil's Walk, by Professor Porson*. London: Marsh and Miller, 1830.

Prentice, Archibald. *A History of the Anti-Corn Law League*. London: W. & F. G. Cash, 1853.

Sheridan, Richard Brinsley. *Substance of the Speech of the Late Right Honourable Richard Brinsley Sheridan at a Meeting of the Electors of the City of Westminster, At the Crown and Anchor Tavern, Sept. 18, 1806*. London: James Ridgway, 1806.

Sheridan, Richard Brinsley. *Speeches of the Late Right Honourable Richard Brinsley Sheridan*. London: Patrick Martin, 1816.

Simple, Peter. *The Horrible Cruelty of the New Poor Law, Or, A Scene in the Bath Union Bastile*. London: Miss Williams, 1837.

Stanhope, Charles, Earl. *Substance of Earl Stanhope's Speech Delivered from the Chair at a Meeting of Citizens at the Crown and Anchor, on 4th February 1795, To celebrate the happy event of the late trials* [1794 treason trials]. London: J. Burks, 1795.

Stanhope, Philip Henry, Earl. *Earl Stanhope's Speech, on the New Poor Law, At a meeting held at the Crown and Anchor tavern*. London: J. Wilson, 1837.

Stoddard, R. H. *Personal Recollections of Lamb, Hazlitt and Others*. New York: Scribner, Armstrong & Co., 1875.

Taylor, Robert. *Swing! Or who are the incendiaries?* London: R. Carlile, 1831.

Thornbury, Walter. 'The Strand (Southern Tributaries)'. *Old and New London*. Vol. 3. London: Cassell, Petter & Galpin, 1878.

Timbs, John. *Curiosities of London: Exhibiting the most rare and remarkable objects of interest in the metropolis, with nearly fifty years recollections*. London: David Bogue, 1855.

Tooke, John Horne. *The Prison Diary of John Horne Tooke*. 1794. Reprinted. A. V. Beedell and A. D. Harvey, eds. Leeds: Leeds Philosophical and Literary Society, 1995.

Towers, Joseph. *Remarks on the Conduct, Principles, and Publications, of the Association at the Crown and Anchor, in the Strand, For preserving liberty and property against republicans and levellers*. London: T. Evans, 1793.

Vizetelly, Henry. *Glances Back through Seventy Years: Autobiographical and other reminiscences*. Vol. 1. London, 1893.

Wakefield, Edward Gibbon. *Householders in Danger of the Populace*. London: Effingham Wilson, 1831.

Wheatley, H. P. *London Past and Present*. London: J. Murray, 1891.

Wilkinson, G. T. *An Authentic History of the Cato Street Conspiracy*. London: Thomas Kelly, 1820.

Wright, Thomas. *Caricature History of the Georges*. London: John Camden Hotten, 1868.

Yorke, Henry Redhead. *These are the Times that Try Men's Souls!: A letter to John Frost, a prisoner in Newgate*. London: D. I. Eaton, 1793.

Secondary sources

Adburgham, Alison. *A Radical Aristocrat: The Rt Hon. Sir William Molesworth, Bart., PC, MP of Pencarrow and his wife Andalusia*. Cornwall: Tabb House, 1990.

Alberti, Samuel J. M. 'Owning and Collecting Natural Objects in Nineteenth-Century Britain'. In *From Private to Public: Natural collections and museums*. Marco Beretta, ed. Sagamore Beach, Mass.: Science History Publications, 2005, pp. 141–54.

Aldred, Guy. *Richard Carlile, Agitator: His life and times*. London: Pioneer Press, 1923.

Alexander, D. *Richard Newton and English Caricature in the 1790s*. Manchester: Manchester University Press, 1998.

Altick, Richard. *The English Common Reader: A social history of the mass reading public 1800–1900*. Chicago: University of Chicago Press, 1957.

Altick, Richard. *The Shows of London*. Cambridge, Mass.: Belknap Press, 1978.

Andrew, Donna T., ed. *London Debating Societies, 1776–9*. London: London Record Society, 1994.

Arnold, Dana, ed. *The Metropolis and its Images: Constructing identities for London, c.1750–1950*. Oxford: Blackwell, 1999.

Babington, Anthony. *The English Bastille: A history of Newgate Gaol and prison conditions in Britain 1188–1902*. London: Macdonald & Co., 1971.

Baer, Marc. *Theatre and Disorder in Late Georgian London*. Oxford: Clarendon Press, 1992.

Baer, Marc. 'Political Dinners in Whig, Radical and Tory Westminster, 1780–1880'. *Parliamentary History*. Vol. 24, no. 1 (2005), pp. 183–206.

Bailey, Peter. 'Will the Real Bill Banks Please Stand Up? Towards a role analysis of mid-Victorian working class respectability'. *Journal of Social History*. Vol. 12 (1977), pp. 336–53.

Bailey, Peter. 'Conspiracies of Meaning: Music-hall and the knowingness of popular culture'. *Past & Present*. Vol. 144 (1994), pp. 138–70.

Bailey, Victor. 'The Fabrication of Deviance: "Dangerous classes" and "criminal classes" in Victorian England'. In *Protest and Survival: The historical experience: essays for E. P. Thompson*. John Rule and Robert Malcolmson, eds. London: Merlin Press, 1993, pp. 221–56.

Banerji, Christiane and Diana Donald. *Gillray Observed: The earliest account of his caricatures in 'London und paris'*. Cambridge, Cambridge University Press, 1999.

Barker, C. 'A Theatre for the People'. In *Nineteenth Century British Theatre*. Kenneth Richards and Peter Thompson, eds. London: Metheun, 1971, pp. 3–24.

Barrell, John. '"An Entire Change of Performances?" The politicisation of theatre and the theatricalisation of politics in the mid-1790s'. *Lumen*. Vol. 17 (1998), pp. 11–50.

Barrell, John. *Imagining the King's Death: Figurative treason, fantasies of regicide, 1793–1796*. Oxford: Oxford University Press, 2000.

Barrell, John. 'Coffee-House Politicians'. *Journal of British Studies*. Vol. 43 (2004), pp. 206–32.

Barrell, John. 'London and the London Corresponding Society'. In *Romantic Metropolis: The urban scene of British culture, 1780–1840*. James Chandler and Kevin Gilmartin, eds. Cambridge: Cambridge University Press, 2005, pp. 85–112.

Barry, Jonathan. 'Bourgeois Collectivism? Urban association and the middling sort'. In *The Middling Sort of People*. Jonathan Barry and Christopher Brooks, eds. London: Macmillan, 1994, pp. 84–112.

Belchem, John. *'Orator' Hunt: Henry Hunt and English working-class radicalism*. Oxford: Clarendon Press, 1985.

Belchem, John. *Popular Radicalism in Nineteenth-Century Britain*. New York: St Martin's Press, 1996.

Benchimol, Alex. 'Remaking the Romantic Period: Cultural materialism, cultural studies and the radical public sphere'. *Textual Practice*. Vol. 19, no. 1 (2005), pp. 51–70.

Bender, John. *Imagining the Penitentiary: Fiction and the architecture of mind in eighteenth-century England*. Chicago: University of Chicago Press, 1987.

Bennett, Tony. *The Birth of the Museum: History, theory, politics*. London: Routledge, 1995.

Bindman, David. *The Shadow of the Guillotine: Britain and the French Revolution*. London: British Museum Publications, 1989.

Bindman, David. 'Prints'. In *An Oxford Companion to the Romantic Age*. Iain McCalman, ed. Oxford: Oxford University Press, 2001, pp. 207–13.

Birrell, Augustine. *William Hazlitt*. London: Macmillan and Co., 1922.

Bloch, Ruth H. 'Inside and Outside the Public Sphere'. *The William and Mary Quarterly*. Vol. 62, no. 1 (2005), pp. 99–106.

Blunden, E., ed. *The Autobiography of Leigh Hunt*. Oxford: Oxford University Press, 1928.

Böker, Uwe. 'Institutionalised Rules of Discourse and the Courtroom as a Site of the Public Sphere'. In *Sites of Discourse—Public and private spheres—legal culture*, Uwe Böker and Julie A. Hibbard, eds. Amsterdam, NY: Rodopi, 2002, pp. 35–66.

Böker, Uwe. 'The Prison and the Penitentiary as Sites of Public Counter-Discourse'. In *Sites of Discourse—Public and private spheres—legal culture*. Uwe Böker and Julie A. Hibbard, eds. Amsterdam, NY: Rodopi, 2002, pp. 211–47.

Booth, Michael R. *English Melodrama*. London: Herbert Jenkins, 1965.

Booth, Michael. *Nineteenth Century Plays*. Vol. 1. Oxford: Clarendon Press, 1969.

Borden, Iain, Joe Kerr, Alicia Pivaro and Jane Rendell, eds. *Strangely Familiar: Narratives of architecture in the city*. London: Routledge, 1996.

Boxer, Marilyn and Jean Quataert. *Connecting Spheres: Women in the Western world, 1500 to the present*. Oxford: Oxford University Press, 1987.

Brett, Peter. 'Political Dinners in Early Nineteenth-Century Britain: Platform, meeting place and battleground'. *History*. Vol. 81, no. 264 (1996), pp. 527–52.

Brewer, John. *Party Ideology and Popular Politics at the Accession of George III*. Cambridge: Cambridge University Press, 1976.

Brewer, John. 'Theatre and Counter-Theatre in Georgian Politics: The mock elections at Garrat'. *History Today*. Vol. 33 (1983), pp. 14–23.

Brewer, John. *The Common People and Politics, 1750–1790s*. Cambridge: Chadwyck Healy, 1986.

Brewer, John. *The Pleasures of the Imagination: English culture in the eighteenth century*. London: Harper Collins, 1997.

Brewer, Luther A. *My Leigh Hunt Library*. New York: B. Franklin, 1970.

Brodie, Marc. 'Free Trade and Cheap Theatre: Sources of politics for the nineteenth-century London poor'. *Social History*. Vol. 28, no. 3 (2003), pp. 346–60.

Brown, Frances. *Joanna Southcott: The woman clothed with the Sun*. Cambridge: Lutterworth, 2002.

Brundage, Anthony. *The English Poor Laws 1700–1930*. New York: Palgrave, 2002.

Bryans, Shane. *Prison Governors: Managing prisons in a time of change*. Cullompton: Willan Publishing, 2007.

Buchanan-Brown, John. *The Book Illustrations of George Cruikshank*. Newton Abbot: David & Charles, 1980.

Bugg, John. 'Close Confinement: John Thelwall and the Romantic prison'. *European Romantic Review*. Vol. 20, no. 1 (2009), pp. 37–56.

Bush, M. L. *What is Love? Richard Carlile's philosophy of sex*. London: Verso, 1998.

Bush, M. L. 'The Women at Peterloo: The impact of female reform on the Manchester meeting of 16 August 1819'. *History*. Vol. 89, no. 2 (2004), pp. 209–32.

Bush, M. L. *The Casualties of Peterloo*. Lancaster: Carnegie, 2005.

Byrne, Richard. *Prisons and Punishments of London*. London: Grafton, 1992.

Calhoun, Craig. *The Question of Class Struggle: Social foundations of popular radicalism during the Industrial Revolution*. Chicago: University of Chicago Press, 1982.

Calhoun, Craig. 'Introduction: Habermas and the public sphere'. In *Habermas and the Public Sphere*. Cambridge, Mass.: MIT Press, 1992.

Campbell, Theophila Carlile. *The Battle for the Freedom of the Press as Told in the Story of the Life of Richard Carlile*. London: A. & H. B. Bonner, 1899.

Caretta, Vincent. *The Snarling Muse: Verbal and visual satire from Pope to Churchill*. Philadelphia, 1983.

Carlson, Julie A. 'Hazlitt and the Sociability of Theatre'. In *Romantic Sociability: Social networks and literary culture in Britain, 1770–1840*. Gillian Russell and Clara Tuite, eds. Cambridge: Cambridge University Press, 2002, pp. 145–65.

Carnell, Geoffrey. 'The Surrey Institution and its Successor'. *Adult Education*. Vol. 26 (1953), pp. 197–208.

Chalkin, C. W. 'The Reconstruction of London's Prisons, 1770–1799: An aspect of the growth of Georgian London'. *London Journal*. Vol. 9, no. 1 (1983), pp. 21–34.

Chalus, Elaine. '"That Epidemical Madness": Women and electoral politics in the late eighteenth century'. In *Gender in Eighteenth Century England: Roles, representations and responsibilities*. Hannah Barker and Elaine Chalus, eds. London: Addison Wesley Longman, 1997, pp. 151–78.

Chalus, Elaine. 'Elite Women, Social Politics, and the Political World of Late Eighteenth-Century England'. *Historical Journal*. Vol. 43, no. 3 (2000), pp. 669–97.

Chancellor, E. B. *The Annals of the Strand: Topographical and historical*. London: Chapman & Hall, 1912.

Chancellor, Valerie E. *The Political Life of Joseph Hume, 1777–1855*. London: V. Chancellor, c. 1986.

Claeys, Gregory. 'Political Economy and Popular Education: Thomas Hodgskin and the London Mechanics Institute, 1823–8'. In *Radicalism and Revolution in Britain, 1775–1848*. Michael T. Davis, ed. London: Macmillan, 2000, pp. 157–75.

Clark, Anna. 'The Queen Caroline Affair and the Sexual Politics of Popular Culture in London, 1820'. *Representations*. Vol. 31 (1990), pp. 47–68.

Clark, Anna. *Struggle for the Breeches: Gender and the making of the British working class*. Berkeley: University of California Press, 1995.

Clark, Anna. 'Class, Gender and British Elections, 1794–1818'. In *Unrespectable Radicals? Popular politics in the age of reform*. Michael T. Davis and Paul A. Pickering, eds. Aldershot: Ashgate, 2008, pp. 107–24.

Clark, Peter. *The English Alehouse: A social history 1200–1830*. London: Longman, 1983.

Clark, Peter. *British Clubs and Associations 1580–1800: The origins of an associational world*. Oxford: Oxford University Press, 2000.

Coburn, Kathleen H. 'S. T. Coleridge's Philosophical Lectures of 1818–19'. *Review of English Studies*. Vol. 10, no. 40 (1934), pp. 428–37.

Cole, G. D. H. *The Life of William Cobbett*. London: Collins, 1924.

Cole, G. D. H. *Richard Carlile, 1790–1843*. London: Fabian Society Pamphlets, 1942.

Colley, Linda. *Britons Forging the Nation 1707–1837*. New Haven, Conn.: Yale University Press, 1992.

Colvin, H. M. *A Biographical Dictionary of British Architects*. Fourth edn. New Haven, Conn.: Yale University Press, 2008.

Connell, Philip. *Romanticism, Economics and the Question of 'Culture'*. Oxford: Oxford University Press, 2005.

Connor, Clifford D. *Colonel Despard: The life and times of an Anglo-Irish rebel*. Conshohocken: Combined Publishing, 2000.

Conolly, Leonard. *The Censorship of English Drama, 1737–1824*. San Marino, Calif.: Huntington Library, 1976.

Cook, Hera. *The Long Sexual Revolution: English women, sex and contraception 1800–1975*. Oxford: Oxford University Press, 2005.

Couture, Tony. 'Feminist Criticisms of Habermas's Ethics and Politics'. *Dialogue*. Vol. 34, no. 2 (1995), pp. 259–79.

Cowan, Brian. 'What was Masculine about the Public Sphere? Gender and the coffeehouse milieu in post-Restoration England'. *History Workshop Journal*. Vol. 51 (2001), pp. 127–57.

Cowan, Brian. 'Mr Spectator and the Coffeehouse Public Sphere'. *Eighteenth-Century Studies*. Vol. 37, no. 3 (2004), pp. 345–66.

Cowan, Brian. *The Social Life of Coffee: The emergence of the British coffeehouse*. New Haven, Conn.: Yale University Press, 2005.

Cowan, Brian. 'Publicity and Privacy in the History of the British Coffeehouse'. *History Compass*. Vol. 5, no. 4 (2007), pp. 1180–213.

Cox, Jeffrey. *Poetry and Politics in the Cockney School: Shelley, Hunt, and their circle*. Cambridge: Cambridge University Press, 1998.

Davis, Michael T. '"Good for the Public Example": Daniel Issac Eaton, prosecution, punishment and recognition, 1793–1812'. In *Radicalism and Revolution in Britain, 1775–1848*. Michael T. Davis, ed. London: Macmillan, 2000, pp. 110–32.

Davis, Michael T., ed. *London Corresponding Society, 1792–1799*. 6 vols. London: Pickering & Chatto, 2002.

Davis, Michael T. '"I Can Bear Punishment": Daniel Issac Eaton, radical culture and the rule of law, 1792–1812'. *Criminal Justice History*. Vol. 18 (2003), pp. 89–106.

Davis, Michael T. 'Le Radicalisme Anglaise et la Revolution Française'. *Annals Historiques de la Revolution Française*. Vol. 342 (2005), pp. 73–99.

Davis, Michael. T. 'The Mob Club? The London Corresponding Society and the politics of civility in the 1790s'. In *Unrespectable Radicals? Popular politics in the age of reform*. Michael T. Davis and Paul A. Pickering, eds. Aldershot: Ashgate, 2008, pp. 21–40.

Davis, Michael, Iain McCalman and Christina Parolin, eds. *Newgate in Revolution: An anthology of radical prison literature in the age of revolution*. London: Continuum, 2005.

de Certeau, Michel. *The Practice of Everyday Life*. Berkeley: University of California Press, 1984.

DeLacy, Margaret. 'Grinding Men Good? Lancashire's prisons at mid-century'. In *Policing and Punishment in Nineteenth Century Britain*. Victor Bailey, ed. London: Croom Helm, 1981, pp. 182–216.

DeLacy, Margaret. *Prison Reform in Lancashire, 1700–1850: A study in local administration*. Stanford: Stanford University Press, 1986.

Derry, John W. *Charles. Earl Grey: Aristocratic reformer*. Oxford: Blackwell, 1992.

Deveraux, Simon. 'From Sessions to Newspaper? Criminal trial reporting, the nature of crime, and the London press, 1770–1800'. *London Journal*. Vol. 32, no. 1 (2007), pp. 1–27.

Dickinson, H. T. *Caricatures and the Constitution 1760–1832*. Cambridge: Chadwyck Healy, 1986.

Dickinson, H. T., ed. *Britain and the French Revolution 1789–1815*. Basingstoke: Macmillan, 1989.

Dinwiddy, J. R. 'Sir Francis Burdett and Burdettite Radicalism'. *History*. Vol. 65 (1980), pp. 17–31.

Dinwiddy, John. *Radicalism and Reform in Britain 1780–1850*. London: Hambleton Press, 1992.

Dinwiddy, John and William Twining, eds. *Bentham: Selected writings of John Dinwiddy*. Stanford: Stanford University Press, 2004.

Dodge, L. Mara. '"One Female Prisoner is of More Trouble than Twenty Males": Women convicts in Illinois prisons, 1835–1896'. *Journal of Social History*. Vol. 32, no. 4 (1999), pp. 907–30.

Doody, Margaret Anne. 'Voices of Record: Women as witnesses and defendants in the Old Bailey Sessions Papers'. In *Representing Women: Law, literature, and feminism*. Susan S. Heinzelman and Zipporah B. Wiseman, eds. Durham, NC: Duke University Press, 1994, pp. 287–308.

Donald, Diana. *The Age of Caricature: Satirical prints in the reign of George III*. New Haven, Conn.: Yale University Press, 1996.

Drummond, Pippa. 'The Royal Society of Musicians in the Eighteenth Century'. *Music & Letters*. Vol. 59, no. 3 (1978), pp. 268–89.

Duffy, Michael. *The Englishman and the Foreigner*. Cambridge: Chadwyck Healy, 1986.

Duffy, Michael. 'William Pitt and the Origins of the Loyalist Association Movement of 1792'. *Historical Journal*. Vol. 39, no. 4 (1996), pp. 943–62.

During, Simon. '"The Temple Lives": The Lyceum and Romantic show business'. In *Romantic Metropolis: The urban scene of British culture, 1780–1840*. James Chandler and Kevin Gilmartin, eds. Cambridge: Cambridge University Press, 2005, pp. 204–26.

Eagleton, Terry. *The Function of Criticism, From the Spectator to Post-Structuralism*. London: Verso, 1984.

Eckersley, Rachel. 'Of Radical Design: John Cartwright and the redesign of the reform campaign, c.1800–1811'. *History*. Vol. 89, no. 296 (2004), pp. 560–80.

Edsall, Nicholas. *The Anti-Poor Law Movement 1834–44*. Manchester: Manchester University Press, 1971.

Eley, Geoff. 'Nations, Publics, and Political Cultures: Placing Habermas in the nineteenth century'. In *Habermas and the Public Sphere*. Craig Calhoun, ed. Cambridge, Mass.: MIT Press, 1992, pp. 289–339.

Elkin, Robert. *The Old Concert Rooms of London*. London: Arnold, 1955.

Elliot, Marianne. 'The "Despard Conspiracy" Reconsidered'. *Past & Present*, vol. 75 (1977), pp. 46–61.

Elliott, Paul. 'The Origins of the "Creative Class": Provincial urban society and socio-political marginality in Britain in the eighteenth and nineteenth centuries'. *Social History*. Vol. 28, no. 3 (2003), pp. 361–87.

Emsley, Clive. 'An Aspect of Pitt's Terror: Prosecutions for sedition during the 1790s'. *Social History*. Vol. 6 (1981), pp. 154–84.

Emsley, Clive. 'Repression, "Terror" and the Rule of Law in England during the Decade of the French Revolution'. *English Historical Review*. Vol. 100, no. 397 (1985), pp. 801–25.

Emsley, Clive. 'The Impact of the French Revolution on British Politics and Society'. In *The French Revolution and British Culture*. Ceri Crossley and Ian Small, eds. Oxford: Oxford University Press, 1989, pp. 31–62.

Emsley, Clive. *Crime and Society in England 1750–1900*. London: Longman, 1996.

Epstein, James. *The Lion of Freedom: Feargus O'Connor and the Chartist movement 1832–1842*. London: Croom Helm, 1982.

Epstein, James. *Radical Expression: Political language, ritual and symbol in England, 1790–1850*. Oxford: Oxford University Press, 1994.

Epstein, James. '"Our Real Constitution": Trial defence and radical memory in the age of revolution'. In *Re-Reading the Constitution: New narratives in the political history of England's long nineteenth century*. James Vernon, ed. Cambridge: Cambridge University Press, 1996, pp. 22–51.

Epstein, James. '"Equality and No King": Sociability and sedition: the case of John Frost'. In *Romantic Sociability: Social networks and literary culture in Britain, 1770–1840*. Gillian Russell and Clara Tuite, eds. Cambridge: Cambridge University Press, 2002, pp. 43–61.

Epstein, James. *In Practice: Studies in the language and culture of popular politics in modern Britain*. Stanford: Stanford University Press, 2003.

Evans, Jessica and Stuart Hall, eds. *Visual Culture: The reader*. London: Sage Publications, 1999.

Evans, Robin. *Fabrication of Virtue: English prison architecture, 1750–1840*. Cambridge: Cambridge University Press, 1982.

Finn, Margot. *The Character of Credit: Personal debt in English culture, 1740–1914*. Cambridge: Cambridge University Press, 2003.

Finn, Margot. 'Henry Hunt's "Peep into a Prison": The radical discontinuities of imprisonment for debt'. In *English Radicalism 1550–1850*. Glenn Burgess and Matthew Festenstein, eds. Cambridge: Cambridge University Press, 2007, pp. 191–216.

Fisher, George. 'The Birth of the Prison Retold'. *Yale Law Journal*. Vol. 104 (1995), pp. 1235–325.

Flynn, Carole Houlihan. 'Whatever Happened to the Gordon Riots?'. In *A Companion to the Eighteenth-Century English Novel and Culture*. Paula Backschreider and Catherine Ingrassia, eds. Malden, Mass.: Blackwell, 2005, pp. 459–80.

Follett, Richard. *Evangelicalism, Penal Theory and the Politics of Criminal Law Reform in England, 1808–30*. Basingstoke: Palgrave, 2001.

Forgan, Sophie. 'Context, Image and Function: A preliminary enquiry into the architecture of scientific societies'. *British Journal for the History of Science*. Vol. 19 (1986), pp. 89–113.

Foucault, Michel. *Discipline and Punish: The birth of the prison*. Trans. Alan Sheridan. London: Penguin, 1991.

Fowler, Simon. 'Pauper Bastille or Pauper Palace? Assessing the success of workhouses'. *Modern History Review*. Vol. 11, no. 3 (2000), pp. 10–13.

Fox, Adam and Daniel Wolfe, eds. *The Spoken Word: Oral culture in Britain, 1500–1850*. Manchester: Manchester University Press, 2002.

Fraser, Nancy. 'Rethinking the Public Sphere: A contribution to the critique of actually existing democracy'. *Social Text*. Nos 25–26 (1990), pp. 56–80.

Frow Ruth and Edmund Frow. *Political Women, 1800–1850*. London: Pluto Press, 1989.

Fulcher, Jonathon. 'Gender, Politics and Class in the Early Nineteenth-Century English Reform Movement'. *Historical Research*. Vol. LXVII (1994), pp. 57–74.

Fulford, Roger. *Samuel Whitbread, 1764–1815: A study in opposition*. London: Macmillan, 1967.

Fuller, Catherine, ed. *The Old Radical: Representations of Jeremy Bentham*. London: University College London, 1998.

Ganguly, Debjani and Mandy Thomas. 'Cultural Politics and Iconography: An introduction'. *Humanities Research*. Vol. XI, no. 1 (2004), pp. 1–7.

Gatrell, V. A. C. *The Hanging Tree: Execution and the English people 1770–1868*. Oxford: Oxford University Press, 1994.

Gatrell, V. A. C. *City of Laughter: Sex and satire in eighteenth-century London*. New York: Walker & Co., 2007.

George, M. D. *Catalogue of Political and Personal Satires Preserved in the Department of Prints and Drawings in the British Museum*. London: The Trustees of the British Museum, 1978.

Gilmartin, Kevin. 'Popular Radicalism and the Public Sphere'. *Studies in Romanticism*. Vol. 33, no. 4 (1994), pp. 549–57.

Gilmartin, Kevin. *Print Politics: The press and radical opposition in early nineteenth-century England*. New York: Cambridge University Press, 1996.

Gilmartin, Kevin. 'In the Theater of Counterrevolution: Loyalist association and conservative opinion in the 1790s'. *Journal of British Studies*. Vol. 41 (2002), pp. 291–328.

Gleadle, Kathryn. *The Early Feminists: Radical Unitarians and the emergence of the women's rights movement, 1831–51*. New York: St Martin's Press, 1995.

Gleadle, Kathryn. 'British Women and Radical Politics in the Late Nonconformist Enlightenment, c.1780–1830'. In *Women, Privilege, and Power: British politics, 1750 to the present*. Amanda Vickery, ed. Stanford: Stanford University Press, 2001, pp. 123–51.

Godfrey, Christopher. 'The Chartist Prisoners, 1839–41'. *International Review of Social History*. Vol. 24, no. 2 (1979), pp. 189–236.

Grass, Sean. *The Self in the Cell: Narrating the Victorian prisoner*. London: Routledge, 2003.

Gregory, Derek and John Urry, eds. *Social Relations and Spatial Structure*. Basingstoke: Macmillan, 1985.

Grimes, Kyle. 'Spreading the Radical Word: The circulation of William Hone's 1817 liturgical parodies'. In *Radicalism and Revolution in Britain, 1775–1848*. Michael T. Davis, ed. London: Macmillan, 2000, pp. 143–56.

Grugel, Lee E. *George Jacob Holyoake: A study in the evolution of a Victorian radical*. Philadelphia: Porcupine Press, 1976.

Habermas, Jürgen. *The Structural Transformation of the Public Sphere: An inquiry into a category of bourgeois society*. Trans. Thomas Burger. Cambridge, Mass.: MIT Press, 1989.

Habermas, Jürgen. 'The Public Sphere: An encyclopedia article'. In *Critical Theory and Society*. Stephen Eric Bronner and Douglas Kellner, eds. New York: Routledge, 1989.

Hadley, David. 'Public Lectures and Private Societies: Expounding literature and the arts in Romantic London'. In *English Romanticism: Preludes and postludes*. Donald Schoonmaker and John A. Alford, eds. Michigan: East Lansing Colleagues, 1993.

Hall, Catherine. 'Private Persons Versus Public Someones: Class, gender and politics in England, 1780–1850'. In *Language, Gender and Childhood*. Carolyn Steedman, Cathy Urwin and Valerie Walkerdine, eds. London: Routledge & Kegan Paul, 1985, pp. 10–33.

Hall, Catherine. *White, Male and Middle-Class: Explorations in feminism and history*. Oxford: Polity Press, 1992.

Hamburger, Joseph. *James Mill and the Art of Revolution*. New Haven, Conn.: Yale University Press, 1963.

Harden, J. David. 'Liberty Caps and Liberty Trees'. *Past & Present*. No. 146 (1995), pp. 66–102.

Hargreaves-Mawdsley, William. *The English Della Cruscans and Their Time, 1783–1828*. The Hague: M. Nijhoff, 1967.

Harling, Philip. 'Leigh Hunt's Examiner and the Language of Patriotism'. *English Historical Review*. Vol. 111 (1996), pp. 1159–81.

Harling, Philip. 'The Duke of York Affair 1809 and the Complexities of War-Time Patriotism'. *Historical Journal*. Vol. 39, no. 4 (1996), pp. 963–84.

Harling, Philip. 'The Law of Libel and the Limits of Repression, 1790–1832'. *Historical Journal*. Vol. 44, no. 1 (2001), pp. 107–34.

Harling, Philip. 'Parliament, the State, and "Old Corruption"'. In *Rethinking the Age of Reform, Britain 1780–1850*. Arthur Burns and Joanna Innes, eds. Cambridge: Cambridge University Press, 2003, pp. 98–113.

Harris, Roy. *Saussure and his Interpreters*. New York: New York University Press, 2001.

Harrison, Brian. 'A Genealogy of Reform in Modern Britain'. In *Anti-Slavery, Religion and Reform: Essays in memory of Roger Anstey*. Christine Bolt and Seymour Drescher, eds. Folkestone: Dawson, 1980, pp. 119–48.

Harrison, J. F. C. *The Second Coming: Popular millenarianism, 1780–1850*. New Brunswick, NJ: Rutgers University Press, 1979.

Hay, William A. 'Henry Brougham and the 1818 Westmorland Election: A study in provincial opinion and the opening of constituency politics'. *Albion*. Vol. 36, no. 1 (2004), pp. 28–51.

Haywood, Ian. *The Revolution in Popular Literature: Print, politics and the people, 1790–1860*. Cambridge: Cambridge University Press, 2004.

Heidegger, Martin. 'Building Dwelling Thinking'. *Basic Writings*. London: Routledge & Kegan Paul, 1978.

Herbst, Susan. *Politics at the Margin: Historical studies of public expression outside the mainstream*. Cambridge: Cambridge University Press, 1994.

Hill, Draper. *Mr Gillray, the Caricaturist: A biography*. London: Phaidon Press, 1965.

Hill, Jonathon. *Occupying Architecture: Between the architect and the user*. London: Routledge, 1988.

Himmelfarb, Gertrude. 'The Haunted House of Jeremy Bentham'. In *Victorian Minds*. London: Weidenfeld and Nicholson, 1968.

Hobsbawm, E. J. *Labouring Men: Studies in the history of labour*. London: Weidenfeld, 1968.

Hollingsworth, Keith. *The Newgate Novel 1830–47: Bulwer, Ainsworth, Dickens, & Thackeray*. Detroit: Wayne State University Press, 1963.

Hollis, Patricia. *The Pauper Press: A study in working-class radicalism of the 1830s*. Oxford: Oxford University Press, 1970.

Holmes, Rachel. *The Hottentot Venus: The life and death of Saartjie Baartman: born 1789—buried 2002*. London: Bloomsbury, 2007.

Hone, J. Ann. *For the Cause of Truth: Radicalism in London 1796–1821*. Oxford: Clarendon Press, 1982.

Hoopes, James, ed. *Peirce on Signs: Writings on semiotics*. Chapel Hill: University of North Carolina Press, 1991.

Hopkins, Eric. *Working-Class Self Help in Nineteenth-Century England*. London: University College London Press, 1995.

Hopkins, James. *A Woman to Deliver Her People: Joanna Southcott and English millenarianism in an era of revolution*. Austin: University of Texas Press, 1982.

Howell, P. 'Public Space and the Public Sphere: Political theory and the historical geography of modernity'. *Society and Space*. Vol. 11 (1993), pp. 303–22.

Huch, Ronald K. and Paul R. Ziegler. *Joseph Hume, the People's MP*. Philadelphia: Diane Publishing, 1985.

Hunt, Lynn. *Politics, Culture, and Class in the French Revolution*. Berkeley: University of California Press, 1984.

Hunt, Tamara. *Defining John Bull: Caricature, politics and national identity in late Georgian England*. Aldershot: Ashgate, 2003.

Ignatieff, Michael. *A Just Measure of Pain: The penitentiary in the Industrial Revolution, 1750–1850*. New York: Columbia University Press, 1980.

Ignatieff, Michael. 'State, Civil Society and Total Institutions: A critique of recent social histories of punishment'. In *Social Control and the State*. Stanley Cohen and Andrew Scull, eds. New York: St Martin's Press, 1983, pp. 75–105.

Ingraham, Barton L. *Political Crime in Europe: A comparative study of France, Germany and England*. Berkeley: University of California Press, 1979.

Inkster, Ian. *Scientific Culture and Urbanisation in Industrialising Britain*. Aldershot: Ashgate, 1997.

Innes, Joanna. 'The King's Bench Prison in the Later Eighteenth Century: Law, authority and order in a London debtors' prison'. In *An Ungovernable People: The English and their law in the seventeenth and eighteenth centuries*. John Brewer and John Styles, eds. London: Hutchinson, 1980, pp. 251–387.

Innes, Joanna and John Styles. 'The Crime Wave: Recent writing on crime and criminal justice in eighteenth-century England'. In *Rethinking Social History: English society 1570–1920 and its interpretation*. A. Wilson, ed. Manchester: Manchester University Press, 1993, pp. 201–65.

Jackson, T. A. *Trials of British Freedom*. London, 1940.

James, Louis. 'Taking Melodrama Seriously: Theatre, and nineteenth-century studies'. *History Workshop Journal*. No. 3 (1977), pp. 151–8.

Jay, Mike. *The Unfortunate Colonel Despard*. London: Bantam Books, 2004.

Johnson, David. *Regency Revolution: The case of Arthur Thistlewood*. Compton Chamberlayne, UK: Compton Russell, 1974.

Johnson, Richard. '"Really Useful Knowledge": Radical education and working-class culture, 1790–1848'. In *Working Class Culture: Studies in history and theory*. John Clarke, C. Critcher and Richard Johnson, eds. London: Hutchison, 1979, pp. 75–102.

Jones, David. 'Women and Chartism'. *History*. Vol. 68, no. 224 (1983), pp. 1–21.

Kalman, Harold D. 'Newgate Prison'. *Architectural History*. Vol. 12 (1969), pp. 50–61 and pp. 108–12.

Karr, David. '"Thoughts that Flash like Lightning": Thomas Holcroft, radical theater, and the production of meaning in 1790s London'. *Journal of British Studies*. Vol. 40, no. 3 (2001), p. 327.

Keane, Angela. 'Richard Carlile's Working Women: Selling books, politics, sex and *The Republican*'. *Literature & History*. Vol. 15, no. 2 (2006), pp. 20–34.

Kent, Christopher. 'The Whittington Club: A bohemian experiment in middle class social reform'. *Victorian Studies*. Vol. 18, no. 1 (1974), pp. 31–55.

King, J. C. H. 'New Evidence for the Contents of the Leverian Museum'. *Journal of the History of Collections*. Vol. 8 (1996), pp. 167–86.

King, Peter. *Crime, Justice, and Discretion in England 1740–1820*. Oxford: Oxford University Press, 2000.

Kirk, Neville. *The Growth of Working Class Reformism in Mid-Victorian England*. London: Croom Helm, 1985.

Kirk, Neville. *Change, Continuity and Class: Labour in British society, 1850–1920*. Manchester: Manchester University Press, 1998.

Klancher, Jon. *The Making of English Reading Audiences, 1790–1832*. Madison: University of Wisconsin Press, 1987.

Knight, Roger. *The Pursuit of Victory: The life and achievement of Horatio Nelson*. Boulder, Colo.: Westview Press, 2007.

Knott, John. *Popular Opposition to the 1834 Poor Law*. London: Croom Helm, 1986.

Koditschek, Theodore. 'The Gendering of the British Working Class'. *Gender & History*. Vol. 9, no. 2 (1997), pp. 333–63.

Kohn, Margaret. *Radical Space: Building the house of the people*. London: Cornell University Press, 2003.

Kurzer, Frederick. 'A History of the Surrey Institution'. *Annals of Science*. Vol. 57 (2000), pp. 109–41.

Landes, Joan. *Women and the Public Sphere: In the age of the French Revolution*. Ithaca, NY: Cornell University Press, 1988.

Landes, Joan. *Women and the Public Sphere in the Age of Enlightenment*. Ithaca, NY: Cornell University Press, 1994.

Landes, Joan. 'The Public and the Private Sphere: A feminist reconsideration'. In *Feminists Read Habermas: Gendering the subject of discourse*. A. Johanna Meehan, ed. New York: Routledge, 1995.

Large, David. 'William Lovett'. In *Pressure from Without in Early Victorian England*. Patricia Hollis, ed. London: E. Arnold, 1974, pp. 105–30.

Latham, Jackie. *Search for A New Eden, James Pierrepont Greaves 1777–1842: The sacred socialist and his followers*. Madison, NJ: Fairleigh Dickinson University Press, 1999.

Latham, Jackie. 'The Political and the Personal: The radicalism of Sophia Chichester and Georgiana Fletcher Welch'. *Women's History Review*. Vol. 8, no. 3 (1999), pp. 469–87.

Latham, Jackie. 'The Bradleys of Birmingham: The unorthodox family of "Michael Field"'. *History Workshop Journal*. Vol. 55 (2003), pp. 189–91.

Lavers, Annette. *Roland Barthes, Structuralism and After*. Cambridge, Mass.: Harvard University Press, 1982.

Lefebvre, Henri. *The Production of Space*. Trans. D. Nicholson-Smith. 1974. Second edn. Oxford: Blackwell, 1996.

Lindebaugh, Peter. *The London Hanged: Crime and civil society in the eighteenth century*. Second edn. London: Verso, 2003.

Lobban, Michael. 'From Seditious Libel to Unlawful Assembly: Peterloo and the changing face of political crime, c.1770–1820'. *Oxford Journal of Legal Studies*. Vol. 10, no. 3 (1990), pp. 307–52.

Lobban, Michael. 'Henry Brougham and Law Reform'. *English Historical Review*. Vol. 115 (2000), pp. 1184–215.

LoPatin, Nancy. *Political Unions, Popular Politics and the Great Reform Act of 1832*. Basingstoke: Macmillan, 1999.

Lyons, H. G. 'The Anniversary Dinner'. *Notes and Records of the Royal Society of London*. Vol. 1, no. 2 (1938), pp. 96–103.

McCalman, Iain. 'Females, Feminism and Free Love in an Early Nineteenth Century Radical Movement'. *Labour History*. No. 38 (1980), pp. 1–25.

McCalman, Iain. 'Ultra-Radicalism and Convivial Debating Clubs in London 1795–1838'. *English Historical Review*. Vol. 102, no. 403 (1987), pp. 309–33.

McCalman, Iain. *Radical Underworld: Prophets, revolutionaries and pornographers in London, 1795–1840*. Cambridge: Cambridge University Press, 1988.

McCalman, Iain. 'Popular Irreligion in Early Victorian England: Infidel preachers and radical theatricality in 1830s London'. In *Religion and Irreligion in Victorian Society*. R. W. Davis and R. J. Helmstadter, eds. London: Routledge, 1992, pp. 51–67.

McCalman, Iain. 'Newgate in Revolution: Radical enthusiasm and Romantic counterculture'. *Eighteenth Century Life*. Vol. 22 (1998), pp. 95–110.

McCalman, Iain. 'Controlling the Riots: *Barnaby Rudge* and Romantic revolution'. In *Radicalism and Revolution in Britain, 1775–1848*. Michael T. Davis, ed. London: Macmillan, 2000, pp. 207–28.

McClellan, Andrew. 'A Brief History of the Art Museum Public'. In *Art and its Publics: Museum studies at the millennium*. Cornwall: Blackwell, 2003.

McCreery, Cindy. 'Satiric Images of Fox, Pitt and George III: The East India Bill crisis of 1783–84'. *Word and Image*. 1993, pp. 163–85.

McCue, D. 'The Pamphleteer Pitt's Government Couldn't Silence'. *Eighteenth-Century Life*. Vol. 5 (1978–79), pp. 38–49.

MacDonagh, Oliver. *O'Connell: The life of Daniel O'Connell, 1775–1847*. London: Weidenfeld and Nicolson, 1991.

Macfie, Alec Lawrence. *The Crown and Anchor Tavern: The birthplace of Birkbeck College*. London: Birkbeck College, 1973.

McGowen, Randall. 'A Powerful Sympathy: Terror, the prison and humanitarian reform in early nineteenth-century Britain'. *Journal of British Studies*. Vol. 25, no. 3 (1986), pp. 312–34.

McGowen, Randall. 'The Well-Ordered Prison: England, 1780–1865'. In *The Oxford History of the Prison: The practice of punishment in Western society*. Norval Morris and David J. Rothman, eds. Oxford: Oxford University Press, 1995, pp. 79–110.

McLaren, Angus. 'Contraception and the Working Class: The social ideology of the English birth control movement in its early years'. *Comparative Studies in Society and History*. Vol. 18 (1976), pp. 238–45.

McLynn, Frank. *Crime and Punishment in Eighteenth-Century England*. London: Routledge, 1989.

Mah, Harold. 'Phantasties of the Public Sphere: Rethinking the Habermas of historians'. *Journal of Modern History*. Vol. 72, no. 1 (2000), pp. 153–82.

Mander, Raymond and Joe Mitchenson. *Lost Theatres of London*. London: New English Library, 1976.

Manning, Peter J. 'Manufacturing the Romantic Image: Hazlitt and Coleridge lecturing'. In *Romantic Metropolis: The urban scene of British culture, 1780–1840*. James Chandler and Kevin Gilmartin, eds. Cambridge: Cambridge University Press, 2005, pp. 227–45.

Manogue, Ralph A. 'The Plight of James Ridgway, London Bookseller and Publisher, and the Newgate Radicals 1792–1797'. *Wordsworth Circle*. Vol. 27 (1996), pp. 158–66.

Markus, Thomas. *Order and Space in Society: Architectural form and its context in the Scottish Enlightenment*. Edinburgh: Mainstream, 1982.

Marlow, Joyce. *The Peterloo Massacre*. London: Rapp & Whiting, 1969.

Marlow, Joyce. *The Tolpuddle Martyrs*. St Albans, Herts: Panther, 1974.

Marsh, Joss. *Word Crimes: Blasphemy, culture, and literature in nineteenth-century England*. Chicago: University of Chicago Press, 1998.

Massey, Doreen. *For Space*. London: Sage, 2005.

Mee, Jon. '"Examples of Safe Printing": Censorship and popular radical literature in the 1790s'. *Essays and Studies*. Vol. 46 (1993), pp. 81–95.

Mee, Jon. '"Reciprocal Expressions of Kindness": Robert Merry, Della Cruscanism and the limits of sociability'. In *Romantic Sociability: Social networks and literary culture in Britain, 1770–1840*. Gillian Russell and Clara Tuite, eds. Cambridge: Cambridge University Press, 2002, pp. 104–22.

Mellor, Anne K. 'Joanne Baillie and the Counter-Public Sphere'. *Studies in Romanticism*. Vol. 33, no. 4 (1994), pp. 559–67.

Miles, Dudley. *Francis Place 1771–1854: The life of a remarkable radical*. Brighton: Harvester, 1988.

Miller, John. *Religion in the Popular Prints, 1600–1832*. Cambridge: Chadwyck Healy, 1986.

Miller, Naomi C. 'Major John Cartwright and the Forming of the Hampden Club'. *Historical Journal*. Vol. 17, no. 3 (1974), pp. 615–19.

Milsome, John. 'Arthur Thistlewood and the Cato Street Conspiracy'. *Contemporary Review*. Vol. 217 (1970).

Mitchell, Leslie G. *Charles James Fox*. Oxford: Oxford University Press, 1992.

Moody, Jane. *Illegitimate Theatre in London, 1770–1840*. Cambridge: Cambridge University Press, 2000.

Morris, A. D. *James Parkinson: His life and times*. Boston: Birkhauser, 1989.

Nead, Lynda. *Victorian Babylon: People, streets and images in nineteenth-century London*. New Haven, Conn.: Yale University Press, 2000.

Neale, R. S. *Class in English History. 1680–1850*. Oxford: Blackwell, 1981.

Newey, Katherine. 'Reform on the London Stage'. In *Rethinking the Age of Reform, Britain 1780–1850*. Arthur Burns and Joanna Innes, eds. Cambridge: Cambridge University Press, 2003, pp. 238–53.

Nicholson, Eirwen E. C. 'Consumers and Spectators: The public of the political print in eighteenth-century England'. *History*. Vol. 81, no. 261 (1996), pp. 5–21.

Nicholson, John. *The Great Liberty Riot of 1780*. London: Panther Press, 1995.

Nowlan, Kevin B. and Maurice R. O'Connell, eds. *Daniel O'Connell: Portrait of a radical*. Belfast: Appletree Press, 1984.

O'Connell, Philip. *Romanticism, Economics and the Question of Culture*. Oxford: Oxford University Press, 2001.

O'Gorman, Frank. 'Campaign Rituals and Ceremonies: The social meaning of elections in England, 1780–1860'. *Past and Present*. Vol. 135 (1992), pp. 79–115.

Oliver, W. H. 'John Ward—the messiah as agitator'. *Prophets and Millennialists: The uses of biblical prophecy in England from the 1790s to the 1840s*. Auckland: Auckland University Press, 1978.

Osborne, John. *John Cartwright*. Cambridge: Cambridge University Press, 1972.

Palk, Deidre. '"Fit Objects for Mercy": Gender, the Bank of England and currency criminals, 1804–1833'. *Women's Writing*. Vol. 11, no. 2 (2004), pp. 237–58.

Palk, Deidre. *Gender, Crime, and Judicial Discretion, 1780–1830*. Woodbridge: Boydell Press, 2006.

Parolin, Christina. '"Let Us Have Truth and Liberty": Contesting Britishness and otherness from the prison cell. *Humanities Research*. Vol. xiii, no. 1 (2006), pp. 71–83.

Parolin, Christina. 'The "She-Champion of Impiety": A case-study of female radicalism'. In *Unrespectable Radicals? Popular politics in the age of reform*. Michael T. Davis and Paul A. Pickering, eds. Aldershot: Ashgate, 2008, pp. 185–200.

Parssinen, T. M. 'The Revolutionary Party in London, 1816–20'. *Bulletin of the Institute of Historical Research*. Vol. 45 (1972), pp. 266–82.

Patten, Robert L. *George Cruikshank's Life, Times and Art*. 2 vols. New Brunswick, NJ: Rutgers University Press, 1992.

Peirce, Lewis K. 'Axioms for Reading the Landscape'. In *The Interpretation of Ordinary Landscapes*. D. W. Meinig, ed. Oxford: Oxford University Press, 1979.

Peltz, L. 'Aestheticizing the Ancestral City: Antiquarianism, topography and the representation of London in the long eighteenth century'. *Art History*. Vol. 22, no. 4 (1999), pp. 472–94.

Philp, Mark. *Godwin's Political Justice*. Ithaca, NY: Cornell University Press, 1986.

Philp, Mark, ed. *The French Revolution and British Popular Politics*. Cambridge: Cambridge University Press, 1991.

Philp, Mark. 'Vulgar Conservatism, 1792–2'. *English Historical Review*. Vol. 110, no. 435 (1995), pp. 42–69.

Pickering, Paul A. 'Class Without Words: Symbolic communication in the Chartist movement'. *Past & Present*. No. 112 (1986), pp. 144–62.

Pickering, Paul A. '"Irish First": Daniel O'Connell, the native manufacture campaign, and economic nationalism, 1840–44'. *Albion*. Vol. 32, no. 4 (2000), pp. 598–616.

Pickering, Paul A. *Feargus O'Connor: A political life*. London: Merlin, 2008.

Pickering, Paul A. '"Peaceably if We Can, Forcibly if We Must": Political violence and insurrection in early-Victorian Britain'. In *Terror: From tyrannicide to terrorism in Europe, 1605–2005*. B. Bowden, ed. St Lucia: University of Queensland Press, 2008, pp. 114–33.

Pickering, Paul A. and Alex Tyrrell. '"In the Thickest of the Fight": The Reverend James Scholefield and the Bible Christians of Manchester and Salford'. *Albion*. Vol. 26, no. 3 (1994), pp. 461–82.

Pickering, Paul A. and Alex Tyrrell. *The People's Bread: A history of the Anti-Corn Law League*. London: Leicester University Press, 2000.

Pincus, Steve. '"Coffee Politicians Does Create": Coffeehouses and Restoration political culture'. *The Journal of Modern History*. Vol. 67, no. 4 (1995), pp. 807–34.

Poole, Robert. 'The March to Peterloo: Politics and festivity in late Georgian England'. *Past & Present*. No. 192 (2006), pp. 109–53.

Porter, Roy. 'Science, Provincial Culture and Public Opinion'. *British Journal for Eighteenth Century Studies*. Vol. 3 (1980), pp. 20–46.

Porter, Roy. 'Seeing the Past'. Review article. *Past and Present*. Vol. 118, no. 1 (1988), pp. 186–205.

Porter, Roy. *Doctor of Society: Thomas Beddoes and the sick trade in late Enlightenment England*. London: Routledge, 1992.

Pratt, John. 'The Disappearance of the Prison'. *Isolation: Places and practices of exclusion*. London: Routledge, 2003.

Pred, Allan. *Making Histories and Constructing Human Geographies*. Colorado: Westview Press, 1990.

Priestman, Martin. *Romantic Atheism: Poetry and freethought, 1780–1830*. Cambridge: Cambridge University Press, 1999.

Prothero, Iowerth. *Artisans and Politics in Early Nineteenth Century London, John Gast and his Times*. Folkestone: Dawson, 1979.

Prothero, Iowerth. 'William Benbow and the Concept of the "General Strike"'. *Past & Present*. Vol. 63 (1974), pp. 132–71.

Qureshi, Sadiah. 'Displaying Sara Baartman, the "Hottentot Venus"'. *History of Science*. Vol. 42 (2004), pp. 233–57.

Radzinowicz, Leon. *The History of the Criminal Law and its Administration Since 1750*. 5 vols. London: Stevens, 1948–86.

Radzinowicz, Sir Leon and Roger Hood. 'The Status of Political Prisoner in England: The struggle for recognition'. *Virginia Law Review*. Vol. 65 (1979).

Rendall, Jane. *The Origins of Modern Feminism: Women in Britain, France and the United States 1780–1860*. London: Macmillan, 1985.

Rendall, Jane. '"A Short Account of My Unprofitable Life": Autobiographies of working class women in Britain c.1775–1845'. In *Women's Lives/Women's Times: New essays on auto/biography*. Trev Lynn Broughton and Linda Anderson, eds. New York: State University of New York Press, 1997, pp. 31–50.

Rendall, Jane. 'Women and the Public Sphere'. *Gender & History*. Vol. 11, no. 3 (1999), pp. 475–88.

Rendell, Jane. *The Pursuit of Pleasure: Gender, space and architecture in Regency London*. London: Athlone Press, 2002.

Rendell, Jane, Barbara Penner and Iain Borden. *Gender Space Architecture: An interdisciplinary introduction*. London: Routledge, 2000.

Rickword, Edgell. *Radical Squibs and Loyal Ripostes: Satirical pamphlets of the Regency period, 1819–1821*. Bath: Adams and Dart, 1971.

Roberts, Sir Howard and W. H. Godfrey, eds. *Survey of London*. Vol. xxii. Bankside: London County Council, 1950.

Roberts, John Michael. 'Spatial Governance and Working Class Public Spheres: The case of a Chartist demonstration at Hyde Park'. *Journal of Historical Sociology*. Vol. 14, no. 3 (2001), pp. 305–35.

Roberts, Michael. *The Whig Party*. London: Macmillan, 1939.

Roberts, Michael. 'The Society for the Suppression of Vice and its Early Critics, 1802–1812'. *Historical Journal*. Vol. 26, issue 1 (1983), pp. 159–76.

Roberts, Stephen. *The Chartist Prisoners: The radical lives of Thomas Cooper 1805–1892 & Arthur O'Neill 1819–1896*. Oxford: Peter Lang, 2008.

Robinson, John Martin. *The Dukes of Norfolk*. Second edn. Chichester: Phillimore & Co., 1995.

Robinson, Nicholas. *Edmund Burke: A life in caricature*. New Haven, Conn.: Yale University Press, 1996.

Rodrick, Anne. *Self-Help and Civic Culture: Citizenship in Victorian Britain*. Aldershot: Ashgate, 2004.

Rogers, Helen. *Women and the People: Authority, authorship and the radical tradition in nineteenth-century England*. Aldershot: Ashgate, 2000.

Rogers, Nicholas. *Crowds, Culture, and Politics in Georgian Britain*. Oxford: Clarendon Press, 1998.

Rorty, Adrian. 'Architecture as Punishment'. Review essay. *Art History*. Vol. 6 (1983), pp. 481–4.

Rose, Jonathon. *The Intellectual Life of the British Working Classes*. New Haven, Conn.: Yale University Press, 2001.

Rose, June. *Elizabeth Fry, A Biography*. Philadelphia: Quaker Books, 1994.

Rosen, F. 'Jeremy Bentham's Radicalism'. In *English Radicalism 1550–1850*. Glenn Burgess and Matthew Festenstein, eds. Cambridge: Cambridge University Press, 2007, pp. 217–40.

Rowe, D. J. 'Class and Political Radicalism in London, 1831–2'. *Historical Journal*. Vol. 13, no. 1 (1970), pp. 31–47.

Rowe, D. J. *London Radicalism 1830–1843: A selection from the papers of Francis Place*. London: London Record Society, 1970.

Royle, Edward. 'Mechanics Institutes and the Working Classes, 1840–1860'. *Historical Journal*. Vol. 14 (1971), pp. 305–21.

Royle, Edward. *Radical Politics 1790–1900: Religion and unbelief*. London: Longman, 1971.

Royle, Edward. *Victorian Infidels: The origins of the British secularist movement 1791–1866*. Manchester: Manchester University Press, 1974.

Royle, Edward and James Walvin. *English Radicals and Reformers 1760–1848*. Brighton: Harvester, 1982.

Rudé, George. 'The Gordon Riots: A study of the rioters and their victims'. In *Paris and London in the Eighteenth Century*. New York: Viking Press, 1971, pp. 268–92.

Russell, Gillian. *The Theatres of War: Performance, politics, and society, 1793–1815*. Oxford: Clarendon Press, 1995.

Russell, Gillian. '"Burke's Dagger": Theatricality, politics and print culture in the 1790s'. *British Journal for Eighteenth Century Studies*. Vol. 20 (1997), pp. 1–16.

Russell, Gillian. 'Spouters or Washerwomen: The sociability of Romantic lecturing'. In *Romantic Sociability: Social networks and literary culture in Britain, 1770–1840*. Gillian Russell and Clara Tuite, eds. Cambridge: Cambridge University Press, 2002, pp. 123–44.

Russell, Gillian. 'Recent Studies in Late Georgian Theater and Drama'. Book review. *Journal of British Studies*. Vol. 42, no. 3 (2003), pp. 396–405.

Russell, Gillian. *Women, Sociability and Theatre in Georgian London*. Cambridge: Cambridge University Press, 2007.

Russell, Gillian. 'The Theatre of Crim. Con.: Thomas Erskine, adultery and radical politics in the 1790s'. In *Unrespectable Radicals? Popular politics in the age of reform*. Michael T. Davis and Paul A. Pickering, eds. Aldershot: Ashgate, 2008, pp. 57–70.

Russell, Gillian and Clara Tuite. 'Introducing Romantic Sociability'. In *Romantic Sociability: Social networks and literary culture in Britain 1770–1840*. Gillian Russell and Clara Tuite, eds. Cambridge: Cambridge University Press, 2002, pp. 1–24.

Saisselin, Remy G. 'Architecture and Language: The sensationalism of Le Camus De Mezeieres'. *British Journal of Aesthetics*. Vol. 15, no. 3 (1975), pp. 239–53.

Sanderson, Michael. *Education, Economic Change and Society in England 1780–1870*. Second edn. Basingstoke: Macmillan, 1991.

Scholfield, Philip. 'Jeremy Bentham, the French Revolution and Political Radicalism'. *History of European Ideas*. Vol. 30, no. 4 (2004), pp. 433–61.

Schürer, Norbert. 'The Storming of the Bastille in English Newspapers'. *Eighteenth-Century Life*. Vol. 29, no. 1 (2005), pp. 50–81.

Sennet, Richard. *The Fall of Public Man: On the social psychology of capitalism*. Cambridge: Cambridge University Press, 1978.

Shapiro, Ann-Louise. *Breaking the Codes: Female criminality in fin-de-siecle Paris*. Stanford: Stanford University Press, 1996.

Sharpe, J. A. *Crime and the Law in English Satirical Prints*. Cambridge: Chadwyck Healy, 1986.

Shaw, Robert. *Cato Street*. London: Chatto and Windus, 1972.

Sheehan, W. J. 'Finding Solace in Eighteenth-Century Newgate'. In *Crime in England 1550–1800*. J. S. Cockburn, ed. London: Metheun, 1977, pp. 229–45.

Shelley, Henry C. *Inns and Taverns of Old London*. Boston, 1909.

Sikes, Hershel Moreland, ed. *The Letters of William Hazlitt*. London: Macmillan, 1979.

Smith, E. A. 'Charles, Second Earl Grey and the House of Lords'. In *Lords of Parliament Studies, 1714–1914*. R. W. Davis, ed. Stanford: Stanford University Press, 1995, pp. 79–96.

Smith, Olivia. *The Politics of Language, 1791–1819*. Oxford: Clarendon, 1984.

Soja, Edward W. 'The Spatiality of Social Life: Towards a transformative retheorisation'. In *Social Relations and Spatial Structure*. Derek Gregory and John Urry, eds. Basingstoke: Macmillan, 1985.

Spater, George. *William Cobbett: The poor man's friend*. 2 vols. Cambridge: Cambridge University Press, 1982.

Spence, Peter. *The Birth of Romantic Radicalism: War, popular politics, and English radical reformism, 1800–1815*. Aldershot: Scholar, 1996.

Stallybrass, Peter and Allon White. *The Politics and Poetics of Transgression*. Ithaca, NY: Cornell University Press, 1986.

Stephens, Michael and Gordon Roderick. 'The Working Classes and Mechanics' Institutes'. *Annals of Science*. Vol. 29, no. 4 (1973), pp. 349–60.

Stevenson, John. 'The Queen Caroline Affair'. In *London in the Age of Reform*. John Stevenson, ed. Oxford: Blackwell, 1977, pp. 117–48.

Stewart, Robert. *Henry Brougham, 1778–1868: His public career.* London: Bodley Head, 1986.

Strachan, John. 'Gifford and the Della Cruscans'. *British Satire 1785–1840.* Vol. 4. London: Pickering and Chatto, 2003.

Streicher, Lawrence H. 'On a Theory of Political Caricature'. *Comparative Studies in Society and History.* Vol. 9, no. 4 (1967), pp. 427–45.

Taylor, Antony. '"Commons-Stealers, "Land-Grabbers" and "Jerry-Builders": Space, popular radicalism and the politics of public access in London, 1848–1880'. *International Review of Social History.* Vol. 40, no. 3 (1995), pp. 383–407.

Taylor, Antony. '"A Melancholy Odyssey among London Public Houses": Radical club life and the unrespectable in mid-nineteenth century London'. *Historical Research.* Vol. 78, no. 199 (2005), pp. 74–95.

Taylor, Barbara. *Eve and the New Jerusalem: Socialism and feminism in the nineteenth century.* London: Virago, 1983.

Taylor, Miles. 'John Bull and the Iconography of Public Opinion in England c.1712–1929'. *Past & Present.* No. 134 (1992), pp. 93–128.

Thale, Mary. 'London Debating Societies in the 1790s'. *Historical Journal.* Vol. 32, no. 1 (1989), pp. 57–86.

Tholfsen, T. *Working Class Radicalism in Mid-Victorian England.* London: Croom Helm, 1976.

Thomas, J. E. *House of Care: Prisons and prisoners in England 1500–1800.* Nottingham: University of Nottingham, 1988.

Thomis, Malcolm and Jennifer Grimmett. *Women in Protest 1800–1850.* London: Croom Helm, 1982.

Thompson, Dorothy, ed. *The Early Chartists.* London: Macmillan, 1971.

Thompson, Dorothy. 'Women and Nineteenth-Century Radical Politics'. In *The Rights and Wrongs of Women.* Juliet Mitchell and Ann Oakley, eds. London: Penguin Books, 1976.

Thompson, E. P. *The Making of the English Working Class.* London: Penguin, 1968.

Thompson, E. P. 'Patrician Society, Plebeian Culture'. *Journal of Social History.* No. 4 (1974), pp. 382–405.

Tilly, Charles. 'Spaces of Contention'. *Mobilization: An International Quarterly*. Vol. 5, no. 2 (2000), pp. 135–59.

Turner, Michael. '"Arraying Minds Against Bodies": Benthamite radicals and revolutionary Europe during the 1820s and 1830s'. *History*. Vol. 90, no. 2 (2005), pp. 236–61.

Turner, Simon. 'William Holland's Satirical Print Catalogues, 1788–1794'. *Print Quarterly*. Vol. 16 (1999), pp. 127–38.

Van Wyhe, John. *Phrenology and the Origins of Victorian Scientific Naturalism*. Aldershot: Ashgate, 2004.

Vernon, James. *Politics and the People; A study in English political culture c.1815–1867*. Cambridge: Cambridge University Press, 1993.

Vernon, James, ed. *Re-Reading the Constitution: New narratives in the political history of England's long nineteenth century*. Cambridge: Cambridge University Press, 1996.

Vicinus, Martha. '"Helpless and Unfriended": Nineteenth-century domestic melodrama'. *New Literary History*. Vol. 13 (1981), pp. 127–43.

Vickery, Amanda. 'Golden Age to Separate Spheres? A Review of the Categories and Chronology of English Women's History'. *Historical Journal*. Vol. 36, no. 2 (1993), pp. 383–414.

Vincent, David. *Testaments of Radicalism: Memoirs of working class politicians 1790–1885*. London: Europa Publications, 1977.

Vincent, David. 'The Decline of the Oral Tradition in Popular Culture'. In *Popular Culture and Custom in Nineteenth Century England*. Robert Storch, ed. London: Croom Helm, 1982, pp. 20–48.

Vincent, David. *Literacy and Popular Culture: England 1750–1914*. Cambridge: Cambridge University Press, 1989.

Vincent, David. *The Rise of Mass Literacy: Reading and writing in modern Europe*. Cambridge: Polity Press, 2000.

Voskuil, Lynn M. 'Feeling Public: Sensation theater, commodity culture and the Victorian public sphere'. *Victorian Studies*. Vol. 44, no. 2 (2002), pp. 245–74.

Waldstreicher, David. 'Two Cheers for the "Public Sphere"...And one for historians' skepticism'. *William and Mary Quarterly*. Vol. 62, no. 1 (2005), pp. 107–12.

Walker, Garthine. *Crime, Gender and Social Order in Early Modern England*. Cambridge: Cambridge University Press, 2003.

Walvin, James, ed. *Slavery and British Society 1776–1848*. London: Macmillan, 1982.

Wang, Orrin N. C. 'Romancing the Counter-Public Sphere: A response to Romanticism and its publics'. *Studies in Romanticism*. Vol. 33, no. 4 (1994), pp. 579–88.

Watts, Ruth. 'Rational Religion and Feminism: The challenge of Unitarianism in the nineteenth century'. In *Women, Religion and Feminism in Britain, 1750–1900*. Sue Morgan, ed. New York: Palgrave Macmillan, 2002, pp. 39–52.

Weinstein, Benjamin. 'Popular Constitutionalism and the London Corresponding Society'. *Albion*. Vol. 34, no. 1 (2002), pp. 37–57.

White, R. J. *Waterloo to Peterloo*. Harmondsworth: Penguin, 1968.

Whitehead, Andrew. 'Dan Chatteron and his "Atheistic Communistic Scorcher"'. *History Workshop Journal*. Vol. 25, no. 1 (1988), pp. 83–99.

Whittet, T. D. 'The Crown and Anchor and the Arts and Sciences, Part 1'. *Pharmaceutical Historian*. Vol. 13, no. 3 (1983), pp. 2–6. And 'Part 2'. *Pharmaceutical Historian*. Vol. 13, no. 4 (1983), pp. 5–8.

Whittet, T. D. 'The Crown and Anchor and Gas Lighting'. *Pharmaceutical Historian*. Vol. 14, no. 3 (1984), pp. 4–7.

Wiener, Joel. *Radicalism and Freethought in Nineteenth-Century Britain: The life of Richard Carlile*. Westport, Conn.: Greenwood Press, 1983.

Wiener, Joel. *William Lovett*. Manchester: Manchester University Press, 1989.

Wilkinson, George. *The Newgate Calendar*. Vol. 3. Leeds: Panther, 1965.

Williams, Gwyn. *Rowland Detrosier; A working-class infidel 1800–34*. York: St Anthony's, 1965.

Williams, Raymond. *Culture and Society 1780–1950*. 1953. Reprinted. New York: Columbia University Press, 1983.

Wilson, Linda. '"Constrained by Zeal": Women in mid-nineteenth century nonconformist churches'. *Journal of Religious History*. Vol. 23, no. 2 (1999), pp. 185–202.

Wittman, Richard. 'Architecture, Space, and Abstraction in the Eighteenth-Century French Public Sphere'. *Representations*. Vol. 102, no. 1 (2008), pp. 1–26.

Wood, Marcus. *Radical Satire and Print Culture, 1790–1822*. Oxford: Clarendon, 1994.

Woodfine, Philip. 'Debtors, Prisons, and Petitions in Eighteenth Century England'. *Eighteenth-Century Life*. Vol. 30, no. 2 (2006), pp. 1–31.

Worrall, David. *Radical Culture: Discourse, resistance and surveillance 1790–1820*. New York: Harvester, 1992.

Worrall, David. *Theatric Revolution: Drama, censorship and Romantic period subcultures 1773–1832*. Oxford: Oxford University Press, 2006.

Yeo, Eileen. 'Robert Owen and Radical Culture'. In *Robert Owen: Prophet of the poor*. Sidney Pollard and John Salt, eds. London: Macmillan, 1971, pp. 84–114.

Yeo, Eileen. 'Will the Real Mary Lovett Please Stand Up?: Chartism, gender and autobiography'. In *Living and Learning, Essays in Honour of J. F. C. Harrison*. Malcolm Chase and Ian Dyck, eds. Brookfield, Vt: Scolar Press, 1996, pp. 163–81.

Yeo, Eileen, ed. *Radical Femininity: Women's self-representation in the public sphere*. Manchester: Manchester University Press, 1998.

Zedner, Lucia. *Women, Crime and Custody in Victorian England*. Oxford: Clarendon Press, 1991.

Zedner, Lucia. 'Wayward Sisters: The prison for women'. In *The Oxford History of the Prison: The practice of punishment in Western society*. Norval Morris and David J. Rothman, eds. New York: Oxford University Press, 1995, pp. 295–324.

Zegger, Robert E. *John Cam Hobhouse: A political life, 1819–1852*. Columbia: University of Missouri Press, 1973.

Biographical dictionaries

Biographical Dictionary of Modern British Radicals. Joseph Baylen and Norbert Gossman, eds. Vols 1–2. Sussex: Harvester Press, 1979.

Jones, W. D. 'Jones, John Gale'. Vol. 1, pp. 269–73.

Prochaska, Alice. 'Brooks, Samuel'. Vol. 1, pp. 65–6.

Prothero, Iowerth. 'Davenport, Allen'. Vol. 1, pp. 111–13.

Royle, Edward. 'Taylor, Robert'. Vol. 1, pp. 467–70.

Weisser, Henry. 'Cleave, John'. Vol. 2, pp. 138–41.

Wiener, Joel. 'Carpenter, William'. Vol. 2, pp. 124–7.

Wiener, Joel. 'Hassell, Richard'. Vol. 1, pp. 213–15.

Wiener, Joel. 'Hibbert, Julian'. Vol. 1, pp. 221–2.

Wiener, Joel. 'Perry, Thomas Ryley'. Vol. 1, pp. 372–3.

Oxford Dictionary of National Biography. H. C. G. Matthew and Brian Harrison, eds. Oxford: Oxford University Press, 2004. Online edn Lawrence Goldman. [All entries refer to the online edition.]

Baird, John D. 'Cowper, William 1731–1800'.

Beaver, S. A. 'Roebuck, John Arthur 1802–1879'.

Beckett, J. V. 'Curwen, John Christian 1756–1828'.

Bowdler, Roger. 'Dance, George, the Younger 1741–1825'.

Kell, P. E. 'Lever, Sir Ashton 1729–1788'.

McConnell, Anita. 'Wood, Sir Matthew, First Baronet 1768–1843'.

Moss, David J. 'Wakefield, Edward Gibbon 1796–1862'.

Olleson, Philip. 'Wesley, Samuel 1766–1837'.

Richardson, Terence. 'Feinaigle, Gregor von 1760–1819'.

Smith, G. B. Revised. Anita McConnell. 'Gurney, Sir Goldsworthy 1793–1875'.

Torrens, H. S. 'Parkinson, James bap. 1730, d. 1813'.

Webb, Timothy. 'Hunt, John 1775–1848'.

Wiener, Joel H. 'Hetherington, Henry 1792–1849'.

Unpublished theses

Kinraide, Rebecca Brookfield. The Society for the Diffusion of Useful Knowledge and the Democratization of Learning in Early Nineteenth-Century Britain. Unpublished PhD dissertation. The University of Wisconsin, Madison, 2006.

McCalman, Iain. Popular Radicalism and Freethought in Early Nineteenth Century England. Unpublished MA thesis. The Australian National University, Canberra, 1975.

Parolin, Christina. Radicalism as Theatre: The Blackfriars Road Rotunda 1830–32. Unpublished Honours thesis. The Australian National University, Canberra, 1989.

Internet sources

Hüttner, Johann Christian. *London und Paris*. 1798. Quoted from web site of the National Portrait Gallery, London. <http://www.npg.org.uk/live/arccari5.asp>

Kucich, Greg. '"The Wit in the Dungeon": Leigh Hunt and the insolent politics of Cockney coteries'. *Romanticism on the Net*. Vol. 14 (1999). <http://users.ox.ac.uk/~scat0385/cockneycoteries.html>

'Lever's Museum Consisting of Natural Curiosities and Productions of Art. Petition of Sir Ashton Lever'. *Journal of the House of Commons*. 1803 reprint, 1784/06/07, vol. 40, <http://www.bopcris.ac.uk/bop1688/ref1572.html>

Old Bailey Proceedings Online. <www.oldbailey.org>

Paley, Morton. 'The Devil's Walk' and 'The Devil's Thoughts'. Conference paper. Romantic Circles Conference, October 1997. <http://www.rc.umd.edu/villa/vc97/paley.html>

Paley, Morton, ed. Online edition of the poem *The Devil's Thoughts*. <http://www.rc.umd.edu/editions/shelley/devil/dev29vs35.html>

The Diaries of John Cam Hobhouse. <http://www.hobby-o.com/newgate.php>

Index

Adkins, Governor 67, 74, 75, 76
Adkins, Mrs 96
Alderson, Amelia 28
Anti-Corn Law League 167, 168, 170, 171, 201, 281
Aris, Thomas 56, 74, 75
Attwood, Thomas 233, 239

Bamford, Samuel 67, 68, 69, 146, 164, 176, 177
Banks, Sir Joseph 191
Bastille, the 22, 23, 80, 81, 116, 119
   see also French Revolution
Beccaria, Cesare 28, 196
Benbow, William 231, 232, 233, 236, 272n.125
Bentham, Jeremy 28, 29, 56, 58
Bewick, William 195, 197
Binns, John 1
Birmingham Political Union 233, 239
Black Dwarf 70, 71, 80, 98, 140
Blackburn Female Reform Society 91
Blackburn, William 58, 72
Blackfriars Road Rotunda 3, 162, 177, 181, 182, 188, 201, 211, 216, 217, 239, 257, 258, 259, 260, 261, 267–8, 269–70, 276–7, 280, 283
   and public unrest 179, 180, 183
   and religion 217, 218, 219, 220, 222, 243, 244, 246, 257, 261, 263, 264
   as a dissenting chapel 215, 217, 219, 237, 238
   as a public venue 14, 207, 208, 215, 220, 227, 228, 242
   as a theatre 222–3, 224, 225, 226, 227, 241
   as an educational venue 203, 205–6, 208, 218, 231, 241
   as an outlet for radical press 210
   as radical space 14, 156, 157, 158, 180, 182, 200, 206, 213, 215, 216, 227, 228, 229, 231–3, 235–7, 260, 280, 281–2, 285
   as threat to society 157, 166, 233, 234, 235, 237–8, 258
   attempt to revitalise 243, 244, 245, 249, 250, 253
   conflict within 229–30, 235–6, 265
   decline of 243, 265, 276–9
   events at 3, 156–7, 206–7, 210
   immunity from prosecution 238
   in mainstream press 156, 166, 233–5, 263
   official action against 240, 241
   origins 183–4, 189, 191, 192, 193, 198, 199, 200
   performances 222, 225, 227
   personalities 4, 14, 157, 180, 182, 200n.105, 206, 207, 221–2, 256
   popularity of 210, 255, 282
   Rotunda radicalism 182, 183, 211, 220, 234, 243, 244, 247, 248, 249, 251, 256
   Rotunda radicals 166, 206, 219, 225, 230, 232, 234, 235, 258, 260, 272, 283
   'Rotunda revolutionists' 156, 233, 234
   'Rotundanist' 157, 234, 235
   women's involvement 14, 242, 247–53, 256, 258–9, 260, 261–3, 264, 266, 267–8, 271–2, 285
Blasphemous and Seditious Libels Act 5
blasphemous libel, *see* libel
blasphemy 36, 39, 41, 43, 44n.118, 55n.25, 62, 71, 72, 77, 85, 86, 87, 90, 91, 93, 102, 157, 200, 216, 220, 221, 227, 240, 241, 244n.6, 246, 260, 261
   see also devilry, libel—blasphemous, sacrilege
Boyle, Humphrey 34, 35, 37, 42, 47, 70, 73, 75, 79, 89n.30
British Forum 2, 3, 4
Britishness 57, 78, 80, 88n.25, 106, 127, 135, 137, 146, 153, 282
Brookes, John 167, 170
Brooks, Samuel 151
Brougham, Henry 164, 202
Burdett, Jones 152

Burdett, Sir Francis 105, 106, 152
   at Crown and Anchor 114, 121n.47, 129, 163, 164, 177
   creation of National Political Union 162
   depictions of 127, 128, 130–1, 132, 140, 142, 144
   electoral campaigning 49, 51, 78, 80, 150, 225
   electoral victories 50, 51, 114, 128, 147
   imprisonment 154, 163
   prison advocacy 51, 53, 54, 61n.47, 62, 64, 66, 72
   support for John Gale Jones 2, 3, 154
Burke, Edmund 25, 26, 123, 137, 157, 172, 196
Burton, James 183, 185
Byng, George 131

Campion, William 34, 39, 40, 45, 46, 47
Carlile, Jane 33, 83, 84n.8, 86, 88, 89, 90n.32, 93, 94, 95, 97, 98, 99, 246, 248, 265
Carlile, Mary-Ann 86, 90, 91, 94, 98, 99
Carlile, Richard 3, 4, 14, 33, 38n.92, 41, 47, 84, 89, 94, 98–9, 101, 182, 205, 231, 236, 240, 280
   anti-religious sentiment 41, 72, 102, 206, 208–9, 220, 228, 244, 247, 258, 264n.88
   arrest (1830) 240, 241
   attitudes to theatre 222–3, 224, 225, 226, 243
   bookshop 33, 34, 71, 86, 100
   conflict with William Haley 41, 73
   conflict with radical community 41, 70n.91, 102, 228, 229, 230, 235, 236, 265
   death 270
   dissemination of radicalism 216
   expectations for his workers 41, 73
   fight for press freedom 204, 208
   free speech 209
   freethinking 207
   ideas 205, 206, 207, 231, 252, 256, 257
   imprisonment 41, 44n.118, 86, 204, 243, 246, 265
   imprisonment of shop workers 34, 35, 42, 55, 70, 71, 83, 89
   influences on 38n.92
   lack of support from radical community 240n.137
   legacy 271
   philosophies on sex and birth control 102, 252, 257, 265, 266
   praise for Richard Hassell 41–2
   print culture depictions of 140, 142
   publications 43, 73, 202, 210
   relationship with Eliza Sharples 244, 245, 246, 247, 248, 249, 250, 253, 265, 266, 272
   relationship with Susannah Wright 83, 84, 85, 86, 89, 99–100, 101–2, 247, 266
   shop workers 55, 70, 71, 72, 73, 83, 86, 89, 95n.57, 173n.99
   support for fellow radicals 41–2, 70n.86
   supporters 36, 45, 101n.86, 102, 204, 259
   tour of England 199
   'Westminster Committee of 200' 158, 161
   women in Carlile circle 84, 99, 258
   see also Jane Carlile, Eliza Sharples. Susannah Wright
   writings 35, 79, 86, 205, 240
   see also Prompter, Republican, Blackfriars Road Rotunda
Carpenter, William 216, 231
Cartwright, Major John 107, 140, 151, 152
Castlereagh, Lord 2, 55, 65, 92n.44, 97, 137
Cato Street conspirators 70n.86, 97n.68, 159n.42, 161, 215
Chartism 11, 163, 168, 175, 209, 223, 270–1, 272, 282, 284

demonstrations 12n.53
origins 4, 166
pre- 8n.31, 177
see also People's Charter
Chartists 79, 163, 166, 168, 177, 254, 262, 269, 270, 272, 282
   Convention (1839) 232
   imprisonment of 55n.25, 76
Chesterton, George Laval 56, 63, 74, 75, 81n.143, 273
Christopher, John 34
Clarke, John 34, 39, 45, 47
Cleave, John 216, 231, 236, 271
Cobbett, William 30, 31, 32, 33, 35, 45, 68, 69, 106, 151, 152, 153, 164, 174, 180, 207, 229, 259n.72
Cobbett's Weekly Political Register 2n.7, 30
Cochrane, Lord 131, 132
Cochrane, William 34
Cockerill, Edward 39, 40, 41
coffee houses
   as political sites 7, 8, 9, 12, 28, 45, 68, 86, 148, 149, 210, 213, 214, 215, 225, 227, 236, 255, 285
Coldbath Fields House of Correction 2, 3, 13, 48, 49, 51, 53–7, 59–71, 73–6, 79, 81, 82, 84, 96, 97, 103, 107, 121, 154, 163, 195, 225, 273, 274, 280, 281
   see also prison reform
Coleridge, Samuel Taylor 54, 56, 113, 194, 196
Combination Act 239
countertheatre 225, 226, 238, 241, 244, 260, 261
   see also theatre
courts
   as gendered spaces 88, 93, 96
   as political spaces 82, 85
Cowper, William 233
Crown and Anchor tavern 1, 2, 3, 13–14, 147, 157, 158, 168, 181, 195, 204, 213, 232, 233, 268n.106, 276, 280, 282, 283
   as a political space 126, 150, 151, 153, 154, 155, 156, 157, 158, 164, 165, 166–7, 168, 169, 170, 171–2, 175, 177, 281
   as a radical space 14, 107, 112, 122, 128, 137, 148, 149–50, 158, 161–2, 163, 166, 167, 170, 171, 177, 201, 285
   as a symbol in print culture 107–8, 121, 169, 179, 280, 281
   centre of loyalist network 64, 121, 122, 134, 168
   demise 274, 275, 276
   descriptions of 108, 109, 110, 111, 113, 176, 177, 214, 276
   Great Assembly Room 112, 113, 130, 159, 174, 176
   in mainstream press 107, 147, 153, 157, 161, 165, 166, 167–8, 171, 172, 175, 281
   politics 114, 126, 151, 152, 153, 156, 159, 160, 161, 163, 164, 167, 169, 231
   public commitment to 106
   radical dinners 105, 111–14, 119, 121n.47, 126, 128, 131, 149, 150, 154, 155n.28, 161, 164, 172, 174, 177
   representation in visual culture 116–23, 125–6, 127, 128, 129, 130–3, 135, 136, 141, 144–7, 150, 169, 170, 233, 280, 281
   tenants 147–8, 153, 165, 166, 168
   women's involvement 173, 174, 175, 214–15
   see also Sir Francis Burdett, Charles James Fox, John Cam Hobhouse
Cruikshank, George 91n.39, 135, 136, 138, 141, 142, 145
Curwen, John Christian 154

Dance, George the Younger 20, 22, 25, 26, 29, 30n.51, 59n.40, 273
   see also Newgate prison
Davenport, Allen 90, 98, 102
De Wilde, Samuel 131, 132, 144
Defoe, Daniel 24, 83
Della Cruscans 119, 120
Despard, Colonel Edward Marcus 51, 53, 64, 65, 66, 68, 76, 121, 128

Devil's Pulpit 210
devilry 117, 121, 146, 147
   see also blasphemy, sacrilege
Dickens, Charles 24n.25
Dissenters 116, 196, 197, 215, 219, 255, 268n.106

Eardley-Wilmott, Sir 77n.126
education 77, 78, 249, 252
   in prison 38n.92, 42, 46, 47, 97
   middling classes 195
   popular forums of 197, 201, 203, 205, 207, 210, 218, 268
   radical 208, 209, 219
   rights to 203
   working classes 44, 183, 201, 202, 203, 204, 205, 210, 211
   Zetetic 204–5
Edwards, George 161n.49
elections 49, 50, 78, 80–1, 114, 141, 147, 152, 163, 169
   and aristocratic women 51n.10
   and Crown and Anchor dining 121n.47, 128, 149, 162, 164, 172
   and plebeian women 51n.10
   theatre 225
   see also reform—electoral, suffrage
Erskine, Thomas 122, 220n.34
Evans, Thomas 158, 161
Evans, Thomas John 158

Feinaigle, Gregor von 194, 195
Female Reform Associations 254
Fitch, Josiah 219, 220, 268n.106
Foucault, Michel 13, 56, 56n, 57, 63, 64, 72
Fox, Charles James 1, 28, 80, 114, 117, 120, 121, 125, 127, 128, 129, 130, 131, 144, 150, 154, 177
freethought 85, 86n.86, 142, 180, 183, 200, 207, 214, 218, 219, 220, 246, 248, 256
   see also Richard Carlile, Eliza Sharples, Susannah Wright, Zetetic movement

French Revolution 1, 22, 92, 123, 135, 156, 207
   radical response to in Britain 116, 181, 228–9, 230
   radical symbols 80, 119, 127, 142, 146, 182
   see also Bastille
Fry, Elizabeth 30n.51, 83, 92, 94n.52

Gast, John 231
Gifford, Sir Robert 70
Gillray, James 53, 117–18, 119, 120, 121, 122, 123, 129, 133, 134, 136, 145
Godwin, William 27, 28, 134n.98, 195, 222
Gordon, Lord George 19, 26, 30, 122n.52
Gurney, Sir Goldsworthy 192

habeas corpus 5, 34, 51n.11, 97n.68, 106, 136, 137
Habeas Corpus Suspension Act 31
Habermas, Jürgen 8–11, 43, 57, 82, 129, 148, 153, 172, 184, 191, 196, 206, 211, 213–14, 288, 283, 284
Haley, William 34, 35, 41, 42, 72, 73
Haliburton, James, *see* Burton, James
Hall, Abel 73n.104, 215, 220, 221, 227, 230, 243, 246, 249, 250, 251, 252, 257, 258, 259, 261, 263–4, 265
Hampden Club 152, 153, 155, 166, 168
Hassell, Richard 34, 38, 39, 42, 45, 46
Haydon, Benjamin Robert 195
Hazlitt, William 61n.46, 67, 113, 195, 197, 261
Hetherington, Henry 164, 166, 207n.138, 231, 236, 271
Hibbert, Julian 101, 200, 231, 234, 250, 257
Hobhouse, John Cam 32, 33, 34, 35, 36, 45, 68, 69, 105, 106, 107, 111, 126, 149, 163
Holcroft, Thomas 223
Holmes, William 34, 38, 89, 106
Holyoake, George J. 42, 101, 233, 269, 270, 276

Home Office 8, 73n.104, 161n.49, 172, 173n.100, 182, 215, 216n.17, 219, 227, 230, 237, 240, 243, 247, 250, 252, 257n.62, 264, 265, 271
Hone, William 91n.39, 136, 137, 138, 141, 142, 144, 145, 146, 150, 195, 238, 239
House of Commons 2, 32, 46, 51, 53, 54, 65, 69, 72, 78n.127, 91, 103, 114n.20, 152, 165, 169, 170, 171, 177, 180, 192, 200, 281
Howard, John 18, 19, 28, 29, 54, 56, 58n.33, 58n.37, 59, 61, 94n.52, 108, 125n.61
Huddesford, George 130
Hume, Joseph 91n.38, 162, 163, 165
Humphrey, Hannah 133, 134
Hunt, Henry 3, 164, 174, 229
  ascension of 151,
  at Peterloo 158,
  at the Rotunda 180, 216
  campaigns 152, 154, 163
  depictions of 140,
  imprisonment 39,
  Radical Reform Association 207, 228, 230
  return to London 159, 160, 161, 173
  supporters 234, 256
  see also Radical Reform Association
Hunt, John 55, 61n.46, 66, 67, 68, 69, 75, 76, 195
Hunt, Leigh 55, 66, 67, 75, 76, 78n.128, 224
Hunter, John 216

Irish Uprising (1798) 2, 97n.68
Isis 210, 244, 245, 246, 247, 249, 250n.34, 276, 280

Jeffries, Thomas 34, 39
Jerrold, Douglas 175, 274
John Bull 118, 129, 131, 135
Jones, B. B. 34, 84, 85, 87, 88, 95, 96, 100, 253

Jones, John Gale 1, 2, 3, 4, 11, 12, 159, 173, 205, 285
  at the Rotunda 180, 206, 207, 213, 230, 231, 262–3
  imprisonment 55, 65–6, 68, 77, 78, 79, 85, 86, 154
  views 203, 232
  wife 3, 65, 66, 85

Keats, John 195
King George III 120–1, 125, 126, 149
King George IV 36n.81, 100, 106, 121, 174, 179, 229, 233
Kitchen, Alice 91

lecturing 174, 180, 196, 205, 207, 215, 218, 219, 227, 258, 269, 270
  and authorities 199, 216n.17, 237
  literary 113, 191, 194, 195, 196, 197
  political 207, 213, 229, 231, 249
  religious 241, 243, 244, 249, 268
  scientific 113, 191, 192, 203, 205, 252
  venues 183, 192, 193, 194, 195, 199, 200, 201, 207, 208, 210
  women 175, 245n.9, 246, 247, 249, 250, 251, 252–3, 257, 259, 261, 262, 263, 268, 270
Leroux, Jacob 58, 59
Lever, Sir Ashton 183, 184, 185, 188, 190, 191, 217
Leverian Museum 14, 183, 185, 186, 187, 188, 189, 190, 191, 198, 201, 224, 251, 280
libel 2, 36, 37, 55, 65, 66, 77, 88n.25, 134, 172, 238, 241
  blasphemous 35, 73n.103, 240, 241
  seditious 5n.17, 30, 55, 62, 240
  see also Blasphemous and Seditious Libels Act, sedition
liberty 26, 121, 131
  in print culture 121, 125, 127, 131, 137, 141, 142
  principle of 88
  symbols of 116, 119, 123, 127, 181–2, 230

London Corresponding Society (LCS) 1, 2, 51, 54n.19, 65
London Working Men's Association 166
Louis XVI 80, 121, 127
Loveless, George 166n.74
Lovett, William 166, 231

Macauley, Eliza 174, 267, 268
Mainwairing, William 49n.5, 78n.127
Martin, Emma 270, 271n.122, 276
Martineau, Harriet 175n.115, 268
Mayhew, Henry 31n.59, 224, 260
Mechanics Institutes 203, 203n, 204
Melbourne, Lord 237
Merry, Robert 119–120
Metropolitan Political Union (MPU) 228, 231
Middlesex magistrates 49, 54, 56, 65, 76, 77, 78n.127
middling classes 97, 102n.90, 133, 148, 152, 161, 166, 168, 175, 179, 188, 189, 191, 195, 196, 198, 202, 203, 204, 223, 228, 231, 240, 248, 254, 257, 258, 259, 260, 261, 264, 272, 283
millenarianism 206, 243, 244, 255
Molesworth, Sir William 164
monarchy 81, 101, 121, 123, 125, 129, 137, 141, 184, 233
Montesquieu, Baron de 28, 196
museums 184, 185, 188, 189, 190, 191, 192, 251
  see also Leverian Museum

National Political Union (NPU) 162, 173, 235, 236n.114
National Union of the Working Classes (NUWC) 101n.86, 157, 180, 182, 206, 207, 208, 210, 215–16, 231–6, 239, 242, 243, 249, 264, 269, 271, 272, 284
Neild, James 28, 92
Nelson, Lord (Horatio) 64, 137
New Poor Law Act 167
Newgate Monthly Magazine 43, 44, 47, 72, 75

Newgate prison 2, 13, 17–49, 51, 54, 58, 59, 61, 63, 65, 68, 70–6, 79, 81–4, 88, 92–7, 99, 103, 105, 107, 120, 125n.60, 234, 264, 273, 274, 280
  see also prison reform
Newspaper Stamp Duties Act 5
Norfolk, Duke of 108, 125, 126, 127, 131, 149, 176

O'Brien, Bronterre 166, 270
O'Connell, Daniel 164, 165, 166n.74, 169, 170, 180, 207, 228
O'Connor, Feargus 79, 130, 163, 166n.74, 168
Owen, Robert 255n.57, 256, 267
Owenism 166n.76, 174, 234, 245n.9, 250, 254, 256, 267, 268, 270, 271

Paine, Thomas 3, 26, 27, 31, 45, 46, 98, 99, 117, 122, 203, 222, 245, 250
panopticon 29, 58
Parkinson, James 27, 183, 184, 185, 188, 190, 191, 192
Parkinson, Joseph T. 192, 193, 194
Patmore, Peter George 67, 195
Paul, Sir George Onesiphorus 28, 29, 56
Peel, Sir Robert 41, 70, 167, 169, 170, 171, 179, 237
People's Charter, the 166, 167, 168, 231
  see also Chartism, Chartists
Perry, Thomas Ryley 34, 44, 45, 46, 47
Peterloo massacre 2, 3, 14, 32, 33, 36, 39, 105, 136, 137, 141, 158, 160, 173, 230
petitioning 3, 26, 39, 41, 44, 46, 91n.38, 140, 151, 152, 165, 166, 174, 184, 239
Pitt, William 26, 30, 49, 80, 121, 123n.56, 125, 135, 137, 174
Place, Francis 101, 131, 132, 156, 157, 158, 162, 167, 177, 202, 204, 213, 232, 233, 235, 236, 260
police 51, 62, 63, 101, 164, 170, 173, 179, 180, 182, 216, 237
political reform 2, 4, 105, 106, 114, 141, 144, 146, 152, 153, 158, 159, 161, 163, 183, 206, 213, 239, 271, 281

agenda 107, 122, 156, 229
  campaign for 107, 131, 166
  demand for 4, 103, 122, 125
  reformers 116, 117, 118, 119, 121, 122, 127, 128, 130, 131, 144
  spying on reformers 123
  see also reform, *Reform Act*
Preston, Thomas 159
print culture 24, 25, 33, 36–7, 43, 116, 122, 128, 129, 133, 134, 136, 146, 147, 157, 173, 208, 209, 233, 247, 263, 281
  and visual satire 14, 32, 91n.39, 114, 115, 116, 117, 119, 125, 126, 128, 129, 130, 131, 135, 136, 141, 144, 145, 146, 150, 169, 233, 281
Prison Act 274
prison reform 28–30, 36, 39, 43, 44, 47, 55, 56, 63, 81–2, 85, 103
  architecture 29, 58, 61, 62, 83
  boom 59
  prison economy 62, 95
  movement 13, 18, 71, 91, 101
  principles of 19, 20, 29, 40, 42, 58, 59, 74, 280
  prison labour 59, 74n.108
  reformers 19, 29–30, 36, 37, 42, 54, 56, 57, 63, 85, 91
  resistance to 29, 32, 33, 273, 280
  separation of sexes 30n.51, 29, 60, 94n.52, 97n.64
  women's conditions 92, 95 *see also* Jane Carlile, Susannah Wright
  see also Coldbath Fields House of Correction, Newgate prison, religious—instruction in prison
Prompter 200, 210, 222, 235, 240, 241
public sphere 4, 5, 8–9, 12, 13–14, 15, 33, 79, 82, 107, 114, 115, 121, 131, 144, 145, 148, 153, 156, 168, 171–73, 175, 177, 181, 183, 184, 189, 196, 201, 210, 211, 228, 235, 251, 280, 282–3
  and gender 11, 14, 92n.43, 99, 103, 190n.36, 242, 248, 251, 253, 254, 260, 262, 263, 266, 284
  bourgeois 9, 10, 11, 43, 79, 129, 148, 153, 188, 191, 197, 206, 214, 228, 283
  counter-sphere 10, 172, 228n.70, 283
  plebeian 9, 10, 11, 132, 148, 206, 283, 284
  radical 44, 47, 79, 85, 99, 103, 282
  see also Jürgen Habermas

Quakers 92, 95, 196, 264
Queen Caroline 36, 174
Queen Charlotte 121, 165

Radical Reform Association (RRA) 207, 213, 228, 229, 230, 231
Reeves, John 64, 121, 122, 123, 134, 168
reform 1, 3, 126, 146, 183, 200, 203, 216, 232, 233, 268, 283
  age of 1, 7
  Crown and Anchor reformers 132, 137, 149, 151, 153, 160, 168, 281
  electoral 206
  movement 28, 179, 230, 231, 235, 240n.137, 254, 255, 266, 284
  see also political reform, prison reform, Radical Reform Association
Reform Act 14, 147, 155, 161, 162, 163, 164, 165, 232, 239n.128
religion 39, 102, 213, 220, 256, 264, 266, 268
  and radicalism 204, 215, 218, 219, 220, 247, 251, 261
  and women 85, 87, 88, 90, 91, 94, 95, 97, 102, 244, 247, 248, 251, 257
  attacks on 201, 206, 208, 217, 228, 246, 249, 251, 263
  countering 205, 206, 218, 220, 246, 263
  radical 255
  see also blasphemy, devilry, sacrilege
religious
  conversion of radicals 41, 72, 247
  despotism 200
  dissent 11, 19, 33, 85, 95, 206, 247n.17, 249, 256, 258, 267, 282
  dogma 201, 220
  freedom 163, 280

instruction in prison 29, 39, 42, 56, 58–9, 68, 71, 72, 280
licences 215, 238
motivations of reformers 57, 74
offences 35, 47, 55, 64, 71, 82
opposition to radicals 100–1
Renwick, Adam 98
Republican 43, 44, 45, 75, 86, 89, 96, 97, 98, 99, 101, 208
republicanism 3, 45, 99, 231, 244, 271
Reveley, Maria 28
Rhodes, Joseph 34, 38
Rich, Mary 53, 78
Richards, Georgiana 257n.64, 259n.72, 264
Robinson, Henry Crabb 195, 196
Roebuck, John 164, 281
Romilly, Sir Samuel 28
Rotunda, *see* Blackfriars Road Rotunda
Royal Academy of Arts 194
Royal Academy of Music 194
Royal Circus 224
Royal Institution 191, 192, 194, 196, 252
Royal Society 113

sacrilege 260
    see also blasphemy, devilry, religion
Saull, William Devonshire 200, 257
Scientific institutions 191n, 218
    see also Royal Institution, Surrey Institution
Scott, John 65
secret service 8
    see also spies
sedition 1n.3, 5n.17, 26n.34, 36, 39, 55, 77, 121, 145, 146, 147, 156, 172, 214, 216, 227, 237, 238, 240, 260, 281
seditious libel, *see* libel—seditious
Seditious Meetings Act 1, 5, 172, 237, 239
Sharples, Eliza 102, 180, 205, 206, 207, 208, 210, 218, 238, 243–53, 257–60, 262, 263, 265, 266, 267, 268n.106, 271, 272
Sheridan, Richard Brinsley 80, 117, 121
Six Acts 34, 97n.68, 141, 214, 239

Smith, J. T. 130, 132, 144
Smith, William 131
Society for the Diffusion of Useful Knowledge (SDUK) 202, 203, 204
Society for the Suppression of Vice 86, 121
Southey, Robert 54
spies 5, 106, 123, 161n.49, 172, 173n.100, 215, 227, 230, 237, 243, 247
    see also Hall, Abel
Stanhope, Charles, Earl 167
Stoddart, John 91
Strand, the 1, 50, 73n.103, 108, 109, 110, 120, 147, 155, 164, 175, 179, 228n.70
suffrage 152
    universal male 3, 151, 152, 155, 163, 206–7, 229, 232, 231, 234, 271
Surrey Institution 14, 183, 185, 191, 193–8, 201, 207, 224, 228, 252, 261, 280, 283

taverns 7, 8, 9, 12, 14, 28, 45, 46, 68, 86, 133, 148, 159, 160, 172, 173, 174, 219, 213, 214, 215, 216, 227, 254, 255, 256, 283, 284, 285
    see also Crown and Anchor tavern
Taylor, Reverend Robert 4, 5, 180, 182, 199, 200, 201, 205–8, 210, 213, 216–22, 224–7, 230, 231, 232, 238, 240, 241, 243–6, 248, 250, 251, 255, 257–60, 263–5, 269
Temple Club 276, 277
theatre 207, 222, 223, 224, 225, 226, 241, 277, 284
    Patent, 223, 224, 225, 226
    political 225, 227
    radical 223
    see also Blackfriars Road Rotunda, countertheatre, Richard Carlile—attitudes to theatre, working classes—theatre
Thistlewood, Arthur 159, 161, 168
Tocker, Mary Ann 88n.25
Tolpuddle Martyrs 166n.74, 174
Tooke, John Horne 120, 122

Towers, Joseph 116, 117
treason 51, 68, 77, 122n.52, 125, 165, 172, 182
Treasonable Practices Act 1, 5
Tunbridge, William 34, 55, 70, 71, 73, 74, 75, 79, 95n.57
Twort, Charles 180, 206, 243

Vice Society, *see* Society for the Suppression of Vice
Vickery, Governor 74, 75, 96
Volney 27, 99, 213, 219, 220

Waddington, Samuel 55, 73, 75, 159, 160
Waithman, Robert 131
Wakefield, Edward Gibbon 234, 256
Wakefield, Gilbert 39
Ward, John 'Zion' 180, 206, 207, 208, 243–4, 246, 255, 260
Ward, John 106
Watson, James 55, 71, 75, 97, 159, 231, 249n.25
Wellington, Lord/Duke of 137, 169, 179, 237
Wesley, Samuel 194
'Westminster Committee of 200', *see* Richard Carlile—'Westminster Committee of 200'
Whitbread, Samuel 154, 155
White Lion Tavern 159, 160, 161
Whittington Club 175, 176, 274, 275, 276
women
    and crime 93
    and legal system 87, 88, 90, 91, 92, 93
    and mainstream press 90–2, 263
    imprisonment of 82, 85, 92, 94–5, 97–8
    in public life 5, 7–8, 11, 13, 85, 190, 199, 251–2, 260
    marginalisation 11, 14, 86, 247, 253–4, 259, 261–2, 271, 284–5
    participation in radical culture 14, 84, 85, 99, 103, 173, 175, 242, 246–8, 251, 254, 256, 262, 265–6, 271, 272, 280, 284
    political involvement 51n.10, 92, 174, 175, 179, 206, 244, 249, 253, 255, 256, 270, 282
    radical male attitudes to 98, 102, 103, 215, 252, 253, 257, 263, 265, 271, 272, 284
    radical women as prostitutes 13, 91, 92, 92n, 258, 263, 264,
    working-class 94, 253, 254, 258, 261, 266, 267n.103, 282
Wood, Matthew 30, 131
working classes 7, 174, 213, 219, 232, 233n.97, 236, 237, 240n.137, 244n.3, 257n.60, 258, 260–1, 283
    and religion 219, 220, 258
    class consciousness 7, 202, 204, 284
    class distinctions 161n.51, 259
    culture 202, 241, 261, 282
    education 183, 201, 202, 203, 204, 205, 209, 210–11, 241
    emancipation 183, 205, 206
    exclusion 162n.55, 254
    movements 11, 272, 284
    public sphere 10, 254
    radical press 163, 164
    radicalism 14, 157, 161, 162, 202, 203, 204, 216, 227, 231, 235, 241, 256, 266, 272
    theatre 224, 226, 227
    see also Chartism, London Working Men's Association, National Political Union, National Union of the Working Classes, women—working class
Wren, Christopher 108
Wright, Susannah 13, 34, 55, 79, 82–103, 106, 147, 248, 251, 153, 263, 266, 281, 282, 285
Wright, William 85, 96, 100

yeomanry 2, 137, 141, 158
Yorke, Charles 2

Zetetic societies 204, 205

www.ingramcontent.com/pod-product-compliance
Lightning Source LLC
Chambersburg PA
CBHW041244240426
43670CB00025B/2976